SPECTACLES OF DEATH IN
ANCIENT ROME

SPECTACLES OF DEATH IN ANCIENT ROME

Donald G. Kyle

Routledge
Taylor & Francis Group

LONDON AND NEW YORK

First published 1998
by Routledge
2 Park Square, Milton Park Abingdon, Oxon OX14 4RN

Simultaneously published in the USA and Canada
by Routledge
711 Third Avenue New York, NY 10017, USA

Routledge is an imprint of the Taylor & Francis Group, an informa business

Typeset in Garamond by Florencetype Ltd, Stoodleigh, Devon

British Library Cataloguing in Publication Data
A catalogue record for this book is available from the British Library

Library of Congress Cataloging in Publication Data
Kyle, Donald G.
Spectacles of death in ancient Rome / Donald G. Kyle
p. cm.
Includes bibliographical references and index.
1. Death–Social aspects–Rome. 2. Funeral rites and ceremonies–
Rome. 3. Violence–Rome–History. 4. Gladiators–Rome–History.
5. Christian martyrs–Rome–History 6. Rome–Social life and
customs. I. Title.
HQ1073.5.R66K95 1998
306.9–dc21   97–43475
CIP

ISBN 0415248426

CONTENTS

CONTENTS

ILLUSTRATIONS

PREFACE

This project originated several years ago when I taught my first course on ancient sport, a service course established to woo non-majors into embarking on more 'serious' ancient studies. Usually such courses only cover Greek sport, but I decided to add the Roman experience, reasoning that Greek athletics continued under Rome, and that races in the circus and physical recreation in the baths – and perhaps even the games of the arena – can be studied as sport. However reprehensible, whatever activities a given society participates in or watches for the sake of disportment, entertainment, recreation, and leisure are sport for that society. I knew that a rousing rendition of the 'horrors of the Colosseum' would maintain student interest in the latter part of the course; but I was not going to indulge in any simplistic, stark contrast of Roman bloody, decadent, spectator games with the purity and inspiring virtue of less bloody (but hardly bloodless) Greek sport, for I knew that Romans were open to exercise and in time even to Greek sport, and that Greek sport was not free of corruption, abuse, and violence.

There I was, disgusting students with horrific 'true stories' of bloody beast-fights, gladiatorial gore, and cruelty to Christians. As I read out famous accounts of the astounding numbers of casualties in the spectacles, a usually lethargic student suddenly blurted out: 'But what did they do with all those bodies?' There it was. I answered perfunctorily with something that I recalled vaguely from some classical handbook, but I felt uneasy and suspected that the student's innocent question went well beyond sport. The nagging sense that this was a valuable question stayed with me long after the course was over. Some years later, after having done research primarily on Greek sport, I returned to that student's question and embarked like a detective on a trail of scattered clues. From pagan literature to Roman law to Christian martyrology, from the Colosseum to the Capitol, from the Forum to the suburbs of Rome, I delved deeper and deeper into the case of the missing bodies.

Given the many episodes of brutality in recent world history and the escalating violence in the modern, especially American, media, it is not surprising that a new wave of scholarship in English has begun focusing on the Roman amphitheater – its archaeology, art, and architecture, and its symbolism or cultural significance. In 1992 at the meeting of the Archaeological Institute of America and the American Philological Association a joint panel on the Roman arena (abstracted in *AJArch.* 97 (1993) 304–6) showed that the scholarly community was ready for new perspectives on spectacles. As I was working on the project, impressive interdisciplinary studies appeared, including Wiedemann's 1992 *Emperors and Gladiators*, Brown's 1992 'Death as Decoration: Scenes from the Arena on Roman Domestic Mosaics', and Barton's 1993 *Sorrows of the Ancient Romans*, all of which offer new depths of investigation into what the gladiator and the arena meant to the Romans. Also in 1993, Hornum's *Nemesis, the Roman State, and the Games* related the state and the games to punishment and social order. Recently, Plass' 1995 *The Game of Death in Ancient Rome* pursues further the role of institutionalized violence in Roman society, and ties both the arena and political suicide to a desire for order and security. Finally, 1996 saw the appearance of valuable interpretive studies on the social and cultural significance of the arena: an article by Gunderson in *Classical Antiquity* and chapters by Edmondson and others in Slater, ed., *Roman Theater and Society*.

Even with these fine studies my student's question remained instructive. What follows began as a limited investigation of the specific question of how bodies were disposed of from the Roman spectacles. Questions that appear to be simple, at least from a rationalist, modernist perspective, however, need not have simple or trivial answers, and they can lead to other complex questions and multi-faceted problems. Consider the logistical and symbolic problems that the modern world faces concerning the disposal of garbage, nuclear waste, and human tissue from medical procedures. As the specific question of arena disposal led me to examine broader Roman patterns of institutionalized violence and the disposal of the dead, the issue of disposal became a heuristic conceit for locating the phenomenon of deadly spectacles within Roman society and civilization at large.

For a title I had considered 'Death, Disposal and Damnation', and one colleague wryly suggested 'Corpses, Carcasses and Christians'. Instead, I adapted the publisher's suggestion of *The Spectacle of Death in Rome* as *Spectacles of Death in Ancient Rome* in order to avoid any suggestion of reductionism, for Rome knew a variety and hierarchy of spectacular deaths and disposals.

Am I gravely serious and in deadly earnest about this? Has something driven me from learned to lurid history, from 'bread and circuses' to blood and carcasses? Should I lay my necrology to rest before I make a spectacle of myself? Might my digging in this pathological pursuit of dead meat and the ungrateful dead lead to a dead end? Once hooked, did I get carried away? I must not drag this out, but some things still haunt me. Is my work the pits, are my findings a washout? Enough. Nothing in past human experience is beyond the scope of history. Some of Thucydides' most powerful and insightful writing deals with the horrors of the plague, of atrocities in cities in internal upheaval, and of military defeat. History is not always –

or even often – pretty, and we must consider basic and repulsive ingredients in the mélange or miscellany that is our human heritage.

My intended audience is broad and eclectic. As a teacher I hope that the text of the work is reasonably accessible to students and non-experts interested in the history of Rome, violence, and death. For scholars of Roman history and society interested in the development of arena violence and the options for disposal, I have tried to cite ancient testimonia and modern scholarship adequately but not exhaustively, despite their length, in my notes. My documentation on broad and diverse topics such as Roman festivals, law, and food, and Christian persecutions is meant to be helpful, not comprehensive. Interdisciplinary scholars of violence, law, and sport will find that the symbolism of violence done to human and animal bodies at Rome bears comparison with many other cultures. While the study is, I hope, not conceptually barren, it is not theory-driven or hermeneutically adventuresome. As a historian I note and apply various approaches and interpretations, but I try not to stray too far from the evidence, the scattered and limited pieces of the puzzle. The project has made me reconsider disturbing but essential features of Roman life and death, and I hope that the book has a similar effect on its readers.

In the notes I have abbreviated the names of ancient authors and texts, journals, corpora of evidence, and reference works, generally following the systems of the *Oxford Classical Dictionary*³, *L'Année Philologique*, or the *American Journal of Archaeology* (occasionally with further self-evident abbreviation, e.g. Eusebius' *Hist. eccl.* = *HE*; Cassius Dio = Dio. Also U. = University/U. of/ U. Press). For convenience I have generally used translations from the Loeb Classical Library (cited in notes as 'Loeb'). Passages from the following are reprinted by the kind permission of the publishers and the Loeb Classical Library: Dio Cassius, *Roman History*, vols. 7 and 8, translated by Earnest Cary, 1924–5; Livy, vol. 5, translated by B. O. Foster, 1929; *Scriptores Historiae Augustae*, vols. 1 and 2, translated by D. Magie, 1922, 1924; Seneca, *Epistulae Morales*, vol. 4, translated by R. G. Gummere, 1917; Suetonius, *The Lives of the Caesars*, vols. 1 and 2, translated by J. C. Rolfe, 1914; Tacitus, *Annals*, vols. 4 and 5, translated by John Jackson, 1937; Tertullian, *Apology* and *De Spectaculis*, translated by G. H. Rendall, 1931; all of these: Cambridge, Mass.: Harvard University Press. Standard editions of ancient texts are used, and textual problems and other translations are acknowledged in the notes. Some citations of Dio indicate both the numbers of the Loeb book (first) and of the Greek text (in parentheses, e.g. Dio 73(72).20.3). Once cited in full in a note, secondary works appearing in the list of references are later cited by author and date. The list of references lists important and repeatedly cited works; a full bibliography of all works consulted or cited would be of greater length than value. Many well-illustrated works on the spectacles are now readily available (e.g. Golvin and Landes, Golvin, Brown, Wiedemann, Pearson, Quennell), so I saw no need for extensively illustrating this volume.

PREFACE

My acknowledgements include my sincere thanks (but certainly no imputed blame for errors or omissions) to various persons who have discussed or read all or part of the work: S. Brown, N. Crowther, D. G. Geagan, J. Kushma, D. Quertermous, S. Reinhardt, T. F. Scanlon, and C. Wells. I especially thank Thomas Wiedemann for his helpful comments on the typescript, Larry Tritle for our discussions of the value of studying disturbing historical topics, Ingomar Weiler for encouraging me to publish earlier versions of parts of chapter 6 as 'Animal Spectacles in Ancient Rome: Meat and Meaning', *Nikephoros* 7 (1994) 181-205, and Nick Bateman of the Museum of London Archaeological Service for his correspondence and hospitality in London. Research in progress was presented at various forums: the Iaonnides Memorial Lecture at the University of Western Ontario in 1989, the North American Society for Sport History in 1991 and 1994, and a joint session of the AIA/APA in 1992. I wish to thank the College of Liberal Arts at the University of Texas at Arlington for a faculty development leave in the fall of 1991 and also a summer research stipend in 1996 in aid of my writing. The help of the UTA interlibrary loan office was, in a word, invaluable, and I am very grateful to the tireless and resourceful staff of that office. For a Visiting Humanities Fellowship in the summer of 1993, I thank the Humanities Research Group of the University of Windsor. My sincere thanks go to Richard Stoneman and Routledge for encouraging this study with an advance contract in 1992, and for their patience and support. My friend and wife, Adeline, assisted me in Italy, and, as always, her faith in me kept me going. For their curiosity and vitality, I dedicate this book to our sons Cameron and Colin.

1

INTRODUCTION:
VIOLENT SPECTACLES AND
ROMAN CIVILIZATION

Life becomes transparent against the background of death,
and fundamental social and cultural issues are revealed.
(Metcalf and Huntington, *Celebrations of Death* (1991) 25)

The death of humans (and sometimes even of animals) usually constitutes a
spectacle, a disturbing sight which is awful in both senses of the word, an eerie
yet intriguing phenomenon demanding acknowledgement and attention.
When confronted, as it must be, death makes us come to terms, individually
and collectively, with our powers and our limitations – with our humanity and
our mortality. Witnessing natural deaths of the aged and infirm is distressing,
but far more disturbing are premature, forced, and unnatural deaths. Yet
throughout human history some beings have been killed so that others might
live, prosper, or feel safe or superior. Violence and destruction are (or have
been) necessary for survival and security; empires always have exploited and
intimidated. All societies witness natural death and all societies kill, whether
directly in war, state executions, blood sacrifice, hunting, or the butchering
of animals for meat, or indirectly via oppressive poverty, insidious pollution,
or various 'combat' or 'blood sports' wherein the abuse and death of humans
and animals are either intentional or probable. Rome, however, remains extraordinary for the scale and the method of its violence, and for applauding skill,
artistry, and diligence in the punishment and destruction of creatures.

From our origins as humans we have dealt with the activity, the responsibility, and the aftermath of death. Paleolithic man advanced as a species
in part by developing tools and techniques to improve his killing abilities,
to expand his capacity to destroy and control nature and other men; but
we still have not evolved past the sensation that killing is a symbolically
charged act, something necessary but something to be done in certain
prescribed contexts and ways, with certain appropriate actions before and
after the killing. Killing must not be random or simply for its own sake;
it must be justified in some way, e.g. to protect the community from threats
or to provide resources for survival. However swift and intelligible the
death, killing normally evokes a profound sense of anxiety. All societies use

1

culturally appropriate rituals of separation or rites of passage to come to terms with the emotional intensity of killing and death, to lay the dead to rest, and – more importantly, since societies privilege the living above the dead – to restore the social fabric and let the living move on.[1]

Like any city ancient Rome dealt daily with normal and natural death, but Rome also killed on an enormous scale, with efficiency, ingenuity, and delectation. In the infamous arenas of Rome, in amphitheaters, circuses, and other sites, blood shows (*munera*) included gladiatorial combats (*spectacula gladiatorum, munera gladiatoria*) and animal hunts (*venationes*), and increasingly under the Empire there were also ritualized and even mythologized executions. From the third century BC through the late Republic and into the early Empire, political opportunism, imperial resources, and social needs greatly expanded these spectacles of death and changed their emphasis from private rites or necessary punishments into public entertainments. Of pre-modern cultures, perhaps only the Maya and Aztecs of Mesoamerica rivalled Rome in the extent and duration of their ritualized killing in religious and imperial contexts.

This study looks at unnatural, public death at Rome – the intentional, orchestrated, and spectacular killing of non-loved ones, the slaying of humans and the slaughter of beasts seen as foes, outsiders, outlaws, threats, or prodigies. Our subject is life-taking violence allowed or ordered, sanctioned or staged by the state in public areas. For Romans this killing was not clandestine, nor was it to be ignored: the killers, the killing, the dying, and the dead all were to be seen. As Seneca protested, Romans saw the turning of a man into a corpse as a 'satisfying spectacle' (*satisque spectaculi*: *Ep.* 95.33).[2] In fact, the dedicatory inscription for the earliest known amphitheater, that at Pompeii of ca. 70 BC, calls the facility a *spectacula*.[3] Away from the battlefield, Rome killed at home in sacrifices, festivals, *munera*, proscriptions, and executions. The famous spectacles of the arena were largely expanded, embellished versions of earlier forms of killing adapted for the comfort and entertainment of the spectators. The allure of violence and death was not unique to classical Rome,[4] but Rome revelled in killing as in the thrills and the reassurance, the self-validation, of a love affair. Death became a spectator sport at Rome, and the viewers, the viewed, and the venues of viewing deserve continued study.

Ancient and modern attitudes

In its many forms, death in the arena was public, official, and communicative; and, when properly conducted, spectacles of death were comforting and entertaining for Romans of all classes. Spectacles played a major role in the festival calendar, the social life, and the public space of ancient Rome for over a millennium. With industry and pride, Rome scoured the Empire for victims, built monumental facilities, orchestrated events, and immortalized

2

these performances in art, architecture, and literature. Thanks to martyrology, historians such as Edward Gibbon, artists such as J.-L. Gérôme, novels and Hollywood epics such as *Quo Vadis*, the enduring image of Rome will forever be stained with the blood of the arena.[5]

From the emperors who took pride in the productions, to the spectators (high and low) who flocked to the shows, Romans of all classes attended, approved of, and enjoyed the games.[6] Romans of different stations and from different viewpoints found something redeeming or entertaining about the games, be it how well gladiators faced death, the punishment of malefactors, the ability to interact with the emperor, or the viewing of foreign peoples and animals. The seating at the Colosseum, with tiered levels of spectators from senators to women and slaves, is often used as a metaphor for Rome's hierarchically ordered society.[7] Indeed, as social functions, arena spectacles were an occasion, as Tertullian said, for 'seeing and being seen', for seeing performances of skill and courage, and punishments and domination of foes, and for being seen – as producers and patrons of games sitting at prominent vantage points, as citizens of status in seats of privilege, as citizen-spectators participating and sanctioning the rules and rulers of Rome, or even as a potential lover.[8]

For the state the killing in the arena symbolized power, leadership, and empire, but the 'blood sports' did not have the same, singular meaning or attraction for all Romans of all classes in all eras. Individually, Romans were drawn to the arena by the allure of violence, by the exotic and erotic sights, and by an appreciation of the skill and courage of some participants or by the anticipation of the harsh but necessary punishment of others.[9] Attentive and knowledgeable, some spectators, including some emperors, were true fans – or fanatics; some arguably were sadists, some went for the crowd and the gambling as well as the killing, and many perhaps went to escape their deplorable living conditions. As in modern sports, many different people attended for many different reasons.[10] When in Rome, it was 'the thing to do'.

Passages in some Roman authors, notably Seneca and Cicero, seem to be criticisms of the arena, but they must be interpreted carefully. Writing in the wake of Caligula and Claudius, emperors notorious for cruel punishments, Seneca condemned certain arena spectacles:

> Man, an object of reverence in the eyes of man, is now slaughtered
> for jest and sport (*per lusum ad iocum*); and those whom it used to
> be unholy to train for the purpose of inflicting and enduring wounds,
> are thrust forth exposed and defenceless.[11]

Laudable but atypical, this passage concerns ritualized executions in the 'midday shows' (*meridiani*), not true gladiatorial combats. Moreover, Seneca was discomforted less by the effect of blood sports on the viewed than on the viewers. As a recent study clarifies, 'There is no compassion in the modern sense of the word for those who act in the arena; Seneca worries about the spectators.'[12] He condemned the corruptive, brutalizing influence on the individual of contact with emotionally intense crowds at executions. Yet Seneca was open to shows as diversions (e.g. *Helv.* 17.1), he did go to the arena, and he praised the virtues of gladiators. Seneca and his circle often commented on the slaughter in the arena, but from an elite, intellectual perspective. Philosophers even applauded the games as useful educational demonstrations of military valor or stoic fortitude (see ch. 3 below).

Depending on the genre, context, or purpose of a statement, authors could be ambivalent or inconsistent about spectacles.[13] Cicero used 'gladiator' as a term of derision, but he felt that gladiators were a good investment.[14] His famous criticism of Pompey's games of 55 BC also is atypical:

> But what pleasure can it possibly be to a man of culture, when either a puny human being is mangled by a most powerful beast, or a splendid beast is transfixed with a hunting spear? And even if all this is something to be seen, you have seen it more than once; and I, who was a spectator, saw nothing new in it. The last day was that of the elephants, and on that day the mob and crowd was greatly impressed, but manifested no pleasure. Indeed the result was a certain compassion (*misericordia*) and a kind of feeling that that huge beast has a fellowship with the human race.[15]

Cicero knew what to expect but still attended, and any sense of the 'fellowship' of men and beasts was not strong enough to save the animals.[16]

Indictments of the Romans, especially of the lower classes, for their enthusiasm for games clearly represent a minority ineffectually condemning what was popular and persistent. As in other societies, the intelligentsia criticized the popular culture of the masses, using soon commonplace themes of social and moral debasement.[17] Christian writers predictably saw spectacles as idolatrous and corruptive, yet even they testify to the widespread popularity of the games.[18] Aside from Stoic and Christian authors' concerns about crowd passions and idolatry, criticisms of the games were often of specific examples of a leader's injustice or excess – not of the custom in general. Common Romans resented emperors who were miserly about spectacles, and elite Romans were disturbed when emperors or the upper classes perverted the customs of the circus and arena.[19] Criticisms of aberrations or elements (e.g. *meridiani*) do not amount to opposition to the phenomenon in general. There simply was no widespread opposition to the inhumanity of the games.[20] If the games were held for the people and not for the emperor himself, and if they were performed with some propriety and some sporting interest, they were welcomed and applauded.

4

The blood sports and deadly spectacles fascinate moderns as, on the surface, a glaring contradiction of Rome's image as a civilizing power.[21] Modern scholars have long pondered how civilized Romans could condone and even enjoy, make sport of, watching hundreds and even thousands of humans and animals being killed in elaborate public spectacles. Yet violence was omnipresent in Roman society and history. From animal sacrifice and slaughter to the disciplining of slaves and children to the brutalities of ancient warfare, the Romans had long grown accustomed to regarding creatures of lowly status, others and outsiders without reason or rights, as legitimate objects of violence. In the modern West, however, we have difficulty coming to terms with the spectacles because of modern, 'civilized' conventions and sensibilities about violence and sport. Ironically, until all too recently, in the context of poverty, violence, and poor life expectancy, western societies tolerated and enjoyed watching the tormenting and destruction of creatures in brutal spectacles, including public hangings, bull and bear baiting, cockfights, and more. Sociologists Norbert Elias and Eric Dunning suggest that, to the degree that we moderns now feel reservations about such customs, we have been influenced by a 'civilizing process' whereby there has been a broad change in manners and notions of decent behavior since the late Middle Ages. In recent centuries external factors, such as modern police and penitentiaries, and an internal factor, a conditioned psychology of abhorrence of excess violence, have contributed to a gradual shift in the parameters of embarrassment and shame, including reduced levels of interpersonal violence, increased sensitivity to pain, and an aversion to cruelty.[22] Most moderns are conditioned to feel that the viewing of actual life-threatening violence in public should be distasteful and should be discouraged by the social order. The civilizing process, nevertheless, remains incomplete. Just as ancient criticisms had only limited and late effect on death sports at Rome, the banning of modern blood sports and animal baiting has not been quickly or totally achieved.

Not unique but culturally distinctive, Roman spectacles of death must be viewed in their own and not in a modern cultural context. For example, in these days of animal rights, of protests against the cruelty of hunting, rodeos, and lab experiments on animals, of vegetarianism and distrust of red meat, the beast spectacles of ancient Rome seem an alien and disturbing topic; but we should try to comprehend as well as condemn Rome's killing of beasts by men and/or beasts in 'games' or 'hunts'. Moderns struggle to understand the meaning and attraction of beast shows for Romans, first of all, because we misapply our view of animals and of sport hunting to antiquity. An authority on ancient art, J. M. C. Toynbee, finds it paradoxical

> that a people that was so much alive to the interest and beauty of
> the animal kingdom ... that never seemed to tire of the sight
> of rare and unfamiliar specimens, that displayed such devotion to

its pets, should yet have taken pleasure in the often hideous sufferings and agonizing deaths of quantities of magnificent and noble creatures.[23]

The paradox is perhaps more modern than Roman. Modern European and American empathy with the suffering of animals stands out awkwardly against a long history of brutality.[24]

Any inconsistency between beast spectacles and the Roman love of nature, pets, and zoological rarities did not undermine beast spectacles. Romans admired wild animals and also saw them as predators or game. Animals were to be controlled or killed, as threats or nuisances, as beasts of burden, as sources of materials (hides, fur, wool, or feathers and bone, horn, or ivory), and as food (meat, marrow, and brains). Wild or domesticated, hunted or raised, animals were seen by virtually all Romans as a sub-human part of nature.[25] As Matt Cartmill states, 'No intrinsic value was attributed to the lives of beasts in ancient Greece and Rome ... In a world where philosophers could seriously argue that human slaves are only detached parts of their masters' bodies, and where grotesquely awful deaths were regularly meted out to human victims to amuse the arena-goers, few concerned themselves with the lives of beasts.'[26]

Is it impossible for us, as Church fathers warned early Christians, to get close to the arena and feel its thrill without losing our dignity and innocence, without corruption or guilt? Total historical objectivity is admittedly an illusion, and yet we must confront and reconstruct the past. Traditionally, well-intentioned scholars have felt compelled to minimize or to condemn the games with passionate but anachronistic editorial flourishes. Experts distanced themselves from this face of Rome, declaring that the arena could not or must not happen again.[27] Still widely used in introductory Roman civilization courses, J. Carcopino's text declares:

> Revisiting the arenas of Rome after nearly 2,000 years of Christianity, we feel as if we were descending into the Hades of antiquity. The amphitheatre demands more than reproach. It is beyond our understanding that the Roman people should have made the human sacrifice, the *munus*, a festival joyously celebrated by the whole city.[28]

Otto Kiefer moralized that: 'Those orgies of hate and cruelty were *bound* to produce the gospel of love ... the whole of Roman sadism is a necessary step towards a new, a truly noble [Christian] state of humanity.'[29] Historically, however, the decline of the Roman Empire brought the decline of the Roman spectacles, not vice versa. Also, condemning Roman spectacles by comparison with Greek sport is satisfying for Hellenists but unenlightening.[30] Beginning with the premise of some unique, unfathomable Roman dispensation or perversity will not help,[31] for Rome's blood sports and aggravated executions have too many analogues in other cultures and times.[32] Brutality is in the eye of the beholder.

Interpretations of Roman violence and spectacles

To explain the widespread popularity of violent sports, anthropologists speculate about innate aggression and violence in human nature, and sociologists theorize about how societies accommodate and use symbolic and real violence. Violence and blood sports seem to be a universal legacy from the long prehistory of man as a hunter and killer that all societies retain in sublimated or ritualized form. Some suggest that all social order is ultimately based on violence. To reinforce the social order violence must be performed or proclaimed in public, and public violence tends to become ritualized into games, sports, and even spectacles of death. In early societies violence (against man or beast) and the sacred are linked, and homicide and blood sports often occur in sacral or funerary contexts.[33] Groups use violence to protect themselves and also, in a deeply emotional way, to avenge themselves (or to appease their dead) through punishment. Greek sport itself perhaps went back to human sacrifice ritualized into funeral games, and Rome's brutal inclinations in spectacles give support to theories of violence, vengeance, or sacrifice (for the dead, for the gods, or for the dead as gods) as original impulses, with agonism, sport, and craft as secondary or epiphenomenal.[34] As cultural media, when they have some element of danger, drama, or unpredictability, some symbolic reassurance of moral viability, some identification with players, and some emotional investment in winners and losers, games both reveal power and have power themselves.[35] Skill and suspense turn homicide or beast slaughter into sport or craft — the spectacle becomes something to be watched and not just seen.

Scholars agree on the importance of deadly games in Roman society, but predictably they disagree on the primary nature or meaning of the games. Explaining a complex phenomenon like the spectacles entails the use of interpretations, theories, or 'models' — what M. I. Finley explains as conceptual schemes, non-mathematical explanatory constructs, or simplifying assumptions, which help control the subject of discourse by selecting variables to be studied.[36] Models of the origins, nature, and function of the spectacles have ranged without consensus from pagan piety to human sacrifice and from sadism to imperial politics.[37] Racial and moral explanations have had their day, some traditional models retain value, and some recent explanations have become increasingly theoretical and interpretive.

A religious model follows Tertullian's argument (e.g. *De spect.* 12) that all spectacles were inherently idolatrous because they originated as sacrifices to venerate the gods or to honor and appease the spirits of the dead. Religious roots and overtones are undeniable for the early games, and even as the spectacles became politicized the religious overtones continued in rituals,

7

popular piety, and the overlap of religion and politics in office-holding and the provision of ceremonies. Rome was never a secular state, and the Christian and modern distinction between church and state had virtually no meaning for pagan Romans. G. Ville asserted that gladiatorial games under the late Empire were pure spectacles without cultic significance, but anthropologically any games involving violence and death remain sacred.[38]

Warfare and games are often seen as analogous, and another model ties the arena to Roman militarism and imperialism. Various festivals (*ludi*) began as military thanksgivings, and military triumphs included the presentation of foreign beasts and captives and the staging of spectacular deaths. Both gladiatorial combats and the earliest amphitheaters arose in contexts of Roman militarism under the Republic.[39] Moreover, there were 'mock' mass combats on land and water, and gladiators provided emotional conditioning (as well as actual instruction at times) for the soldier-citizen. Certainly warfare familiarized Romans with violence, and violent spectacles escalated with, and symbolized, the territorial expansion of the empire. Finally, blood sports perhaps acted as a surrogate for war during the Pax Romana.[40]

It has become more acceptable to see the spectacles as 'sport' or 'leisure' – from the perspective of the spectators and even some of the participants. Sport is a human universal with cultural adaptations and significance in any society, and the Roman games, including the arena, do fulfill a broad definition of sport as a means whereby members of a society disport or entertain themselves.[41] While some earlier works strained apologetically at times to stress the popularity of the chariot races over gladiatorial fights or to downplay the cruelty of the hunts, other works almost turn gladiators into athletes by emphasizing their training, esprit de corps, and rewards.[42] Some scholars still balk at the notion of spectacles of death as sport or as 'sporting', but their prominence in Roman leisure and recreation cannot be denied any more than the prominence of violence – symbolic, fake, and real – in modern sport.[43]

Spectacles, obviously but not solely, were political devices used by leaders to gain support under the Republic and by emperors to appease the masses under their autocratic system in the age of 'bread and circuses'. Moralists and Marxists condemn spectacles for turning productive citizen-workers into idle subject-consumers of mass culture. A more sympathetic model of political sociology shows, however, that the relationship was not simply one-dimensional manipulation. To look beyond the vulnerability of an underemployed urban population to the hegemonic political aims of rulers, this model points out the assertiveness of massed spectators and the vulnerability of the popularity of leaders at spectacles. Under the Republic the aristocratic tradition of munificence (euergetism) put leaders under obligation to give games as gifts of appreciation to their community.[44] Later, under the Empire, an implicit contract existed whereby the emperor was expected to give games and gifts as a demonstration of his generosity (*liber-alitas*), to enjoy such shows, and to tolerate and attend to expressions of the popular will voiced in the context of spectacles.[45] At spectacles crowds of commoners had a sense of confidence and power, and a dialogue took place between the provider and the consumers of the games. The 'spectacle' unfolded publicly within a threefold interactive dynamic involving the crowd and the authority figure(s) as well as the direct participants or victims. As a recent study concludes, 'The urban crowd did not simply sit back to be entertained by displays of aristocratic largesse and power; it actively inter-vened to determine the course of the events and, at times, the participants.'[46]

Following Foucault's ideas on punishment as a confirmation of social order, some scholars see the games as symbolic demonstrations or perfor-mances, as rituals or 'shows' of power.[47] Martial (*Spect.* 5.65) claimed that the games showed imperial power and control even over nature, and with the variety and multitude of species and races involved, the games were a microcosm of the territorial extent and imperial majesty of Rome. Like festivals, processions, drama, and games in other societies, spectacles were ritualized performances that communicated, restored, consolidated, and sometimes helped change the communal order. Not mere entertainments or distractions, they were systems of meaning or cultural performances by which socio-cultural orders (i.e. values, norms, status relationships) were formulated and reformulated.[48]

Some works have extended ideas from A. W. Lintott's pioneering analysis of violence in Roman history, attitudes, and law. Lintott traces the early ideal of communal self-help, and the assumption of a natural right to self-defense: *Vim vi repellere licet.* He shows that violence in politics and Roman legal procedures were originally modelled on ritualized self-help. Rome could be callous or indifferent to the suffering of inferiors, but not out of cruelty (*crudelitas*). Spectacular violence in spectacles was accepted as a policy of expediency against worthless victims.[49] Similarly, R. Auguet views Roman spectacle violence not as sadistic but as pragmatic, as a demonstration of the power of the empire and a destruction of irreconcilable foes.[50] Recently K. Coleman has discussed the punitive and deterrent aims of 'fatal charades' or mythologized violence in the early Empire, and M. Hornum has detailed a strong correlation between the state and its arena games and the cult of the goddess Nemesis as an expression of the state's power to control and punish.[51] In urban Rome the arena, in effect, provided spectacular civics lessons in schools of death. The games taught the Romans who they were and how they were to behave.

Some recent studies relate the arena to broad themes of desire, death, and disorder. Carlin Barton offers a psychological examination of the Roman 'physics' of desire, despair, envy, and fascination concerning the pervasive images of the gladiator and the monster (abnormal or deformed creatures). In the transition from Republic to Empire, Roman society was in moral and political flux, consumed with angst and anomie. 'The paradox of the social pariah, the irrevocably socially debased creature, exalted by its commitment to its own annihilation, became increasingly familiar, even insistent, in the literature of the imperial period.'[52] Barton suggests that Rome needed negative extremes to balance its formal emphasis on control and propriety; it needed to strike and to embrace the monster and the monstrous. Irresolvable tensions in Roman society (e.g. between hierarchy and collectivity, violence and harmony) found compensatory channels, not solutions, in the imagery of the despised and the obscene.

Exploring the arena 'in the context of Roman ideas about society, morality and mortality', Thomas Wiedemann views the killing of beasts and humans in the games symbolically as a defense of civilization and social order against nature, barbarism, and criminality. The arena was a marginal, liminal site where Romans confronted the limits of the human versus the natural world in beast combats, the limits of morality, law, and social order in executions, and the limits of human mortality in the gladiatorial *munus*.[53] Wiedemann also emphasizes the role of bloody spectacles as fundamental to Rome's cultural identity or Romanness (*Romanitas*) in the process of Rome's unification of Italy and expansion overseas.

Paul Plass relates the arena to the universal problem of social violence. For Plass 'violence, or more generally, disorder falls under an axiom of anomaly, that is, an abnormal or disruptive factor formally institutionalized in one way or another to be internalized, in a process characteristic of any immune system'.[54] He argues that, as components of one social system, both arena sport and political suicide had a social purpose in dealing with problems of security and survival (i.e. either external danger or internal political conflict). As socially sanctioned violence and controlled disorder, both addressed social anomaly by incorporating disorder into order, restoring social routine, and (re)affirming security. Plass finds the arena's excessive violence consistent with the antithetical logic of liminal institutions which incorporate potential dysfunction to assure proper function. Spectators gather in an amphitheater away from normal life, they vicariously participate in combat, and they then return to normalcy.[55]

Somatics and necrology: the problem of disposal

Even with these valuable models the spectacles remain enigmatic as a pluralistic and polysemic phenomenon. With a long and complex history, they included multiple elements, and neither the victims nor the viewers were uniform. Sophisticated theoretical and symbolic interpretations of the arena in metaphorical, allegorical, or abstract terms take a rather intellectualist, cerebral aproach to a social phenomenon that was primarily visual and atavistic. By now the theoretical parameters are broad enough for most audiences,[56] and this study essays no impressive new interpretation of the whole

10

phenomenon of the spectacles or of violence at large in Roman society. However, it offers what may be an instructive perspective from which to apply or supplement these models.

Perhaps new light may be shed on the spectacles by reexamining the historical development of the spectacles and the social history of their victims, and by investigating an understudied but fundamentally relevant problem – the treatment and disposal of the arena's dead victims. Robust, afflicted, or broken, costumed, branded, or nude, pure, continent, or corrupted, in Roman and early Christian society bodies were profoundly symbolic.[57] As Florence Dupont writes, 'The Roman citizen consisted of a name and a body ... The body of a citizen was the man himself, the "embodiment" of the truth about him.'[58] The anthropological constant that a society's patterns of disposal of the dead are of profound cultural significance can be applied to the spectacles. The treatment and disposal of the dead victims of the arena formed an integral stage in the tripartite process of a death spectacle: the acquisition, the public violence, and the disposal. Humans and animals were collected alive, but most of them had to be removed dead from the arena. That this last consideration has been largely ignored in modern scholarship does not mean that it was insignificant to the ancients.[59] It's simply another way in which we have viewed Rome through our modern eyes. Traditionally, academics have been reluctant to investigate such indelicate aspects of human experience. Only recently have we viewed ancient sexuality through non-Victorian eyes, and shifted our focus from generals and heroes to cannon fodder and casualties. Most moderns in the urban West seldom think about the derivation or processing of their meat or drinking water. As well as delaying or even denying death, modern societies prefer to hide, sanitize, and hush up the process of disposal.[60] Ancients were generally far more candid about how people died and what happened to the remains.[61]

A necrological investigation of the problem of disposal may seem somewhat morbid, coldblooded, or vulgar, but it can assist our understanding of Roman attitudes and the fundamental, though not singular, nature of their spectacles of death. I shall examine various forms of intentional killing in arenas (sites and buildings) at Rome from the early Republic until the early fourth century AD. This includes the killing of humans from mass slaughters of captives and criminals to individual duels of elite gladiators, but I exclude accidental deaths in chariot races or Roman versions of Greek combat sports.[62] As in modern motor sports, the possibility of deaths in such dangerous events added excitement, but death was not essential to these contests. I focus on spectacles in which probable or certain death took center stage, 'blood sports' in which violence and the likelihood of injury and death for men and beasts were arranged for and appreciated by Romans. Given the symbolic value of animals in ancient culture, I discuss both animal and human killers and victims. There were significant analogies in the recruitment, hierarchy, and even death of men

11

and beasts, and consideration of both beasts and humans is called for by the post-modernist reevaluation of humanity and of our relationship to nature and animals behind ethology, socio-biology, and the animal rights movement.[63] Constantine's reign offers a serviceable endpoint because he legalized Christianity and legislated, however ineffectively, against gladiatorial spectacles. Socially entrenched and popular, spectacles of death did not die easily or soon, but the decline of Rome's power and resources gradually ended the most lavish and deadly spectacles.[64] Pragmatically, my main focus is on urban Rome, but at times I integrate important Italian and provincial evidence. Although procedures outside Rome probably yielded to local variations and the discretion of local officials, spectacles were an urban and imperial phenomenon, Rome was the model, and ritual patterns were widespread.

This study goes beyond natural deaths and normal burials and disposal to examine the public, premature, and violent deaths and the disposal of all types of victims from diverse spectacles and arenas at Rome. While fine studies have detailed the origins (recruitment, collection, hunting), preparations, and modes of death of the human and animal victims, we also need to study the destinations – the procedures, means, and facilities that were necessary for disposing of the corpses and carcasses from the arena. Understandably, studies of Roman burial practices usually concentrate on private arrangements for individuals and pay little attention to the mass and usually anonymous victims of the games. For example, Keith Hopkins provides masterful syntheses on spectacles and on the symbolism of death and burial, but he does not pursue the relationship of disposal to the spectacles.[65] Authoritative studies of the life, training and death of gladiators exist, and recent works have pursued the symbolic depths of gladiatorial combats; but, as argued below in ch. 3, the deaths of gladiators were outnumbered by those of animals and untrained, doomed human victims (noxii).[66]

The study of ritualized modes of death and disposal in Roman blood sports requires interdisciplinary investigation into the legitimization of violence, religious pollution and purification, patronage and public beneficence, the sociology of the arena, and the topography of the city. Like other aspects of the games and festivals, disposal had traditional roots and ritual continuities; and it must have been officially sanctioned or supervised, especially as the spectacles grew under the Empire. In the era of 'bread and circuses', mass entertainment including blood sports was an institutionalized social service, an obligation accepted by most emperors. Rulers increasingly had to be concerned with issues such as finance, public services, and popular attitudes.

Arena disposal must be approached as both a logistical and a symbolic problem. Rome had to dispose of the potentially great pollution of many thousands of corpses and carcasses, from regular and extraordinary spectacles, and from various sites, over hundreds of years. Disposal entailed the removal and deposition or destruction of the flesh to end the whole procedure and to avoid pollution – both disease and religious contamination.[67] Pragmatically, the numbers, methods, and sites of disposal posed logistical challenges. Roman urbanization, the development of facilities for spectacles, and increased demands on sites for burial and disposal must be considered. Hypothetically and historically, options for disposal at Rome were limited by both material and moral considerations. Burial, deposition, or exposure on land, burning, consumption, and deposition in water will all be examined.

Beyond the logistics lie the more intriguing cultural, symbolic, and emotional dimensions of disposal. From paleolithic times, man as a hunter and killer has never felt that he was finished when the foe or the game was killed. The sense that there was more to be done led to rituals of sacrifice and reconstitution as well as rituals of consumption and conviviality. The symbolic dimensions of violence and killing did not end with death, for, as R. Parker says of the Greeks, 'Treatment of corpses remained one of the means by which men could hurt, humiliate, or honor one another, express contempt or respect.'[68] How Homer's Achilles treated Hector's corpse reveals Achilles' state of mind more dramatically than how he treated Hector before he killed him. Romans might rationally feel justified in spectacular homicides of non-citizens, but proper disposal and, irrationally, the threat of haunting by vengeful spirits were serious concerns. As François Hinard points out, in modern societies all aspects of punishment, both the execution and the disposal, are specified in law, but in Republican Rome the modes of execution were largely determined by *fas* or sacred tradition.[69] Symbolic aspects of disposal are related to phenomena ranging from archaic rituals to legalized abuse, theatricalized executions, proscriptions, and persecutions.

For ancient peoples disposal of dead humans was to some degree a religious problem as well as an administrative one. Rome credited its success to pious attention to the *pax deorum*, and homicide always involved the sacred. The condemnation of persons to the arena to face death in ways tantamount to torture and corpse abuse raised concerns about justification, purification, and avoidance of contamination or religious pollution. It was not difficult, but it was necessary that the Roman community somehow assured itself that the killing was acceptable and even positive and therapeutic – that the victims were justly executed criminals, traitors, prisoners of war, paid volunteers, or dangerous heretics.[70] The Romans must also have assured themselves that the dead victims were disposed of in a way that precluded any further threats or contamination. Rome's earliest law code, the XII Tables, established a lasting ban on the burial or burning of human bodies 'within the city'. As damned abominations (*noxii, damnati* or *sacri*), most arena victims were seen as pollutions that must not contaminate sacred areas (*res religiosae*), which included all territory within the city's sacred boundary (*pomerium*) and normal burial areas beyond it.[71] Also, disposal was a symbolic act that communicated significant messages about the dead to the living. To read those messages we must study the victims

13

of the spectacles up to and beyond the point of death. The allowance, provision, and denial of proper burial all reveal fundamental attitudes to the games and their victims. How Rome disposed of expensive animals and undesirable humans helps explain why Rome killed them in such numbers and in such spectacular ways.

A wealth of archaeological, artistic, legal, epigraphical, and literary evidence bears witness to the prominence and longevity of the spectacles, but ancient sources say little specifically about disposal, perhaps because procedures were taken for granted.[72] Roman writers often use metaphors or examples from the games, and we too often have glossed over the brutalities used artistically in Roman humor, satire, and panegyric. Countless books on Roman life invoke Juvenal's indictment of 'bread and circuses' (*panem et circenses*),[73] of circus games as the opiate of a politically moribund plebs, but fewer acknowledge that that phrase comes in the midst of an account of the killing, corpse abuse, and denial of burial of Sejanus. Petronius, Apuleius, and a minor oration by Pseudo-Quintilian help reveal procedural details of the arena, and imperial histories by Suetonius and Dio use many relevant arena anecdotes to characterize the reigns of rulers.[74] Similarly but less reliably, the *Historia Augusta*, a late collection of biographies of emperors of the second and third centuries, often claims to record incidents of spectacular violence.[75] Both pagan (Martial, Suetonius) and Christian (Tertullian, Cyprian, Novatian) authors wrote works on spectacles;[76] and, ironically, some of the most valuable evidence on disposal comes from Christian authors, including Tertullian and Eusebius, who wrote highly charged polemics, apologies, and martyrologies in which they, as outsiders, condemned Rome's arena killing and disposal as actions that they could not enjoy or abide.[77]

From the XII Tables on, law codes and imperial decrees trying to regulate punishment and burial, though not always enforced, show intended societal norms.[78] Epigraphy provides abundant testimony from the epitaphs of gladiators to municipal regulations about games and graves.[79] Especially valuable are some municipal inscriptions concerning corpse disposal and undertakers, an edict of AD 19 from Larinum on the theater and the arena, and an edict of AD 177 concerning the prices of gladiators. Art and architecture, from mosaics to amphitheaters, have much to offer. From North Africa the Zliten mosaic alone graphically reveals many features of the arena and its killing (see figure 1, a and b).[80] Some dramatic discoveries have been made recently, and archaeology has clarified some topographical questions (e.g. about the cemetery on the Esquiline). Nevertheless, the problem of disposal may never be resolved indisputably because most of the evidence no longer exists to be found.

This study is organized as an investigative pursuit of an unconventional question. After a look at the phenomenon of spectacles historically and socially, a discussion of the problem of death and disposal in Roman society leads into an investigation of various options and their viability and

Figure 1a Gladiatorial combat in the arena, with an appeal for release from death (*missio*) in the center and a bier or stretcher (*sandapila*) in background right. Detail from a mosaic from Zliten, Libya.

Figure 1b The exposure of condemned men to beasts (*damnati ad bestias*) to the left and a beast hunt (*venatio*) in the center and right.

implications. In chapter 2 an overview shows that from its beginnings Rome housed various spectacles of death, and that the later, more famous spectacles in the arena were expansions of early customs. For example, animal spectacles had long ties back to hunting and beast-baiting traditions. While much scholarly attention has been devoted to the possible non-Roman origins of gladiatorial combats before their introduction to Rome in 264, and to the growth of such phenomena in the late Republic and early Empire, this study presents the middle Republic (roughly from the 260s to the 130s BC) as crucial to understanding the ideology and dynamics of gladiatorial games. As expansions of earlier customs, later developments, notably the domination of the phenomenon by the emperors, and variations, such as staged battles on land and water and mythologically enacted executions, increasingly became compounded, in sequence, in what might be called multi-dimensional or 'conglomerate' spectacles.

Chapter 3 examines the typology, procurement, and preparation of arena victims to clarify certain distinctions. Enormous quantities of beasts and humans from all over the Empire were brought to Rome as materials for spectacles, but not all victims faced the same treatment before, in, or after the arena. While they get the most attention, true gladiators – that is, trained weapons fighters who had made an oath and 'voluntarily' faced the prospect of killing or being killed – comprised only an elite minority among victims. Preoccupied with the involvement of volunteers – either freeborn citizens or reenlisting freedmen gladiators – scholarship has paid less attention to the masses of condemned humans executed in shows. Most of these victims were slaves and prisoners of war, when available, or convicts supplied (in increasing numbers and with increasing facility) by Rome's provincial and legal systems.

Chapter 4 has two parts. After discussing Roman attitudes and practices concerning the normal dead, customs reflective of a hierarchical and hegemonic society, the first part shows that, before and outside the spectacles of the arena, Rome had a strong vengeful tradition of abusing the bodies and denying the proper burial of hated or terrifying foes. The second part offers a brief cross-cultural excursus on 'blood sports', human savagery, and violence in various cultures beyond Rome: Assyrian brutality, punishments in Greece, human sacrifices in Mesoamerica, and abuse of captives by Indians in North America. The aim is explanatory – not to assert deterministic or psychic universals but to suggest some ritual analogies, to raise the issue of disposal, and to suggest some options and considerations.

Chapter 5 begins with a discussion of some rituals of the arena, their chthonic overtones, and the differential removal of victims. An investigation of options follows, focusing on the use of proper burial, mass depositions in pits, fire, and crucifixion. Archaeology, topography, and ancient literature suggest that the confirmation of the social order symbolized by the ritual killing in the arena continued on into differential treatment of corpses, and

Figure 2 Tombstone of the gladiator Martialis, a *retiarius* who fought with a net and a trident, from Smyrna.

INTRODUCTION

into allowance, non-provision, or denial of burial rights. As in society at large, victims of the arena were granted rights and privileges in proportion to the good or harm that they did for Rome. Rome's desire to protect itself and punish its foes went beyond death.

The ultimate disposal of gladiators reflects their social 'marginality' and Rome's ambivalent attitudes toward them. Although gladiators were despised socially, relatives or undertakers paid by the gladiator's burial society could claim their corpses and provide decent burial and even commemorative epitaphs for these trained and talented fighters (see figure 2). Unclaimed arena corpses, especially those of executed convicts, were perhaps dumped for a time, like those of slaves and paupers at large, in potter's fields outside the city and exposed to carrion animals (dogs and birds). However, potter's fields like that on the Esquiline Hill do not adequately account for arena disposal. Moreover, crucifixion accounts for relatively few arena victims, and fire was not an efficient means of mass disposal.

Chapter 6 presents the disposal of animal carcasses from arenas as symbolically and economically significant. An investigation of the possible consumption of the flesh of arena victims by animals and/or humans argues that humans did not eat human victims, nor did arena animals feast on human or animal flesh to the degree commonly assumed. However, a comparison with Spanish bullfighting, and consideration of other aspects of Roman festivals and society, suggests that some animal meat from the arena was eaten by the populace of Rome. As well as representing the breadth of Rome's imperial power and the control of its frontiers, arena hunts were popular as demonstrations of hunters' skills and as symbolic reconstructions of a rural past. If the games led to distributions of meat, the emperor/patron as a master hunter was providing game as well as games for his people.

Returning to the disposal of humans, chapter 7 argues that an efficient, early, and enduring custom involved throwing bodies into the Tiber River. By tradition, after brief stays in Rome's ancestral prison, criminals and captive enemies were executed and, after a period of corpse abuse and public exposure, their bodies were disposed of via the Tiber. Proscriptions and imperial 'reigns of terror' continued this custom. Also of interest, an ancient form of execution in which parricides were tied in sacks and thrown into the river and an ancient ritual which included throwing effigies of men into the Tiber each spring show that Rome traditionally used the waters of the Tiber to purge and purify itself.

The study necessarily extends to the controversial area of Christian persecutions and martyrology, and chapter 8 discusses Christians as persecuted victims and perceptive reporters of the spectacles. Compared to pagan victims, relatively few Christians actually died in arenas, but their bodies may have received especially harsh treatment because of Roman reactions to Christian defiance and the Christian concept of resurrection. Finally, a

19

brief conclusion notes recurrent themes, including punishment, pollution, and protection.

NOTES

1 P. Green, *Classical Bearings* (London: Thames and Hudson, 1988) 63: 'Anxiety about death dictates many of our fundamental beliefs and behaviour patterns . . . To study any group's attitudes to death becomes, in a very real sense, a refraction of their ideas about life, their social conventions and priorities, their more persistent sustaining myths.' P. Metcalf and R. Huntington, *Celebrations of Death: The Anthropology of Mortuary Ritual*, 2nd ed. (Cambridge: Cambridge U., 1991) begin their survey of mortuary rituals with valuable discussions, esp. 1–39, of the theories of E. Durkheim, A. van Gennep, and others who see disposal of the dead as a ritualized process of deep cultural significance. For an early anthropological approach, see J. G. Frazer, *The Fear of the Corpse in Primitive Religion* (London: Macmillan, 1933). A. van Gennep, *The Rites of Passage*, trans. M. Vizedom and G. Caffee (Chicago: U. Chicago, 1960) 1–13, 146–65, sees contests as appropriate for funerals: honors and spectacles appease the dead and reintegrate the community after the loss of a member. On European customs, see Philippe Ariès, *The Hour of Our Death*, trans. H. Weaver (New York: Vintage Books, 1982, orig. 1977) 18–19, passim, and, in brief, his *Western Attitudes Toward Death*, trans. P. M. Ranum (Baltimore: Johns Hopkins U., 1974), on facing death through ritualized public ceremony.

2 Further on Seneca, see ch. 3 below. Tacitus, *Hist.* 3.84, Loeb, comments on the abuse of Vitellius: 'With his arms bound behind his back, his garments torn, he presented a grievous sight (*foedum spectaculum*) as he was led away. Many cried out against him, not one shed a tear; the ugliness of the last scene had banished pity.' Juv. 10.66–7: 'Sejanus is being dragged along by a hook, as a show and a joy to all (*spectandus, gaudent omnes*).' Eusebius, *HE* 8.10, says that after numerous horrific tortures the wounded, naked bodies of martyrs in Alexandria were presented to onlookers as a spectacle (*spectaculum*).

3 *CIL* 10.852 (= *ILS* 5627); see L. Richardson, Jr, *Pompeii: An Architectural History* (Baltimore: Johns Hopkins U., 1988) 134–8. On the terminology, see Katherine Welch, 'The Roman Arena in Late-Republican Italy: A New Interpretation', *JRA* 7 (1994) 59–80, discussed below.

4 Two famous examples are often cited. Plato, *Resp.* 4.439e–440a, writes of a man encountering an executioner and the bodies of some criminals outside the walls of Athens. He knew that it was disgusting, but wanted to look; his desire overcame his aversion, and he approached the bodies, telling himself to stare at the 'lovely spectacle'. Centuries later, Augustine, *Conf.* 6.8, writes of a pupil Alypius succumbing to crowd enthusiasm in an amphitheater at Rome: he closed his eyes but not his ears, and moved by the crowd's roar when a gladiator was wounded, he opened his eyes, became fascinated with the bloodshed, and became a fanatic eager to attend more shows.

5 On films and the arena, see M. Eloy, 'Les Gladiateurs dans le spectacle moderne', 277–94, in C. Domergue, C. Landes, and J.-M. Pailler, eds., *Spectacula -I: Gladiateurs et amphithéâtres: Actes du colloque tenu à Toulouse et à Lattes les 26,27,28 et 29 mai 1987* (Lattes: Editions Imago, Musée archéologique Henri Prades, 1990). Jean-Claude Golvin and Christian Landes, *Amphithéâtres et gladiateurs* (Paris: Éditions du CNRS, 1990), 'Histoire et fiction', 15–21, discusses films and novels, and, passim, uses various works by Gérôme on amphitheatral themes as illustrations.

6 L. Friedländer, *Roman Life and Manners Under the Early Empire*, Eng. trans. J. H. Freese and L. A. Magnus, 4 vols. (New York: Barnes and Noble, 1965) 2:16–17: 'But the spectacles did not occupy only the masses, for whom they were intended. The impression of these exciting scenes of might fascinated all, infected the intellect of Rome, even the highest and most cultured circles, and especially the women.' Cic. *Mur.* 40, noted in P. Plass, *The Game of Death in Ancient Rome: Arena Sport and Political Suicide* (Madison: U. Wisconsin, 1995) 66, says that some may pretend not to, but everyone enjoys the shows.

7 Erik Gunderson, 'The Ideology of the Arena', *Cl. Ant.* 15 (1996) 113–51, at 123–6, discusses the prominence and hierarchical arrangement of the seating for the nobility at spectacles, and sees, 125, seating at the arena as 'an ideological map of the social structure of the Roman state'. Seeing a similar but more dynamic construction of society, J. C. Edmondson, 'Dynamic Arenas: Gladiatorial Presentations in the City of Rome and the Construction of Roman Society during the Early Empire', 69–112, in William J. Slater, ed., *Roman Theater and Society*, E. Togo Salmon Papers I (Ann Arbor: U. Michigan, 1996), at 82, comments: 'Audiences too were a cross section of Roman society: from emperor to slave, from senator to peasant, from citizen soldier to foreign tradesman, from vestal virgin to common prostitute.' Edmondson, 84–95, discusses in detail the status distinctions and segregation of spectators by location of seating – a subject of recurrent imperial legislation, costume, type of seats, access (entrances, passageways, staircases), and possible food or gifts; see further on Edmondson below. Earlier discussions include: J. Kolendo, 'La Répartition des places aux spectacles et la stratification sociale dans l'empire romain: A propos des inscriptions sur les gradins des amphithéâtres et théâtres', *Ktèma* 6 (1981) 301–15; Monique Clavel-Lévêque, *L'Empire en jeux: Espace symbolique et pratique sociale dans le monde romain* (Paris: Éditions du CNRS, 1984) 154–73; E. Rawson, '*Discrimina Ordinum*: The Lex Julia Theatralis', *PBSR* 55 (1987) 83–114; and Paul Zanker, *The Power of Images in the Age of Augustus*, trans. A. Shapiro (Ann Arbor: U. Michigan, 1988) 147–53; but cf. Ian Morris, *Death-Ritual and Social Structure in Classical Antiquity* (Cambridge: Cambridge U., 1992) 11–12, with cautions about social interpretations.

8 Tert. *De spect.* 25, Loeb: 'That sharing of emotions, that agreement, or disagreement in backing their favourites, makes an intercourse that fans the sparks of lust. Why, nobody going to the games thinks of anything else but seeing and being seen (*nisi videri et videre*).' On 'seeing and being seen', on theatricality as a prominent feature of social and public life, see Florence Dupont, *L'Acteur-roi, ou, Le théâtre dans la Rome antique* (Paris: Les Belles Lettres, 1985). On courting at shows, see n. 10 below.

9 Tertullian, *Apol.* 49.4, charges that the Roman commons exulted in the abuse of Christians, and that magistrates used the punishment of Christians in shows to win the favor of the masses and to glorify themselves.

10 Ovid recommends gladiatorial shows as well as the circus and theater as places of amatory opportunity: *Ars am.* 1.164–70, trans. Rolfe Humphries, *The Art of Love* (Bloomington: Indiana U., 1957):

> There is another good ground, the gladiatorial shows.
> On that sorrowful sand Cupid has often contested,
> And the watcher of wounds often has had it himself.
> . . .
> He is a victim himself, no more spectator, but show.

Similarly, Ovid, *Ars am.* 1.99, trans. Humphries, says that women throng the festival games: 'Hither they come, to see; hither they come, to be seen.' Ovid,

Ars am. 3.395–8, trans. Humphries, suggests that women seeking attention should:

> Go and look at the games, where the sands are sprinkled with crimson,
>
> . . .
>
> 'Out of sight, out of mind'; and out of mind, out of longing.
> What good are looks, unseen? Nothing is gained if you hide.

Keith Hopkins' suggestion, *Death and Renewal* (Cambridge: Cambridge U., 1983) 26, that crowds were drawn by gambling as the 'emotional glue' of the gladiatorial shows is perhaps overstated.

11 *Ep.* 95.33, Loeb. A similar passage, *Ep.* 7.2–5, is discussed in ch. 3 below. On both, see Plass, (1995) 68–70; Carlin A. Barton, *The Sorrows of the Ancient Romans: The Gladiator and the Monster* (Princeton: Princeton U., 1993) 23–4.

12 A thorough discussion of all of Seneca's relevant comments, Magnus Wistrand, 'Violence and Entertainment in Seneca the Younger', *Eranos* 88 (1990) 31–46, quote at 42, argues that Seneca was not opposed to gladiatorial or punitive spectacles in principle. However, as in *Ep.* 95.33, he was critical of executions that amounted to mere slaughter, which offered no positive diversion or inspiration to virtue. For Seneca, 42: 'Death in the arena should be designed as instructive *exempla* to demonstrate *virtus*, or to be terrifying warnings. Executions with the sole purpose of entertaining were objectionable.' On the acceptance of blood sports by the Romans, see Magnus Wistrand, *Entertainment and Violence in Ancient Rome: The Attitudes of Roman Writers of the First Century A.D.* (Göteborg, Sweden: Acta Universitatis Gothoburgensis, 1992) esp. 15–29, who, 18, declares: 'There is, in fact, no direct criticism of arena entertainment as an institution in Seneca's writings.' Similarly, Richard A. Bauman, *Crime and Punishment in Ancient Rome* (London: Routledge, 1996) 80–1, 142–3, explains that Seneca was not against the death penalty but that he was against excessively cruel executions used as a public entertainment, and modes of execution dictated by anger. Moreover, as he notes, 162, 'Seneca's attack on nasty modes of execution failed to lessen the allure of the arena.'

13 *Pace* Barton (1993), 4, who discounts traditional historians' concerns about issues of rhetoric, fiction, context, and historicity: 'But for my purposes, the "truth", "sincerity", or "authenticity", of the ancient statements or stories that I repeat is largely irrelevant . . . What makes things seem real or unreal to a Roman at a particular moment is of greater concern to me than what was (or is) real . . . For my purposes, all of the sources are equally true and equally false.'

14 Derision: e.g. Cic. *Phil.* 6.5.13; cf. A. A. Imholz, 'Gladiatorial Metaphors in Cicero's *Pro Sex. Roscio Amerino*', *CW* 65 (1972) 228–30. Investment: e.g. *Att.* 4.46. He approved of the discipline of gladiators (*Tusc.* 2.41), but he was not an enthusiast (*Fam.* 7.1.3; *Att.* 2.1.1); he accepted shows as a tradition but opposed the politically motivated escalation of the spectacles (*Off.* 2.57; *Mur.* 77). On the apparently ambivalent feelings of Cicero and Seneca on the arena, see Gunderson (1996) 137–8; G. Ville, *La Gladiature en Occident des origines à la mort de Domitien* (Rome: Ecole française de Rome, Palais Farnèse, 1981) 447–57.

15 *Fam.* 7.1.3, Loeb. On the incident: Dio 39.38.2–4; Sen. *De brev. vit.* 13.6; Plin. *HN* 8.21. David Potter, 'Martyrdom and Spectacle', 53–88, in Ruth Scodel, ed., *Theater and Society in the Classical World* (Ann Arbor: U. Michigan, 1993) n. 6 on 73, feels that the audience did pity the beasts; but Thomas Wiedemann, *Emperors and Gladiators* (London: Routledge, 1992) 60, 139–41, cautions that here Cicero was consoling a friend, who missed the spectacle, by downplaying its appeal. Cf. J. Aymard, *Essai sur les chasses romaines des origines à la fin du siècle*

des Antonins (Cynegetica) (Paris: É. de Boccard, 1951) 81–2; J. M. C. Toynbee, *Animals in Roman Life and Art* (Ithaca: Cornell U., 1973) 22–3; Ville (1981) 92. Wonder, not pity, was evoked when animals were coerced away from their natural instincts – when deer fought or lions fetched rabbits in their mouths without harming them (e.g. Mart. 1.48). Plass (1995), 119, sees a 'subliminal message about unexercised imperial power' here and elsewhere; cf. *Mart.* 1.6, 14, 22, 60, 104.

16 Shelby Brown, 'Death as Decoration: Scenes from the Arena on Roman Domestic Mosaics', 180–211, in Amy Richlin, ed., *Pornography and Representation in Greece and Rome* (Oxford: Oxford U., 1992) 200, comments on the realism of depictions of suffering beasts in the arena: 'The goal is to invite, not sympathy for the animals, but respect and gratitude for the *editor.*'

17 E.g. Messala in Tac. *Dial.* 29, Loeb: 'Again, there are the peculiar and characteristic vices of this metropolis of ours . . . the passion for play actors, and the mania for gladiatorial shows and horse-racing; and when the mind is engrossed in such occupations, what room is left over for higher pursuits?' Chariot racing drew more criticism in literature (e.g. Plin. *Ep.* 9.6; Juv. 11.197) partly because it drew greater crowds and intellectuals decried what they saw as plebeian fanaticism at the circus; see Wistrand (1992) 41–7. Countering the elitists' image (e.g. in Tacitus and Juvenal) of the mob as vulgar, politically impotent, and easily bribed, Z. Yavetz, *Plebs et Princeps* (repr. New Brunswick, N.J.: Transaction Books, 1988, orig. London: Oxford U., 1969) 34, says that the plebs were not brutish, insolent or fickle: 'the masses were able to distinguish between good and evil, between right and wrong, between clemency and strict justice. The people did not always behave cruelly and bloodthirstily.' Gunderson (1996) suggests that criticisms of the arena in elite sources tend to focus on the enthusiasm of the masses for watching or the enthusiasm of some members of the upper classes for participating in spectacles. As he notes, 114, 'the disgust expressed in literature for partisans of the games is especially strong when a self-consciously refined member of the elite like Messala sees members of his own class betraying his idealized conception of nobility'.

18 R. MacMullen, 'What Difference did Christianity Make?', *Hist.* 35 (1986) 322–43, argues that the level of judicial savagery continued and even grew under Christian rulers. Christians accepted judicial savagery and were not uncomfortable with cruel punishments in the arena.

19 E.g. Tiberius' parsimony was not popular (Suet. *Tib.* 47.1). On this and abuses such as elite participation or the forcing of spectators into the arena, see ch. 3 below.

20 Wiedemann (1992), 128–53, thoroughly discusses the conventional and elitist character of criticisms, which represent specific groups or contexts: philosophers condemned the emotionalism and loss of reason of the crowds, the elite criticized the expense and danger, and Christians, as well as repeating philosophical criticisms, added their moral and religious arguments about the evil nature, impiety, and idolatry of games as the work of Satan. He shows that criticisms, even by Greeks, Jews, and Christians, do not show humanitarian concerns about cruelty to animals or humans. Similarly, Wistrand (1992), 16, remarks that even Seneca and Cicero did not attack gladiatorial shows as an institution: 'virtually no one criticized this form of entertainment before the Christians'.

21 How could the same Rome applauded for its legacy for western civilization also be the cruel persecutor of Christian historiography and a negative example for the modern West? S. Dill, *Roman Society from Nero to Marcus Aurelius* (New York: Meridian, 1956, orig. 1904) 234, makes a typical remark: 'It is difficult for us now to understand this lust of cruelty among a people otherwise highly

civilised.' On contradictory images of Rome in the modern mind, see Peter Bondanella, *The Eternal City: Roman Images in the Modern World* (Chapel Hill: U. North Carolina, 1987). Patrick Brantlinger, *Bread and Circuses: Theories of Mass Culture and Social Decay* (Ithaca: Cornell U., 1983) 53–81, suggests that modern moralizations depicting the spectacles as symptoms and factors in the fall of Rome demonstrate a 'negative classicism', often comparing modern society with Rome's 'bread and circuses' – the classical form of mass culture.

22 The growing central power of the state, the demilitarization of the aristocracy, and the nature of modern life and work are said to have led to new social and moral constraints on interpersonal expressive violence among the European nobility, and this internalization of codes of self-restraint and gentility in sport and society filtered down the social ladder. See N. Elias, *The Civilizing Process: Sociogenetic and Psychogenetic Investigations*, vol. 1, *The History of Manners*, vol. 2, *State Formation and Civilization* (Oxford: Basil Blackwell, 1978); and N. Elias and E. Dunning, *Quest for Excitement: Sport and Leisure in the Civilizing Process* (Oxford: Basil Blackwell, 1986), including Elias, 'An Essay on Sport and Violence', 150–74, and Dunning, 'Social Bonding and Violence in Sport', 224–44. On shifting attitudes to hunting and the death of animals, see below.

23 Toynbee (1973) 21.

24 Concern about cruelty to animals is a quite recent development; the SPCA was not established until 1824. On animal baiting, cockfighting, and the tossing of animals to death as early modern English and European entertainments, see Keith Thomas, *Man and the Natural World: A Study of Modern Sensibilities* (New York: Pantheon, 1983); and Allen Guttmann, *Sports Spectators* (New York: Columbia U., 1986) 54–62. Matt Cartmill, *A View to a Kill in the Morning: Hunting and Nature through History* (Cambridge, Mass.: Harvard U., 1993) 104–8, discusses eighteenth-century abuses and the development of moralistic criticisms of animal suffering. James Turner, *Reckoning with the Beast: Animals, Pain, and Humanity in the Victorian Mind* (Baltimore: Johns Hopkins U., 1980) esp. 15–38, explains that nineteenth-century defenders of pit sports (with bulls, dogs, and rats) argued that the sports taught inspiring noble lessons about bravery, enduring pain, and facing death. On menageries and brutal, wasteful big-game hunting as symbols of imperial domination over territory and over the lower orders (beasts and savages), see Harriet Ritvo, *The Animal Estate: The English and Other Creatures in the Victorian Age* (Cambridge, Mass.: Harvard U., 1987) 243–88; Cartmill (1993) 134–7; or John M. Mackenzie, *The Empire of Nature: Hunting, Conservation and British Imperialism* (Manchester: Manchester U., 1988) 158–60. The debate about man's relationship to nature continues; now see Jan Dizard, *Going Wild: Hunting, Animal Rights, and the Contested Meaning of Nature* (Amherst: U. Massachusetts, 1994).

25 Richard Sorabji, *Animal Minds and Human Morals* (Ithaca: Cornell U., 1993), on the moral status of animals in western culture, shows that, while the Pythagoreans and Plutarch discussed the injustice of animal abuse and the virtues of vegetarianism, the ancients generally had no broad concept of animal rights. Further on Plutarch: S. T. Newmyer, 'Plutarch on Justice Towards Animals: Ancient Insights on a Modern Debate', *Scholia* n.s. 1 (1992) 38–54. Animals lacked reason and so were to be used as objects (M. Aur. *Med.* 6.23). Cf. Plutarch's story, *Per.* 1.1, Loeb, that, upon seeing wealthy foreigners in Rome carrying and fondling pet puppies and monkeys, Augustus asked them if women in their country did not bear children, 'thus in right princely fashion rebuking those who squander on animals that proneness to love and loving affection which is ours by nature, and which is due only to our fellow-men'.

26 Cartmill (1993) 40–1. Wiedemann (1992) 62: 'Pre-industrial societies cannot afford to be squeamish about the slaughter of animals, either domestic or wild.'

27 As Brown (1992), 180–1, says: 'To evaluate the violent acts of another culture in an objective way is a difficult, perhaps impossible, task, especially when the acts are completely unacceptable within one's own society.' Similarly, Hopkins (1983) 29: 'The cultural divide makes the modern historian's normal tactic of empathetic imagination particularly difficult.' Cf. Barton (1993) 7, who suggests that understanding the Roman games 'can help us articulate our own "physics" of despair, desire, fascination, and envy.' She, 5, sees 'the assumption of a provisional compatibility of human experience' as the key to understanding the spectacles.

28 Jérôme Carcopino, *Daily Life in Ancient Rome*, ed. H. T. Rowell, trans. E. O. Lorimer (Harmondsworth: Penguin, 1975) 254; cf. 267: 'Despite all the extenuations we may urge, the Roman people remain guilty of deriving public joy from their capital executions by turning the Colosseum into a torture-chamber and a human slaughter-house.' J. P. V. D. Balsdon, *Life and Leisure in Ancient Rome* (London: Bodley Head, 1969) 308: on throwing victims to the beasts: 'No one can fail to be repelled by this aspect of callous, deep-seated sadism which pervaded Romans of all classes.'

29 Otto Kiefer, *Sexual Life in Ancient Rome* (London: Abbey Library, 1934) 106. Kiefer's classic study, 99–106, sees the Romans as 'cruel by nature', a 'morbid' and 'sadistic' nation, who expressed their will to power as sadism in sex and the sadistic enjoyment of savage spectacles.

30 Revisionists have debunked the traditional contrast between positive, participatory Greek sportsmen and sinister, spectatory Romans. In fact the Romans traditionally favored exercise and games, and they developed a sincere appreciation of Greek athletics. See e.g. Nigel Crowther, 'Greek Games in Republican Rome', *Ant. Class.* 52 (1983) 268–73. Furthermore, violent and deadly sports were not a Roman preserve; see Michael B. Poliakoff, *Combat Sports in the Ancient World* (New Haven: Yale U., 1987). M. Gwyn Morgan, 'Three Non-Roman Blood Sports', *CQ* n.s. 25 1 (1975) 117–22, shows that cockfighting, quailfighting, and partridge-fighting were more common among Greeks than Romans. Greeks were especially fond of cockfights and felt that they inspired military vigor and a determination to fight to the death; e.g. Lucian *Anach.* 37; Plut. *Mor.* 1049a and other references in Eric Csapo, 'Deep Ambivalence: Notes on a Greek Cockfight (Part I)', and 'Parts 2–4', *Phoenix* 47 (1993) 1–28, 115–24.

31 See Barton (1993) n. 4 on 11, for more modern condemnations of gladiatorial shows as incomprehensible, alien, and sadistic.

32 E.g. the history of public, ritualized lynchings in modern America, as the result of legal procedures and mob violence, is an obvious and sobering comparison; see J. William Harris, 'Etiquette, Lynching, and Racial Boundaries in Southern History: A Mississippi Example', *AHR* 100 (1995) 387–410; W. Fitzhugh Brundage, *Lynching in the New South: Georgia and Virginia, 1880–1930* (Urbana: U. Illinois, 1993); George C. Wright, *Racial Violence in Kentucky, 1865–1940: Lynchings, Mob Rule, and 'Legal Lynchings'* (Baton Rouge: Louisiana State U., 1990).

33 The problem of violence in human society, the debate over primitive instincts versus acquired traits, has fascinated writers from Freud to Konrad Lorenz and Desmond Morris, and the debate continues. On the origins and institutionalization of violence, see David Riches, ed., *The Anthropology of Violence* (Oxford: Basil Blackwell, 1986), which, 1–3 and passim, explains the legitimization of violence by the established order as for the common good; Walter Burkert, *Homo Necans*, trans. P. Bing (Berkeley: U. California, 1983); and R. G. Hammerton-Kelly, ed., *Violent Origins: Walter Burkert, René Girard, and Jonathan Z. Smith on Ritual Killing*

and Cultural Formation (Stanford: Stanford U., 1987), which discusses Burkert's theories on paleolithic hunting rituals, Girard's ideas on locally adapted sacral rites, and Smith's modern views on social reconstruction through violence. Burkert examines the actual process of killing, treatment, and disposal in blood sacrifice, theorizing that the ritual reconstitution of animal victims harked back to paleolithic concerns. Burkert writes, 1, that 'all orders and forms of authority in human society are founded on institutionalized violence . . . Thus, blood and violence lurk fascinatingly at the very heart of religion.' Postulating enduring religious concerns rooted in primal acts of violence, René Girard, *Violence and the Sacred*, trans. P. Gregory (Baltimore: Johns Hopkins U., 1977), suggests that societies use public rituals of violence to confront the threat of disorder from social violence. Scapegoats – marginal, ambivalent figures – are used to discharge society's elemental predisposition to violence, and such sacred rites can evolve into stylized sports. For divergent views see Cartmill (1993) 1–27 and passim, who on paleoanthropological grounds rejects the 'hunting hypothesis', which asserts the influence of paleolithic hunting on essential human nature; and Lawrence H. Keeley, *War Before Civilization: The Myth of the Peaceful Savage* (Oxford: Oxford U., 1995), who argues that the brutality and frequency of pre-historic warfare show that man never was a peaceful, noble savage.

34 In 1922 H. J. Rose, 'The Greek Agones', repr. in *Arete (Journal of Sport Literature)* 3 (1985) 169–70, suggested a pattern in the worship of the dead from Australian aborigines to Greece and Rome: 'The most acceptable offering to the dead is blood; and among a warlike people a natural way to provide this is by means of combat over the grave.' Greece: Hom. *Il.* 23.801–25: funeral game combat in arms; Plut. *Mor.* 675c: the original games at Olympia were duels to the death. Hdt. 5.8: at funerals of wealthy Thracians, after laying out the dead, sacrificing, feasting, lamentation, the actual burial and building of the burial mound, there were all sorts of contests and the greatest prizes were offered for single combat. K. Meuli, 'Der Ursprung der Olympischen Spiele', *Die Antike* 17 (1941) 189–208, saw the origin of Greek funeral games in the ritualistic identification or selection of a man guilty of homicide; but now see Poliakoff (1987) 149–57.

35 Clifford Geertz' classic exercise in interpretive sociology, 'Deep Play: Notes on the Balinese Cockfight', 1–37, in C. Geertz, ed., *Myth, Symbol, and Culture* (New York: Norton, 1974), explains that the intense involvement of specta-tors in blood sports as 'deep play' goes beyond diversion to a deeper symbolism about danger and social order. See ch. 3 below on the gladiatorial paradox.

36 M. I. Finley, *Ancient History, Evidence and Models* (New York: Viking, 1985) 60, defines a model as: 'a simplified structuring of reality which presents suppos-edly significant relationships in a generalized form'.

37 E.g., surveying interpretations of gladiators, Hopkins (1983) 27–30, notes the social psychology of the crowds, Romans' exposure to cruelty, games as devices of discipline and control, as by-products of warring traditions, as confirmations of public order, and as 'a psychic and political safety valve' for the release of tensions. In her perceptive review essay on Wiedemann (1992), S. Brown, 'Explaining the Arena: Did the Romans "Need" Gladiators?', *JRA* 8 (1995) 376–84, comments, 383: 'A scholarly consensus as to 'the' explanation for the arena, especially across a wide geographical extent and a history of more than 700 years, is surely impossible.'

38 On spectacles and religion, see A. Piganiol, *Recherches sur les jeux romains* (Strasburg: Librairie Istra, 1923); and M. Le Glay, 'Les Amphithéâtres: *Loci religiosi?*', 217–29, in Domergue et al. (1990). G. Ville, 'Les Jeux de gladiateurs dans l'empire chrétien', *MÉFRA* 72 (1960) 273–335, suggests, 289, that games

held under Constantine and other Christian emperors were not associated with the pagan gods or the cult of the dead. In 'Savage Miracles: Redemption of Lost Honor in Roman Society and the Sacrament of the Gladiator and the Martyr', *Representations* 45 (1994) 41–71, C. Barton argues that, by the very nature of sacrifice and consecration, gladiators were always sacred. See further below in ch. 3.

39 Hopkins (1983) 1–2, 29, suggests that the arena turned war into a game or drama in the 'domesticated battlefield of the amphitheatre' set up in memory of Rome's warrior traditions. However, now see the arguments of Welch (1994) for games and amphitheaters as major social functions promoting military virtue during the Republic. She concludes, 80, that: 'The stone amphitheatre was born during a time of military activity and cannot, therefore, be explained as a substitute for warfare or as a symptom of collective *ennui* . . . The Romans' interest in the arena had much to do with their conception of themselves as a military people, that is, their conception of what it meant to be Roman.' See further on Welch below.

40 Johan Huizinga, *Homo Ludens: The Study of the Play Element in Culture* (repr. Boston: Beacon Press, 1950, orig. 1938) 9–10, 89–104, sees games as surrogate war, struggles as a means of reconciliation with defeat and death.

41 Defining sport thus, 13, H. A. Harris, *Sport in Greece and Rome* (London: Thames and Hudson, 1972), discusses Roman chariot racing but excludes arena spectacles. Poliakoff (1987), and J. K. Anderson, *Hunting in the Ancient World* (Berkeley: U. California, 1985) exclude Roman gladiatorial and hunting spectacles on the grounds of morality and purpose. Poliakoff, 7, sees the spectacles as 'a form of warfare for spectators'. Arguing that when neolithic man began sacrificing domesticated animals the earlier ritual element of expended energy in the paleolithic hunt was henceforth sacrificed in the form of sport as an enduring ritual and an offering to the gods, D. Sansone, *Greek Athletics and the Genesis of Sport* (Berkeley: U. California, 1988) 61–2, 116–17, sees Roman gladiatorial fights simply as an intensified form of 'sport'. On violence in sport and its impact on spectatorship at Rome and in general, see Guttmann (1986) 19–27 and passim, and his 'Roman Sports Violence', 1–19, in Jeffrey H. Goldstein, ed., *Sports Violence* (New York: Springer-Verlag, 1983). J. P. Toner's recent work, *Leisure and Ancient Rome* (Cambridge: Polity Press, 1995) 34–52, discusses spectacles within a broader context of Roman leisure.

42 E.g. Balsdon (1969), 248 and 268, stresses the predominance of theater shows and the interest in chariot races, saying that Romans seldom saw gladiators. L. Robert, *Les Gladiateurs dans l'Orient grec* (repr. Amsterdam: Hakkert, 1971, orig. 1940) 250–3, notes that documents in the eastern Empire refer to gladiators with terms similar to those applied to boxers and other heavy athletes. J. Pearson, *Arena: The Story of the Colosseum* (New York: McGraw-Hill, 1973) 107–12, feels that the development of style and skill in fighting, a star system, and the participation of free volunteers turned gladiatorial combat into 'modern-style mass sport'. See below on the interest in the volunteerism of gladiators as perhaps a new version of apologia.

43 In addition to football, boxing, hunting, rodeo, auto racing, and professional wrestling, the television show *American Gladiators* and the recent rise of 'Ultimate Fighting Championships' (purportedly a modern version of the Greek *pankration*) speak volumes about not just the acceptability but the appeal of violence in modern 'sports'. As Ernest Hemingway, *Death in the Afternoon* (New York: Scribners, 1960, orig. 1932) 22, commented: 'We, in games, are not fascinated by death, its nearness and its avoidance. We are fascinated by victory and we replace the avoidance of death by the avoidance of defeat. It is a very

nice symbolism but it takes more cojones to be a sportsman when death is a closer party to the game.'

44 In his *Res gestae, Mon Anc.* 22–3, Augustus carefully listed the entertainments which he provided as 'Princeps'. Cic. *Sest.* 106, 124: the masses express themselves at assemblies, elections, games (*ludi*), and gladiatorial contests. The role of the assemblies of Romans at games and spectacles as (unofficially) political, as forums for the effective expression of public opinions – rather than as diversions for the politically impotent – has been well established (especially concerning theaters and the circus). See, e.g., A. Cameron, *Bread and Circuses: The Roman Emperor and his People* (London: Oxford U., 1974); A. Cameron, *Circus Factions* (Oxford: Oxford, 1976) 156–92; T. Bollinger, *Theatralis Licentia: die Publikumsdemonstrationen an den öffentlichen Spielen im Rom der früheren Kaiserzeit und ihre Bedeutung im politischen Leben* (Winterthur: Hans Schellenberg, 1969) 24–71; and Yavetz (1988) esp. 18–24. Hopkins (1983), 14–20, says that bloody spectacles can be seen as 'political theatre', as dramatic reconfirmations of the emperor's power and ritual reestablishments of the moral and political order. Broadly on euergetism, politics, and social order, see Paul Veyne, *Bread and Circuses: Historical Sociology and Political Pluralism*, abridged with an Introd. by O. Murray, trans. B. Pearce (London: Allen Lane, Penguin, 1990, orig. 1976) esp. 701–30.

45 Wiedemann (1992), 165–83, sees spectacles as a forum revealing the ambiguity of imperial versus popular sovereignty; the emperor's provision of shows and his attendance were obligations, and popular sovereignty was expressed through condemnations and reprieves decided by the crowd. Similarly, see F. Millar, *The Emperor in the Roman World* (Ithaca: Cornell U., 1992, orig. 1977) 368–75; Gunderson (1996) 126–33.

46 See David Potter, 'Performance, Power, and Justice in the High Empire', 129–60, in Slater (1996) esp. 147–55, quote at 159, on the theatrical aspects of the exercise of authority at spectacles. Potter thoroughly demonstrates the ability of the crowd, especially by using chants as expressions of the popular will, to influence public trials, executions, and arena spectacles. Further on the complexities of interactions between emperors and spectators in theaters, amphitheaters, and society and politics at large, see Shadi Bartsch, *Actors in the Audience: Theatricality and Doublespeak from Nero to Hadrian* (Cambridge, Mass.: Harvard U., 1994), who pursues the paradigm of theatricality – where audiences are forced to applaud and act in response to the performance of an oppressive autocrat – in Roman culture and politics. Especially under Nero and in Tacitus, autocracy reverses the roles of actor and audience; but Bartsch also shows that spectators could resist by means of innuendo and doublespeak. Recently, Wilfried Nippel, *Public Order in Ancient Rome* (Cambridge: Cambridge U., 1995) 87–8, 93–5, relating interaction at shows to the maintenance of public order, adds an intriguing reference, 21–2, from Macrob. *Sat.* 2.61, to an edict of 56 BC ordering that only fruit and not stones might be thrown into the arena. As shown below in ch. 8, in varying degrees the authority figures, the crowd, and the victims themselves might also influence the final spectacular act – the disposal of victims.

47 Michel Foucault, *Discipline and Punish: The Birth of the Prison*, trans. A. Sheridan (New York: Pantheon, 1977). On arenas and amphitheaters as symbolic urban spaces that housed games as ideological rituals of integration and hegemony, shows that communicated discipline, a hierarchical social order, submission, and protection, see Clavel-Lévêque (1984a); similarly her 'L'Espace des jeux dans le monde romain: hégémonie, symbolique et pratique sociale', *ANRW* (Berlin: De Gruyter, 1986) 2.16.3: 2406–563, and her 'Rituels de mort et

28

consommation de gladiateurs: Images de domination et pratiques imperialistes de reproduction', 189–208, in Hélène Walter, ed., *Hommages à Lucien Lerat* (Paris: Les Belles Lettres, 1984).

48 Not just 'functional' in Durkheim's sense of the demonstration of social order, games could act as social drama, disrupting and altering the social order. On rituals, spectacles, power, and community in general, see the fundamental works on symbolic anthropology by Victor Turner and Clifford Geertz. On rituals and power in modern society, see, e.g., D. I. Kertzer, *Ritual, Politics and Power* (New Haven: Yale U., 1988). On performance theory, see J. J. MacAloon, *Rite, Drama, Festival, Spectacle: Rehearsals Toward a Theory of Cultural Performance* (Philadelphia: U. Pennsylvania, 1984); and Paul Connerton, *How Societies Remember* (Cambridge: Cambridge U., 1989). On the Roman use of images and ceremonies, see, e.g., S. Price, *Rituals and Power: The Roman Imperial Cult in Asia Minor* (Cambridge: Cambridge U., 1984); or Zanker (1988). Most recently, Edmondson (1996), esp. 98–112, approaches 'gladiatorial presentations' as 'cultural performances' at which emperors and participants (in both the stands and the arena) did not merely passively reflect the status quo but rather could make 'dynamic contributions' to the active construction of Roman cultural values and social relationships.

49 A. W. Lintott, *Violence in Republican Rome* (Oxford: Clarendon Press, 1968) 6–21, Latin quote at 23 from *Dig.* 43.16.1.27. He shows, 35–51, that Romans extended sympathy only in proportion to one's worth and deserts (*dignitas*).

50 Roland Auguet, *Cruelty and Civilization: The Roman Games* (repr. London: Routledge, 1994, orig. 1970) 15, feels that, somewhat ironically, the utilitarian and practical Roman mind was averse to destroying potentially valuable items, but it was in favor of useful calculated cruelty for political ends. Potter (1993) 65: death in the arena was 'a political as well as a juridical ritual, a ceremony which served to reinforce the existing power structure by reducing the condemned to the level of an object. The body of the condemned became a vehicle for the reaffirmation of the public order.'

51 See K. M. Coleman, 'Fatal Charades: Roman Executions Staged as Mythological Enactments', *JRS* 80 (1990) 44–73, who concludes, 73, that increasingly autocratic emperors demonstrated their power of life and death by turning myths into reality. See ch. 3 below on Michael B. Hornum, *Nemesis, the Roman State, and the Games* (Leiden: Brill, 1993). Cf. Gunderson (1996) 149: 'Nearly every major theme of the Roman power structure was deployed in the spectacles: social stratification; political theater; crime and punishment; representations of civilization and empire; repression of women and exaltation of bellicose masculinity.'

52 Barton (1993) 30. Barton, 59, even suggests, empathically, that in delighting in terrible suffering, Romans 'were both victims and victimizers, and thus, in a sense, *neither* victims nor victimizers'.

53 Wiedemann (1992) xvi, 46–7, passim. Ibid., 179: 'The arena was where Roman society dealt not just with the chaos represented by wild beasts and crime, but also the chaos of death. It was a symbol of the ordered world, the cosmos; it was the place where the civilized world confronted lawless nature.' Cf. Jean Maurin, 'Les Barbares aux arènes', *Ktèma* 9 (1984) 102–11.

54 Plass (1995) 9. Plass, 56–8, at 58, sees gladiatorial combat as part of a 'common process of publicly acknowledging and working through in ritual form dangers that perpetually threaten order'. Plass, n. 11 on 208–9, also applies Girard's theory of violence to gladiatorial combats.

55 Ibid., 25–8, applies the ideas of V. Turner about liminoid states and van Gennep's model of a three-stage process of separation, transition (ordeal), and

reintegration through which societies recognize, deal with, and dispose of threats. Rome resolved anomaly, 25: 'by confirming social order through disorder, controlling violence by means of violence, injecting fear into entertainment, and transforming ritual into reality through actual death'.

56 For a recent and detailed extension of theoretical discussions, see Gunderson (1996), focusing on the value and meaning of the arena for the elite classes in the early Empire. Applying Foucault's Panopticon, Gunderson suggests, 115–16, that the arena acts as 'a social organ of sight', 'an apparatus which not only looks in on a spectacle, but one which in its organization and structure reproduces the relations subsisting between observer and observed'. Also applying ideas from Louis Althusser, Gunderson approaches the arena, 117, as 'an Ideological State Apparatus in Rome, and hence a vehicle for the reproduction of the relations of production. Most importantly, the arena serves to reproduce the Roman subject and thus acts as an instrument of the reproduction of Romanness as a variously lived experience.'

57 See, e.g., Peter Brown's brilliant work, *The Body and Society: Men, Women, and Sexual Renunciation in Early Christianity* (New York: Columbia U., 1988).

58 Florence Dupont, *Daily Life in Ancient Rome*, trans. C. Woodall (Oxford: Basil Blackwell, 1989) 240–1. Morris (1992) 31: 'The body is a uniquely powerful medium for ritual communication, furnishing a set of "natural symbols", as some would call them.' Cf. C. P. Jones, '*Stigma*: Tattooing and Branding in Graeco-Roman Antiquity', *JRS* 77 (1987) 139–55. Plutarch, *Rom.* 27.5, tells a story that the first senators of Rome killed Romulus, dismembered him, and distributed pieces to each senator to carry away. W. Burkert, 'Caesar und Romulus-Quirinus', *Hist.* 11 (1962) 356–76, at 365–8, sees this as a metaphor for the transfer of power from the king to the senators at the establishment of Rome's social order. Bruce Lincoln, 'Of Meat and Society, Sacrifice and Creation, Butchers and Philosophy', *L'Uomo* 9 (1985) 9–29, at 14–16, relates this sociogony to the Indo-European practice of sacrificial dismemberment.

59 F. Hinard, 'Spectacle des exécutions et espace urbain', 111–25, in *L'Urbs: Espace urbain et histoire (Ier siècle av. J.-C.–IIIe siècle ap. J.-C.)*, CÉFR 98 (Rome: Palais Farnèse, 1987), has pursued the question of the disposal of corpses of executed individuals in the late Republic, but not those from arena spectacles. His topographical suggestions stress the influence of custom but underestimate logistical considerations. J.-P. Callu, 'Le Jardin des supplices au Bas-Empire', 313–59, in *Du châtiment dans la cité: Supplices corporels et peine de mort dans le monde antique*, CÉFR 79 (Rome: Palais Farnèse, 1984) 337–8, notes that sometimes executions might be reinforced by abuse of the corpse, and he does pay attention to the disposal of Christians, but I disagree with him on various points.

60 Ariès (1974), 39–44, contrasts our modern, 'wild', or frightful death, with its horror of physical death and decomposition, with, 1–24, the 'tame death' of medieval times as calm, collective, and familiar, a death accepted without great fear or awe. Christian Europe saw death as natural and found comfort in the belief in collective resurrection; but the development of individualism from the thirteenth to the fifteenth century brought anxiety about the death of the self and individual judgement: 103–7. Modern death became seen as a break, an unacceptable separation. By the mid-twentieth century, 85–103, death had become a shameful and forbidden taboo. On North American peculiarities (e.g. embalming, beautification of the corpse for display, horror of putrescence) and the commercialism of funeral practices, see Ariès (1982) 596–601; and Metcalf and Huntington (1991) 26–7, 191–214, with further bibliography.

61 Scholarly examinations include: G. Gnoli and J.-P. Vernant, eds., *La Mort, les morts, dans les sociétés anciennes* (Cambridge: Cambridge U., 1982); and Morris

(1992) on antiquity; and broader works, e.g. Metcalf and Huntington (1991) and S. C. Humphreys and Helen King, eds., *Mortality and Immortality: The Anthropology and Archaeology of Death* (London: Academic Press, 1981). Recent works on Roman death rites include: François Hinard, ed., *La Mort, les morts, et l'au-delà dans le monde romain* (Caen: Centre de Publications de l'Université de Caen, 1987); François Hinard, ed., *La Mort au quotidien dans le monde romain* (Paris: De Boccard, 1995); see further below in ch. 4. Interest in necrology, thanatology, or what Hinard (1987a) 5, calls 'les études ultérieures', has revived, in part influenced by modern medical resources and emergency treatments and the recent 'death awareness' movement; see Metcalf and Huntington (1991) xi, 22, 25–7. Publications range from the psychological to the sensationalistic: e.g. E. Kübler-Ross, *Death: The Final Stage of Growth* (Englewood Cliffs, N.J.: Prentice-Hall, 1975); Kenneth V. Iverson, *Death to Dust: What Happens to Dead Bodies?* (Tucson, Ariz.: Galen Press, 1994).

62 I exclude preliminary warm-up fights (*prolusiones*) with wooden weapons or whips, displays by military cadets (*iuvenes*, see Ville (1981) 216–20), and harmless theatrical entertainments (e.g. comedy, mimes, music, acrobats). However, I include spectacles of death which occurred in theaters and 'fatal charades' or mythologized executions staged in arenas; see ch. 2 below.

63 E.g. Michael H. Robinson and Lionel Tiger, eds., *Man and Beast Revisited* (Washington: Smithsonian Institute, 1991); Aubrey Manning and James Serpell, eds., *Animals and Human Society: Changing Perspectives* (London: Routledge, 1993).

64 Constantine forbade gladiatorial games but they continued; see Ville (1960) 314–16. On shows in the late Empire, see ch. 2 below.

65 Hopkins (1983) 'Murderous Games', 1–30, and 'Death in Rome', 210–56. Hinard (1987a) has twenty-seven articles, many of them excellent, on normal death, but none on the arena. The twenty essays in Hinard (1995) include a few relevant essays (e.g. on executions, suicide, and funerary rituals), but none on arena death and disposal.

66 Herein the term *noxii* (as in Tert. *Apol.* 15.4) refers to hated and doomed victims (slaves, criminals, captives, and deserters), as distinct from trained (and somewhat rehabilitated) gladiators; cf. ch. 3 below.

67 Plass (1995), e.g. 26, 36, 71, sees the arena in symbolic terms as a 'disposal area' for the expulsion of social outsiders through death, but there was also the practical problem of ultimate disposal.

68 R. Parker, *Miasma: Pollution and Purification in Early Greek Religion* (Oxford: Clarendon Press, 1983) 46.

69 Hinard (1987b) 111.

70 Potter (1996) 155: 'Public executions are only effective rituals if there is agreement that the sentence is just.' Cf. Sen. *De ira* 2.2.4, Loeb: 'our minds are perturbed by a shocking picture and by the melancholy sight of a punishment even when it is entirely just' ('movet mentes et atrox pictura et iustissimorum suppliciorum tristis adspectus').

71 Legal, moral, and sacral aspects of crime and punishment remained intertwined from the earliest days of the Roman community. On the rich Roman terminology, including concepts of contagion, purification, and expiation, see Gabriele Thome, 'Crime and Punishment, Guilt and Expiation: Roman Thought and Vocabulary', *A. Class.* 35 (1992) 73–98, esp. 77–8. Also see Thome, 76, 79–80, on *noxius*, in the sense of *damnosus*, as a derivative of *noxa*, *noxia*, with connotations of damage, injury, and guilt.

72 Alexander Scobie, 'Slums, Sanitation and Mortality in the Roman World', *Klio* 68 (1986) 399–433, at 399–400, points out that Vitruvius virtually ignores disposal of human and other wastes: 'Perhaps decorum precluded discussion of

such topics, and it is possible that presumed knowledge of normal practice made such discussion unnecessary.' Scobie, 'Spectator Security and Comfort at Gladiatorial Games', *Nikephoros* 1 (1988) 191–243, at 196–7, suggests that Vitruvius' decorum inclined him to places of *dignitas*, not *infamia*. A lack of explicit documentation does not prove the insignificance of a problem or a procedure in Rome or Greece; e.g. Robert Garland, *The Greek Way of Death* (Ithaca: Cornell U., 1985) x, 36, points out that we do not know whether a regular liturgy accompanied the disposal of the body in Greek funerals.

73 Juv. 10.78–81; with a parallel in Fronto, *Ep.* 2.216. Plutarch, *Mor.* 802D, also criticizes leaders who influence the masses by giving banquets, money, and gladiatorial and other shows.

74 We must be cautious about accepting specific 'facts' literally from sources, but we can use sources to suggest general attitudes and practices. Ancient writers present the character and rule of emperors via their behavior concerning spectacles; see K. R. Bradley, 'The Significance of the *Spectacula* in Suetonius' *Caesares*', *RSA* 11 (1981) 129–37; R. F. Newbold, 'Cassius Dio and the Games', *Ant. Class.* 44 (1975) 589–604; and Wiedemann (1992) 130–5, 171–5. Suetonius includes abundant references to spectacles for biographical ends, as emperors' displays of wealth and imperial power, and as a technique of evaluation, one means of estimating an emperor's performance of his duties to his subjects at Rome. Bradley, 132, notes that Suetonius generally approves of imperial spectacles, and he tends to record his spectacles in a positive context when listing commendable items of a reign. Mainly concerned with status, propriety, and economics, Dio discusses an emperor's games (e.g. his cruel or indecorous behavior or his disregard for the treasury) as part of the evaluation of that emperor; as Newbold suggests, 604: 'An emperor's games policy provided a convenient yardstick for measuring his performance as a whole.' Edmondson (1996), 75–9, offers the best recent discussion of historians' accounts of imperial spectacles, noting, for example, that Tacitus and Dio saw spectacles as beneath their historiographical dignity. On the problems of moralistic, elitist, and rhetorical influences on sources concerning emperors and their actions, see R. Saller, 'Anecdotes as Historical Evidence for the Principate', *G&R* 27 (1980) 69–83; and more generally, Catharine Edwards, *The Politics of Immorality in Ancient Rome* (Cambridge: Cambridge U., 1993).

75 A long debate continues over the authorship, purpose, and reliability of the *Scriptores Historiae Augustae*, which purports to have been written by six authors in the late third and early fourth centuries AD. See T. D. Barnes, *The Sources of the Historia Augusta*, Collection Latomus 155 (Brussels: Latomus, 1978), who argues for a single author of ca. AD 395–9, now the general opinion among scholars. Since the author(s) fabricated documents and probably whole biographies (i.e. Avidius Cassius, the lesser emperors after Alexander Severus), the SHA must be used with caution, but its use here is unavoidable. Whatever our skepticism about the quantitative dimensions of spectacles of death in the SHA, the qualitative aspects of the accounts were intelligible to a Roman audience and find corroboration in Dio and Suetonius. For a detailed discussion of capital punishment in the SHA, see Callu (1984), esp. 327–33, 352–7.

76 Tert. *De spect.* 5.8 and Suda s.v. mention a lost work by Suetonius, the *Ludicra historia*. In his philological study of the attitudes of nine first-century AD Roman authors, Wistrand (1992), 15, 55, suggests that most writers, except Martial, felt that entertainments were not a proper subject for literature.

77 Most martyrological references herein are cited from H. A. Musurillo, *The Acts of the Christian Martyrs* (Oxford: Clarendon Press, 1972). Further on source problems, see ch. 8 below.

78 Roman legal history is daunting for the non-expert, and this study has been greatly assisted by the recent appearance of three excellent works: Bauman (1996); O. F. Robinson, *The Criminal Law of Ancient Rome* (Baltimore: Johns Hopkins U., 1995); Nippel (1995).

79 Major studies include: P. Sabbatini Tumolesi, *Gladiatorum paria: Annunci di spettacoli gladiatorii a Pompeii* (Rome: Edizioni Quasar, 1980); P. Sabbatini Tumolesi, *Epigrafia anfiteatrale dell'Occidente Romano I: Roma* (Rome: Edizioni Quasar, 1988); Gian Luca Gregori, *Epigrafia anfiteatrale dell'Occidente Romano II: Regiones Italiae VI–XI* (Rome: Edizioni Quasar, 1989). See further below in ch. 5.

80 On mosaics and the arena, see Katherine M. D. Dunbabin, *The Mosaics of Roman North Africa* (Oxford: Clarendon Press, 1978) 65–87; and Brown (1992) on arena art from inexpensive media (e.g. lamps) to commissioned works (e.g mosaics) for the wealthy. She also notes, 188–92, that scenes in art tend to be tripartite and ranked thematically: men against men, men against beasts, and last beasts against beasts. The rankings reflect the degree of certainty of outcome from herbivores against carnivores to equally matched gladiators. Further on art and victims, see ch. 2 below. On amphitheaters: A. Hönle and A. Henze, *Römische Amphitheater und Stadien: Gladiatorenkämpfe und Circusspiele* (Zurich: Atlantis, 1981); Jean-Claude Golvin, *L'Amphithéâtre romain: Essai sur la théorisation de sa forme et de ses fonctions*, 2 vols. (Paris: É. de Boccard, 1988); Golvin and Landes (1990) 85–153; David L. Bomgardner, 'The Carthage Amphitheater: A Reappraisal', *AJA* 93 (1989) 85–103 and his 'An Analytical Study of North African Amphitheaters', 2 vols., his unpublished dissertation, U. Michigan, 1985. Cf. Wiedemann's excellent survey of art and architecture (1992) 188–92.

2

THE PHENOMENON:
THE DEVELOPMENT AND
DIVERSITY OF ROMAN
SPECTACLES OF DEATH

One of the simplest things of all and the most fundamental
is violent death.
(E. Hemingway, *Death in the Afternoon*, 1960 (1932) 2)

Rome violently and publicly killed human and animal victims in a variety
of 'games' or 'shows'.[1] These entertainments became more elaborate and
complex over time but danger and death were not stylized and reduced, as
in modern violent sports, but intensified and actualized. Even after Olympics,
Superbowls, and World Cups, moderns are still amazed not just by the
brutality but by the extent and the diversity of the Roman spectacles. For
example, Caesar's triumphal games in 46 BC were a truly spectacular combination of theatrical, equestrian, athletic, and gladiatorial events held on
several sites in front of large crowds:

> He gave entertainments of diverse kinds: a combat of gladiators and
> also stage-plays in every ward of the city . . . as well as races in the
> circus, athletic contests, and a sham sea-fight . . . [military dances,
> theatrical events, equestrian contests, and the Game of Troy (an
> equestrian performance) also were held] . . . Combats with wild beasts
> were presented on five successive days, and last of all [in the Circus
> Maximus] there was a battle between two opposing armies, in which
> five hundred foot-soldiers, twenty elephants, and thirty horsemen
> engaged on each side . . . [three days of athletic competitions took
> place in the Campus Martius] . . . For the naval battle a pool was dug
> in the lesser Codeta and there was a contest of ships . . . Such a throng
> flocked to all these shows from every quarter, that . . . the press was
> often such that many were crushed to death, including two senators.[2]

To open the Flavian Amphitheater in AD 80 Titus gave extravagant spectacles lasting for a hundred days:

animals both tame and wild were slain to the number of nine thousand . . . several [men] fought in single combat and several groups contended together both in infantry and naval battles. For Titus suddenly filled this same theater with water and brought in horses and bulls and some other domesticated animals . . . He also brought in people on ships, who engaged in a sea-fight there . . . and others gave a similar exhibition outside the city . . . There, too, on the first day there was a gladiatorial exhibition and a wild beast hunt . . . On the second day there was a horse-race, and on the third day a naval battle between three thousand men, followed by an infantry battle.[3]

In AD 107, as an entertainment and a celebration after his Dacian campaigns, Trajan held 23 days of games in which 11,000 animals were killed and 10,000 gladiators fought.[4] Such *spectacula* were things seen in public, spectacular things in scale and action, things worth seeing and meant to be seen, put on by elite representatives of the community to reinforce the social order, which included their own status. When resources permitted, emperors put on spectacles as impressively as they could, and the obligation on the leader and the appreciation by the people continued into the Christian era.

This chapter surveys the historical development and growing diversity and pervasiveness of the phenomenon of spectacles of death in which creatures were intentionally and violently killed in 'arenas' at Rome.[5] The early roots and natures of different types of spectacles of death suggest enduring religious concerns and punitive motives. Like other peoples, from its origins Rome saw the public killing of animals in sacrifices and humans in executions as vital to the security of the city as an ordered society and as a sacral community. Over time the categories of sacrifice, ritual killing, execution, and hunting became blurred, especially as they increasingly overlapped in what might be called the 'conglomerate' or multi-dimensional spectacles of the first century BC.

Festivals, punishments, celebrations, and games

From its earliest days Rome celebrated festivals or holidays (*feriae*) concerned with fertility and harvest, fields and lustration. These rustic ceremonies (e.g. Saturnalia, Lupercalia) were moved into the emerging city, held close to temples and shrines, and added to the official festival calendar. The fundamental rite was the sacrifice of domesticated animals to honor the gods. A proper sacrifice was one in which an unblemished animal was induced to suggest its willingness by stretching forward its neck. The meaning of beast sacrifices in antiquity has been interpreted in many sophisticated ways, but at its core was the sense that the community was dependent on the good will of the gods. Convinced that they had to give up things in order to

35

get things, ancient peoples regularly and ritually offered blood sacrifices for the welfare of the community. Some sacrifices were done discreetly by priests, but most were performed in public after a procession of the victims. Wanting to know that the rites had been performed properly, people participated indirectly as witnesses, and some of the meat might be distributed to be eaten by worshippers. Other things, such as grain, were sacrificed as well, but in the ancient mind blood and death were intimately associated with fertility and regeneration. Holidays with sacrifices reinforced social and cosmic hierarchies, and ritual violence, security, and the sacred were insep-arable.[6] For centuries Romans saw sacrifices of animals as essential to the vitality of the group, and their magnitude and splendor were a reflection of the sacrificial group's status. Done regularly and properly, sacrifices of flawless, willing beasts provided few problems, psychological or logistical, for pagan Rome.[7]

At this point a digression on the question of whether Rome practiced human sacrifice is called for on various accounts: human sacrifice is a wide-spread phenomenon in human history, Romans knew of human sacrifice and may have performed it symbolically and regularly via surrogates or occasion-ally in actuality, Christian sources repeatedly accuse Rome of performing human sacrifices (at funerals, in festivals, and at *munera*), and some scholars associate gladiatorial spectacles with aspects of human sacrifice.[8] As we shall see, while human sacrifice was a motif in Roman literature,[9] and while some groups within the Empire did practice it,[10] Rome did not routinely perform human sacrifice in a conventional sense. Nevertheless, the ritualized killing of humans in the arena was not without religious overtones and concerns, for homicide in antiquity always involved the sacred.

Human sacrifice was the most extreme form of sacrifice of a living crea-ture, but unfortunately the term is often used very generally of any killing of a human in a religious context. In the most obvious examples, as among the Aztecs, human lives were offered regularly to seek the gods' help in ensuring continued security (e.g. via fertility, rainfall, success in war) for the community.[11] More specifically, we should distinguish between human sacrifice and ritual killing. In human sacrifice societies feel that a god or its cult requires the regular offering of human life. In ritual killing (or ritu-alized murder), in reaction to circumstances (e.g. crises, crimes, prodigies), societies carry out the killing of humans in ritualized and sacralized ways, in hopes that the consecration of the victim to the god(s) will sanction or legitimize the violence, prevent pollution, and bring a restoration of order. In human sacrifice the gods (or the dead) are thought to demand the sacrifice, while in ritual killing the gods (or the dead) accept, approve of, or appre-ciate the killing as an honorific gesture. Both of these forms of homicide enlist divine aid in preventing or resolving a crisis (e.g. famine or pestilence), and in purifying the community – on a regular basis or by removing a particular offense to the gods and the related disruption to the social order.[12]

36

Human sacrifice tended to be regular and preventive, while ritual killing tended to be occasional and reactive. Such distinctions are difficult, however, because descriptions of ritualized killing often appropriate the vocabulary of sacrifice.[13] For example, in the ritual killing or expulsion of a 'scapegoat' a person, often a criminal or a scapegoat who the community feels must be executed (or exiled), is consecrated or devoted to infernal or chthonic deities and then executed or driven off to a symbolic death. While 'scapegoat' phenomena are often associated with human sacrifice, if scapegoats are actually killed, they are better seen as examples of ritual killing – unless the scapegoat ritual is institutionalized on a regular basis, as in a recurring festival, in which case it would be better seen as human sacrifice.[11]

Recently J. Rives has shown convincingly that recurrent charges and counter-charges of human sacrifice between Christians and Romans were not historically reliable accounts but rather were a feature of an extensive Graeco-Roman discourse about civilization and religion. Pagan claims that Christians performed human sacrifices, killed babies, and drank blood seem to have been a phenomenon of the second half of the second century AD used against a group that rejected central features of Roman religion (e.g. blood sacrifice) and society (e.g. spectacles). Accusations were noted from Justin Martyr (e.g. *Apol*. 11.12.5) in the 150s on, and reversed and applied against pagans by Tertullian (*Apol*. 9), Minucius Felix (*Oct*. 30), and others. Well into the fourth and fifth centuries Christians continued to indict Rome as moved by demons to sacrifice humans – to Saturn in the annual gladiatorial games in December and to Jupiter in the Feriae Latinae (see below). Accusers on both sides used such charges (and related charges of cannibalism) as signs or cultural markers to assert their cultural superiority, to establish cultural distance, and to malign their opponents as 'the other' – as barbaric rather than civilized, and as worshippers of bad rather than proper religion.[15] On neither side were the accusations based on actual customary human sacrifices.

We do not know whether Latins ever practiced human sacrifice in prehistory, but by historical times any such Roman traditions had normally been stylized via effigies and surrogates.[16] Human sacrifice was condemned as a non-Roman and barbaric rite, but sources claim that some examples of human sacrifice, or more probably ritualized killing, took place in Rome.[17] In the earliest purported example, Livy says that in 356 BC the Tarquinians sacrificed 307 Roman captives in the forum of Caere, and in revenge 358 captives from the noblest Tarquinian families were sent to Rome in 355 and flogged in the Forum and beheaded.[18] The Tarquinians may have been enacting an Etruscan form of human sacrifice, but the Roman response – if historical – was an act of vengeance, not a cultic obligation.

In a probably historical but exceptional case, Rome later reportedly buried alive various Celtic and Greek couples as well as certain Vestal Virgins. In 228 BC, alarmed by a Sibylline oracle and the prodigy of lightning striking

37

the Capitoline Hill, the senate felt compelled to order an uncharacteristic rite and buried alive a Celtic couple and a Greek couple in the Forum Boarium, the old cattle market (see map 1).[19] In 216 BC terrifying news of the defeat at Cannae added to religious anxiety about recent bad omens and prodigies. Convicted of unchastity, one Vestal had committed suicide and another was executed in the customary (indirect) fashion: she was buried alive near the Colline Gate in a chamber and provided with food to absolve the executioners of responsibility for the taking of a consecrated life. Also, the Pontifex Maximus had beaten to death the secretary of the Pontiffs, who had violated a Vestal, in the place of assembly (*comitium*). Livy further says that, to propitiate the gods, on the orders of the Sibylline Books, 'a Gaulish man and woman and a Greek man and woman were buried alive in the Cattle Market, in a place walled in with stone, which even before this time had been defiled with human victims, a sacrifice wholly alien to the Roman spirit'.[20] Later, in 114/13 three Vestals caught in a sexual scandal were apparently executed by being buried alive. Subsequently a consultation of the Sibylline Books ordered the burial alive of a Greek and a Celtic couple in the Forum Boarium as a sacrifice to some non-Roman gods.[21]

The traditional interpretation of these incidents is that scandals concerning the Vestals led to the sacrifices in the traditonal manner of punishing unchaste Vestals. However, this does not explain the selection of the victims, and there is no certain evidence for Vestal impropriety for 228, so A. M. Eckstein argues that the Vestal scandals were merely great *prodigia* which, in combination with other portents, led the senate to consult the Sibylline Books, which ordered the killings. Since Rome was not actually at war with Celts or Greeks at the time of the killings, Eckstein revises the old interpretation of human sacrifices at Rome as a *Kriegsopfer*, a magical diffusion of the military power of current enemies. Rather, perhaps as part of the legacy of Etruscan influence, Rome was trying to ward off future military disasters by offering Celts and Greeks, as former and likely future foes, who appropriately represented 'enemies' in a general way.[22] In other words, while the deaths of the Celts and Greeks may have been highly unusual human sacrifices ordered by the Sibylline Books, the deaths of the Vestals were more conventional ritual executions.

In the late Republic, rather than being part of a broad cultural discourse, charges that individuals performed human sacrifices refer to acts of political vengeance thinly disguised or justified as sacrifices, or the charges were simply figments of political slander. For example, when some of Caesar's soldiers rioted during his games in 46, three of them were executed. Dio says they were killed 'as a sort of ritual observance . . . the Sibyl made no utterance and there was no other similar oracle, but at any rate they were sacrificed in the Campus Martius by the pontifices and the priest of Mars, and their heads were hung up near the Regia'.[23] Clearly not responding to the expressed will of the gods, Caesar at best was trying to sacralize a

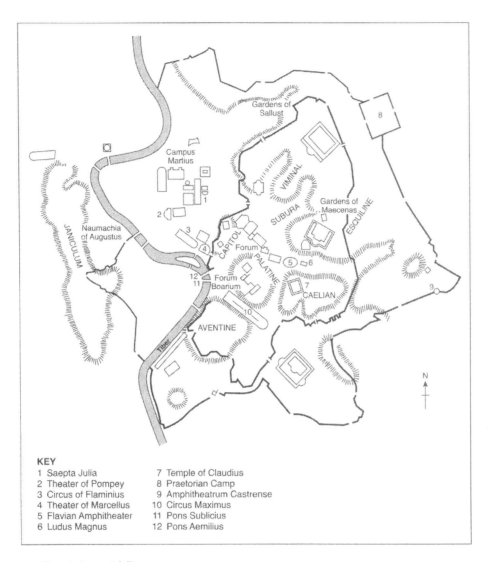

Map 1 Imperial Rome

military punishment. Despite some possible examples *in extremis*, then, Rome did not routinely perform human sacrifices; but, as in the burial alive of corrupted Vestals, Rome did ritually execute threatening or disruptive humans and assign them to the gods of the underworld. Execution, punishment and revenge were primary; dedication to the gods was secondary.[21]

As Rives says, in Christian polemic the 'canonical example of Roman human sacrifice' was the festival of Jupiter of Latium (Latiaris), the Feriae

Latinae, an old Latin festival which was celebrated at Rome from the fourth century. By the first century BC the festival included some sort of games, and Christian sources charge that blood from the human victims was poured on the statue of Jupiter as a sacrifice.[25] Tertullian (*Apol.* 9.5, Loeb) said that at Rome there 'is a certain Jupiter, whom they drench with human blood at his own games. "Yes, but only the blood of a man condemned already to the beasts", you say?' Following Tertullian, Minucius Felix (*Oct.* 30.4, Loeb, cf. 23.6) claims that 'even to-day a human victim is offered to Jupiter Latiaris, and, as becomes the son of Saturn, he battens on the blood of a criminal offender (*mali et noxii hominis*)'. In the third century Novatian (*De spect.* 4.1–2, cf. 5.1) says that all spectacles are sacrifices dedicated to the dead; idolatry is the mother of all the games (*ludorum omnium matrem*), and blood from the throat of a victim is thrown from a libation cup and given to an idol to drink. The Christian tradition is long and lurid but, on both sides, the charges were part of a discourse of cultural differentiation.[26] Christians did not sacrifice humans, and the Romans did not regularly perform human sacrifice. By the Christian era spectacular executions at this festival may have recalled an early tradition of human sacrifice,[27] but it is more likely that Christians misunderstood or misrepresented 'gladiatorial' games (which they saw as deriving from human sacrifices at graves – see below) as a traditional part of the festival rather than a later addition.[28]

Despite Christian claims that Rome regularly performed human sacrifices and that gladiatorial combat was human sacrifice, homicides in Roman spectacles are better understood as ritualized or sacralized killings – preceded and followed by ceremonies, performed to some degree in stylized fashion, and associated with gods or spirits of the dead. No Roman god required human sacrifice as a regular act, and it is unlikely that early Romans felt that the spirits of their dead required human sacrifice as a funeral rite.[29] While *munera* were prominent in the age in which Christianity emerged, the killing in public of humans, supposedly as a duty or offering to the spirit of the dead, at a funeral at Rome is not attested until 264 BC. Even if the early, private funeral *munus* required human life, the gladiatorial *munus* was not a regular part of the official festival calendar until the late first century BC. The gladiatorial *munus* was not purely a secular event, but human sacrifice in the arena was not a traditional element of official Roman religion.

The earliest institutionalized ritualized homicides at Rome were not rooted in prehistoric traditions or Christian rhetoric, but were sacro-legal executions. As societies become more complex, dealing with dysfunctional community members becomes a greater problem. If disobedient and dangerous elements arise within small groups, they can simply be cast out and driven away. In larger communities, however, such persons are punished in public to demonstrate the power of the state, to reassure the obedient, and to deter the potentially disobedient. Long before the first *munus* in 264, ritual killings as executions, both punitive and sacral, were entrenched in law and ritual. Even official executions retain sacral overtones, but when states become autocracies and empires, demonstrations of state power become even more mandatory and spectacular. Such executions were exacerbated rather than mollified over time, and their continuance and expansion formed a major dimension of Roman spectacles.

Along with Livy, the XII Tables of 451 BC show that in early Rome, while executions were not common, those convicted of treasonous acts (e.g. arson, parricide, breaking patronage by defrauding a client, moving boundary stones, etc.) were declared *sacri* and could be killed with impunity. Such men were devoted or consecrated to the nether gods, usually Ceres.[30] Treason – a threat or an affront to the social and religious order – was treated as a religious crime and required expiation. As J.-L. David notes, archaic execution rituals go back to an age when penal law and religious punishment could not be distinguished.[31] Under Table VIII, 'Sacred Law', adults who pastured or harvested by night another's crops received 'capital punishment and, after being hung up, death as a sacrifice to Ceres'.[32] Men who bore false witness or slaves who committed theft were thrown from the Tarpeian Rock.[33] Debtors might suffer capital punishment, or be delivered across the Tiber, or the creditors might 'cut shares' of them.[34]

In early Rome the *fasces*, each a bundle of rods with an axe, carried by the lictors, symbolized the political and sacral power of the highest officials to punish and execute.[35] A citizen of status condemned to death, if his appeal to the assembly failed and he declined to go into exile, faced summary execution by the sword (*gladio*). Floggings in the 'ancient fashion' (*more maiorum*) and executions were often done in public in the center of town, the Forum.[36] An expert on Sulla and proscriptions, François Hinard suggests that executions under the Republic were sacral ceremonies with set times and places, and set roles for executioners and attendants: the trial took place in the Forum, possibly involving the torture of slaves, the magistrate condemned the criminal and called a crowd together, a procession led to the place of execution, lictors, musicians, and heralds attended, the magistrate pronounced the sentence, the execution took place, and the body was mutilated and removed.[37] As we shall see, the punishment and execution of malefactors continued in the area of the Forum but increasingly shifted to the arena.

Roman games (*ludi*) arose as celebrations of religious rites with sports or shows, acts of communal thanksgiving to the gods for military success or deliverance from crises. Inherently popular, they increased over time and became annual and state financed as supplements to traditional *feriae*. *Ludi* usually included *ludi circenses* or chariot races, begun, according to tradition, in the Circus Maximus by the Etruscan king Tarquin, and *ludi scaenici* or theatrical performances. The Ludi Romani, the oldest games, begun in 366, and the Ludi Apollinares, instituted during the Second Punic War, each presented both circus and theater games.[38] Neither type was originally or primarily deadly, but ultimately spectacles of both animal and human death took place in *ludi* in Roman circuses (chariot-racing facilities) and even in theaters.[39]

Triumphs, the highest honor a Roman could achieve (Livy 30.15.12), were spectacles of military victory and death. Since the right to put on these parades of captives and booty was awarded only after a set number (apparently 5,000) of foes were killed on campaign, triumphs functioned as visible 'proof' of deaths.[40] As well as the procession of the successful general (the *triumphator*) in the guise of Jupiter, triumphs included the ritual public murder of the captured enemy leader in the Forum, representing the vanquishing of the threat to Rome (see ch. 7 below). As Rome's frontiers expanded, displays of foreign beasts were added (to symbolize foreign enemies and lands), and later large numbers of captives were displayed and killed directly at Rome. Ludi Magni Votivi originated as triumphal games vowed by generals to Jupiter before a campaign. Paid for by the victorious general out of his spoils of war, they were put on at the end of triumphal processions, further demonstrating the extent and glory of the victory. Originally occasional, some votive *ludi* were institutionalized as regular annual games, such as the Ludi Victoriae Sullae from 82 and the Ludi Caesaris from 46 BC, and the days of *ludi* grew accordingly.[41]

Offensive and yet impressive to us, the great beast spectacles of Rome must be understood in the changing context of Rome's history from humble rural roots to imperial power.[42] From the first exhibition of elephants in 275 to the first 'hunt' (*venatio*) in 186 BC to the great triumphal shows of Pompey and Caesar, the beast spectacles became more and more popular.[43] During the second half of the first century BC exotic animals (e.g. giraffes, crocodiles) were apparently merely displayed as curiosities and not killed, but probably before and certainly later the beasts that appeared in *venationes* were routinely killed.[44] These 'hunts' spread from state festivals to funeral games and shows (*munera*), they expanded in size with imperial excesses from Augustus to Commodus and beyond, and they outlived the decline and fall of gladiators and of Rome itself.

As well as having native hunting traditions, from early times Romans regularly killed animals in blood sacrifices, and the ritual process continued beyond the killing. Most of the flesh of the victims was eaten, and sometimes the skins, blood, and head were used for ritual purposes, as in the Lupercalia and the October Horse.[45] Moreover, in certain festivals, in addition to chariot races and theatrical performances, early Romans also hunted, baited, or abused animals.[46] In the Ludi Cereales, the games of the ancient Italian fertility goddess Ceres, dating from before 202 BC, foxes with burning brands tied to their tails were let loose in the Circus Maximus.[47] Pliny mentions an annual sacrifice of dogs who were crucified live and carried about in a procession.[48] In the Ludi Piscatorii fish from the Tiber

were thrown live into a fire in the Forum.[49] From 173 BC the games of
Flora, an ancient Italian fertility goddess of flowers and vegetation, were
celebrated with the drinking and social license typical of festivals of fertility
and dissolution, and they also included hunts of harmless small wild animals
(roe deer and hares) staged in the Circus.[50] The killing of such animals may
represent the elimination of vermin that threatened the cultivated lands,
but Italians also hunted such animals for food and for sport. Such public
animal-baiting ceremonies were not normal sacrifices of domesticated
animals. Even before it expanded overseas, Rome brought dogs and wild
beasts from the local countryside into the heart of the city and publicly
tormented or hunted them.[51] When *venationes* became an official part of
state festivals in 169 BC, in addition to traditions of public sacrifice and
rustic subsistence hunting, customs like the games of Ceres and Flora no
doubt made Romans more receptive to the carnage of beast spectacles in
the arena.

As Rome conquered Italy and embarked on overseas expansion, Roman
hunting took on new dimensions. Under Greek influence and consistent
with changes in society, well-to-do Romans took up sport hunting in the
Italian countryside as an elitist recreation.[52] Moreover, from Macedon and
the Hellenistic East, which had learned it from Egypt, Assyria, and Persia,
Rome also adopted the custom of 'royal hunts', of collecting and transporting
large numbers of beasts, often unusual and foreign ones, to be displayed or
usually killed as a demonstration of imperial power and territorial control.[53]
Roman generals adapted this practice as a natural expansion of votive games
and triumphal celebrations. The collection of the animals was equivalent
to a circumambulation ritual of 'beating the bounds' to lay claim to hunting
territory, and the exotic animals were paraded like exotic prisoners of war.[54]
Since hunting in the wilds was seen as a good preparation for warfare,[55]
and exposure to the blood and death of humans in the arena was considered
a positive acculturation for citizens of this warrior nation, exposure to the
blood and death of animals in hunts in the arena would have been seen to
have similar benefits.[56]

Munera: rites and spectacles

The prime occasions for abundant human death were the *munera*, which
were originally violent rites associated with funerals as duties or tributes
owed to dead ancestors.[57] Tertullian gives the standard Christian position
on the origin of gladiatorial *munera*:

> The ancients thought that by this sort of spectacle they rendered
> a service to the dead, after they had tempered it with a more
> cultured form of cruelty. For of old, in the belief that the souls of
> the dead are propitiated with human blood, they used at funerals

> to sacrifice captives or slaves of poor quality whom they bought.
> Afterwards it seemed good to obscure their impiety by making it
> a pleasure. So after the persons procured had been trained in such
> arms as they had and as best they might – their training was to
> learn to be killed! – they did them to death on the appointed day
> at the tombs. So they found comfort for death in murder.[58]

As we have seen, rituals of condemnation, execution, and sacrifice all existed
at Rome before the introduction of gladiatorial games. At the earliest level
sacrifice and punishment overlap in that both seek security for the community. Death spectacles were a way to punish criminals, to dispose of captives,
to venerate the dead, and to demonstrate munificence. As Tertullian says,
these 'sacrifices' and executions were ritualized into entertainments and
performances; Rome turned the *munus* into a 'pleasure' and a 'more cultured
form of cruelty'. As well as punishments and sacrifices, *munera* became entertainments.

Romans may always have staged contests or, less likely, human sacrifices
at the funerals of prominent men, but the earliest recorded gladiatorial
combat at Rome was not until 264 BC. Violence was essential to the *munus*:
blood could be spilled in the *spectacula gladiatorum* and later the *venationes*,
the beast fights, overflowed from *ludi* to *munera*. In early *venationes* wild
animals faced skilled and well-equipped hunters, and over time in *munera*
beasts were set against other animals or set upon (almost or fully) defenseless victims. Though subject to state regulations by the first century, *munera*
at Rome were organized privately by individuals or families until the end
of the Republic. They became politically expedient and even essential, but
they were not part of a magistrate's official duties.[59]

Traditionally, works have assumed that Rome adopted gladiators from the
Etruscans.[60] As Wiedemann notes, moderns were long willing to blame
the 'oriental' Etruscans for corrupting the European Romans.[61] Sixth-century
Etruscan tomb paintings depict a blindfolded man with a club or lash being
attacked by a dog and attended by a masked figure named Phersu with a whip
or leash. The involvement of a beast and some hindrance or abuse of the victim
are intriguing, but it remains uncertain whether the 'game of Phersu' was an
execution, sacrifice, contest, or performance.[62] Exponents of an Etruscan origin
for gladiators feel that this was a form of funerary human sacrifice turned into
a ritual competition. By the fourth century scenes of the killing of bound
captives, especially attended by the death demon Charon, were prominent,[63]
but the Phersu 'game' at best was a precursor to Roman beast combats.

Although it is unlikely that gladiatorial combats per se came to Rome
solely through Etruscan influence, it is likely that the legacy of Etruscan
rule contributed in significant ways to Roman spectacles of death. As well
as their enthusiasm for spectator sports, most notably chariot racing, the
Etruscans passed on to Rome their preference for foreign, slave, or captive

performers, and the notion that good citizens watched rather than performed in public games. Like the Etruscans, the Romans believed in social stratification in this world and beyond.[64]

Scholarship now tends to reject an Etruscan origin for gladiators in favor of a Campanian, Sabellian, or Samnite one. Fourth-century tomb paintings and vase paintings from Campania seem more obviously to depict armed single combats, and sources do refer to Campanian combats at banquets.[65] Suggesting that gladiatorial games originated in South Italy or Campania among Oscans and Samnites in the early fourth century or earlier, Ville argues that Campania had gladiatorial fights as part of funeral games. In these fourth-century combats elite volunteers competed for prizes, but fought mainly to expend energy and only to the point of first bloodshed. From Homer's *Iliad* 23 Ville suggests that the original combats were not to the death, but that death became common as slaves and captives were used. From their armament, prizes, and organization, he argues that gladiators were professionalized under the Etruscans: men might be spared for doing a good professional job to the point of injury or incapacity, or they were killed as a penalty for a poor job.[66] However, certain evidence for gladiatorial prizes, decision ceremonies and volunteerism at Rome does not appear until at least a century after 264 (see ch. 3 below).

The origin of gladiatorial and beast combats is probably not a historical question answerable in terms of a single original location (e.g. Etruria or Campania), a single original context (e.g. sacrifice, contests, vengeance, scapegoats), and a simple linear transmission (e.g. Etruria to Rome). Combats, sacrifices, and blood sports were simply too widespread in antiquity. Before the first gladiatorial fight in 264 Rome had already been exposed, directly or indirectly, to all the suggested original influences. By then Rome already knew other spectacles of death: animals sacrificed, tormented, or hunted in festivals, criminals consecrated to Ceres and executed, and countless acts of brutality in war. Since the adoption of imported cultural features such as sports and spectacles usually involves cultural adaptation, whatever the origins or precursors beyond Rome, the best historical approach is to concentrate on the context of Rome's adoption and development of the gladiatorial spectacle.[67]

Romans apparently became familiar with Campanian gladiatorial combats in the late fourth century. Livy writes of a battle in 308 of Romans and Campanians against Samnites, who fought with inlaid shields, plumed helmets, and greaves on their left leg. In battle the Samnites 'dedicated themselves in the Samnite manner' (see 10.38.2–4 on the *devotio* and oath of the Samnite troops) and C. Junius Bubulcus attacked them 'declaring that he offered these men as a sacrifice to Orcus (Pluto)'.[68] Celebrating the victory, the Romans adorned the Forum with the captured arms.

> So the Romans made use of the splendid armour of their enemies
> to do honour to the gods: while the Campanians, in consequence

of their pride and in hatred of the Samnites, equipped after this fashion the gladiators who furnished them entertainment at their feasts (*gladiatores, quod spectaculum inter epulas erat*), and bestowed on them the name of Samnites.

(Livy 9.40.17, Loeb)

The Romans did not use the spoils for gladiatorial entertainments at banquets in Campanian fashion, but the incident exposed them to elements of the later *munus*: gladiatorial entertainment, *devotio* (positively by Samnites, negatively by Romans), Samnite gladiatorial armor, and 'Samnite' – like later 'gladiator' – as a hateful insult for a foe.[69]

After the Samnite Wars and Rome's further expansion to the south, to honor their dead father the sons of Decimus Junius Brutus Scaeva, another member of the Junii, gave the first gladiatorial *munus* at Rome in 264 BC, a modest affair with three pairs of gladiators in the Forum Boarium. 'Pairs', presumably each with a loser and a victor, is suggestive, but there is no mention of later standard elements: crowds, a special facility, training and skills, appeal for *missio*, manumission, etc. Campanian influence, however, is suggested by the Campanian experience of the earlier Junius, the consul of 317.[70]

The Romans had not adopted gladiators in 308 BC, but did so by 264. Significantly, the first display of animals, elephants captured in warfare shown by a general, had taken place in Rome in 275, and in 270 there had been a public execution of rebel soldiers in the Roman Forum (see below). The military demands of the conquest of Italy had been great, spotlighting successful generals and facilitating the political gains of the Struggle of the Orders. Constitutionally the Struggle ended Rome's old caste system: the plebeians shared the consulship, they dominated the Tribal Assembly, and by 287 they could legislate. After centuries of stratified hierarchy and with the entrenched conservative ideology of *mos maiorum*, Rome did not become egalitarian, nor did its elite welcome upward mobility in politics. In this age of political readjustment the Roman elite reformulated itself as the 'nobles' (*nobiles*), a class of descendants of office-holders.[71] The nobles included successful plebeian families, but like the old patricians the nobles saw themselves as an exclusive elite entitled to run the state. Since non-nobles were no longer formally excluded from higher offices, to establish and maintain their legitimacy, to stay on top in the competitive world of popular politics, the new elite had to compete and dominate in the political arena. They could no longer rely simply on birth. Along with a number of para-political devices such as clientship, marriage, factions, and bribery, they had to restore the deferential tendencies of the now potentially dominant masses by active competitive demonstrations of their worthiness for leadership. As Roman social and political dynamics became more complex, the elite shifted from personal single combats and military exploits, as a way

46

to display valor essential to political power, to more indirect devices including the provision of military displays in triumphs, *venationes*, and *munera*.[72]

Political anthropology, stressing the effectiveness of gestures, symbols, and ceremonies, has noted the widespread use of displays of power, wealth, generosity, and clemency in the 'Roman Revolution', but such use of *munera* developed in the third century. Elite Romans had long used elaborate funerals to reinforce familial claims to status, and they would later use imposing monuments and tombs as more enduring symbols. Just as the feasting and circus and theatrical games of triumphal *ludi* were vindications of awarded *dignitas*, the innovation of the gladiatorial *munus* on a limited, almost experimental, basis in 264 allowed families, under the pretext of honoring a dead relative, to display their claim to status.[73] With the wars against Carthage and with elite families vying for consulships and thus generalships, demonstrations of the destruction of foreign captives, rebel slaves or deserters, or exotic beasts from the expanding limits of Roman power seemed entirely appropriate for the military leaders of a burgeoning empire. Through the era of the Punic Wars, often called 'the age of senatorial ascendency', the nobles entrenched their control. From the magnitude of the Punic Wars to the Roman atrocities in Spain, Romans fought 'total' wars against non-Italians and became more tolerant and even expectant of public brutality.[74] In the same period *munera* and *venationes* expanded in scope and frequency as the provision of spectacles of death was becoming more and more politically advantageous.

The symbolic dynamics of the gladiatorial combat – what its actions and participants 'meant' to the Romans beyond the demonstration of the status of the provider – emerged (or were 'constructed') as despair forced adaptation in the wake of the defeat at Cannae in 216 BC.[75] Cannae and its aftermath crystallized the ideology of military virtue, of enlistment, endurance, and elevation, that Rome traditionally expected of its soldiers in battle and now demanded of gladiators in the arena. Hannibal's legacy included an intensified need for Rome to show foes and rebels being destroyed in public on a grand scale, a need to demonstrate that poor fighters would be punished and good soldiers rewarded,[76] and a need to entertain and communicate with urbanized and underemployed masses. Politicians and generals soon cultivated these needs into a peculiarly Roman social institution.

Cannae brought a national crisis of both mass despair and depleted resources.[77] Of the same family that introduced the gladiatorial combat in 264, the Dictator Marcus Junius Pera,[78] and his Master of the Horse, Tiberius Sempronius Gracchus, proclaimed a levy of young men over 17, sent to the allies and Latins for troops, and even turned to using slaves.

> They gave orders that armour, weapons and other equipment should
> be made ready, and took down from the temples and porticoes the

47

ancient spoils of enemies. The levy wore a strange appearance, for, owing to the scarcity of free men and the need of the hour, they bought, with money from the treasury, eight thousand young and stalwart slaves and armed them, first asking each if he were willing to serve. They preferred these slaves for soldiers, though they might have redeemed the prisoners of war at less expense.

To these slave volunteers, Valerius Maximus explains, Rome administered an oath that they would bear arms and serve courageously as long as the enemy was in Italy.[79] As long as they individually expressed volition, Rome preferred slaves, selected for their fighting potential and equipped with the dedicated spoils of earlier wars, to free men who had already surrendered and broken their oaths.[80] Through virtue and fidelity to their oaths even the lowliest men could serve Rome by fighting and by inspiring free young recruits.[81]

Recounting the debate over whether to ransom the Roman captives from Cannae, Livy repeats the commonplace of Rome's disdain for prisoners who failed their oaths and surrendered. An envoy of the prisoners admits (22.59.1, Loeb) 'that no state ever held prisoners of war in less esteem than ours', but he argues that they had been brave and deserved to be spared, and that they valued their honor above life.[82] Titus Manlius Torquatus had intended to say little, merely to warn Rome (22.60.7) 'to hold fast to the tradition of our fathers and teach a lesson necessary for military discipline', but he felt that the envoy's speech almost boasted of their surrender.[83] In disgust Torquatus (22.60.14–15, Loeb) said, 'You lack even the spirit to be saved! . . . you have forfeited your status, lost your civic rights, been made slaves of the Carthaginians. Do you think to return, for ransom, to that condition which you forfeited by cowardice and turpitude?'[84] True to Rome's tradition of showing the 'scantiest consideration for prisoners of war' (22.61.1–3), the senate declined to ransom the captives. The envoy had said that slaves by their lack of civil rights were unworthy and despised, but the senate decided that slaves, by their willingness to serve Rome well, rose – morally if not legally – beyond their status and became admirable and preferable to men of status who had disgraced themselves and reduced them-selves – morally if not legally – to the level of slaves.[85]

Cannae left a legacy of insecurity, a need for reassurance through brutality, and a willingness to see moral exempla beyond the ranks. After 216 the escalation of gladiatorial spectacles at Rome was almost geometrical.[86] The practice of pitting men against each other in contests to the death appealed to the warring Romans, and it grew quickly because it was politically effec-tive. So popular were such displays that generals held them beyond Rome and foreign leaders experimented with them in their own domains.[87]

Soldiers – and probably early gladiators – were expected to win or die.[88] The arena's military morality plays reenacted the lessons of Cannae: gladiators faced death in the arena like those slave volunteers and like the heroes who died in battle.[89] Roman deserters and rebels, however, were beyond hope and were to die miserably.[90] In 270, 300 or more Campanian troops who rebelled and took over Rhegium in South Italy were sent to Rome, paraded into the Forum, bound to stakes, scourged in public, and executed by having the back of their necks cut with an axe.[91] In 214, 370 deserters caught in southern Italy were publicly scourged in the place of assembly (*comitium*) and thrown from the Tarpeian Rock at Rome, and in the same year Claudius Marcellus, the Roman commander of Sicily, stormed pro-Carthaginian Leontini and beheaded 2,000 troops as deserters.[92] Using an even more spectacular form of execution, in 167 Lucius Aemilius Paullus had non-Roman deserters trampled to death by elephants, and in 146 Scipio Africanus Minor, as well as crucifying Roman and beheading Latin deserters at Carthage, threw non-Roman deserters and runaway slaves to wild beasts at public shows at Rome.[93] The brutal destructions of Carthage and Corinth in 146 were emphatic demonstrations that Rome would tolerate no insubordination, that it would eliminate perceived threats and punish affronts with utmost severity and without remorse. Such messages increasingly moved from the military frontier to the artificial confrontations in arenas at Rome.

Late Republic: power, proscriptions, and multi-dimensional spectacles

In origin rituals of piety, punishment, or reassurance, spectacles of death, through expansion and recurrence, became ritualized entertainment.[94] On the decline of morality after 146 owing to excessive prosperity, Florus (1.47.10, Loeb) says that the excessive size of slave establishments led to Servile Wars: 'How else could those armies of gladiators have risen against their masters, save that a profuse expenditure, which aimed at winning the common people by indulging their love of shows, had turned what was originally a method of punishing enemies into a competition of skill (*supplicia quondam hostium artem faceret*)?' In other words, politics turned damned victims into performers. Pliny tells us that Gaius Terentius Lucanus, who celebrated his grandfather's death with a show of thirty pairs in the Forum in the second half of the second century, began the practice of publicly exhibiting commissioned pictures of gladiatorial shows.[95] Displays were effective. In 122 Gaius Gracchus, seeking popular support as tribune, took down the barriers built around an arena in the Forum for a gladiatorial show and opened spectatorship without payment to all Romans.[96] Politicians responded to the Romans' desire to watch gladiators, and punitive performances in spectacles developed a hierarchy of craft or entertainment value.

With the escalation of combats, gladiatorial virtues and skills became more appreciated, the worlds of the gladiator and soldier were increasingly correlated, and the facilities used to house the combats took on characteristic and monumental features. Rutilius Rufus as consul of 105 BC began the practice of using gladiatorial trainers to instruct landless army recruits;[97] this was formerly misinterpreted as the introduction of official *munera*.[98] Recently, Welch has tied the emergence and spread of gladiatorial shows and amphitheaters to military training and the interests of military veteran colonists in the first century BC. Rejecting the conventional interpretation of the amphitheater as a Campanian invention, she makes a convincing argument that amphitheaters spread not from Campania to Rome but from the Roman Forum to Campania and elsewhere with the establishment of military colonies, as at Pompeii and Capua. She associates the model for the oval amphitheater with gladiatorial shows (from the third century on) in the Forum at Rome, where temporary wooden seating for gladiatorial shows was adapted to the trapezoidal space of the Forum and led to the typical elliptical shape of amphitheaters.[99] She feels that the amphitheater at Pompeii of around 70 BC was made specifically for veteran colonists, that the idea was familiar from shows in the Roman Forum, and that such amphitheaters made statements about Roman power and cultural distinctiveness.[100]

From Marius and Sulla to Octavius and Antony, rival warlords and triumvirs established a parasitical perversion of earlier spectacles of death-proscriptions. Violence and homicide had erupted somewhat spontaneously against the Gracchans earlier, but these new homicides were planned and orchestrated. Now citizens of status – not criminals and slaves – were condemned and killed publicly in artificially ritualized public spectacles. Early rituals of execution were adapted for vengeance and political intimidation, there was no reassurance for the community, and the terror was long remembered.[101] Proscriptions, the collapse of the façade of the Republic, and the autocratic power of generals with client armies all added to the disruption and despair of the civil war era.

In the first century BC rival generals expanded and conflated existing spectacles and imported or invented variations to court popular support. The actual activities, the range of spectacular killing, became very similar in *munera* and triumphal *ludi*. In theory or pretext *munera* under the Republic were apparently always associated with death and funerary honors, but aspiring politicians clearly had to provide spectacles of death, whether officially in *ludi* or unofficially in *munera*.[102] A law of 63 made it *ambitus* (electoral corruption) to give gladiatorial shows, banquets, or cash within two years of candidacy, but candidates sidestepped the law.[103] In the 60s and 50s politicians also extensively used gangs of gladiators for protection.[104]

Dynasts, and soon emperors, put on grander and more complex shows, using funeral and triumphal honors and the festival calendar as excuses. By the late first century BC Rome had what might be called 'conglomerate spectacles', what Ville calls *munera legitima*, multi-dimensional entertainments combining any or all of the once distinct elements discussed above.

Different events were held in sequence throughout the day: *venationes* in the morning gave way to *meridiani*, the midday games – essentially executions – and *munera* followed in the afternoon.[105] Such conglomerate spectacles conflated pretexts (e.g. funerals, victory *ludi*, magisterial duty, electoral largesse, hunts, public banquets, patronage, punishment, vengeance) and were soon institutionalized by autocracy. From the circus to the theater, formerly separate elements continued in combination, with violence as the common mortar.

In numerous ways the career of Julius Caesar signalled the end of the Republic and the need for a transition to Empire. In the history of the spectacles Caesar was innovative in scale, context, and content. He got past the need for the recent death of a male relative: in 65 he held games for his long-dead father (with gladiators and a combat of criminals with silver weapons against beasts) and in 45 he held a *munus* for his daughter, who had died eight years earlier.[106] He kept gladiatorial troops at Capua and assembled so many gladiators at Rome (320 pairs) in 65 that a bill was passed limiting the number that a person could keep in the city. After the civil wars his triumphal games outdid even those of Pompey.[107] As well as a *venatio* with 400 lions and the first display of a giraffe at Rome, as Suetonius (above) shows, Caesar's spectacles compounded many earlier activities (e.g. gladiators, stage-plays) with new variations such as athletic contests, Thessalian bullfighting, the Game of Troy, and mock battles both on land and on water.[108] In his games in the Circus in 46 Caesar put on a mock battle with 500 troops, thirty horsemen, and twenty elephants in each army. Rather than harmless military displays or even combats of professional gladiators, these 'mock battles' were spectacular mass executions of captives.[109]

In his triumphal spectacles of 46 BC, Julius Caesar gave the first naumachy or 'mock sea battle' at Rome.[110] *Naumachiae* meant both the artificial sites and the spectacles – large shallow basins with banks of seats for spectators, and the 'mock' naval battles staged thereon with large numbers of victims and mass killing.[111] Caesar had a special basin dug in the Campus Martius, and 4,000 oarsmen and 2,000 fighters in costume recreated a battle between Tyrians and Egyptians.[112] In 2 BC Augustus built a large naumachy on the right bank of the Tiber (see map 1) to mark the dedication of the Temple of Mars Ultor, and 3,000 fighters staged the battle of Salamis with Athenians against Persians.[113] Titus staged one on Augustus' lake (along with other water spectacles) in which 3,000 men put on the battle of the Athenians against the Syracusans, and another one in the Colosseum in AD 80 with Corcyreans against Corinthians.[114] As Coleman suggests, emperors tried to outdo each other by producing such technologically miraculous spectacles. Symbolically, the recreation of ancient naval battles in Rome was meant to demonstrate the emperor's power over history and nature, and thus confirm his claim to eventual apotheosis.[115]

Apparently Caesar's legacy also included the first associations of *munera* with state expenditure and with the duties of officials. Contrary to Wiedemann's argument that all Republican *munera* were held in private contexts (see above), Welch notes that Caesar's municipal legislation ordered that public funds were to pay part of the cost of *munera* given by *duoviri*. She also argues that gladiatorial combat was part of the Quinquatrus festival to Minerva at Rome by 43 BC.[116] Gladiatorial *munera* were officially organized (if perhaps not institutionalized) in 44 in the sense that the senate ordered that Caesar be given a special day of his own in association with all gladiatorial games at Rome and in Italy.[117]

In political history the pivotal role of Augustus in the transition from Republican politics to imperial rule has always been recognized. Recently cultural and social historians increasingly have stressed his role in orchestrating changes in Rome's perceptions of its own cultural identity, its social customs, and its images of power.[118] Wiedemann argues that Augustus monopolized the symbolic value of *munera* for the Principate, that he institutionalized and centralized *munera* on an official basis with legislation, imperial gladiatorial schools (*ludi*), and an imperial administration, and that he expanded and dispersed these spectacles of death through the emperor cult.[119] Wiedemann further shows that gladiatorial combats, which had became emblematic of Romanness (*Romanitas*) during the unification of Italy, were exported and emulated throughout the empire. Under Augustus *munera* were established even in the Greek East by provincial elites trying to proclaim their *Romanitas*. Wiedemann also ties Augustus to the tripartite format of morning hunts, midday executions, and afternoon gladiatorial combats, and to the concentration of *munera* on a few days near the winter solstice and in March.[120]

As Suetonius (*Aug.* 43.1, Loeb) says, Augustus 'surpassed all his predecessors in the frequency, variety and magnificence of his public shows'. Wanting to dominate the giving of *munera*, in 22 BC Augustus limited the praetors to two shows while in office, with a maximum of 120 gladiators.[121] He also seems to have crafted an efficient empire-wide administrative system using procurators (*procuratores familiae gladiatoriae*).[122] His system of conglomerate spectacles of death at Rome continued under the Julio-Claudians and Flavians and remained intimately tied to the imperial regime. The bureaucracy and the facilities used expanded into elaborate imperial schools and the Flavian Amphitheater.[123] Under the Empire the amphitheater and the circus became forums for the definition of the limits of popular and imperial sovereignty. Although not officially a requirement, magnificent, properly held games were a necessary if not sufficient condition for the popularity of emperors.

Spectacular punishments:
summa supplicia and 'fatal charades'

With the institutionalization of conglomerate spectacles came variations on ritualized public executions of criminals (and in time Christians).[124] Rome did not execute everyone the same way. Quick and unaggravated, decapitation at the edge of town was the most discreet form of execution, a privilege for citizens of status.[125] For a host of crimes Rome punished criminals of low status with aggravated or ultimate punishments (*summa supplicia*), which included exposure to wild beasts, crucifixion, and burning alive.[126] One could also be condemned to become a gladiator, or sent for life to the mines (*metallum*) or public works (*opus publicum*).[127] From the time of Augustus on, various forms of executions were performed on an increasingly spectacular basis in the arena. The victim's lasting agony and death provided a terrifying and exemplary public spectacle.[128] Some of the punishments have precedents under the Republic (see above), but under the Empire the torture and aggravated death of criminals became a standard part of *munera*.

According to the XII Tables men might be bound, beaten, and burned alive (*vivicomburium*, *damnatio ad flammas*, *vivus uri*, *crematio*) as an ancient penalty for treachery and arson.[129] This was rare under the Republic, but the Roman masses knew the violent use of fire as a threat and as vengeance.[130] More common under the Empire, execution by fire was mostly for slaves and the lower orders (*humiliores*) for arson, desertion, magic, and treason, and it was an especially common punishment for Christians (see ch. 8 below). Used earlier in the Near East and probably invented by Persia,[131] crucifixion at Rome seems to have developed from a form of punishment (the public carrying of a cross, being bound to it, and whipped) to a form of execution (being attached to a cross and suspended).[132] Usually this form of execution was authorized by the Roman court; the victim was stripped and scourged; a horizontal beam was placed on his shoulders; and he was marched to the execution site, usually outside the city walls, where a vertical stake was set in the ground and the man was bound or nailed to the cross.[133] The normal form of execution for criminal slaves, crucifixion was used frequently against rebellious Jews and Christians.[134] For exemplary effect, crucifixions were held at well-travelled public roadways, offering a stark contrast to the hallowed burials of good citizens nearby.[135]

As we have seen, Roman generals had killed deserters and runaway slaves via beasts in the second century, and exposure to beasts (*damnatio ad bestias*) became a supplement to *munera*. Little known under the Republic, it became more common than fire or crucifixion under the Empire. Criminals were led into the arena almost or fully naked, with a rope or chain around their necks, sometimes bearing the verdict (*titulus*) attached to them. Their condemnation was proclaimed, and, tied to posts or without weapons, they were exposed to beasts. Beasts (see figures 1b and 4) were a common penalty for slaves, foreign enemies, and free men guilty of a few heinous offenses, but Severan sources show more use concerning rustling, murder, and sacrilege.[136]

Such aggravated punishment might even be compounded. In Apuleius (*Met.* 6.31–2, Loeb) a group of men debate how to punish and gain revenge upon a girl. Some suggest that she should be burned alive, thrown to the beasts, hanged on a gibbet, or flayed alive with tortures (*tormentis excarnificari*). Another man, saying that she deserves more than these sudden deaths, proposes that the girl be stripped and sewn into the belly of an unreliable ass, with only her head exposed:

> Then let us lay this stuffed ass upon a great stone against the broiling heat of the sun ... she shall have her members torn and gnawed with wild beasts, when she is bitten and rent with worms; she shall endure the pain of the fire, when the broiling heat of the sun shall scorch and parch the belly of the ass; she shall abide the gallows, when the dogs and vultures shall drag out her innermost bowels.

Such images might be dismissed as figments of literary imagination, but they were inspired by familiarity with horrific historical punishments.[137]

Executions became even more spectacular and dramatic in what Coleman calls 'fatal charades' – 'the punishment of criminals in a formal public display involving role-play set in a dramatic context; the punishment is usually capital'.[138] Coleman's definition is based on Tertullian (*Ad nat.* 1.10.47; also *Apol.* 15.4–5) concerning criminals in mythological roles in *meridiani*: crowds laughed as an Attis was castrated or a Hercules was burned to death.[139] In the earliest known example, probably in the late 30s BC, Selurus, a Sicilian brigand, was placed on a model of Mount Etna at Rome, which collapsed and dropped him into a cage of wild beasts.[140] Such incidents actually took place, for myths and legends became real punishments in the arena. For his crimes, Laureolus, as the character Prometheus in a play, was crucified and mauled to death by a bear on stage in the amphitheater.[141] Most evidence for charades comes from the second half of the first century AD, notably Martial's *On the Spectacles*, and concerns events mostly under Nero and Titus. As motives Coleman suggests an increased taste for realism on stage, the demonstration of absolute, autocratic power, and possibly scapegoat (e.g. dressing up in costumes as an honorific ritual prior to punishment) or compensatory reactions to disasters (e.g. Vesuvius, fires).[142] As factors in the psychological appeal of fatal charades, Coleman suggests the audience's endorsement of just punishment of deserving victims, the reinforcement of social inequality, and a fascination with horror.[143] The state as rule-enforcer cooperated with the audience as sanctioners by their participation: authoritarian power was approved by mass disapproval of the breaking of social norms. Feeling morally superior and distant, the spectators showed no humanitarian sentiment or sympathy. Crowd reactions were ones more of pleasure than revulsion, amusement rather than terror.

Against the perspective of *summa supplicia* and fatal charades, the actual methods of execution of Christians in the persecutions seem less bizarre or extreme. Punishment of Christians was not unique, nor was it the greatest element in Roman spectacles of death, but special animosity or abuse was possibly involved (see ch. 8 below). Under the Empire Rome's legal system clearly sanctioned violence against the lowly or the disloyal, and more and more victims were punished in spectacularly brutal ways. Arena death became both banal and surreal, and it continued throughout the history of the Empire and even later.

After Christian protests about gladiatorial fights as idolatrous and demonic, Constantine forbade them in 325, but the ban probably only applied to the eastern Empire and it was in vain. Gladiatorial combats continued on for many years.[144] Rejecting anachronistic perceptions of the end of gladiatorial combats as a simple legislative *fait accompli*, like the modern abolition of slavery, Wiedemann offers a cultural explanation for the eventual decline of the shows. He suggests that Christians were uncomfortable with the Roman imagery of gladiatorial salvation and resurrection, that gladiatorial survival in this world was a symbolic rival for Christian resurrection beyond this world. He points out that in the fourth century imperial gladiatorial combats were concentrated at the winter solstice and in March, times which Christians later claimed for Christmas and Easter, that the end of gladiatorial combats does not coincide with the triumph of Christian emperors, and that combats continued through the fourth century despite local or temporary bans. He concludes that the combats were not killed but rather died off gradually in the fifth century as the Christian sacraments provided a Christian, less urban, less Mediterranean-based society with a more satisfactory model of resurrection.[145] In more mundane terms, gladiatorial games had been dependent on imperial (economic and legal) structures and munificence for centuries; with a few exceptions (e.g. the Northwest) they ended with the demise of emperorship in the West. While beast shows and executions continued on a reduced scale, gladiatorial combats, as the most expensive and infrequent spectacles, were vulnerable to the systems collapse of the western Empire.

NOTES

1 My use of 'victim' is modern, not Roman. From out point of view even the justifiable killing of the guiltiest man or the fiercest beast in the arena involved inappropriate abuse of the sufferers and enjoyment by the spectators. From the Roman point of view, however, the victims deserved their treatment, and Rome deserved the entertainment.

2 Suet. *Iul.* 39, Loeb; on Caesar, see below.

3 Dio 66.25.1–5, Loeb; cf. Suet. *Tit.* 7.3; Mart. *Spect.*

4 Dio 68.15.1. Edmondson (1996) 70–1, with nn. 4–7, clarifies that this was preceded by another show organized by Hadrian in 106 (SHA *Hadr.* 3.8), adds the testimony of a calendar of public events from Ostia (*Inscr. Ital.* 13.1, no. 5, frags. 21–2) including details of another show by Trajan in AD 108–9.

5 Herein I use arena (*harena (arena)*: sand, sanded place) as the generic word for any site (e.g. from the Forum to amphitheaters) where blood sports were held. For overviews of the spectacles, and compendia of evidence, the works of Friedländer (1965), vol. 2; Robert (1940); Ville (1981); Balsdon (1969) 244–313; K. Schneider, 'Gladiatores', *RE* Suppl. 3 (1918) 768–84; and G. Lafaye, 'Gladiator', Dar.–Sag. 2 (1896) 1563–99, remain starting points for lesser derivative studies like this one. Auguet (1972) and M. Grant *Gladiators* (London: George Weidenfeld and Nicolson, 1967, repr. New York: Barnes and Noble, 1995) are readable but without footnotes. Recent treatments include Wiedemann (1992); Golvin and Landes (1990); Clavel-Lévêque (1984a) and others noted in ch. 1.

6 On sacrifice: Burkert (1983), esp. 1–22, and now his *Creation of the Sacred: Tracks of Biology in Early Religions* (Cambridge, Mass.: Harvard U., 1996); *Le Sacrifice dans l'antiquité* (Geneva: Fondation Hardt, 1981); J. Scheid, 'Sacrifice, Roman', *OCD³* (1996) 1345–6. Cf. ch. 1 above. Lincoln (1985), 9–29, interprets Indo-European sacrifice as a ritual repetition of creation, both cosmogony and sociogony, tied to a myth of creation through dismemberment. Some pieces of the victims were distributed differentially and eaten to represent the social order and some pieces were dispersed to the cosmos (e.g. through fire) to relate the microcosm to the macrocosm; see further in his *Myth, Cosmos and Society: Indo-European Themes of Creation and Destruction* (Cambridge, Mass.: Harvard U., 1986).

7 On Roman festivals and cults, see H. H. Scullard, *Festivals and Ceremonies of the Roman Republic* (Ithaca: Cornell U., 1981). Christian objections led Constantine to forbid beast sacrifices as idolatrous: Euseb. *Vit. Const.* 4.25; *CTh* 16.10.2.

8 Suggesting that gladiators devoted themselves to gods, or that victims for execution were consecrated to gods or spirits of the dead, some see stylized or attenuated forms of human sacrifice in the arena. E.g. H. S. Versnel, *Inconsistencies in Greek and Roman Religion*, vol. 2, *Transition and Reversal in Myth and Ritual*, 2nd ed. (Leiden: Brill, 1994) 210–17, feels that human arena victims were still seen to some degree as sacrifices even under the Empire. Cf. Barton (1994) on the sacralization of victims; and further below in ch. 3.

9 Like Achilles' sacrifice of the Trojan captives on the pyre of Patroclus, Aeneas captured eight enemy warriors alive to pour their blood on the flames of the pyre of Pallas as offerings to his shade: Verg. *Aen.* 10.517–20. See S. Farron, 'Aeneas' Human Sacrifice', *A. Class.* 28 (1985) 21–33.

10 A. Rouselle, *Porneia: On Desire and the Body in Antiquity*, trans. F. Pheasant (Oxford: Basil Blackwell, 1988) 112–21, 124–8, argues that human sacrifice, especially of children, to gods such as Saturn, Ceres, Cybele, and Baal continued in Syria and North Africa under Rome into the third century. Cf. Piganiol (1923) 126–36. For a detailed study, see Shelby Brown, *Late Carthaginian Child Sacrifice and Sacrificial Monuments in their Mediterranean Context*, JSOT/ASOR Monograph Series no. 3 (Sheffield: JSOT Press, 1991). Cf. further in J. Rives, 'Tertullian on Child Sacrifice', *MH* 51 (1994) 54–63. On human sacrifice and *trinqui* in Gaul, see ch. 8 below.

11 On Aztec and Mayan sacrifices, see ch. 4 below. See Patrick Tierney, *The Highest Altar: Unveiling the Mystery of Human Sacrifice* (New York: Penguin, 1989) for an anthropological demonstration that the rite continues in modern South

America. We generally assume, from an evolutionary and modernist perspective, that in most cultures human sacrifice has usually become mollified over time and stylized into the offering of surrogates or symbolic effigies or into the staging of contests and duels involving exertion and often bloodshed but usually not death. For a general survey using a broad definition, see Nigel Davies, *Human Sacrifice in History and Today* (New York: William Morrow, 1981).

12 Greek myth and legend viewed human sacrifice as a ritual of expiation to appease the gods and as a way to honor or avenge a dead friend or relative. Dennis D. Hughes, *Human Sacrifice in Ancient Greece* (London: Routledge, 1991) 1–8, approaches human sacrifice – the killing of a human offered to a superhuman recipient – as but one type of ritual killing of humans, which he defines, 3, as 'a killing performed in a particular situation or on a particular occasion (a religious ceremony, a funeral, before battle, etc.) in a prescribed stereotyped manner, with a communicative function of some kind'. Hughes notes the recurrence of the motif of human sacrifice in literature and myth (e.g. Iphigenia), but sees almost no sound, clear archaeological evidence of the practice in Greece. Similarly, A. Henrichs, 'Human Sacrifice in Greek Religion: Three Case Studies', in *Le Sacrifice* (1981) 195–235, sees no undeniable evidence of human sacrifice in Greek or Latin literature, but suggests that the idea still had influence.

13 Vocabulary: J. Rives, 'Human Sacrifice among Pagans and Christians', *JRS* 85 (1995) 65–85, at n. 9 on 66. Davies (1981), 52, explains that premodern societies did not see execution as distinct from sacrifice: 'In general terms, throughout the history of mankind, sacrifice, vengeance and penal justice were not separate notions but different facets of the same process, needed alike to protect the state against the wrath of the gods.'

14 Accepting violence as universal and cyclical, Girard (1977) theorizes that primitive societies used human sacrifice to resolve great 'sacrificial crises', that the killing (or exiling) of a victim or scapegoat resolved social tensions and restored (social and cosmic) order until the next cycle of crisis and solution. James G. Frazer, *The Golden Bough: A Study in Magic and Religion* (repr. London: Macmillan, 1957, orig. 1922) 756–8, notes that in ancient cultures scapegoats (sometimes criminals) might be scourged (to rid them of maleficent influences), killed, driven beyond bounds, stoned, or thrown into the sea (or burned and their ashes thrown into the sea) to purify the community. In Greece the scapegoat (*pharmakos*) was elevated, honored, and then expelled (but probably not killed) as atonement for the community: see Jan Bremmer, 'Scapegoat Rituals in Ancient Greece', *Harv. Stud.* 87 (1983) 299–320, esp. 315–18; W. Burkert, *Structure and History in Greek Mythology and Ritual* (Berkeley: U. California, 1979) 59–77; Hughes (1991) 139–65.

15 See Rives (1995), esp. 74–7, for testimonia and discussion. Also see Versnel (1994) 211–16. On the symbolism of human sacrifice and its relationship to accusations of cannibalism, see Andrew McGowan, 'Eating People: Accusations of Cannibalism Against Christians in the Second Century', *JECS* 2 (1994) 412–42, esp. 433–4, 437–8; cf. ch. 6 below. On Ausonius *Ecl.* 23.33–7 on gladiatorial games to Saturn/Cronus, see Wiedemann (1992) 47, and ch. 8 below.

16 The classic example, made famous in Frazer's *Golden Bough*, concerns the Latin sanctuary of Diana at Nemi, where a stylized version of the traditional sacrifice of kings was practiced to protect the crops; the underlying myth was that of the slain god (or priest king) correlated with the cycle of crops. On effigies, see below. Rives (1995) 66: 'certainly in historical times human sacrifice did not regularly feature in either Greek or Roman religion'.

17 See J. S. Reid, 'Human Sacrifices at Rome and Other Notes on Roman Religion',

JRS 2 (1912) 34–45; J. P. V. D. Balsdon, *Romans and Aliens* (Chapel Hill: U. North Carolina, 1979) 245–8; Farron (1985); A. M. Eckstein, 'Human Sacrifice and the Fear of Military Disaster in Republican Rome', *AJAH* 7 (1982) 69–95; and D. Porte, 'Les Enterrements expiatores à Rome', *Rev. Phil.* 58 (1984) 233–43.

18 Livy 7.15.10, 7.19.2–3. Farron (1985), 23, feels that the incident was probably not historical. Cf. the treatment of rebel soldiers from Rhegium in 270 BC described below. On Etruscan human sacrifices, see L. Bonfante, 'Human Sacrifice on an Etruscan Funerary Urn in New York', *AJArch.* 88 (1984) 531–9; and L. Bonfante, ed., *Etruscan Life and Afterlife* (Detroit: Wayne State U., 1986) 262, 265.

19 Plut. *Marc.* 3.3–4; Dio, frag. 50; Oros. *Adv. Pag.* 4.13.3. Eckstein (1982), 76, puts the first human sacrifice in November of 228, a year and a half after the latest date for the Vestal scandal and trial in Livy *Per.* 20. See further in his Appendix, 82–7. On the location: Hinard (1987b) 112–13, 117.

20 Livy 22.57.2–6, Loeb; cf. Min. Fel. *Oct.* 30.4; Plut. *Fab.* 18.3. Plutarch, *Num.* 10.4–7, describes the traditional punishment of Vestals. On the burial of the Vestals as ritual expulsions of prodigies, see A. Fraschetti, 'La sepoltura delle Vestali e la Città', 97–129, in *Châtiment* (1984); and Eva Cantarella, *I supplizi capitali in Grecia e a Roma* (Milan: Rizzoli, 1991) 136–40. For a recent discussion, see Bauman (1996) 92–7, who sees Domitian's execution of Vestals (Suet. *Dom.* 8.3–4; Plin. *Ep.* 4.11.5) as a device to publicize his message of moral reform.

21 Livy *Per.* 63; Plut. *Quaest. Rom.* 83.

22 Traditional interpretation: C. Cichorius, 'Staatliche Menschenopfer', in his *Römische Studien* (Berlin: Teubner, 1922) 7–21. Eckstein (1982), 72, feels that Rome was restoring the *pax deorum* 'not in order to expiate the *prodigia* themselves, but in order to avert the impending danger'. Later Rome possibly continued to sacrifice Greeks symbolically via straw effigies; see ch. 7 below.

23 Dio 43.24.3–4, Loeb. Hinard (1987b) 15, 124, arguing for a sacralized execution ceremony at Rome, takes this as a ritual sacrifice to Mars. On displaying heads and on ritualized killings in proscriptions as abuses of rituals, see ch. 7 below. Allegations (e.g. Suet. *Aug.* 15; Dio 48.14.4; accepted by Sen. *Clem.* 1.11.2) that Octavian sacrificed 300 captive rebels (a conventional number) from Perusia at the altar of Caesar in 40 BC are rejected by Farron (1985) 26–7, as an exaggeration or invention from anti-Octavian propaganda. As well as showing revulsion (4.765–97), Silius Italicus (11.249–51, noted by Farron (1985) 30) says that a false accusation of human sacrifice was a way to slander an enemy. As McGowan (1994) 431–2, and Rives (1995) 73, observe, suggestions (Sall. *Cat.* 22; Plut. *Cic.* 10.4; Dio 37.30) that Catiline and his conspirators sanctified an oath by drinking human blood, or even sacrificing a human, were made to condemn Catiline as a barbarous and conspiratorial threat to Roman order, and thus to justify his punishment. Rives further notes, n. 67 on 79, that charges of human sacrifice were made against 'bad' emperors beginning with Didius Julianus. E.g. SHA, *Heliogab.* 8.1–2, claims that Elegabalus, raised to be a priest of Baal, shocked Rome as emperor by trying to introduce the sacrifice of children whose parents were alive, and he even had their entrails examined.

24 A problem remains concerning Pliny's comment (*HN* 28.2.12) that human sacrifice had taken place in Italy in his own time. Plutarch, *Marc.* 3.4, however, says that the human sacrifice of 228 was commemorated every November, implying that actual homicides were not performed. Eckstein (1982), n. 59 on 93, notes that, if Pliny is accepted, the senate's ban of 97 BC (Plin. *HN* 30.1.12)

was not being upheld. Possibly Pliny was referring to illegal magical practices or to incidents of *devotio*, self-sacrifices vowed *pro salute* and enforced under Caligula. See ch. 7 below.

25 Rives (1995) quote at 76. Testimonia include Justin *Apol.* 2.12.5; Tatian *Ad Gr.* 29; Tert. *Scorp.* 7.6; Lactant. *Div. inst.* 1.21.3; Athan. *Gent.* 25; and more in Rives, n. 52 on 75. On the festival: H. J. Rose, 'De Iove Latiari', *Mnemos.* 55 (1927) 273–9.

26 Later Christians increasingly generalized about executions of criminals ritually dedicated to infernal deities. E.g. in the fourth century, Prudentius, *C. Symm.* 1.379–98, Loeb, wrote:

> Look at the crime-stained offerings to frightful Dis, to whom is sacrificed the gladiator laid low on the ill-starred arena, a victim offered to Phlegethon in misconceived expiation for Rome . . . Why, Charon by the murder of these poor wretches receives offerings that pay for his services as guide, and is propitiated by a crime in the name of religion. Such are the delights of the Jupiter of the dead (*Iovis infernalis*) . . . Is it not shameful that a strong imperial nation thinks it needful to offer such sacrifices for its country's welfare? . . . With blood, alas, it calls up the minister of death from his dark abode to present him with a splendid offering of dead men . . . human blood is shed at the Latin god's festival (*Latiari in munere*) and the assembled onlookers there pay savage offerings at the altar of their own Pluto.

Clavel-Lévêque (1984b), 190–3, 201, generalizes from such testimonia to argue that gladiatorial spectacles were always at some level a form of human sacrifice to revitalize the spirit of a family or to assure the safety of the state. On Charon, Dis, and *sacri*, see ch. 5 below.

27 Scullard (1981), 111–15, feels that the little puppets of humans hung in the trees during the Feriae Latinae were perhaps just charms against evil spirits or offerings to Jupiter to spare the living, but ancient writers saw these effigies (*oscilla*: Plut. *Quaest. Rom.* 86; Dion. Hal. *Ant. Rom.* 1.38.2; Schol. Bob. ad Cic. *Planc.* 23), typically thrown into the Tiber later, as substitutions for earlier human sacrifices. Cf. below on *oscilla* and hanging in ch. 4.

28 Another possibility is that Christians (e.g. Min. Fel. *Oct.* 30.5) misunderstood or misrepresented what seems to have been the occasional but actual use of blood from gladiatorial combats or executions in potions or rituals (see ch. 6 below).

29 Wiedemann (1992) 34: 'there is no evidence that the Romans in any period thought that any such human sacrifices [as at Perugia] were appropriate in connection with funerals'.

30 See A. Watson, *Rome of the XII Tables* (Princeton: Princeton U., 1975); T. Mommsen, *Römisches Strafrecht* (Leipzig: Dunker und Humblot, 1899, repr. Darmstadt: Wissenschaftliche Buchgesellschaft, 1961) 899–905; Cantarella (1991) 290–305; Claire Luvosi, 'La peine de mort au quotidien', 23–9, in Hinard (1995).

31 J.-M. David, 'Du Comitium à la Roche Tarpéienne: Sur certains rituels d'exécution capitale sous la République, les règnes d'Auguste et de Tibère', 131–76, in *Châtiment* (1984) 145.

32 A. C. Johnson et al., *Ancient Roman Statutes, a Translation with Introduction, Commentary, Glossary, and Index* (Austin: U. Texas, 1961) Doc. 8.8.9, 8.8.24b, repeats this and adds that sacrifice to Ceres was 'a punishment more severe than homicide'. Rome already conceived of punishments worse than death.

33 False witness: Johnson (1961) Doc. 8.8.23; slaves: Doc. 8.8.14; freemen were flogged and adjudged to the injured party for compensation. On the use and topography of the Tarpeian Rock, see Cantarella (1991) 238–63; T. P. Wiseman, 'Topography and Rhetoric: The Trial of Manlius', *Hist.* 28 (1979) 32–50 (= *Roman Studies* (Liverpool: F. Cairns, 1987) 225–43); L. Richardson, Jr, *A New Topographical Dictionary of Ancient Rome* (Baltimore: Johns Hopkins U., 1992) 68, 377–8. David (1984), 131–8, sees the use of the Tarpeian as a typical archaic type of execution, i.e. as a form of consecration or abandonment to the gods, a ritual expulsion of a criminal performed with communal involvement in the center of Rome; those who survived would be spared further execution. On the execution procedure: Gell. *NA* 20.1.53; Sen. *Controv.* 1.3; Livy 6.20.12; Festus 458L; Tac. *Ann.* 6.19; [Aur. Vict.] *De vir. ill.* 24.6, 66.8. The exact location has long been debated, but the Tarpeian was probably in full view of the Forum and near the Comitium, Carcer, and Scalae Gemoniae (see map 2 and ch. 7 below); see Wiseman; David (1984) 135; and now Richardson.

34 Johnson (1961) Doc. 8.3.5–6. Some sources (Gell. *NA* 20.1.52; Quint. *Inst.* 3.6.84; Tert. *Apol.* 4.9) feel that cutting shares meant actually cutting up the debtor's body; see M. Radin, '*Secare Partis*: The Early Roman Law of Execution against a Debtor', *AJPhil.* 43 (1922) 32–48.

35 A. J. Marshall, 'Symbols and Showmanship in Roman Public Life: the Fasces', *Phoenix* 38 (1984) 120–41.

36 Appeal to the assembly (*provocatio*) was a legal safeguard but also a way to dissipate blood guilt. On flogging, see W. A. Oldfather, 'Livy i, 26 and the *Supplicium de More Maiorum*', *TAPA* 39 (1908) 49–72, on Livy 1.26.6; Suet. *Ner.* 49.2, *Dom.* 11.2–3, *Claud.* 34.1. Livy, 2.23.3–6, Loeb, tells a story, set in 495 BC, as an example of the 'binding over' of debtors to creditors, of an aged impoverished debtor who appeared suddenly in the Forum and was 'carried off by his creditor, not to slavery, but to the prison and the torture-chamber (*in ergastulum et carnificinam*)'. On the later executions of citizens by beheading at the edge of town, see ch. 5 below.

37 Citing Sen. *Controv.* 9.2.12 and Cic. II *Verr.* 5.169, Hinard (1987b) 111–25, esp. 111–12, 121–5, stresses the influence of *mos* (custom) and *fas* (sacral law). Influenced by the Annales school and often drawing parallels to ceremonial executions as social diversions under *ancien régime* France, Hinard sees a process of social restoration, a release of collective violence, and the exclusion of the criminal; he also asserts a symbolic correlation of the site of punishment with the nature of the crime and he feels that the ceremony turned sites (e.g. the Campus Sceleratus, Esquiline, Campus Martius, Forum, and Tiber) into spaces of communal action and resolution. However, as an early practice, his elaborated execution ceremony rests on inadequate sound evidence and it recalls later well-attested procedures concerning the Carcer and martyrdoms. Hinard suggests that the traditional ritual was perverted during the Civil Wars, and that a shift to the use of the Carcer and Gemoniae, and the arena, followed. On the procedures and sites, see ch. 7 below.

38 The other five fixed Republican games began in the half-century after 220 BC; Balsdon (1969) 245–8; see further in Scullard (1981).

39 For insights into the 'spectacular' nature of violence in theaters as well as arenas, see various chapters, esp. Edmondson, in Slater (1996).

40 W. V. Harris, *War and Imperialism in Republican Rome 327–30 B.C.* (Oxford: Clarendon Press, 1979) 25–6, on triumphs, cites Polybius, 6.15.8, saying that the *triumphator* in effect recreated for citizens the spectacle of his achievements on campaign. Harris also suggests that through most of the middle Republic about one consul in every three celebrated a triumph.

41 H. S. Versnel, *Triumphus: An Inquiry into the Origin, Development and Meaning of the Roman Triumph* (Leiden: E. J. Brill, 1970) 101–14, rejects the idea that Ludi Romani were an original part of the triumphal ceremony. Versnel, 396–7, sees Greek and Etruscan strands in the triumph: the Greek myth of the epiphany of Dionysus and Etruscan ceremonies (a new year's festival with the king acting as a god, and a festival of victory) developed into a Roman ceremony with elements of victory, new beginnings, and the coming of the bearer of good fortune. E. Künzl, *Der römische Triumph: Siegesfeiern im antiken Rom* (Munich: Beck, 1988), shows the shift under the Empire from a religious celebration of Jupiter to a celebration of the emperor as conqueror. C. Nicolet, *The World of the Citizen in Rome*, trans. P. S. Fulla (Berkeley: U. California, 1980) 352–6, notes the politicization and the shifting focus of triumphs from the religious celebration to the victor; he sees triumphs, like funerals, as 'alternative institutions' which developed beyond their original purpose into political and spectacular occasions. Clavel-Lévêque (1984a), 40–5, compares the triumph to the parade of participants entering an arena.

42 *Venationes* were associated with *ludi* and triumphs under the Republic, but they were increasingly associated with *munera* under the Empire. For overviews, see Friedländer (1965) 2:62–74, 4:181–9; G. Jennison, *Animals for Show and Pleasure in Ancient Rome* (Manchester: U. Manchester, 1937) 44–59, on early shows to 30 BC, 60–98, on the Empire; Aymard (1951) 74–85, 185–99, 537–58; Auguet (1972) 81–106; Ville (1981) 51–6, 88–94, 106–16, 123–8; Toynbee (1973) esp. 17–22; G. Lafaye, 'Venatio', *Dar.–Sag.* 5 (1914) 680–709, on arena hunts, 700–9; Balsdon (1969) 302–13; A. M. Reggiani, 'La *venatio*: origine e prime raffigurazioni', 147–55, in A. M. Reggiani, ed., *Anfiteatro Flavio: immagini, testimonianze, spettacoli* (Rome: Edizioni Quasar, 1988); Clavel-Lévêque (1984a) 78–86; Wiedemann (1992) 55–67.

43 In 275 BC M. Curius Dentatus exhibited four elephants, taken from Pyrrhus at Beneventum, in his triumph (Sen. *De brev. vit.* 13.3). In 251 the proconsul Lucius Caecilius Metellus brought 142 elephants to Rome and exhibited them as spoils of war in the Circus Maximus (Polyb. 1.84). In 186 Marcus Fulvius Nobilior, after the war with the Greeks, held the first *venatio* at Rome, with a hunt of lions and panthers (Livy 39.22.1–2). Aymard (1951), 74–6, feels that the hunt of 186 is simply the first recorded *venatio*, and that it was preceded by a longer history. He points out, 79–80, that the lifting by 170 of the senate's ban of 186 (Plin. *HN* 8.64) on the importation of African beasts indicates that animal shows were already very popular. In 169 the curule aediles, Scipio Nasica and P. Lentulus, gave a show in the Circus Maximus with 63 leopards, 40 bears and elephants (Livy 44.18.8).

44 K. M. Coleman, 'Ptolemy Philadelphus and the Roman Amphitheater', 49–68, in Slater (1996) at 61–3, suggests that later some of the beasts from the spectacles at Rome may have been taken to the imperial game park south of Rome, but she notes that the mere display of exotic species at Rome (e.g. Suet. *Aug.* 43.11) was short-lived (i.e. from the 50s to 2 BC). On the fate of beasts at Rome, see ch. 3 below.

45 At the Lupercalia priests clad in the bloody skins from a sacrifice of goats (unusually, dogs were also sacrificed) ran about flogging spectators. Also, in the Equus October held in the Campus Martius, possibly in the Circus Flaminius, the right-hand horse of the victorious team in a chariot race was sacrificed. The ritual included a contest among regions of the city for the head of the horse victorious in a preceding race. Paulus (in Festus 246L) says that the tail of the sacrificed racehorse, dripping blood, was carried to the Regia in a rite to bless the crops. The Vestals saved some of the dried blood for later

use in the Parilia. Whatever the custom meant, it somehow combined elements of sacrifice, contest, and carnival melée. On these rituals, see Scullard (1981) 76–8, 193–4. C. Bennett Pascal, 'October Horse', *Harv. Stud.* 85 (1981) 61–91, sees a superimposition of religious trappings onto a popular contest.

46 Jennison (1937) 3, 42, sees the origin of beast shows in the hunting or baiting of native Italian animals in the Circus Maximus in the festivals of Ceres and Flora. Similarly, Aymard (1951), 77–9, associates the *venationes* with ancient rites of the field and fertility among Romans and other Italian peoples.

47 Ovid, *Fast.* 4.681–712, Loeb, offers a fanciful tale to explain the custom: at Carseoli, a fox, wrapped in straw and set afire by a farmboy as punishment for stealing chickens, escaped and set crops afire; therefore (711–12) 'to punish the species a fox is burned at the festival of Ceres, thus perishing itself in the way it destroyed the crops'. Scullard (1981), 102–3, thus suggests a punishment or a warning to other vermin to keep away from farms.

48 *HN* 29.57; see more testimonia in Scullard (1981) 170.

49 According to Festus (274L; Ov. *Fast.* 6.235–40), this represented a sacrifice to Volcanus of fish instead of human victims; Scullard (1981) 148. As Scullard, 179, notes, according to Varro, *Ling.* 6.20, at the Volcanalia in August people threw animals into the fire as substitutes for themselves (*pro se*).

50 The Sibylline Books ordered these games in 283 BC to end a drought (see n. 73 below), and they were held annually from 173. See Ov. *Fast.* 5.371–4; and Scullard (1981) 110–11, with testimonia. Martial, 8.67.4, says that the arena still exhausts the animals at Flora's games (*et Floralicius lasset harena feras*). Prostitutes claimed the Floralia as their feast, and Juvenal's lady fencers (6.247–67) may have been preparing for the Floralia (6.250) or for more serious combats.

51 Timothy Mitchell, *Blood Sport: A Social History of Spanish Bullfighting* (Philadelphia: U. Pennsylvania, 1991) 15–25, notes that rural Spanish festivals often involve violence, animal baiting, and mass participation in touching, killing, or 'running' with beasts. Activities include the killing of chickens, calves, and bulls, and the driving through the streets of bulls with firebrands or flares attached to their horns.

52 See Anderson (1985) 83–100; Aymard (1951) 43–63; and Dunbabin (1978) 46–64. Certainly there were Greek influences, but Rome was also experiencing other historical factors (e.g. urbanization, *latifundia*) which led wealthy urbanites to maintain villas and fashionable ties to the countryside.

53 Anderson (1985), 57–83, discusses Persian royal hunts, and says that Rome learned great hunts from the Greek East. Great imperial hunts, even of Pharaohs, go back to tribal concerns about providing food and defending the community; see W. Decker, *Sports and Games of Ancient Egypt*, trans. A. Guttmann (New Haven: Yale U., 1987) 147–67. In the great royal hunts of Assyria recorded in inscriptions and palace reliefs, the kings, hunting from horseback or chariots, delighted in brutal, self-glorifying hunts. Ashurbanipal did hunt in the wild, but sometimes game was driven to the king or brought to him in cages and then released to be killed by him before spectators in a display of royal prowess. Similar to their boasts of brutality and heaps of bodies in war (see ch. 4 below), kings' descriptions of their hunting exploits suggest that hunting was a royal and a religious duty (i.e. to protect subjects, herders, and their cattle and sheep) aided by the gods (hunts ended with libations over the victims laid out in rows). Persian kings adopted the Assyrian hunting imagery of empire and royal protection, and also used stocked animal parks or paradises. See Anderson (1985) 6–10, 14, 63–70. On the symbolism of such hunts, see Leo Bersani and Ulysse Dutoit, *The Forms of Violence: Narrative in Assyrian Art and Modern Culture* (New York: Schocken Books, 1985) esp. 3–39.

54 Coleman (1996), 57–68, discusses the display of animals in processions in Ptolemaic Alexandria compared to the use of beasts in spectacles at Rome. In both cases foreign fauna could symbolize territorial control, but, unlike Rome, the Ptolemies killed animals only in sacrifices; 64: 'Slaughter for the sake of spectacle is unattested.'

55 See Anderson (1985) on the value of hunting for education and warfare in Greece, 17–18, 26–7, 30, 37, 87, and in Rome, 87, 101–2, 151, with testimonia including Hor. *Sat.* 2.29ff., and Plin. *Pan.* 81.1–3. The analogy between hunting and war was well established: e.g. Cic. *Nat. D.* 2.64.161; Veg. *Mil.* 1.7; see further in Aymard (1951) 469–81.

56 The rise and expansion of the *venationes* corresponds in time, especially after Hannibal, to a demographic shift of Romans toward urbanization and away from rustic subsistence farms intimately associated with the countryside. Yeomen Romans, with long traditions of rural hunting and of service in the army, found themselves in urban settings and, before Marius, often ineligible for the army after losing their farms. However contrived, the hunts of the arena were an attractive surrogate for the violence of the hunt and the battlefield. Moreover, as the Empire expanded, Rome incorporated other peoples with native hunting traditions.

57 Servius (*Ad Aen.* 3.67 quoting Varro; *Ad Aen.* 10.519–20) says that gladiators developed out of human sacrifice to the dead and through forced contests between prisoners of war at funerals.

58 Tert. *De spect.* 12, Loeb; but recall Rives' cautions (above) about a discourse on human sacrifice. Cf. Hopkins (1983) 4–12; Ville (1981) 1–19; L. Malten, 'Leichenspiel und Totenkult', *MDAI(R)* 38/9 (1923–4) 300–40.

59 Balsdon (1969), 250, notes that *munera* might include other games but were distinguished from festival *ludi*. Like Balsdon, Wiedemann (1992), 6–7, rejects earlier assumptions about 105 BC and feels that gladiators fought only at privately produced *munera* during the Republic. On these issues, see below.

60 Athenaeus, 4.153f–154a, Loeb, quotes Nicolaus of Damascus (*FGrH* 90, F78 = *FHG* iii.264) on Roman gladiatorial fights (*monomachias*) during banquets:

> The Romans staged spectacles of fighting gladiators not merely at their festivals and in their theatres, borrowing the custom from the Etruscans, but also at their banquets. . . some would invite their friends to dinner . . . that they might witness two or three pairs of contestants in gladiatorial combat . . . when sated with dining and drink, they called in the gladiators. No sooner did one have his throat cut than the masters applauded with delight at this feat.

Note, however, that Athenaeus mentions this within an eclectic discussion (4.153e–154d) of deadly combats and games among Campanians, Celts, or Mantineans (as well as Etruscans), and he also mentions duels, self-sacrifice for prizes, a Thracian game involving a noose and a knife, and more esoterica. Livy, 39.42.7–43.5, Loeb (cf. Plut. *Cat. Mai.* 17.1–5, *Flam.* 18.4–10), tells two versions of a story that the proconsul L. Quintius Flamininus in Gaul personally killed a prisoner at a dinner party. Cf. SHA *Heliogab.* 25.7.8 and *Verus* 4.9 for combats held before or during banquets.

61 Etruscan origins are accepted e.g. by Auguet (1972) 248–9; Carcopino (1975) 208; and Schneider (1918) 760–1. Malten (1923–4), 304–5, 317–18, 328–30, feels that gladiatorial combats originated in the cult of the dead in Etruria but reached Rome via Campania (when under Etruscan rule); cf. Ville (1981) n. 32 on 8, on Suet. *De regibus.* Wiedemann (1992), 33, says that the ascription

of an Etruscan origin 'has to be explained as a result of Roman ambivalence about the games, and not vice-versa'.

62 Ville (1981), 2–6, feels that this contest (*agon*) was an element in funeral games, and that the object was to spill blood and not to kill the man. L. B. van der Mere, 'Ludi scenici et gladiatorum munus: A Terracotta Arula in Florence', *BaBesch.* 57 (1982) 87–99, discusses Phersu and scenes in Etruscan art of the second and first centuries BC, and asserts an Etruscan origin for the gladiatorial *munus*. On three depictions of Phersu in Etruscan tomb frescoes, see J.-P.Thuillier, *Les Jeux athlétiques dans la civilisation Étrusque* (Rome: Palais Farnèse, 1985) 124, 267, 338–40, 587–90, who argues that the 'game' of Phersu is not a gladiatorial combat, that the *munus* came to Rome from the South, and that the Phersu figure was acting as an executioner in an Etruscan version of exposing a doomed victim to a beast. Cf. Thuillier's similar conclusions in his 'Les Origines de la gladiature: une mise au point sur l'hypothèse étrusque', 137–46, in Domergue et al. (1990). Plass (1995), 57–8, sees a combination of gladiatorial combat and exposure to animals with Phersu playing the role of a circus master orchestrating the violence. On Phersu and various aspects of sport and spectacle in Etruria, now see L'École française de Rome, *Spectacles sportifs et scéniques dans le monde étrusco-italique*, CÉFR 172 (Rome: Palais Farnèse, 1993), esp. Jean-René Jannot, 'Phersu, Phersuna, Persona. A propos du masque étrusque', 281–320.

63 A punitive and malicious adaptation of the Greek ferryman, the Etruscan Charon conducted shades to the lower world and tormented the souls of the guilty; see Emeline Richardson, *The Etruscans: Their Art and Civilization* (Chicago: U. Chicago, 1976) 229. J. M. C. Toynbee, *Death and Burial in the Roman World* (Ithaca: Cornell U., 1971) 13, n. 14, see pls. 1–2, says that of the hideous Etruscan male demons, 'Charon, beak-nosed, blue-fleshed, grasping or swinging a hammer or clutching a pair of menacing snakes, is by far the most grisly.' Roughly contemporary with historical examples of slaughters of Roman and Tarquinian captives (see above), scenes of Charon in fourth-century depictions of stylized executions of helpless captives (e.g. the Trojan captives) were popular in Etruscan art; see J. Heurgon, *Daily Life of the Etruscans*, trans. J. Kirkup (London: Weidenfeld and Nicolson, 1964) 210–11; Toynbee (1971) 13. Against the association of the Etruscan Charon with the Roman arena, see ch. 5 below.

64 See Toynbee (1971) 11–14, and ch. 4 below.

65 E. T. Salmon, *Samnium and the Samnites* (Cambridge: Cambridge U., 1967) 60–1, noting that gladiatorial combats do not appear in Etruscan art until the third century, suggests that Samnites introduced gladiators to Rome in 264. Cf. Ville (1981) 19–35; Golvin (1988) 15–17. S. P. Oakley, 'Single Combat in the Roman Republic', *CQ* 35 (1985) 392–410, argues, 398, that duels were common at Rome and in Campania; see below. Paintings of fighters: M. W. Fredericksen, *Campania*, ed. N. Purcell (London: British School at Rome, 1984); P. C. Sestieri, 'Tombe dipinti di Paestum', *RIA* 5–6 (1956–7) 65–110; Gigliola Gori, 'Elementi Greci, Etruschi e Lucani nelle pitture tombali a soggetto sportivo di Paestum', *Stadion* 16 (1990) 73–89 at 78–9, with pls. 4–6. Banquets: Strabo 5.4.13; Ath. 4.153f–154a (quoted above in n. 60); cf. Livy 9.40.17 (below) and Sil. *Pun.* 11.51–4 on third-century banquets. Christopher P. Jones, 'Dinner Theater', 185–99, in William J. Slater, ed., *Dining in a Classical Context* (Ann Arbor: U. Michigan, 1991) 193–4, feels that such practices were cited as 'proof of Campanian decadence' in the middle Republic. On gladiators and imperial banquets, see ch. 6 below.

66 Ville (1981) 7, 35–42. He feels the finger gesture in this context would be an admission of defeat, as in Greek combat sports, not an appeal for mercy in later Roman fashion.

67 Wiedemann (1992), 33–4, surveys theories about the original gladiatorial context and suggests that Rome's motives for adoption may have differed from the original purpose of *munera* elsewhere.

68 Consul in 317, 313, and 311, C. Junius Bubulcus in 311 held a command in Samnium, retook Cluviae, took Bovianum, and celebrated a triumph; see T. R. S. Broughton, *The Magistrates of the Roman Republic*, 3 vols. (New York: American Philological Association, 1951–2, repr. Atlanta: Scholars Press, 1986) 1: 155, 158, 160.

69 Wiedemann (1992), 33, feels that gladiatorial combats were borrowed from Campania and cites this passage on the moral uncertainties of foreign borrowing and on the 'Samnite' type of gladiator. One of the four standard types of gladiators (see Plin. *HN* 7.81), 'Samnite' gladiators probably were actually associated with Samnium. On types of gladiators, and on *devotio*, see ch. 3 below.

70 Livy *Epit*. 16; Val. Max. 2.4.7; Auson. *Griphus ternarii numeri* 36–7. See Ville (1981) 42. Decimus Junius Brutus Pera, son of Decimus Junius Brutus Scaeva (consul of 292), was consul in 266, campaigned in Umbria, and celebrated a triumph over Sassina; Broughton (1951–2) 1: 201. Balsdon (1969), 249, suggests that the 'gladiators' may have been captives from his campaigns. Van der Mere, op. cit., 91, asserting an Etruscan origin for the gladiatorial *munus*, suggests that captives from Etruscan territory and gladiatorial combats arrived in Rome at the same time, but he ignores the earlier experience of the family in Campania. Note that Valerius Maximus, 2.4.7, further remarks that Marcus Scaurus added a 'contest of athletes' to the ceremony. From its inception, a 'gladiatorial *munus*' was distinguished from a 'contest of athletes'.

71 See Matthias Gelzer's classic study, *The Roman Nobility*, trans. R. Seager (Oxford: Basil Blackwell, 1969); and P. A. Brunt, '*Nobilitas* and *novitas*', *JRS* 72 (1982) 1–17.

72 Oakley (1985), 400–1, shows that military single combats (when champions of armies accept formal challenges to fight) were a primitive tradition throughout Italy, and that they continued for Rome through the middle and late Republic to 45 BC; cf. Harris (1979) 38–9. These duels were a 'sideshow', a display allowing individuals to show initiative and win glory, not a way to settle wars. Oakley suggests that such duels took place every year in the middle Republic and several times a year during the Hannibalic war, but, significantly, there is only one known combat by a *nobilis* (in 101) after that of Scipio Aemilianus.

73 On the politicization of early as well as later *munera*, see E. Baltrusch, 'Die Verstaatlichung der Gladiatorenspiele', *Hermes* 116 (1988) 324–37. Similarly, Plass (1995) 46–55, on expensive and violent games as conspicuous consumption, notes symbolic largesse as a traditional means of exercising power. For a counter-argument, that the expansion of the number of days of *ludi* was influenced by sincere religious sentiment and not just political manipulation, see M. Gwyn Morgan, 'Politics, Religion and Games in Rome, 200–150 B.C.', *Philol.* 134 (1990) 14–36, who suggests that the development of the Floralia from a *feria* to the annual Ludi Florales in 173 BC was a religious response to a crop blight and an epidemic.

74 After urging Rome to continue the war effort, perhaps in 249 BC, M. Atilius Regulus returned to his Carthaginian captors, who supposedly cut off his eyelids and tortured him to death in a barrel lined with spikes: Cic. *Off*. 3.99–101, Hor. *Carm*. 3.5, and Val. Max. 9.2.5. Acquiring more and more imperial subjects, becoming more overtly imperialistic and intolerant of defiance, Romans showed less and less sensitivity to the suffering of enemies and inferiors. Harris (1979), 50–3, suggests that the brutality of Romans in war, 51, 'sprang from an unusually pronounced willingness to use violence against alien peoples'. He

relates Roman ferocity in war to the regularity of their warfare, which, 53, gave it 'a pathological character'. At the fall of New Carthage in Spain Scipio ordered that the soldiers kill everyone they met, as was customary, before they could plunder goods. Even dogs were cut in two and animals were dismembered: Polyb. 10.15.4–5. Cf. further examples in Harris (1979) 263–4.

75 Barton (1993) posits a 'physics' of desire and despair to explain the 'inverse elevation' of gladiators, and she ties that elevation and ambivalence to the crises of the late Republic. Perhaps Livy retrojected the ideology of the arena as a moral lesson for contemporary Rome, but his account of the Hannibalic war is more firmly grounded than his stories of legendary heroics in early Rome. The pivotal significance of Cannae in Roman history suggests that Romans understood the elevation of the lowly by demonstration of military *virtus* and *amor mortis* much earlier than the late Republic. On the gladiatorial paradox, see ch. 3 below.

76 To teach his men glory of victory or death in battle rather than in captivity, in 218 Hannibal invited prisoners captured in the mountains to use Gallic weapons and to fight duels with the possibility of death or freedom, and thus avoid death as a slave or captive: Livy 21.42–3; Polyb. 3.62–3. Hannibal was less successful when he staged a fight between an elephant and a captive (Plin. *HN* 8.18). Hannibal had agreed to let the prisoner go free if he killed the beast, but when he did so to the dismay of the Carthaginians, Hannibal had the man killed, lest news of the event diminish fear of elephants. Barton (1993), 20–2, notes Hannibal's duels and emphasizes the analogous virtues of soldiers and gladiators; see ch. 3 below. Gunderson (1996), 138–40, feels that in 21.42 and 28.21 (on Scipio's games at New Carthage, see n. 87 below) Livy has reworked his material to present idealized gladiatorial combats using a Roman and Augustan-era model of the noble gladiator.

77 The news of Cannae brought panic and religious fervor – the introduction of the cult of Magna Mater, even 'human sacrifice' (see above); on the possible introduction of 'the sack', see ch. 7 below. Plutarch, *Fab.* 18.3, says that rituals used after Cannae were meant to propitiate the gods and avert further evil omens. Plass (1995), 38–40, sees the taste for brutal entertainments as a function of insecurity in Roman history in general: gladiatorial violence evoked and exorcised military danger and built morale.

78 Before becoming dictator after the news of Cannae, Marcus Junius Pera had been consul in 230 and censor in 225; Broughton (1951–2) 1: 226, 231, 248.

79 Livy 22.57.9–12, Loeb. Valerius Maximus, 7.6.1, says that a commission was chosen to purchase 24,000 slaves. He comments that Rome now turned to slaves even though before it had rejected free men without property as soldiers.

80 Livy, 22.38.1–5, points out that in 216 immediately before Cannae the military oath was changed from a voluntary agreement not to desert the field of battle into a mandatory and legally binding oath (*sacramentum*) formally made before the military tribune. The oath gave commanders the power to put deserters and disobedient soldiers to death without trial. In a later version, probably true to earlier practice, the soldier swore enthusiastic allegiance to the emperor and promised never to desert or to resist death for Rome: Veg. *Mil.* 2.5. See G. R. Watson, *The Roman Soldier* (Ithaca: Cornell U., 1969) 44, 49–50. On the gladiator's oath, see ch. 3 below.

81 Cf. Claudius' remark in AD 48 that Rome had a traditional policy of bringing conspicuous merit to Rome from whatever origins: Tac. *Ann.* 11.24. Elitist authors remarked on humble individuals who showed virtue beyond that associated with their status. Tacitus, *Ann.* 15.57, applauds the virtue of the

freedwoman Epicharis, who endured torture and committed suicide: she set a
'noble example' – beyond freedmen, knights, and even senators who had cracked
and revealed accomplices in the conspiracy of Piso against Nero. See Anton J.
L. Van Hooff, *From Autothanasia to Suicide: Self-Killing in Classical Antiquity*
(London: Routledge, 1990) 18–20, who explains that Tacitus and others used
accounts of suicides by lowly individuals as lessons for their noble contempo-
raries. Dio, 51.7.2, says that the gladiators of Antony and Cleopatra were
despised for their status but that they fought bravely and loyally. SHA *Marc.*
21.7, 23.5, Loeb: Marcus Aurelius, facing a manpower shortage against the
Marcomanni, trained slaves for military service, whom he called Volunteers,
and he 'armed gladiators also, calling them the Compliant (*obsequentes*), and
turned even the bandits of Dalmatia and Dardania into soldiers'.

82 He even claims, 22.59.19, that if they were ultimately spared by Hannibal,
this would be no blessing if the Romans showed displeasure with them and
found them unworthy of ransom.

83 A successful general himself, Torquatus was from a military family renowned
for single combats against enemies; see Oakley (1985) nos 6 and 8. These 7,000
armed men had not tried to fight their way through the enemy despite a good
opportunity during the night, and they refused to join the 600 men who forced
their way through and returned themselves to their country free and armed.
Instead they negotiated the price for ransom and surrendered. Torquatus,
22.60.12, also recalls the earlier call to *devotio* by Marcus Calpurnius Flamma
in the First Punic War.

84 Livy, of course, embellished his speeches, and he used heroic deeds of early
Romans to provide moral exempla for his own age; but the actions of the senate
after Cannae are not in doubt. Before Cannae *munera* seem to have included
the simple killing of slaves and captives, but after Cannae and the refusal to
ransom the prisoners of war, *munera* came to embrace the notions of elevation
and *missio* crucial to the later gladiatorial paradox; see ch. 3 below.

85 Arguing, 22.59.12, that the prisoners would fight well out of gratitude if
ransomed, that their numbers are roughly the same as those of the recruited
slaves, and that their ransom would cost no more, the envoy adds: 'I make no
comparison between our worth and theirs, for that would be to insult the name
of Roman.'

86 Detailed in Friedländer (1965) 2:41 and Toynbee (1971) 56 and nn. 219–22
on 294; 216 BC: 22 pairs of gladiators fought in three-day funeral games at
the funeral of Marcus Aemilius Lepidus given by his sons in the Forum: Livy
23.30.15; 200 BC: 25 pairs at four-day funeral games given in the Forum by
his sons for Marcus Valerius Laevinus: Livy 31.50.4; 183 BC: three-day funeral
ludi with 120 gladiators and *visceratio data* at the funeral of Publius Licinius:
Livy 39.46.2; 174 BC: a four-day *munus* with 74 fighters *cum visceratione epuloque
et ludis scaenicis* at the funeral of the father of Titus Q. Flamininus: Livy 41.28.11.
Providers of circus and theatrical shows found that audiences wanted them
supplemented with more violent events. Terence, *Hec.* prologue 31, as
Wiedemann (1992) 145 notes, complains that his play had to compete with a
gladiatorial combat in 164.

87 On Scipio's games at New Carthage in 206, see ch. 3. Livy, 41.20.10–13,
writing of gladiatorial spectacles 'in the Roman style' held by Antiochus
Epiphanes in Syria in 175 BC, says that some combats went only to the point
of wounds but others were without quarter, and that local volunteers came to
be used instead of imported and expensive gladiators from Rome. See
Wiedemann (1992) 42, who notes that Antiochus had been a prisoner at Rome.

88 Death and victory were probably the only options for the first gladiators; sparing

losers (*missio*) arose later as a way for spectators to express appreciation or as an economic measure by editors not wanting to waste valuable resources; see ch. 3 below. On the correlation between the virtues of gladiators and soldiers, see ch. 3 below. Cicero, *Off.* 3.32.114, says that the senate did not ransom the captives from Cannae in order to teach soldiers that they must conquer or die. Similarly, the speech by Regulus in Horace, *Carm.* 3.5.18–40, says that surrendered soldiers are not worth ransoming. On the Roman tendency to blame defeats on the soldiers rather than their generals, see Nathan Rosenstein, *Imperatores Victi: Military Defeat and Aristocratic Competition in the Middle and Late Republic* (Berkeley: U. California, 1990). Later, Crassus decimated some 500 troops defeated by Spartacus; Plut. *Crass.* 10.2–3, Loeb: he put to death one of every ten chosen by lot, 'thus reviving after the lapse of many years, an ancient mode of punishing the soldiers. For disgrace also attaches to this manner of death, and many horrible and repulsive features attend the punishment, which the whole army witnesses.' Crassus went on to defeat Spartacus and to crucify 6,000 slaves along the Appian Way as a means of improving 'the morale of the Roman citizens'. *Fustuarium*, a purification rite for military failure, involved forcing soldiers to club their comrades to death; see Polyb. 6.38.1–2 and Lintott (1968) 41–3 with testimonia. Suetonius, *Aug.* 24.2, says that this was Augustus' standard punishment for mass cowardice.

89 Livy, 22.51.5–8, describes the battlefield at Cannae strewn with corpses; some soldiers still alive, but incapacitated with their thighs and tendons slashed, bared their necks and throats (i.e. for the death blow); some committed suicide by burying their heads in holes which they dug in the ground. Cf. Cic. *Tusc.* 2.17.41: gladiators show discipline and a desire above all to please their masters; offering an education in pain and death, they sustain wounds, they die with honor, and when defeated they offer their necks for the death blow. Florus, 2.8.14, Loeb, says that Spartacus' men fought to the death (*sine missione*) as befitted men led by a gladiator.

90 Legal sources reflect the disgust that Rome felt toward deserters. It was considered treason possibly worthy of capital or even aggravated punishment if a soldier deserted, attempted to desert, retreated from an entrenchment, or betrayed information to the enemy. See Robinson (1995) 18, 45–6, 76, with testimonia. For soldiers, even attempted suicide without a valid justification was seen as desertion and was punishable by death: *Dig.* 49.16.6.7; see Van Hooff (1990) 84, 172; M. R. de Pascale, 'Sul suicido del *miles*', *Labeo* 31 (1985) 57–61.

91 Polybius, 1.7.12, cf. 1.10.4, says that they were killed 'according to the Roman custom' for breaking faith with Rhegium and to restore the good name of Rome among the allies. See also Dion. Hal. *Ant Rom.* 20.16.2. In 206 BC Scipio recalled that 'some time ago' a rebellious legion of 4,000 men sent to garrison Rhegium were executed in the Roman Forum: Livy 28.28.3. Such executions were customary, according to Dion. Hal. 20.5.5 (concerning an earlier rebellion at Rhegium), who, 20.16.2, puts the total killed in 270 at Rome, by a unanimous vote of all the tribes, at 4,500; see Harris (1979) 188. On the disposal of the bodies, see n. 34 in ch. 4 below.

92 Livy 24.20.6, 24.30.6. Also in 214, the people of Henna in Sicily were massacred by the Roman garrison to prevent any revolt: Livy 24.39.1–5.

93 Val. Max. 2.7.12–14, who approved of such disciplinary acts as beneficial (*utilissimo exemplo*); Livy *Per.* 51; Lintott (1968) 43; Ville (1981) 232–40. Cf. the story in *III Macc.* 4.11, 5.1–6.21 that Jews who resisted the orders of Ptolemy IV (221–203 BC) that they worship Dionysus were herded into a hippodrome to be trampled to death by 500 elephants intoxicated by wine and incense, but

miraculously the beasts turned on Ptolemy's troops instead; cf. J. H. Humphrey, *Roman Circuses: Arenas for Chariot Racing* (Berkeley: U. California, 1986) 509–10. SHA *Claud. Goth.* 11.8, Loeb: when some of his soldiers were delinquent in their duties, turning to plundering and letting themselves be routed by a smaller force, Claudius 'seized all those who had shown a rebellious spirit, and he even sent them to Rome in chains to be used in the public spectacles'.

94   Plass (1995), 29–45, suggests that, in the context of war and militarism, games dealt with tensions and insecurity, and became stylized into a celebration of civic power. Ritual violence to outsiders reassured insiders of their security; 29: 'Games were essentially ceremonies for the living, not sacrifice for the dead.'

95   Plin. *HN* 35.52; Friedländer (1965), 2:41, suggests a date around 145; Wiedemann (1992), 15, suggests the late second century.

96   Plut. *C. Gracch.* 12.3–4. Wiedemann (1992), 20, suggests that Gracchus presented the show, but the passage does not say so.

97   A fifth-century AD writer, Ennodius, *Panegyricus dictus regi Theodorico* 213.25 (ed. Vogel) cited, e.g., in Barton (1993) 22, claims that the consuls of 105, Rutilius and Manlius, put on the first publicly sponsored gladiatorial games to give common Romans a sense of the battlefield. As Balsdon (1969) 250; Ville (1981) 46–7; Wiedemann (1992) 6–7; and Edmondson (1996) n. 39 on 79, correctly note, this was not an institutionalization of state *munera*.

98   Val. Max. 2.3.2. From the school of Aurelius Scaurus (cons. 108) at Capua, the earliest recorded private gladiatorial school, the instructors taught skills and also possibly the virtue of facing death without surrendering. In 105 the Roman defeat at Arausio by the Cimbri and Teutones was the worst since Cannae, and the Romans in crisis turned to Marius and to gladiatorial instructors. Frontinus, *Strat.* 4.2.2, comments that Marius preferred the troops trained by Rutilius to his own. Vegetius, *Mil.* 1.11, asserts the importance of training with weapons at stakes for both soldiers and gladiators. On the development in 105, now see Welch (1994) 62–5, who argues that gladiatorial instruction continued on a regular basis in the post-Marian army. On the enduring conservative opposition to the use of professional gladiatorial weapons trainers, see Watson, op. cit., 55–7.

99   Welch (1994); also see her 'Roman Amphitheaters Revived', *JRA* 4 (1991) 272–81, esp. 274–7. Cf. Golvin (1988) 24, 42–67, 301–13, on the origin of the shape of the arena in forums where *munera* were held, and on the influence of the wooden seating in the Roman Forum on the amphitheatral architecture. Welch (1994) 61, 78, notes that the facilities at Pompeii and in the Roman Forum both were referred to as *spectacula*. Cf. Welch's proposed reconstruction of the facilities in the Forum: figs 6–8 on 73–75, rejecting that by Golvin (1988) pl. Vb. Note that this site is just southeast of the Comitium, Carcer and Scalae Gemoniae; see ch. 7 below.

100 Welch (1994) 80: 'For ancient Romans the games were entertaining because of the dramatic and uncertain outcome of the highly skilled combat, and useful because they promoted military courage, *virtus* – a key ingredient of the Roman self-image.'

101 See chs. 4 and 7 below.

102 Wiedemann (1992) 5–7; Ville (1981) 72–88.

103 Cic. *In Vat.* 37, *Sest.* 64.133–5, Loeb: Vatinius 'knew what the people wanted' and 'foresaw their applause'.

104 Milo's gang included the well-known gladiators Eudamas and Birria; on these and others, see Lintott (1968) 83–5. As Susan Treggiari, *Roman Freedmen during the Late Republic* (Oxford: Clarendon Press, 1969) 142, suggests, probably these gladiators were (or were promised that they would become) freedmen.

105 Ville (1981) 125–6, 236 and n. 21, 379, 393; cf. Suet. *Claud.* 21.4: *munus iustum atque legitimum*. Cf. Wiedemann below crediting Augustus with the tripartite arrangement; but Edmondson (1996), n. 21 on 74, via W. J. Slater's suggestion, points out that App. *B Civ.* 2.118 (on the aftermath to the assassination of Caesar) suggests that gladiatorial combats were already taking place in the afternoon in 44 BC. Edmondson, 76–9, noting the diversity of spectacles and their context, appropriately warns, 77, that, because leaders combined various elements in different ways, it is 'dangerous to attempt to reconstruct a "typical" *munus*'. He suggests that the format of *munera* was not standardized until the completion of the Flavian Amphitheater in AD 80.

106 Metcalf and Huntington (1991), 144–51, note that the Berawan people of Borneo build mausoleums as a means of conspicuous display, but by local custom leaders may not prepare a tomb for someone not yet dead (including themselves). Therefore, to achieve self-aggrandizement while alive, leaders build tombs for obscure relatives, and in honoring them they ennoble themselves.

107 Pompey had dedicated his theater in 55 with a *venatio* in which 20 elephants and 500 or 600 lions and some 400 other African beasts died: Dio 39.38.2; cf. Cicero's comments in ch. 1 above. Cf. further in Balsdon (1969) 256, 269, 303, 306–7, 310; Jennison (1937) 51–5.

108 Sources on Caesar's spectacles include: Suet. *Iul.* 39, quoted at the start of this chapter; Suet. *Iul.* 10.2, 26.2; Plut. *Caes.* 5.4; Dio 43.22–3; App. *B Civ.* 2.102; Plin. *HN* 8.22, 33.53. On Caesar's games, see Ville (1981) 68–71, 93–4; Jennison (1937) 56; Wiedemann (1992) 6. Welch (1994), 71, associates Caesar with the development of subterranean shafts in the area of the Forum used for gladiatorial shows; see further in G. F. Carretoni, 'Le gallerie ipogee del foro e i ludi gladiatori forensi', *BCAR* 76 (1959) 23–44.

109 On mock battles, see Ville (1981) 228–31, esp. his nos. 45 (Caesar in 46) and 65 (Augustus); cf. further in ch. 3. Coleman (1990), 71–2, sees such battles as an extension of triumphal processions; see also Versnel (1970) 95–6.

110 Suet. *Iul.* 39.4; Dio 43.23.4, 45.17.8; App. *B Civ.* 2.102. Welch (1991), 279, notes, from Livy 29.22, that Scipio Africanus held a mock sea battle with his fleet in Sicily in 204 BC.

111 K. M. Coleman, 'Launching into History: Aquatic Displays in the Early Empire', *JRS* 83 (1993) 48–74, thoroughly discusses the venues, logistics, and purposes of *naumachiae*, comparing the deadly realism of reenacted sea battles with that of 'fatal charades' (see below) in the arena. She suggests, 49, that an aspect of the Roman *mentalité* was 'a passion for novel and elaborate ways of mounting spectacle, which in turn generates the notion of enhancing mortal combat by staging it in a theatrical setting'. As Wiedemann (1992), 89–90, explains, naumachies were usually elements of triumphs, not of *munera*. Further, see Joël Le Gall, *Recherches sur le culte du Tibre* (Paris: Presses Universitaires de France, 1953) 84, 115–16, 271, 282, 314; J.-C. Golvin and M. Reddé, 'Naumachies, jeux nautiques et amphithéâtres', in Domergue et al. (1990) 165–77; Richardson (1992) 265–6, 292; Friedländer (1965) 2:74–6; Balsdon (1969) 328–9. On the participants, see ch. 3 below. On aquatic displays (e.g. erotic water ballets, dressage or chariot races in water), see Coleman (1993) 64–7; G. Traversari, *Gli spettacoli in acqua nel tardo-antico* (Rome: L'Erma di Bretschneider, 1960).

112 Dio, 45.17.8, says that the site was filled in three years later by senatorial order because of an epidemic. Richardson (1992) 265: 'It is not clear whether this was a measure of hygiene or a gesture of atonement.'

113 *Mon. Anc.* 23; Suet. *Aug.* 43.1; Dio 55.10.7; Vell. Pat. 2.100.2; Tac. *Ann.*

14.15.3. On Claudius, see ch. 3 below. Nero had his new wood amphitheater designed so that the arena could be flooded, and gave one (Persians versus Athenians) or possibly two naumachies: Suet. *Ner.* 12.1. Dio 61.9.5 and 62.15.1 may concern separate or the same events. On locations and construction of facilities, see Coleman (1993) 50–60.

114 Suet. *Tit.* 7.3; Dio 66.25.2–4; cf. Mart. *Spect.* 24–6, 8, who marvels at land turned into sea and vice versa, and that the naumachy houses spectacles of both circus and amphitheater.

115 Coleman (1993) 57, 63, 68–74. Domitian dug a new facility near the Tiber: Suet. *Dom.* 4.1–2; Dio, 67.8.2–3, claims that in Domitian's naumachy virtually all the fighters died. Trajan apparently also built a naumachy; see Richardson (1992) 266. Finally, in AD 247 Philip the Arab's millennial games included water spectacles and possibly naumachies on an artificial lake across the Tiber: SHA *Heliogab.* 23.1; cf. Aur. Vict. *Caes.* 28.

116 Welch (1994), 61–2, cites the charter of Urso in Spain of 44 BC (*CIL* 2.5439.70–1 = *ILS* 6087) as the 'earliest surviving evidence of governmental organization of *munera*'. Quinquatrus: ibid., n. 10 on 62, citing Ov. *Fast.* 3.809–14, *Tr.* 4.10.11–14.

117 Dio 44.6.2. Also, note the plebeian aediles' substitution of gladiatorial combats for chariot races in the Cerealia in 42 BC: Dio 47.40.6; which Balsdon (1969), 250, interprets as one of the first 'public' gladiatorial fights. Edmondson (1996) n. 39 on 79, however, cautions that the instances in 44 and 42 were special arrangements and not enduring practices.

118 E.g. Zanker (1988); Karl Galinsky, *Augustan Culture: An Interpretive Introduction* (Princeton: Princeton U., 1996).

119 Wiedemann (1992), 8–10, explains that, while *ludi* remained state occasions paid for by the state and officially part of magistrates' duties, *munera* were the personal gift of the editor; but he admits that public and private, like voluntary and official generosity, blurred under the Empire. Against the usual crediting of the imperial schools to Domitian, Wiedemann, 22, notes that a recent inscription (*AE* (1979) 33) suggests that at least one school existed under Tiberius, and he is inclined to associate the establishment of the imperial *ludi* with Augustus as another tactic of control. K. Welch, 'A Higher Order of Killing: Statilius Taurus and Rome's First Amphitheater' (abstract) *AJArch.* 98 (1994) 326, notes that Rome's first permanent amphitheater, that of Taurus in 30 BC (Suet. *Aug.* 29.5), was the first major building in Rome to be dedicated after Actium (Dio 51.23.1) and that it was completed in time for Octavius' triple triumph of 29. On Augustus' attempt at regulating seating at *munera* (cf. Suet. *Aug.* 44.2) to reinforce his social reforms, now see Edmondson (1996) 88–90, 102–3.

120 *Romanitas* and spread: Wiedemann (1992) 40–6. Tripartite: 55, 59, 67. *Venationes* were regularly associated with gladiatorial *munera* from Augustus on, and the execution of *noxii* also was added by the first century AD. Concentration: Wiedemann (1992) 41, 47, 55, 155–6; see below on decline. The date of the shifting of official *munera* in the calendar is uncertain; these games were possibly held in March under Augustus, but the transfer to December may date to Caligula; see Ville (1981) 102, 119, 159–60, 167–8; Edmondson (1996) 110 and n. 176; and also remarks by D. Potter, reviewing Wiedemann in *JRS* 84 (1994) 229–30.

121 Dio 54.2.4. As Gunderson (1996), n. 67 on 132, points out, if Augustus limited others' shows to 120 gladiators (Dio 54.2.3–4) and he himself gave eight shows with a total of 10,000 gladiators (*Mon. Anc.* 22.1), on average his shows were ten times larger than the legal limit. On imperial legislation

about *munera*, see Ville (1981) 121–3; Balsdon (1969) 261–4; Wiedemann (1992) 132–5. Edmondson (1996) 79–81, esp. n. 45 on 80, asserts that Augustus turned the gladiatorial *munus* into an official state occasion as part of his reordering of Roman society and his redefinition of the relationship between emperor and senate. Tiberius apparently strengthened and then Caligula weakened the rules, and quaestors were put in charge from Claudius on. Recently Coleman (1996), 63, has noted that under Augustus and later emperors animals were killed and no longer just displayed. She interprets the conspicuous consumption of beasts in spectacles, with emperors trying to outdo each other, as an example of the drive of emperors to control (including via death) whatever is extraordinary or spectacular.

122 For epigraphical testimonia on the procurators and imperial training schools, see Edmondson (1996) n. 47 on 81. More broadly on the administration and financing of *munera*, see M. A. Cavallaro, *Spese e spettacoli: Aspetti economici-strutturali degli spettacoli nella Roma guilio-claudia* (Bonn: Habelt, 1984); and now Jean-Jacques Aubert, *Business Managers in Ancient Rome: A Social and Economic Study of Institutores, 200 B.C–A.D. 250* (Leiden: Brill, 1994) 347–68, on public entertainments, esp. 363–5 on amphitheaters.

123 On the Flavian use of games and amphitheaters to legitimize their new dynasty, see Wiedemann (1992) 42.

124 Punitive cruelty was hardly a Roman invention. Sall. *Iug.* 14.15: Jugurtha took Adherbal's relatives captive, some were crucified, some were thrown to wild beasts, and a few were put in dungeons. Among other brutal punishments (e.g. impaling on stakes #153, being burned #25, 157), Hammurabi's laws often order that persons be 'thrown into the water' as an execution (#108, 133a, 143, 155) or an ordeal (#132; cf. Num. 5.11–31); see James B. Pritchard, *Ancient Near Eastern Texts Relating to the Old Testament*, 2nd ed. (Princeton: Princeton U., 1955) 163–77. On water and punishment, see ch. 7 below.

125 See P. Garnsey, *Social Status and Legal Privilege in the Roman Empire* (Oxford: Clarendon Press, 1970) 104, 124 and n. 2, and ch. 3 below. Hadrianic constitutions distinguished simple death (*capite puniri: Dig.* 48.19.28.13–14) from *summa supplicia*.

126 On *summa supplicia* and spectacles, see: Garnsey (1970) 122–36; Cantarella (1991); C. Vismara, *Il supplizio come spettacolo* (Rome: Edizioni Quasar, 1990); C. Vismara, 'L'amphithéâtre comme lieu de supplice', 253–7, in Domergue et al. (1990); Callu (1984), with a detailed analysis of the crimes, punishments, and status of criminals; D. Grodzynski, 'Tortures mortelles et catégories sociales: les *summa supplicia* dans le droit romain au IIIe et au IVe siècles', 361–403, in *Châtiment* (1984); Mommsen (1899) 911–44; Ville (1981) 235–40; U. Brasiello, *La repressione penale in diritto Romano* (Naples: Jovene, 1937) 246–71; and ch. 3 below. Coleman (1990), 46, explains that the offender was to suffer for his offense: 'The humanitarian notion that execution should be carried out with dignity, speed, and discretion is a modern idea.' With increased humanitarian concerns and impersonalization, modern executions may be too distant and impersonal for the masses to associate with the condemned as an individual and thus for significant deterrence to be achieved.

127 Condemnation to public labor (public works, mines, or gladiatorial troop) was an invention of the Principate, generally for the lower classes; it was seen as less severe than execution, but in effect death was usually merely delayed for a time while the state used your body. Free men condemned to public works, mines, or gladiatorial schools lost their liberty as well as citizenship, becoming 'penal slaves'. See Garnsey (1970) 131–4; Bauman (1996) 127–30, 132–5; F. G. Millar, 'Condemnation to Hard Labour in the Roman Empire

from the Julio-Claudians to Constantine', *PBSR* 52 (1984) 125–47. As Millar explains, 130–2, 143–4, *damnatio in metallum* satisfied punitive and economic motives.

128 Grodzynski (1984), 361, emphasizes the effectiveness of the horror of the 'spectacle du corps souffrant'. He shows, 396–403, that such images from the arena persisted into astrological sources of the late Empire. Nippel (1995), 25–6, remarks that the available sources suggest that the use of spectacular punishments of humble persons to deter criminals was a phenomenon of the Empire and not of the Republic.

129 Gaius in *Dig.* 47.9.9 = XII Tables 8.10. Coleman (1990), 46, relates *crematio* to the principle of *talio* by which the punishment suits the crime. E.g. arsonists who committed arson in a built-up area faced *crematio*: *Dig.* 48.19.28.12 (Callistr.).

130 E.g. Dio 54.1.1–3 (cf. 53.33.4): in 22 BC, upset by a series of disasters (flood, famine, plague) and wanting Augustus appointed dictator, the people shut the senators up in the Curia, and threatened to set fire to it. App. *BCiv.* 2.126: after the assassination of Caesar a mob put wood around a house and intended to burn it and Cinna within it.

131 Cf. above on Scipio's crucifixion of Roman deserters in 146 BC. On crucifixion: Garnsey (1970) 126–9; M. Hengel, *Crucifixion in the Ancient World and the Folly of the Message of the Cross* (Philadelphia: Fortress Press, 1978); H.-W. Kuhn, 'Die Kreuzesstrafe während der frühen Kaiserzeit', *ANRW* 2.25.1 (Berlin: De Gruyter, 1982) 648–793; Callu (1984) 336–7; cf. ch. 5 below on inscriptions from Puteoli and Cumae. Constantine banned crucifixion (Aur. Vict. *Caes.* 41.4; Sozom. *Hist. eccl.* 1.8), but replaced it with the 'fork' (*furca*), by which a man was hung by the neck from a wooden fork until dead – a relatively quicker form of execution than crucifixion. On the history of the *crux* versus *furca*, and on what *suspensus* (cf. Plin. *HN* 28.3.12) meant in early Rome, see Grodzynski (1984) 364–7.

132 See Plin. *HN* 18.12; Livy 1.26.6; Plut. *Mor.* 554a; and Oldfather (1908).

133 Procedures: V. Tzaferis, 'Crucifixion – The Archaeological Evidence', *Biblical Archaeology Review* 11.1 (1985) 44–53, at 48–9.

134 On crucifixion of slaves, see Cic. *Clu.* 187, II *Verr.* 5.12; Val. Max. 8.4.2; Livy 22.33.2; Suet. *Dom.* 10.1. For murder of a master by a slave: Mart. *Spec.* 7.8–10. Crucifixion of brigands: Petron. *Sat.* 111.5. Cf. Cic. II *Verr.* 1.13 and 5.161–4 on Verres' improper crucifixion of citizens. Jews: in AD 70 for several months 500 or more Jewish captives were crucified a day in view of the walls of besieged Jerusalem: Joseph, *BJ* 5.450. On Christians, see ch. 8 below.

135 Deterrence as goal: see Coleman (1990) 48–9, who adds that it might be done at the site of the crime so that relatives of the murdered man might gain satisfaction; cf. *Dig.* 48.19.28.15.

136 Beasts: Garnsey (1970) 129–31; Ville (1981) 232–40; H. Leclerq, 'Ad Bestias', Cabrol-Leclercq, *Dict. d'arch. chrétienne* 1 (1907) 449–62; Mommsen (1899) 925–8. Reconstructions from literature and art: Ville (1981) 391–3; Potter (1993) 66–9. On exposure to beasts in art, see ch. 3. Suetonius, *Ner.* 29.1, Loeb, claims that Nero created a perversely erotic game for himself based on such spectacular punishments: 'covered with the skin of some wild animal, he was let loose from a cage and attacked the private parts of men and women, who were bound to stakes'. Cf. Dio 62(63).13.2 and discussion in Bartsch (1994) 57–8.

137 The SHA expands penal precedents into fantastic stories. E.g. Avidius Cassius, *Avid. Cass.* 4.3, Loeb, is credited with a spectacular form of execution: 'after erecting a huge post, 180 feet high, and binding condemned criminals to it

from top to bottom, he built a fire at its base, and so burned some of them and killed others by the smoke, the pain, and even the fright'. Noting examples of punishment used for black comedic effect, Bauman (1996), 68–9, suggests that 'Macrinus was something of a coathanger for unusual penalties.' E.g. SHA *Macrin.* 12.4–5, Loeb: Macrinus punished two soldiers by ordering that two large, live oxen be cut open and one soldier be put into each, with their heads out so that they could talk to each other; SHA *Macrin.* 12.10: co-adulterers were fastened together and burned alive. Bauman explains both of these unreliable examples as inspired by fourth-century legal texts. Cf. Cartmill (1993) 61: by a traditional punishment poachers might be sewn into the fresh skins of deer, then chased and killed by hounds; citing E. P. Thompson, *Whigs and Hunters: The Origins of the Black Act* (New York: Pantheon, 1975) 30–1.

138 Coleman (1990), definition at 44. Cf. Wiedemann (1992) 85–9; Auguet (1972) 99–104; Bartsch (1994) 50–60. The combination of theater and execution in the amphitheater was not theater proper but rather, Bartsch says, 51–2, a 'violation of the theatrical by the actual, or rather a conflation of the two', not a representation but a replication. As she notes, the actual deaths in the charades fulfilled the requirements of both the plot and the penal code. Recently Coleman (1996), 49–52, has compared the use of myth in Roman spectacles with its use in the Grand Procession of Ptolemy Philadelphus in Alexandria in 275/4 BC, but Ptolemy's was not a spectacle of death.

139 Coleman (1990), 61, cites Sen. *Dial. (Cons. ad Marc.)* 6.20.3 on a type of crucifixion whereby the criminal was impaled through the genitals (with self-castration the only way to prevent death). Coleman sees this as a 'mitigated' punishment; cf. Potter's discussion (1993) n. 91 on 84–5.

140 Strabo 6.273C; cf. Coleman (1990) 53–4, 64–5.

141 Real punishments: Mart. *Spect.* 5.4, 7.12; cf. Coleman (1990) 60–6. Coleman, 56, suggests that crucifixion was not very spectacular and might be combined with other punishments, e.g. with fire or exposure to beasts. Laureolus: Mart. *Spect.* 7; this was a famous mime based on the crucifixion of a robber under Caligula; references in Coleman, 64–5, include Suet. *Calig.* 57.4; Joseph. *AJ* 19.1.13; Juv. 8.178f. Cf. Mart. *Spect.* 8 and 21: Daedalus and Orpheus are torn by a bear. Bartsch (1994), 52–4, feels that presentation of 'Laureolus' had a special appeal because a historical incident was turned into a mime (with staged violence) under Caligula and then that mime was turned into a fatal charade (with actual death) under Titus.

142 Coleman (1990) 67–73.

143 Ibid., 57–60. She shows, 44–9 (e.g. via Gell. *NA* 7.14), that public punishments were to allow revenge and to inspire fear. As R. MacMullen, 'Judicial Savagery in the Roman Empire', *Chiron* 16 (1986) 147–66, at 150–1, explains, crowds tolerated and even demanded severe punishments; they felt that cruelty served society's moral ends or they 'simply didn't bother their heads over moral questions and shouted for more, more, without discriminating between the pleasures of violence and vengeance'.

144 Forbade: *CTh* 15.12.1; Euseb. *Vit. Const.* 4.25; ineffectual: see Wiedemann (1992) 156–7. Even this 'Christian' emperor could please his people with cruel punishments of barbarians and criminals in the arena. In AD 315 Constantine allowed *damnatio in ludum gladiatorium* for freeborn individuals convicted of aggravated cases of kidnapping (*CTh* 9.18.1 = *CIust* 9.20.16; slaves and freedmen were to be sent to the beasts), but he later substituted condemnation to the mines; see Robinson (1995) 35. Constantine achieved 'something lovelier even than his victory' when 'for the pleasure of all of us (*ad nostrum omnium voluptatem*)' he had his German prisoners, Bructeri 'too

unreliable to be soldiers, and too savage to be slaves', thrown to the beasts, probably in the amphitheater at Trèves: *Pan. Lat.* xii (ix), 23; see Friedländer (1965) 4:45–6.

145 Wiedemann (1992) ch. 4, 'Opposition and Abolition', 128–64, esp. 147–60, and his 'Das Ende der römischen Gladiatorenspiele', *Nikephoros* 8 (1995) 145–59. Cf. Brown (1995) 378–40, 384, for reservations about Wiedemann's theories of gladiatorial rebirth and its rivalry with Christian ideas of resurrection. Cf. theories about changing tastes, Christian criticisms, etc., in Ville (1960) 273–335, esp. 326–9; Ville, 'Religion et politique: comment ont pris fin les combats de gladiateurs', *Annales (ESC)* (1979) 651–71.

3

THE VICTIMS: DIFFERENTIATION, STATUS, AND SUPPLY

It is a good thing, when the guilty are punished ('Bonum est cum puniuntur nocentes').
(Tertullian *On the Spectacles* 19, Loeb)

The startling quantities and diversity of humans and beasts who performed in Roman spectacles testify to the resources of the empire and to Rome's organizational abilities. Providing, orchestrating, and disposing of the animal and human victims posed a logistical challenge, and also, because of the way the human victims were killed, disposal was not purely a logistical problem.

The body count

We cannot be certain how many creatures Rome killed in spectacles each year, for the city kept no systematic records of arena victims. Even if we collected data on all the known festivals and occasions involving blood sports, plus all the specific numbers explicitly recorded for historical games, we would not have complete and reliable statistical data for the problem of disposal.[1] Cliometrics have limited application for antiquity, for ancient authors cited numbers symbolically, not statistically.[2] Pagan sources seem more concerned with total numbers amassed rather than with specific numbers of casualties and deaths, and martyrologies tend to be late and fervent, dwelling more on bravery and horrors than on objective recording. The public and official nature of most spectacles, and the desire of producers to publicize their generosity, make some claims and numbers seem credible: e.g. announcements of upcoming games, inscriptional records by editors, occasional statements in mosaics, and the multiply attested (though sometimes inconsistent) numbers for the great spectacles of emperors such as Trajan.[3] We do not doubt Augustus' claim in his *Res gestae* that 10,000 gladiators fought in eight shows and 3,500 animals died in twenty-six hunts under his reign.[4] Inaccuracies in such sources would be too obvious and would defeat the purposes at hand (i.e. to glorify the editor's *liberalitas*).

However, other sources, including later imperial biographies, are more suspect.

Imperial histories routinely take note of emperors' games policies, but they tend to emphasize or inflate numbers to praise the largesse or to condemn the brutality of emperors. Dio is pessimistic about any attempt to estimate the number of human and animal victims in Caesar's games for his daughter and for his triumph of 46 BC: 'anyone who cared to record their number would find his task a burden, without being able, in all probability, to present the truth; for all such matters are regularly exaggerated in a spirit of boastfulness'. However skeptical of imperial claims, Dio and others often record specific numbers of victims.[5] Given such problems, many studies simply cite the shocking numbers of victims recorded for extraordinary games – the 9,000 beasts killed in AD 80 in Titus' games to dedicate the Flavian Amphitheater, the 10,000 gladiators who fought and 11,000 animals who were killed in Trajan's games of AD 108–9, or the 3,000 beasts in Probus' show in AD 281. The numbers seem to escalate over time, through competition among editors or exaggeration by authors.

To suggest the scale of the phenomenon, some studies calculate the number of days of festivals (and of games days within these) per year (e.g. sixty-five (under Augustus) and ninety-three (under Claudius) state-funded games days of 159 days of festivals in the early empire; 135 of 230 (under M. Aurelius)). In the Calendar of Philocalus of AD 354 of 200 festival days 176 were show days: 102 theatrical, sixty-four circus, and only ten gladiatorial or venatorial (mostly in December, with some in March). Although only a limited number of days were specifically designated for gladiatorial combats, other festivals included the deaths of animals and executions of criminals. Moreover, normal festival calendars reflect games offered on a regular basis, as voluntary but obligatory contributions by magistrates at Rome, and as compulsory obligations of the office of priests of the emperor cult throughout the empire. Calendars do not reflect the spontaneous and lavish games irregularly put on for triumphs, coming of age celebrations, birthdays, and anniversaries.[6]

Art and literature suggest that, especially under the Empire, the victims killed in the greatest quantities were animals.[7] For economic more than moral reasons, *venationes* were far more common than gladiatorial combats.[8] From early on Rome had exhibits of small numbers of exotic or trained animals, but soon even trained or rare beasts suffered. Although rabbits, goats, and birds appeared, the beasts killed were generally large; most popular were big cats, bulls, and bears, and of course elephants. From the letters of Cicero to the mosaics of Piazza Armerina in Sicily to the letters of the consul Symmachus from the late Empire, abundant evidence reveals the private and imperial arrangements for the hunting and transport of beasts from all over the empire to Rome.[9] As Petronius (*Sat.* 119.14–18, Loeb) wrote: 'The wild beast is searched out in the woods at a great price, and men trouble Hammon deep in Africa to supply the beast whose teeth make him precious for slaying men; strange ravening creatures freight the fleets, and the padding tiger is wheeled in a gilded palace to drink the blood of men while the crowd applauds.'

'Hunting' here meant capturing animals alive for the arena to be used in exhibitions, to fight hunters or other beasts, or to torment and kill human victims.[10] Great importance was attached to catching beasts in the wild, not breeding them in captivity, for shows. Literary sources classify beasts by ferocity and fodder: as wild (*ferae*) or domesticated (*pecudus, mansuetae*), toothed (*dentatae*) like lions and bears or grass-eating (*herbariae, herbaticae, herbanae*) like deer. *Africanae* and *Libycae* were common terms for carnivores.[11] More exotic animals got special treatment with expert handlers and attendants to ensure their health and readiness for their performance. They might also be displayed temporarily or, less likely, kept in menageries before the spectacles for which they were intended. However, most animals, especially commoner species, were collected at Rome, held only briefly, and slaughtered quickly in the arena.[12] Sources may simply say that a certain number of men 'fought' but then provide elaborate, categorized lists of numbers of animals 'killed'.[13] Occasionally, by humanlike courage or talent an animal might win the spectators' admiration, and a star beast might be hailed or mourned – but seldom spared.[14] Studies even speak of the extirpation of species and of ecological changes in patterns of fauna due to hunting to supply the games.[15]

Difficulties in calculations also arise from ambiguous references and loose terminology. Probably, 'gave' or 'exhibited' usually meant 'killed'.[16] The eclectic nature of the imperial spectacles led to a blurring of terms that had once had distinct meanings. Unfortunately, ancient and modern sources sometimes use 'gladiator' broadly to refer to any participant in the arena, any arena victim, even ones without skills, armor, or hope. Compare our modern use of the once specific term 'athlete'. Christian and also pagan sources sometimes speak of 'gladiators' or *bestiarii* when the reference is clearly to non-professionals forced to kill each other, or to victims executed by being thrown to beasts with little or no chance or inclination to put up a decent fight.[17] Gladiators and Christians got the most notice, but they probably represent a minority of the humans killed. Imperial *munera* were generally multi-dimensional spectacles entailing far more than gladiators, and fewer true gladiators than other victims died. The greatest numbers of human victims, nameless *noxii*, get the least attention, but their disposal presented the greatest logistical and symbolic problems.[18]

Cumulative if not Cliometrical evidence confirms that Rome's arenas housed death on a scale perhaps unprecedented (other than in war) in the pre-modern world, certainly often and extensively enough that arrangements for disposal were necessary. The total of human and animal arena victims pales by comparison with the bulk from wars, pestilences, or simply the

78

normal dead – or of sewage and human waste, which was Rome's Augean stables.[19] Nevertheless, arena disposal was a problem and a necessary, final phase of the spectacles. Repetition invites ritualization, as do religious concerns about the dead. Numbers (of victims or days) alone should not be equated with historical significance, for the treatment of even a few bodies can be culturally telling.[20]

Gladiators and beast-fighters: infamy, virtue, and ambivalence

Held in amphitheaters, circuses, forums, and even theaters throughout Rome, the spectacles used an abundance of human victims of different types. Not only did the levels of seating in the stands reflect the social hierarchy in macrocosm, but the arena itself, in microcosm, also had its own social order – from elite gladiators to abject, hopeless victims, with sporting skill and hope as the main criteria of status. That status differentiation extended onto the arena floor is shown in art (e.g. armor, clothing, hair, degree of nudity; see figures 1a and 2) and in advertisements for shows, which distinguish gladiators from hopeless *noxii*. Inscriptions classify gladiators by experience, records of combats, style of fighting, legal status, and nature of combats (e.g. individual or group).[21] We need to differentiate or deaggregate the victims, for Rome was status conscious even in the arena. Not all victims faced the same dangers, death, and disposal.

Different voluntary or involuntary human performers can be distinguished by their training, equipment, and treatment. Originally 'gladiators' (*bustuarii* or *bustum* men) fought in *munera* associated with funerals. By the late Republic, gladiators, i.e. *damnati ad ludum gladiatorum aut venatorium* – as opposed to *ad gladium* (normal execution), or *ad bestias* or other *summa supplicia* (discussed below), had become 'professional', i.e. they were trained, talented, and recompensed (by contracted wages or prizes won). They were specialized weapons fighters, expert craftsmen who bound themselves by a sacred oath to train, suffer, and fight with decorum against men or animals until killed or released.[22] Originally recruited from *damnati* (criminals (*noxii*), slaves, and captives (*captivi*)) but increasingly including *auctorati* (paid contractees), gladiators risked death, but they had the chance of freedom, profit and fame – if they put on a good show. Most gladiators became so against their will, as prisoners of war, victims of kidnapping, slaves, or criminals sentenced to gladiatorial schools (*in ludum damnati*).[23] Sources (see below) claim that professional gladiators wanted to perform and to perform well, to suffer and to die well, to please their masters. There were exceptions and failures, however.[24]

Originally, *venatores* were professional hunters and animal handlers, often imported from Africa, who shot missiles at a distance and often used hunting dogs.[25] Later equated with the *venator*, the *bestiarius* was originally someone armed with knife or spear who was condemned to fight beasts with the probability of death. Over time some *bestiarii* became trained beast-gladiators, and like gladiators they had a chance of survival and even fame. Under the Empire men damned to fight beasts might be sent to the Ludus Matutinus and trained as *bestiarii*-gladiators. Status mobility came with the presentation of skillful, entertaining performances. Like gladiators, *bestiarii* could become stars: Martial (*Spect.* 15.22, 27) praised Carpophorus for his many kills, even comparing him to Hercules.

As a civilized beast man consciously resists but still emotionally attends to violence, and so the position of gladiators in Roman society became increasingly paradoxical over time. Although universally loathed for their lowly social origins or heinous crimes, gladiators were also associated with glory, discipline, and eroticism. Romans condemned them in literature and discriminated against them in legislation, but their combats attracted audiences and even volunteers. The symbolism, allure, and social status of these fighters were paradoxical, anomalous, ambiguous, ambivalent, and even multivalent. Like actors,[26] gladiators were glorified by audiences but not wanted as neighbors, magistrates, or in-laws. Tertullian (*De spect.* 22, Loeb) sees such Roman attitudes as inconsistent, fickle, and confused:

> look at their attitude to the charioteers, players (*scaenicos*), gladiators (*arenarios*), most loving of men, to whom men surrender their souls and women their bodies as well, for whose sake they commit the sins they blame; on one and the same account they glorify them and they degrade and diminish them; yes, further, they openly condemn them to disgrace and civil degradation; they keep them religiously excluded from council chamber, rostrum, senate, knighthood, and every other kind of office and a good many distinctions. The perversity of it! They love whom they lower; they despise whom they approve; the art they glorify, the artist they disgrace (*artem magnificant, artificem notant*).

The paradox and the perversity, the irony and the inconsistency, of the social symbolism of the gladiator have fascinated authors from Rome to today.[27] Recent scholarship offers various explanations of how Romans could see glory or military edification in the deaths of men they despised.

Since Rome was a warrior state accustomed to violence and cruelty, Hopkins stresses the metaphor of gladiators as soldiers. As an 'artificial battlefield' preserving warrior traditions, the amphitheater was legitimized as an inspiration to military virtue.[28] Stoic sources applaud the gladiator's discipline and acceptance of death through training.[29] Over time as Rome moved from survival to imperial security, fewer Romans were personally involved with military action and hence people were increasingly fascinated with military virtues (*gravitas, disciplina*).[30] For Wiedemann the Romans' preoccupation with the combats hinges on the gladiator's possible survival by demonstrating fighting ability and bravery, quintessential elements of Roman military virtue. Beasts and criminals passed from life to death, reassuring society of its security, and despised gladiators – in theory and at times in practice – passed from social death to reintegration into society.[31] Plass feels that gladiators were elevated because they both scared and reassured Romans; Romans loved to hate gladiators 'because of the contraries they hold together in uneasy, potentially dysfunctional tension'.[32]

Barton explains the simultaneous degradation and exaltation of the gladiator in psychological terms of a Roman 'physics' of desire, despair, envy, and fascination. 'The "gladiator madness" of the Romans was simply a distillation of the parching liquors of despair and desire that had, elsewhere within that culture, reached a point of saturation.'[33] As the arena became the new battlefield for demonstrating *virtus*, the volunteerism of the gladiator had additional power because of the Roman notion of *devotio*, as in the ceremonial self-sacrifice of the Republican generals, the Decii. Like the virtuous soldier, the Stoic *sapiens*, and the Christian martyr, the gladiator achieved an 'inverse elevation', an escape from the humiliation of compulsion through enthusiastic complicity, an 'empowerment' by collusion with his masters. He was able to die, unconquered, with honor.[34]

Modern scholarship has increasingly focused on the allure of performing in the arena for free and even noble Romans, but, at least in part, this may be a new form of apologetic commentary on the paradox of cruel spectacles within the highly civilized society of Rome. Older works uncomfortable with the arena emphasized the sporting chariot races, downplayed the frequency of *munera*, or suggested that animals in *venationes* were recaptured and reused. In a more contemporary vein, scholars now write of the Romans' fascination with violence, the forbidden, the other, and mortality. This obsession supposedly led significant numbers of free men and women, and even emperors, to enlist as volunteers (*auctorati*: see below) to perform in the arena. Thus the spectacles may seem less offensive to us because many performers supposedly wanted to risk their lives in public and degrading ways. Two problems, however, must not be overlooked. First, the vast majority of performers in spectacles of death were not present because of 'their own free will'. Non-citizens and lowly subjects were forced into the arena by sale, crime, or capture, and of those who survived to gain their freedom many probably reenlisted, ironically, to earn a livelihood. Secondly, we should not overreact to moralistic comments in Roman literature about free and even elite Romans who 'played' the gladiator. Writers, especially philosophical and satirical ones, were censuring a minor social phenomenon: they were condemning a few examples as a way to reinforce proper social mores. A few debt-ridden, desperate, or decadent citizens did not reverse the traditional and normal Roman attitude to public performance. Performance in the theater was a demeaning occupation for outsiders, and performance in the arena was a punitive spectacle for foreign foes and criminals.

The symbolic paradox of the gladiator, the elevation, glamor, and privileges given to debased men, stems from both the virtues of the actions
and the status of the actors. The paradox should be understood historically,
and the origins and social position of early (and, even later, most) gladiators
remain essential considerations. The honors, the erotic appeal, and the emula-
tion of gladiators grew over time, becoming increasingly inconsistent with
the sociology of that group. As Tertullian said, Romans loved the art (the
growing symbolism of virtue and skill) but continued to hate the artist
(the outsider, the guilty killer). Elements of the symbolism of the gladiator,
while most extensively articulated in the late Republic and early Empire,
historically started to emerge in the crucible of the Second Punic War and
coalesced after the Third Punic War. Conditions and predispositions prior
to the late Republic were crucial to the 'reconstruction' of the gladiator.

Recall Tertullian's comment (*De spect.* 12, Loeb, quoted above in ch. 2)
on the origins of gladiatorial *munera*: 'For of old . . . they used at funerals
to sacrifice captives or slaves of poor quality whom they bought (*captivos
vel mali status servos mercati*).'[35] As Ville notes, performers in *munera* continued
to be selected on moral grounds (i.e. on the basis of status and guilt) as
worthy of punishment.[36] Captives, rebel slaves, and bad soldiers could be
punished and disposed of at the front or in the provinces, but more and
more they were brought to Rome to be killed to set an example and to
reassure the people of their security.

Plutarch (*Mor.* 1099B) records a curious but significant ritual in which,
on the eve of a spectacle, gladiators were given a sumptuous public meal
(*cena libera*) and were put on display for anyone who cared to view them.
The meal has been interpreted as a symbolic compensation to doomed
victims or as a ritual device to turn lowly, vile human sacrificial victims
into worthy, noble sacrifices.[37] Since the banquet was offered to all victims
(gladiators, *bestiarii*, and even Christian *noxii*), it seems to have been retained
as an archaic remnant, and as such it recalls the originally horizontal status
of all arena victims.[38] Like the ambiguous love/hate dynamics of Aztec
sacrifices or Greek scapegoat rituals (discussed in ch. 4 below), this was a
traditional preparation of generic victims, not a privilege acquired by professional gladiators over time.

Roman social traditions stressed a hierarchical social order based on freedom, landownership, and military service; but, as noted in ch. 2 above, out
of the despair of Cannae Rome came to appreciate that even slaves – selected,
sanctified by a voluntary oath, and trained – could contribute positively to
the state by fighting and showing military virtues. According to Roman
mores, those who contributed to the needs of the state came to gain privileges.
As Florus later commented (noted in ch. 2 above), after 146 BC, men whom
the state used to keep from arms became valued as gladiators.

Sources provide no names for gladiators for at least the first century of
munera. Then, in the last third of the second century, Lucilius mentions a

famous victor and a despised loser by name: 'In the public show given by the Flacci was a certain Aeserninus, a Samnite, a nasty fellow, worthy of that life and station. He was matched with Pacideianus, who was by far the best of all the gladiators since the creation of man.'[39] The development of 'stage names', some with superstitious or erotic overtones, like Martial's Hermes (see below), came later when gladiators were becoming stars by fighting and surviving several fights.[40]

By 105 BC gladiatorial training was applied to the military, and *munera* and their arenas soon spread with military colonies. In the first century Cicero voiced an oft-repeated notion that gladiators provided military *exempla* for citizens. The first reference to awarding the *rudis* is from Cicero, by whose time gladiators were an investment, skilled artisans to be rewarded and not to be wasted.[41] Augustus' ban on *munera sine missione*, fights which had no survivors (i.e. winners had to fight again until all were dead) or simply fights that continued until one opponent admitted defeat, shows the elevation of valued performers.[42]

The emergence and specialization of gladiators in the late Republic is an example of 'structural differentiation'. Similarly, cooks had formerly had the status of the lowest slaves, but they came to acquire prestige. What had been scorned as a service came to be acclaimed as an art.[43] The dynamics of a collapsing Republic in the Civil Wars did not create but accelerated a continuing process of elevation; and the increase of privileges for gladiators intensified in the late Republic and early Empire, as in the development of specialized facilities for preparation and performance. The escalation of spectacles brought more and more glory and privileges to gladiators, leading to the ambivalence so often noted in sources of the late Republic and early Empire. Psychology and symbolism apply, but the root of the ambivalence was the disjunction between the Roman view of the type of people who were gladiators – an aboriginal and constant stigma – and the growing status, privileges, and glory won by professional gladiators.[44]

Elite gladiators were increasingly recognized for their skills and training, but from the beginning and always, gladiators were – or, by voluntarily hiring themselves out by contract, they became – stigmatized with *infamia*.[45] As Tertullian said (above), Romans openly condemn gladiators 'to disgrace and civil degradation; they keep them religiously excluded from council chamber, rostrum, senate, knighthood, and every other kind of office and a good many distinctions'. Sources refer to gladiators as low and vile, as *aut perditi homines aut barbari* (Cic. *Tusc.* 2.41), as slaves and criminals (Plin. *Pan.* 33.1), and as killers and criminals guilty of sacrilege, arson, and murder (Ps. Quint. *Decl. Maj.* 9.21). As Barton puts it, 'The gladiator: crude, loathsome, doomed, lost (*importunus, obscaenus, damnatus, perditus*) was, throughout the Roman tradition, a man utterly debased by fortune, a slave, a man altogether without worth and dignity (*dignitas*), almost without humanity.'[46] Cicero sarcastically refers to a family of gladiators as impressive, noble, and magnificent (*speciosam, nobilem, gloriosam*).[47] Whatever fame, money, or erotic allure they achieved by fighting successfully, former gladiators, like *lanistae*,[48] lived at the edge of respectable society. By the Lex Aelia Sentia of AD 4, the Augustan law on manumission, freed slave gladiators or *bestiarii* took the same status as subject foreigners (*peregrini dedicitii*), men who had fought in a war against Rome, were defeated and surrendered (i.e. the original status of many gladiators). They were never to become citizens or Latins, and they were not to make a will or receive anything through a will.[49]

After the rampant escalation of *munera* by dynasts, Augustus tried to control and monopolize gladiators at Rome (see ch. 2 above). The imperial association with gladiators (e.g. via imperial schools run by imperial procurators) heightened their elevation. Just as slaves and freedmen in the imperial bureaucracy, and freedmen in the imperial cult, acquired more status, men selected and trained as imperial gladiators, men worthy of the emperor's shows, were elevated above lesser gladiators and far above hopeless *noxii*. Potential gladiators were selected for their bodies and their temperament, but Rome gave them the training, the skill, and the opportunity to serve Rome, and to be rewarded with, at least, an honorable death, and, at best, riches and freedom.[50]

All gladiators were *infames*, but gladiatorial schools or families were hierarchically structured according to experience (and records of achievements) and legal status (slave, free, *auctoratus*).[51] Although favored by different emperors or fans, a gladiator's fighting style was usually irrelevant to his chances and status. A decree of around AD 177 clarifies a wide range in the expenses and classifications of *munera* and gladiators.[52] Gladiators who fight singly are distinguished from those who fight in teams (*gregarii, sub signo*) (I 36). Within four levels of expenditure for shows (from 30,000–60,000 up to 150,000–200,000 HS and above) gladiators are classified into three to five grades; the maximum price for the cheapest grade of gladiator is set at 3,000 HS and the maximum for the most expensive, the highest and <last> (*summo ac <p>o<strem>o*) grade, is set at 15,000 (I 30–5).[53] The decree (I 35–40) also stipulates proportions and rates for performance of *gregarii* or 'gladiators of the common herd', who were not expected to fight individually: for every show half the combatants were to be *gregarii* and none of these were to fight for less than 1,000 HS.[54]

The living conditions of gladiators were harsh but, as profitable investments, they perhaps lived better than many commoners in terms of food, housing, and medical attention.[55] New or undisciplined men were shackled, and unattended only in the bathroom, but trained gladiators were not always bound, imprisoned, or even confined to barracks.[56] A victorious gladiator's prize money was like the *peculium* or private money of a slave; by acquiring enough of it one could buy his freedom.[57] Gladiators could marry, have children, make inheritance arrangements, and even own slaves.[58]

With the escalation of combats and the military use of gladiators for instruction and inspiration, Romans were becoming knowledgeable and attentive sports 'fans' who recognized skilled performances. Characters in Petronius mock a man for putting on a disappointing show with poor fighters who were flogged for their lack of effort.[59] Critics of the phenomenon themselves attest to what amounts to fan loyalty and mania. As in any spectator sport, the audience's involvement, viewing, and voices influenced the activity itself. Crowds would call for the appearance of certain performers or offer instructions.[60] As fans increasingly identified with gladiators, disassociating them from *noxii*, they wanted the objects of their identification to have hope of survival and honors.[61] Appreciating gladiators as models of martial virtue and as specialized providers of mass entertainment, Romans gave them increased rights and chances of survival for contributing their performances to society.

The eroticism of the spectacles, related to the inherent psycho-sexual allure of violence, should not be overlooked or overemphasized. Many works note the erotic appeal of gladiators,[62] but it seems that 'the gladiator as sex symbol' was an imperial development. References to the eroticism of gladiators are mostly found in the silver Latin of Ovid, Juvenal, and Martial, as well as in graffiti at Pompeii of the first century AD. Tertullian (*De spect.* 22) and Juvenal 6 claim that gladiators were attractive to even noble women,[63] but too much has been made of the woman's skeleton found in the *ludus* at Pompeii.[64] Gladiators might be praised and admired, but Romans became upset if 'good' women fraternized with gladiators.[65]

The analogies between Roman gladiators and the matadors of modern Spain are striking. While the roots of the bullfight are rural, the sociology of matadors is urban: despised but romanticized for their background, they come from the proletariat of the urban slums. They often demonstrate masochistic or suicidal tendencies, they become professionalized over time from the eighteenth to the nineteenth century, and they are obsessed with the taurine code of virtue and with pleasing their spectators.[66] Appealing to aggression and sexuality as human impulses, the matador is a warrior, a taboo-breaker, and a risk-taker who puts honor above life. The masses revere him for his demonstration of *majismo* in manner, body language, dress, honor, and morality, but most Spaniards would not enter the profession even to escape poverty. As at Rome, in the context of aristocratic decline and a wave of plebeianism, moral exemplariness shifted from the upper to the lower classes, and the bullring came to house the charismatic heroes of popular culture. Just as the bullfight is inherently erotic because of its passion and emotionalism and the physiological arousal of the spectators, Roman spectacles were erotic, intoxicating, and voyeuristic. Like matadors, gladiators appealed to spectators as forbidden, déclassé killers: 'The gladiator's hold on the Roman imagination was inseparable from his marginal social status and his proximity to blood, death, and pollution. Thus he was the perfect symbol of the fascinating but threatening power of the prohibited.'[67]

A privileged minority among victims, elite gladiators had a chance, perhaps a good chance, of survival.[68] Augustus had banned *munera sine missione* (see above), and many fights were not to the death.[69] Surviving inscriptions often refer to ties and even losses, suggesting that gladiators did not fight as often as might be expected.[70] Trying to flatter Titus, Martial writes of a pair of gladiatorial opponents who both got prizes and were discharged, but this was probably not as rare as Martial suggests. Martial also wrote an epigram for Hermes, a gladiator skilled at forcing his opponents *ad digitum* without having to kill them.[71] Petronius (*Sat.* 45.4–6, Loeb) mentions the apparently unusual prospect of gladiatorial games in which there would be large numbers of freedmen, plenty of bloodshed, and no quarter: 'not simply a troupe of professional gladiators, but a large number of freedmen (*familia non lanistica, sed plurimi liberti*) . . . He [the sponsor] will give you the finest blades, no running away, butchery done in the middle, where the whole audience can see it (*carnarium in medio*).'

Owners invested time and training in gladiators, and sold or rented them and kept the proceeds (and some or most of the prize money). Such resources were not to be squandered unless for effect. An inscription from Minturnae of AD 249 says that an editor gave a show with eleven bouts in which eleven gladiators died, as if this were unusually generous.[72] Owners used a form of insurance policy against the unwished death of valuable gladiators: in gladiatorial contracts of the second century AD gladiators were worth eighty HS or twenty drachmas if they survived uninjured, but 4,000 HS or 1,000 drachmas if killed or maimed.[73]

The results of some combats or whole *munera* are known,[74] and scholars have tried to suggest the odds of survival of gladiators.[75] Ville estimates that around the first century AD 20 percent of fights brought the death of one of the combatants, but that by the third century the death rate had increased to around 50 percent. A first-century gladiator was therefore unlikely to survive more than ten fights, although stars might win many times, some over 100.[76] The chance of survival decreased in later centuries, perhaps owing to the development of a taste for death and the revival and increased popularity of *munera sine missione*. Nevertheless, it is certain that many gladiators survived the arena to freedom and to retirement.[77]

The importance of hope and privileges is shown by some famous suicides applauded by Seneca to argue that even the lowliest man can find the means for a noble death.[78] A German in a *ludus bestiariorum* was making ready for a morning show (*ad matutina spectacula*) when 'he withdrew in order to relieve himself, – the only thing which he was allowed to do in secret and without the presence of a guard'; and he killed himself by ramming down his throat a stick, tipped with sponge, which was used in the latrine.[79] Another man being taken in a cart under guard to punishment (*ad poenam*) in a morning show managed to break his neck by sticking his head between the spokes of a wheel.[80] Suicide is often rationalized as a protest to give some meaning or defiance to a desperate act. The alternative here was worse – a public, even more agonizing death.[81] Constantly guarded, these men were hopeless and doomed slaves and barbarians, not trained elite, Stoically principled gladiators.

To some degree, because homicide always involves the sacred, gladiators (and probably *noxii*) were sacralized – positively or negatively – as killers and killed. On entering a gladiatorial school recruits swore an oath (*sacramentum gladiatorum*) to be 'burned by fire, bound in chains, to be beaten, to die by the sword'.[82] All these, except the last, were severe affronts to the dignity of a citizen and the integrity of his body. Barton sees this solemn oath as crucial to the 'elevation' and the 'sacralization' of gladiators: 'The *sacramentum* was simultaneously devotion, consecration, and execration (*devotio, consecratio, exsecratio*), putting one's life on deposit to the infernal gods to be redeemed or sacrificed through an ordeal.'[83] She argues that the gladiator's oath symbolically recalled Roman generals' self-consecration (*devotio*): like heroic soldiers and martyrs, they took a voluntary oath to accept death and they became exalted, sacralized sacrifices.[84] By the 'alchemy of the oath', the *sacramentum*, which 'sacralized by binding', turned the soldier into a *miles sacratus* and the gladiator into an *auctoratus*. Establishing their own reality in an unreal world, they escaped compulsion through complicity.[85] This 'voluntary' ritual promise mitigated Rome's responsibility and guilt. As captives or condemned criminals conscripted against their will, most gladiators probably took the oath under coercion, but they were not bound to certain death like hopeless *noxii* who, by the conditions of their purchase, faced only speedy, certain, and brutal death.

Recognized as distinct in ancient sources, *auctorati* or 'contract' gladiators were freeborn men or freedmen (probably mostly released gladiators) who contractually enlisted of their own free will, suspending their freedom and accepting the gladiator's servile status for money or for thrills.[86] Some might join out of bloodlust or the desire for combat, at least according to critical sources, but probably most gambled (but did not necessarily give up) their lives for profit.[87] Free *auctorati* were despised as spendthrifts or as wastrels escaping bankruptcy.[88] If some elite volunteers were drawn by Barton's 'spiral of desire' and saw the *munus* as a 'ritual of empowerment', more men were probably forced by dire circumstances.[89] Victims of debt, despair, or delusion, *auctorati* hired themselves out as gladiators, making a contract (an *auctoramentum*) with specified terms of wages, service, or conditions of appearances, and then taking the oath (*sacramentum*). Barton tends to use *sacramentum* (the gladiatorial oath) and *auctoramentum* (the contract) interchangeably, but she admits that 'Strictly speaking the *auctoratus* had a unique status.'[90] It is important to realize that, as the terms connote, the *sacramentum* was a ritual sacralization while the *auctoramentum* was a legal contract: all *auctorati* made a *sacramentum*, but not all 'gladiators' (i.e. all who take the *sacramentum*) were *auctorati* (i.e. with prior, sincere volition).[91]

87

Figure 3 Marble relief from Smyrna. The beast-fight scene on the lower register suggests that the men above, bound in metal collars attached to ropes, are condemned victims being led by the helmeted men to execution in a spectacle.

The ratio of free to slave gladiators remains uncertain. From epitaphs of the Greek East Robert suggested roughly equal numbers of free and slave gladiators in the second and third centuries AD.[92] Ville, however, properly notes that freedmen had a better chance of leaving epitaphs. Epitaphs, moreover, indicate only status at the time of death, not original status. Ville's sense from the epigraphical evidence of the late Republic and early Empire is that gladiators who were originally slaves were probably more numerous.[93] Clearly, we can only speculate about such proportions by using existing epitaphs and monuments, which tend to reflect the wealthiest and most successful gladiators. In practice, like female gladiators,[94] free volunteers of freeborn or elite status (as opposed to experienced freedmen gladiators) were probably novelties who appeared in limited numbers.[95] Since most *auctorati* would be ex-slave gladiators, five-year veterans of proven skill, they put on good fights.[96]

Not coincidentally, the emergence of *auctorati* and increasing gladiatorial privileges overlap in time. The earliest certain evidence of *auctorati* at Rome seems to be Gaius Gracchus' law of 122 excluding from the courts equestrians who had hired themselves out as gladiators.[97] Cicero seems to contrast the contemporary use of free men and volunteers with an earlier age when criminals fought with swords (*sontes ferro depugnabant*) to the death and taught discipline against pain and death.[98] Possibly the growing numbers of *auctorati* elevated all gladiators, but it is more likely that the elevation of gladiators, the glory, the improved chances of survival, attracted volunteers, whose participation in turn reinforced the elevation.

Volunteerism in the act of facing death inspired Stoic praise of gladiators, but the volunteerism of *auctorati* in enlisting and debasing themselves was hardly praised. Edmondson stresses that the podium wall separating the stands from the arena was a 'real social barrier': 'those who performed down in the arena were socially dead, or, at best, déclassé'. Moreover, as Wiedemann says, 'The ultimate disgrace was for a free citizen to fight as a gladiator.'[99] Most gladiators became so by birth, capture, or other involuntary factors, but *auctorati* were responsible for their own self-debasement and *infamia*. They were men who earlier had had some freedom or status, but had degraded themselves and made a choice to (re)enter the arena. For a contracted period of time they accepted or resumed the servile status of gladiators. Thus they sent mixed signals and got mixed responses.[100]

Sources commenting on the first century BC note the participation of members of the social elite (equestrians and senators) in spectacles, beginning with elite volunteers in Caesar's games in 46.[101] Persons of status might enter the arena on an unpaid basis, to display military prowess (*virtutis causa*), to honor a leader, or to fulfill an oath for an emperor's health, without the stigma of *infamia* attached to entering a contract (*auctoramentum*) with a *lanista* for financial gain (*quaestus causa*). Some became fascinated with gladiators and voluntarily practiced or even fought – though perhaps not to the death – as gladiators, while others were forced, against their will and against all propriety, into the arena with the likelihood or certainty of death.[102]

Participation by the elite as paid contract gladiators was repeatedly prohibited. Enactments in 46, 38, and 22 BC proved ineffective, and the ban was lifted in AD 11. An incomplete senatus consultum of AD 19 on a bronze tablet from Larinum prohibits relatives and connections of knights and senators from appearing on stage or in the arena. Such acts were said (lines 5–6) to be 'contrary to the dignity' of the orders and harmful to the 'majesty of the senate'.[103] The decree upheld previous bans against the participation of the elite as combatants or participants in any way in the arena; they were not to hire themselves out, nor was anyone to hire them for such purposes.[104] By debasing themselves as entertainers and banausic laborers, elite Romans perverted and threatened the social order.[105] Nevertheless, the elite continued to turn up in the arena. Sometimes emperors allowed, encouraged, or even forced such participation, and some emperors even performed themselves.[106] Caligula, Nero, and Commodus were criticized for excess enthusiasm and for forcing decent men to fight.[107]

Although the expansion of the empire and the transition to autocracy added symbolic aspects to venationes analogous to the great hunts of Hellenistic and Near Eastern tradition, there was a fundamental difference in the role of the Roman leader. While a Near Eastern monarch might personally kill game brought to him, a Roman emperor was not supposed to perform in public. In the reenactments of hunts in the arena courage and skill gave the hunter-bestiarius some hope and privileges, but emperors were already supreme and could only demean themselves in the arena. A good emperor, a Trajan or a Hadrian, might hunt for sport virtuously outside the city, but at Rome he was to provide the show indirectly.[108] At Rome, through his power and leadership rather than through his personal hunting skill, the emperor became an imperial pater and patron, indirectly bringing home the prey of his empire-wide hunting to impress his people. Disgracing oneself in the arena by killing collected beasts without personal risk or sport was a travesty. Like Nero, Domitian was disliked for hunting in oriental fashion. At his country estate, from a safe platform and without danger or virtue, he used bow and arrow to kill beasts driven to him.[109] Hunting in a similarly offensive manner, Commodus personally and improperly slaughtered animals not only privately at his estate but publicly in the arena.[110] A dilettante hunter who did not endanger himself, he slew a hundred bears by spearing them from a gallery built for him above the arena, or he shot beasts from a distance with bow and arrow.[111] Like his performances as a gladiator, Commodus' hunting in the arena disgusted both ancient and modern observers.[112]

Noxii: The doomed and the damned

Contrary to popular opinion, most of the arena's dead victims were not true gladiators but doomed convicts (*noxii*), men (and women) sentenced to execution, crucifixion, fire, or the beasts.[113] In the early spectacles all the human victims came from the same class of social outsiders and convicts – uncontrollable slaves, captives, deserters, and heinous criminals – all threatening offenders and abominations to be disposed of quickly, publicly, and brutally. *Damnati* included both gladiators and *noxii*, but there was a hierarchy of skill, virtue, and hope.[114] 'Professional' gladiators were agonistic: theirs was a life or death struggle, but for *noxii* there was 'no contest', for they had not been selected for gladiatorial training (i.e. as *damnati ad ludum gladiatorium* or *venatorium*). As non-citizens beyond the rights and obligations of *mos* and *lex* (e.g. the right to exile, suicide, or normal execution by beheading (*ad gladium*)), *noxii* faced *summa supplicia* – the worst forms of aggravated capital punishment.[115]

Like the original gladiators, the original *noxii* were criminal slaves facing aggravated execution. The killing or punishment of a slave in Rome was more an issue of property than of human rights. Criminal slaves were punished brutally and publicly to reassure the community (and to make sure the slave's owner did not omit the punishment to prevent damage to his human property). In early Rome the killing of a slave was not murder but rather damage to someone's property, but later, possibly by the first century BC, the killing of a slave might lead to criminal charges.[116] In theory the freedom of masters to condemn their slaves to the beasts was restricted by the Petronian law of the first century AD: owners could not send slaves to the beasts without having them condemned before the urban prefect, and it was a crime to accept them for such use without court approval.[117] In practice, however, slaves were extremely vulnerable to violent abuse and exploitation in society at large and, as *noxii*, in the arena.[118]

Pagan and even Christian sources show little sympathy for slave or for formerly free *noxii*.[119] In Apuleius a judge condemns a female poisoner to the beasts, commenting that this was less than she deserved, but there was no more cruel execution for her crime (*Met.* 10.28; cf. 34). Seneca (*De Ira* 2.2.4) accepts the violent execution of criminals in *meridiani* as unquestionably just (*iustissimorum suppliciorum*), and his famous indictment of the arena (*Ep.* 7.3–5, Loeb) focuses more on degenerative crowd involvement than on the victims:

> By chance I attended a mid-day exhibition (*meridianum spectaculum*), expecting some fun, wit, and relaxation, – an exhibition at which men's eyes have respite from the slaughter of their fellow-men. But it was quite the reverse. The previous combats were the essence of

compassion; but now all the trifling is put aside and it is pure murder. The men have no defensive armour. They are exposed to blows at all points, and no one ever strikes in vain ... In the morning they throw men to the lions and the bears; at noon, they throw them to the spectators. The spectators demand that the slayer shall face the man who is to slay him in his turn; and they always reserve the latest conqueror for another butchering. The outcome of every fight is death, and the means are fire and sword. This sort of thing goes on while the arena is empty. You may retort: 'But he was a highway robber; he killed a man!' And what of it? Granted that, as a murderer, he deserved this punishment ... In the morning they cried 'Kill him! Lash him! Burn him! Why does he meet the sword in so cowardly a way? Why does he strike so feebly? Why doesn't he die game? Whip him to meet his wounds! Let them receive blow for blow, with chests bare and exposed to the stroke!' And when the games stop for the intermission, they announce: 'A little throat-cutting in the meantime, so that there may still be something going on!'

As Seneca makes clear, these were not combats of talented gladiators but rather *meridiani*, ritualized executions of pathetic victims.[120]

The killing of *noxii* is shown proudly and unapologetically in Roman art, from mosaics and sculpture commissioned by editors wanting to record their munificence to terracottas and lamps produced for mass consumption.[121] Unlike the flattering, often triumphant poses of usually bloodless gladiators, condemned criminals were depicted in art as helpless, terrified, and bloody. Rather than defiant gladiators, glamorously armored and armed, *noxii* are shown nude or nearly nude, with bound hands or bound to posts, under the control of arena handlers or in the grasp of beasts. The mosaic from a villa at Zliten east of Lepcis Magna in Tripolitania, now in the Tripoli Museum, differentiates gladiators from *noxii*, who are shown bound to stakes or on wheeled carts and exposed to beasts (see figure 1, a and b).[122] Similarly, a mosaic from the Sollertiana Domus at El Djem in Tunisia shows scenes of barbarian prisoners pushed by *bestiarii* to be attacked by leopards.[123]

For Rome *noxii* were a surplus commodity, a leisure resource, a by-product of imperialism. They were totally at Rome's disposal, for Rome's amusement. Josephus (*BJ* 6.418) says that, after the fall of Jerusalem, Titus sent great numbers of Jewish captives to provinces as gifts to be killed in theaters by the sword or by wild beasts.[124] The third-century jurist Modestinus writes that governors were not to release criminals condemned to the beasts to please the crowds; rather if they had enough strength or skill to be worth exhibiting to the people in Rome the governor should consult the emperor.[125] Like slaves, *damnati* convicted of capital crimes were evaluated, sorted, and

92

Figure 4 North African terracotta depicting a condemned woman tied to a bull and being attacked by a leopard. The figure with the shield is probably an arena attendant rather than a beast-fighter (*bestiarius*).

graded, with those showing spirit and skill being sent to the imperial *ludi*. Inferior ones could be sent to the mines or sold to *lanistae* and soon worked or 'used' to death as performers in naumachies or *meridiani* at Rome or in rural *munera*.[126] *Munerarii* applied to authorities for such *damnati*, purchased them for a set and low price, gave an oath that they would be killed within a specified period of time, normally a year, and advertised them as attractions for shows.[127] Some victims fell defenseless to agitated beasts (see figure 3 and 4); others died by fire or crucifixion. Still others perished in Coleman's 'fatal charades', wherein they might be nude, or dressed in animal skins or costumes of gods. The tale of Androcles and the lion shows that survival for a captured runaway slave sent to the beasts was quite unexpected – a marvel. The famous exception proves the rule.[128] In martyrologies miracles might delay the deaths of Christians (see ch. 8 below), but Christian *noxii* were not to survive the arena. Promoters arranged theatrics and props and used large numbers of *noxii*, but, as Seneca shows, terrified and untrained amateurs performed poorly and enraged the crowds.

Treated as a commodity like other *noxii*, fighters in naumachies (*naumachiarii*) and in 'mock' battles on land were not elite gladiators but doomed captives and criminals, who usually fought until all were killed.[129]

Details of Claudius' naumachy on the Fucine Lake in AD 52 indicate that the participants were criminals condemned to die.[130] Tacitus (*Ann.* 12.56.2) says that in order to prevent any escape the circumference of the lake was surrounded by rafts bearing companies of the Praetorian Guard with breast-works, catapults, and balistas. Marines on decked vessels occupied the rest of the lake.[131] Before starting, the fighters hailed Claudius with the now famous words 'Ave imperator, morituri te salutant', and Claudius, perhaps attempting a witticism, answered: 'Aut non'. Ancient sources do not record this supposed 'gladiator salute' in any other context, and it did not come here from true gladiators. Leon concludes that it 'was not a regular and formal salute, but an appeal used only on that occasion in the hope of winning the Emperor's sympathy'.[132] Supposedly Claudius usually enjoyed spectacular executions, even pressing innocent attendants into the fray (Suet. *Claud.* 34.2; Dio 60.13.4). Here, however, surprised and put on the spot by the victims, he stumbled. The words 'Aut non' were taken by the men as a gift of hope, as a change of status, or even a pardon (Suetonius says 'quasi venia data'), and they refused to fight. Upset, Claudius threatened the men with destruction with fire and sword, and pleaded with them to fight. Dio says that when the fighters' salute/appeal failed, they first tried to inflict as few wounds as possible, but then they were forced to kill one another in earnest. Tacitus (*Ann.* 12.56, Loeb) says that 'The battle, though one of criminals, was contested with the spirit and courage of freemen; and, after much blood had flowed, the combatants were exempted from destruction (*occidioni exempti sunt*).' Acting with some initiative and inventing a pseudo-gladiatorial salute, and then fighting well, these men, despite their criminal and non-professional status and their intended extermination, atypically turned themselves into proper gladiators for a day. Hence some survived. The sources remark on the incident, in part, because it was an anomaly in arena practice – a mass Androclean reprieve.

It is also relevant to the status of *noxii* that in their edict on prices of AD 177 (discussed above) M. Aurelius and Commodus, out of need and gratitude, said that *damnati ad gladium* (men to be executed) could be purchased cheaply from the state and used instead of traditional victims (*trinqui*) for human sacrifices in Gaul. The decree acknowledges an established custom even as it applies price controls.[133] Early remarks rhetorically ask about the 'foul and morally offensive revenues' (I 3) made from games:

> The Fiscus, not for itself but in order that it might serve as protection for the butchery in which others engaged, had been invited with an interest amounting to a third or a fourth portion to make the filthy plundering legitimate. And so they took the Fiscus out of the arena completely. After all, why should the Fiscus of Marcus Aurelius and Lucius Commodus be supported by a connection with the arena? All the money of these emperors is clean, not stained

with the splashing of human blood, not soiled with the filth of sordid gains, and it is as innocently produced as it is collected. So away with that revenue, whether twenty or thirty million sesterces a year. Large enough for the empire is the fortune you accumulate by your thrift. 'Let even a part be cut back from the back debts owed by the lanistae, which come to more than five million sesterces, as a free gift to the lanistae . . . let them be invited to serve the public at a fixed rate.'

(I 5–11, Oliver trans.)

The text itself admits that the fisc had been making millions from a sordid business. Clearly the fisc had been taking a significant cut of the profits of *lanistae* and large revenues had been generated – some thirty million HS per year at one-third or one-quarter of, for example, the 1,000 HS per performance of cheap gladiators. The emperors were now easing burdens and, perhaps, ceasing to profit from gladiatorial shows,[134] but they were not ending shows or curtailing their brutality. It is the expense and not the tradition of gladiatorial games that is at issue – a matter of economy, not ideology.[135] Also, the emperors were not discontinuing all profits from the arena: although *damnati* as *trinqui* substitutes were supposedly an exception, these convicts were coldly sold by the state, just as it had collected taxes on gladiators before. Moreover, *lanistae* received remission of a major amount of debt 'as a consolation' for ceasing from their former 'disorderly conduct'. Entrepreneurial *lanistae* had been operating in a laissez-faire climate and the state still needed them, but they were to abide by fixed rates. The emperors were setting up price controls to lessen the burden on elite citizen-buyers, not to aid humble victims.

Law and the arena: demand and supply

To understand how Rome regarded and recruited lowly convicts to be killed in the arena, we must consider the history of Roman criminal law and capital punishment. Roman law overlaps extensively with the spectacles, and both reflect punishment, hierarchy, and hegemony.[136] From early times the legal system sanctioned punitive, public violence to protect the security and rights of citizens, especially elite citizens. Criminal law and sacred law combined to justify spectacularly staged executions aimed at coercion rather than correction, revenge rather than rehabilitation.[137] The idea that the executions of persons of all classes should be equal and merciful is a modern humanitarian notion. For Rome the punishment should fit the crime and the criminal. In the hierarchy of the arena victims' rights, condemnations, and penalties correlated with their crime and status. As lowly, foreign, or threatening criminals and slaves, arena *noxii* had damaged something and they were condemned to be damaged.

95

Throughout its history, Roman society was exceedingly status conscious: it presumed inequality – even before the law. Romans did not believe that 'all men are created equal', nor were any rights 'inalienable'. To Romans the 'self-evident' truths were that people's rights and responsibilities depended on their legal and social status.[138] Roman law held that certain segments of society did or did not deserve privileges in recognition of their status. Even if citizens, Romans of humble social status faced *de iure* and *de facto* legal inequality and suffered quicker and harsher penalties than their social superiors. Lower-class Romans faced *de facto* inequality concerning procedures, self-help, choice of courts, appeals, biases of elite judges, and presumption of guilt; and *de iure* they also received harsher penalties (see below). Inequality and hierarchy were built into the Roman psyche and into social and legal structures.[139]

As Rome grew, the combination of the Roman father's domestic jurisdiction (and the power of life and death over children),[140] the XII Tables' system of private, self-help criminal law, and an early system of assemblies and special commissions became inadequate. The middle Republic had a system of police justice under the jurisdiction of the urban praetor. He left punishment of slaves and humble citizens to the *tresviri capitales*, but death sentences were seldom carried out. Prior to Sulla, Rome had some standing jury courts (*quaestiones perpetuae*) for various types of criminal cases, and Sulla established a system of such courts with statutory penalties.[141] Men of status and means, however, still had access to voluntary exile to escape condemnation.[142]

Variations in penalties were facilitated under the Principate when the standing jury courts disappeared and political crimes faced judicial examination (*cognitio*) before the senate, the emperor, or an official, such as the urban prefect or a provincial governor. Acting *extra ordinem*, without fixed punishments, the judges had enormous power and considerable discretion in determining the nature of the crime and in choosing punishments.[143] Soon, perhaps under Tiberius, more severe sanctions, originally slave penalties, became available for citizens and found increasing use against persons of low status. Penalties could be ordered directly by the emperor himself,[144] or, via delegated punitive authority, by governors, the urban prefect, or the praetorian prefect (see below).

Under the Principate and later, legalized brutality was increasingly applied to the lower orders. Rome developed a dual-penalty system distinguishing between *honestiores*, men of status (*dignitas, honor*) (e.g. senators, knights, decurions (municipal nobles), military veterans), who got lighter penalties, and *humiliores*, all the rest, who got harsher penalties.[145] *Honestiores* retained traditional legal privileges: decurions and above were not supposed to be executed except for parricide and treason, and were exempt from the mines, crucifixion, and burning – and flogging and torture.[146] In effect, criminal condemnations of *humiliores* under the Empire were a matter of potentially arbitrary magisterial discretion, and the problem was exacerbated by the deterioration of methods of appeal. Under the Republic in theory all citizens had the right of *provocatio*, appeal to the people in contexts of death sentences.[147] However, the value of *provocatio* had declined by the time of Trajan, and Caracalla's edict on citizenship further diminished it. The imperial system of *appellatio*, appeals to the emperor, a variation of *provocatio*, was also flawed by status discrimination.[148] In the second and third centuries *humiliores* faced fewer legal rights and harsher penalties, especially concerning the expanding scope of charges of treason.

From its beginnings Rome severely punished treasonous threats to the community. Serious breaches of the moral and religious order of the community were regarded as heinous crimes that merited exceptional judicial condemnation and punishment. The earliest charge of treason (*perduellio*) concerned hostile acts against the state (e.g. arson, temple robbing), which brought the death penalty in the XII Tables. *Maiestas* was established as a somewhat ambiguous crime in 246 or 103 BC, and treason trials in the *quaestio perpetua maiestatis* overlapped with *perduellio* trials in the *comitia* through the 90s and 80s.[149] Sulla's reign saw the end of popular trials for *perduellio* and the establishment of a permanent *quaestio* for *maiestas* in 81. By the Lex Iulia of Caesar or Augustus anyone who, by word or deed, insulted anyone representing the people or the sovereignty of Rome was to be punished as a *vir sacer*.[150] Treason trials were transferred to a senatorial court under Augustus in 19 or 18 BC, and those accused of *maiestas* faced the worst penalties and even fewer or virtually no safeguards – even for the elite.

Maiestas was seen as an extreme category of injury (*iniuria*) to the state; and as the emperor became the state, it grew to encompass insults to the emperor or to magistrates.[151] According to Tacitus (*Ann.* 1.72.3–4; cf. Suet. *Aug.* 55) under Augustus and later, *maiestas* could apply to words as well as deeds; refusing to swear by the spirit of a divine emperor or criticism of the state or its officials became dangerous.[152] Imperial abuses of charges of *maiestas* form a prominent theme in imperial biographies, especially Tacitus, and particularly concerning Tiberius. Seneca charges that under Tiberius:

> there was such a common and almost universal frenzy for bringing charges of treason, that it took a heavier toll of the lives of Roman citizens than any Civil War; it seized upon the talk of drunkards, the frank words of jesters; nothing was safe – anything served as an excuse to shed blood.[153]

In a public society with little privacy, and with secret police about, the danger of *maiestas* was everywhere – from the bathroom[154] to the senate to the stands of the arena.[155] Adding to the potential for abuse, especially in treason trials of the wealthy, was a system of rewarding accusers (*delatores*). Anyone could bring a charge of treason, even those normally barred (e.g. slaves, women, a freedman against his patron); and if a criminal trial brought a conviction, the accuser was rewarded with one-quarter of the defendant's confiscated property. There were laws against calumny (*calumnia*, malicious prosecution) and accusers might be tortured, but opportunistic accusations were inevitable.[156] The senate properly handled most cases of treason, but the emperors reserved the right to protect themselves, and they could easily dominate or bypass senatorial trials. Fear of sedition and assassination compelled many emperors to exceed both the spirit and the letter of the law, and judicial violence could be personalistic, discriminatory, and vengeful.[157]

Under the Empire, conviction for treason brought death, even for citizens, veterans and decurions. Also, men declared enemies of the state lost all rights and were subject to execution without trial.[158] Senators were usually immune, but only at the emperor's discretion. Even the usual exemption of free men from torture did not hold in cases of *maiestas*.[159] Cases under Tiberius (Tac. *Ann.* 4.19–20) make it clear that, barring suicide, conviction for treason, even for *honestiores*, brought execution, confiscation of property, denial of burial, and *damnatio memoriae* – the elimination of a man's name and monuments.[160] Except for suicides under prescribed conditions, even the dead were not safe from criminal proceedings for treason: if a man died under accusation, he was presumed guilty and his estate confiscated.[161] Domitian reportedly used accusations to raise money needed for building programs and entertainments.[162] Marcus Aurelius apparently introduced the practice of charging a dead man formally with treason, and in the later Empire a formal sentence of death could be passed on a dead man, along with the imposition of a blood taint on his family.[163]

The later Empire witnessed a continued pattern of increased savagery and decline of citizens' and even *honestiores'* privileges. The list of capital crimes almost doubled from the Antonines to the third century, and Paulus' *Sententiae* of around AD 300 shows increased severity in penalties (e.g. 5.29.1). Even Constantine used torture and mutilation, the list of capital crimes grew to over sixty crimes during his reign, and he initiated a new form of execution by pouring molten lead down the throat.[164] MacMullen surveys explanations of increased judicial brutality concerning the psychology of increased distance and decreased sympathy, and soldier and slave models of punishment; and he sees the best explanation as the definition of citizenship in terms of culture rather than according to the letter of the law.[165]

With largely unchecked judicial discretion, magistrates – an emperor in terror of conspiracy, in need of resources, or merely on a whim,[166] an urban prefect, or a provincial governor – could unjustly or hastily condemn persons to the arena.[167] Since status-reinforcing mores endorsed it and law allowed it, particularly harsh punishment of the lower orders increased.[168] Also, Christians, as an especially despised group, became victims of summary criminal condemnation.[169] Clearly, then, under the Empire Roman law increased the potential for economic gain and emotional revenge by condemnation of humbler members of the empire to spectacles of death. The ratio of cheap *noxii* and minimal gladiators to expensive true gladiators increased in certain contexts: reigns of terror increased political victims; religious persecutions increased doctrinal victims; economic straits would favor numerous *damnati* over select, elite, expensive performers; and, finally, contexts of despair (e.g. threats on the frontiers, natural disasters) would invite the deaths of increased numbers of *damnati* as diversions or expiations.

Key and probable figures in arena recruitment were the provincial governors beyond Italy, and the urban prefect and the praetorian prefect within Italy and Rome. Even under the Republic, governors supplied non-Roman victims to aediles for games.[170] Somewhat reminiscent of the *tresviri capitales* of the Republic,[171] the urban prefect was an imperial appointee with offices in the area of the Esquiline. Under Nero the urban prefect began adjudicating crimes at Rome with imperially delegated punitive powers, and his jurisdiction widened greatly over time until under the Antonines he could try persons of all classes and sentence capitally. Under the Severans (*Dig.* 1.12.1pr.) all crimes committed in Rome and within a hundred-mile radius in Italy were under his jurisdiction. Similarly, the jurisdiction of the praetorian prefect grew, if more gradually, over time. From the later second century his duties shifted from military to judicial responsibilities, and under the Severans he had independent power of sentencing – like the urban prefect but beyond 100 miles outside Rome. By the end of the third century the prefects independently gave judgements in criminal trials, for which *humiliores* lacked appeal.[172]

Famous accounts of emperors' abuses of the elite in hostile sources may be embellished, and abuses by the prefects of the humble merited less historical attention; but if the elite were vulnerable and attractive for their estates, the lowly, although attractive primarily for their bodies, were even more vulnerable. At the upper levels concerning *honestiores* and people he knew, a megalomaniacal or vengeful emperor might get involved personally in trials and condemnations, but the more likely and numerous condemnations of the faceless lower classes at Rome were normally relegated to the urban prefect.[173] Like the procurator of the decree of AD 177, the urban prefect would be the official at Rome able to sell *damnati* to *lanistae* or *munerarii*. Moreover, the prefect was the personal appointee of the emperor, and their boxes faced each other across the arena of the Colosseum.[174] It seems likely, then, that the law was abused for purposes of graft, to fund civic expenses, or to satisfy an institutionalized need for spectacles.[175]

By the time of Nero the emperor could keep his distance and prefects had the ability to condemn victims rapidly and easily.[176] Anxious to produce scapegoats quickly to quell rumors and to supply his show (see ch. 8 below), Nero did not need an imperial tribunal to condemn Christians; the urban prefect would be the operative official. Just as governors were asked to acquire convicts and beasts for aediles' games under the Republic, urban prefects were probably asked to supply condemned persons, surreptitiously if necessary, for games. The sale of *damnati* extended legal execution into entrepreneurial execution. While the tribunals could use the properties of elite convicts as imperial resources, at the lower level convicted slaves and indigents lacking property were themselves turned into a physical resource for spectacles. Since *noxii*, especially slaves, usually had little or no personal property to be confiscated, not much honor to be taken away, and not much of a name to be eradicated, the state gained advantage and revenge by using them as arena victims and punishing them with aggravated execution.[177]

Legal and religious practices overlapped anew in the worship of Nemesis under the Empire. Michael Hornum's recent study shows that the cult of Nemesis in the Roman Empire was primarily one of comfortable and even elite Roman citizens supporting dramatic displays of the punishment of those who opposed the imperial order. The association of Nemesis with the arena was an originally Roman association, an epiphenomenal aspect of the spread of spectacles to the Greek East from the time of Augustus on, and not a corruption of an earlier Greek cultic or athletic tie. Hornum also disproves earlier assumptions that Nemesis was predominantly a goddess of gladiators, slaves, freedmen, and other individuals of low status. In fact, such persons formed only a small percentage of those who made dedications to Nemesis, and the largest component of dedicators, about one-third, were members of the civil government (e.g. *duoviri*), priests of the imperial cult, or members of the military.[178] Nemesis was seen as especially appropriate to *munera* and *venationes*, and Nemeseia shrines predominated in amphitheaters built for (and in theaters and stadia used for) such games.[179] Hornum explains that symbolically the arena was 'a place where a confirmation of the established state order was displayed in the slaughter of military enemies, criminals, insolent slaves and wild animals'. As a goddess of justice and righteous indignation who suppressed affronts to the Roman order, Nemesis was found at arenas where those who defied or threatened the social order or the majesty of Rome were degraded and punished.[180]

Rituals and resources

The XII Tables and Livy show that criminal punishment was brutal and public in the early Republic, and from 264 on 'gladiators' died in limited *munera* put on privately by the elite as funeral rites and conspicuous expenditure. Under the middle Republic foreign wars, triumphal *ludi*, and an abundance of prisoners of war brought increased games. Like emperors later, Rome's establishment became increasingly paranoid about threats and security, and intolerant and thin-skinned about insults. Early in the late Republic abuse of the Gracchi and Cinna's and Sulla's proscriptions show Rome applying brutality even to its own citizens when they were perceived

100

as threats. In the later stages of the Roman Revolution, popular politics greatly expanded the spectacles, and civil strife led to increased proscriptions as pseudo-legal criminal condemnations. Spectacles and punishments were expanding and overlapping. The arenas needed more and more supplies, and the legal system became more and more accommodating.

Under the Principate the spectacles were fully institutionalized. Better emperors provided sport with professional gladiators and punished only the guilty, but emperors fearful of conspiracies altered legal practice to give more discretion to imperial judges. Various emperors showed that the system could be abused in reigns of terror, but the system and its brutality continued. In good times the state had the resources (e.g. money, prisoners of war) for proper gladiatorial shows; but abusive emperors used the arena to punish treason, and they also used their legal power to supply *damnati* to the shows.

Originally, all arena victims were devoid of status, but the development of gladiatorial combat as a spectator sport elevated gladiators as surrogate soldiers. When gladiators became entertainers, the punitive demands of the arena still had to be met. Spectacular violence against threats and enemies was still necessary, so *noxii* were used in increasing numbers and with increasing brutality. When the empire ceased to expand and acquire new resources, Rome fed its entertainments with its own people. While Republican wars and imperial expansion had filled arenas with large numbers of war captives, the Pax Romana meant fewer prisoners of war. An elaborate system of gladiatorial schools filled the bill when the state could afford such recruitment, but later condemned men and slaves were far more available and convenient. Rome turned from foreign captives as the plunder of a successful military system to *noxii* as perceived internal foes produced by an abusive legal system.[181] Over time emperors sanctioned wider and more frequent application of brutal, inherently spectacular penalties for Rome's own common citizens and subjects. The decline of traditional safeguards and the expansion of spectacles were not causally related, but the latter exploited the former to supply the arena.

Under obligation to provide expiations and entertainments, officials condemned the lowly or the defenseless.[182] Confiscation brought income (via sales of property or of *damnati*), and damnation provided emotionally satisfying insults. A legal system run by the elite to protect the property and security of the elite wasted little remorse on abuses of the poor. In the eyes of the elite, *humiliores*, subjects, and slaves contributed little to the state and thus merited little privilege – except for the few who survived to become star gladiators. The Roman people themselves were not disturbed except by the quality of the performances; as long as victims were condemned by law – justly or not – they were *noxii* without any rights. As Bauman's recent study of punishment at Rome concludes, 'The bottom line is that there were few bleeding hearts in Ancient Rome.'[183]

Changes in the legal system and increased penal brutality complemented the historical development of the spectacles. Judicial changes (e.g. the decline of safeguards) exacerbated the potential for abuse. The ease of pronouncing brutal capital sentences correlated with the increase of spectacular executions of criminals. Quiet decapitations at the edge of town or stranglings in prison declined as brutal executions in public spectacles flourished. With continuing needs for arena resources, and with professional gladiators becoming expensive, emperors sanctioned spectacular use of condemned men.[184] In 177 even the enlightened Marcus Aurelius approved the sale of condemned victims.

Ritualized executions were punitive spectacles. Doomed by their crimes or class, their religion or resistance to Rome, most victims had virtually no hope of avoiding death – or its aftermath. Such men – and women – were officially condemned, brutally killed, and thoroughly damned, all with legal, popular, and religious sanction. Rome was seeking spectacle resources for diversions, but it was also seeking expiation and scapegoats for imperial problems. It was trying to cleanse itself of criminal and blasphemous miasma. The acceptability of judicial violence was aided by, and ultimately outlived, Roman blood sports. Public brutality continued after Rome in sacro-legal punishments – where it began.[185]

NOTES

1 Ville (1981) catalogues 126 *munera* to the death of Domitian, and, 395–9, discusses the question of numbers. Friedländer (1965) 2:62–74; Jennison (1937) 60–3; and Toynbee (1973) 17–9, 21–2, with nn. 9–26, 34–40, give detailed surveys of numbers of beasts in shows from 186 BC to the late Empire. Edmondson (1996), 75–6, notes problems in the literary sources (e.g. inexactitude of detail, imprecision with terms, selective reporting, a focus on imperial spectacles with little or no attention to games given by magistrates and private individuals): 'It is often forgotten that we have evidence for only a tiny percentage of all the *munera* that were staged at Rome.'

2 See Finley (1985) 27–46 on sources. Like Finley, Tim G. Parkin, *Demography and Roman Society* (Baltimore: Johns Hopkins U., 1992) 4–66, esp. 5–19, 41–66, explains the need for skepticism concerning attempts to do statistical investigations using biased and limited ancient sources; even the evidence from tombstones, skeletons, and census figures may be demographically unreliable. Major sources on spectacles are statistically disappointing. Martial is preoccupied with the exotic and the mythological, not with quantification; Tertullian, like Eusebius later, details agonies and heroism, not numbers. Sources mention numbers incidentally, not systematically. E.g. Pliny, *HN* 11.144, discussing eyes and blinking, notes that two of the 20,000 gladiators in training in Caligula's school for gladiators were seen as invincible because only they did not blink under pressure.

3 E.g. the inscription from Minturnae (*CIL* 10.6012 = *ILS* 5062) in which P. Baebius proclaims the number of gladiators and bears killed in his games; see n. 74 below. Some mosaics show a literal count of animals listing numbers and types of beasts; see Brown (1992) 192; Dunbabin (1978) 57, pl. 24. A

third-century mosaic from Smerat in Tunisia commemorates the *munerarius* Magerius with depictions of leopards, hunters (of the venatorial family of the Telegenii), and bags of money: A. Beschaouch, 'La mosaïque de chasse à l'amphithéâtre découverte à Smirat en Tunisie', *CR Acad. Inscr.* (1966) 134–57; Dunbabin (1978) 67–70; Brown (1992) 198–200.

4 *Mon. Anc.* 22.1,3, plus a naumachy with 3,000 combatants: *Mon. Anc.* 23.

5 Dio 42.22.4, Loeb. Newbold (1975), 591, suggests that Dio may be incorporating some history of the games or using numerical standards to suggest an individual's power.

6 Calculations: e.g. Carcopino (1975) 203–6; but see Balsdon (1969) 245–8; and Friedländer (1965) 2:10–12 on the problem. Wiedemann (1992), 11–12, stresses that there were far fewer days with regular gladiatorial games than with *ludi*. Friedländer (1965), 2:11, concludes: 'The number of festival days in the year devoted to the Games cannot be ascertained for any epoch, as the regular spectacles were constantly shifted, and the extraordinary ones incalculable.'

7 Certainly great numbers of animals were killed beyond the arena in normal sacrifices, and special occasions added to the slaughter. During celebrations on the accession of Caligula 160,000 victims were publicly sacrificed in the next three months, or even less time (Suet. *Calig.* 14.1). A zoologist from the Zoological Gardens, Belle Vue, Manchester, Jennison (1937), 62–3, 177–8, admits that the numbers from unexceptional and unrecorded shows must not be overlooked; but he adds an argument, unconvincing until the late Empire, for more progressive spectacles over time, with more performances of trained animals and the recapture of animals for future shows. Similarly, citing examples of tamed, performing animals, Balsdon (1969), 304–5, stresses how often animals were exhibited 'for interest and entertainment alone, and with no thought of killing'.

8 Wiedemann (1992), 16, feels that the growing cost of gladiators influenced increased use of beasts from the Severans onward.

9 The aedile M. Caelius Rufus bothered Cicero, as a provincial governor, seeking beasts, especially panthers, for a show at Rome: Cic. *Fam.* 2.11.2, 8.2.2, 8.4.5, 8.6.5, 8.8.10, 8.9.3, *Att.* 6.1.21; Plut. *Cic.* 36.6. Sending beasts and gladiators for shows was an expected gift between friends: Sen. *Ben.* 1.12.3. On Symmachus, see Balsdon (1969) 263, 298, 304, 312, 314. On mosaics of hunts to supply the arena: Brown (1992) 197 and n. 26 on 210 (with references); cf. n. 41 in ch. 6 below.

10 Jennison (1937) 177–82; cf. bibliographical note on *venationes* n. 42 in ch. 2 above. On logistics, transport, and commerce, see Jennison, 137–53; Ville (1981) 348–52; and F. Bertrandy, 'Remarques sur le commerce des bêtes sauvages entre l'Afrique du Nord et l'Italie (IIᵉ siècle avant J.-C.–IVᵉ siècle après J.-C.)' , *MÉFRA* 99 (1987) 211–41.

11 See Lafaye (1914) 702–3, Balsdon (1969) 308, or Wiedemann (1992) 58–9, citing sources such as Suet. *Ner.* 31.1 and *ILS* 399, 5055, 5062, 5159. E.g. SHA *Gord. Tres* 33.1–2, Loeb:

> There were thirty-two elephants at Rome in the time of Gordian . . . ten elk, ten tigers, sixty tame (*mansueti*) lions, thirty tame leopards, ten *belbi* or hyenas, a thousand pairs of imperial gladiators (*gladiatorum fiscalium*), six hippopotami, one rhinoceros, ten wild lions, ten giraffes, twenty wild asses, forty wild horses, and various other animals of this nature without number. All of these Philip presented or slew (*vel dedit vel occidit*) at the secular games [of AD 248]. All these animals, wild, tame, and savage (*feras mansuetas et . . . efferatas*), Gordian intended for a Persian triumph.

12 Various emperors (e.g. Nero) had pets and menageries, but imperial Rome never had a great zoo. Coleman (1996), 58–68, shows that, while animals were displayed in processions in Ptolemaic Alexandria, at Rome beasts were generally killed, especially under the emperors, as a form of imperial conspicuous consumption.

13 Large animals: e.g. in Caligula's games as consul in AD 37 400 bears and 400 Libyan beasts were killed (Dio 59.7.3); and in AD 38, after the death of Drusilla, Caligula gave a show with 500 bears and 500 *Africanae* (Dio 59.11.3). Killed: e.g. sources on Trajan's games give numbers of humans who participated and of animals 'killed' (see above); cf. Augustus above in ch. 2.

14 Ville (1981), 419–20 and no. 116, suggests that the same rhinoceros appeared in several shows under Titus and Domitian: see Mart. 14.53 and *Spect.* 9, 22; crowds ask for mercy for animals: Mart. 13.98; cf. 11.69. The death of a tamed lion, a favorite of Domitian's, was mourned by the people and senate as if a famous gladiator (Stat. *Silv.* 2.5.25–7). Cf. Mitchell (1991) 90: in the Spanish bullring brave bulls who kill horses or picadors are sometimes spared by crowds. More typical is Dio's simple statement, 60.7.3, that in a show in the circus in AD 41 under Claudius 300 bears and 300 Libyan beasts 'were slain'. Martial, 4.35 and 4.74, marvels that does could be made to fight bravely to the death, but he also shows that they were not spared – dogs and hunters awaited any survivors.

15 E.g. Friedländer (1965) 2:66: 'These hunts went on for centuries, and the parents had to be killed, in order to capture the whelps; hence, the animal kingdom became wholly transformed, wild animals extirpated and driven into wildernesses, and new ground gained for civilization and agriculture.' For ecological discussions condemning the effect of spectacles on fauna, especially in North Africa, see J. Donald Hughes, *Pan's Travail: Environmental Problems of the Ancient Greeks and Romans* (Baltimore: Johns Hopkins U., 1994) 100–8; David Attenborough, *The First Eden: The Mediterranean World and Man* (Boston: Little, Brown, 1987) 112–17. Bertrandy (1987), 234, compares Rome's impact to the imperial hunts in Africa at the turn of the century and to buffalo hunts in America in the second half of the nineteenth century.

16 Concerning the 140 or 142 elephants brought to the Circus at Rome in 252 BC, Pliny, *HN* 8.17, says that sources that say they were not killed have no explanation for what became of them.

17 Ville (1960) 283. Cf. Tertullian's use of 'gladiator' below in ch. 5. SHA, *Prob.* 19.8, says that, in celebrating his triumph over the Germans and Blemmyae (of Ethiopia) in AD 281, Probus presented (*edita*) 300 pairs of gladiators (*gladiatorum*) including Blemmyae who had been led in his triumph, as well as Germans, Sarmatians, and even some Isaurian brigands. Such fighters were captives and criminals forced to fight each other to the death, not elite, true gladiators. SHA, *Aurel.* 33.4–5, Loeb, makes the distinction: Aurelian's triumph in AD 274 included beasts and 1,800 pairs of gladiators 'besides the captives from the barbarian tribes' (e.g. Arabs, Bactrians, Persians), all with their hands bound; 34.6 adds that spectacles in the next few days included hunts, gladiatorial fights, and a naumachy.

18 E.g. SHA, *Hadr.* 17.12, on Hadrian's generosity and gifts, mentions in passing that he sent 300 convicts (*noxios*) to the arena; they were dressed in gold-embroidered cloaks, but probably they all died.

19 See ch. 5 below. Scobie (1986) 399–433, at 413, estimates that Rome's population of 800,000–1,000,000 in early imperial times produced and dumped around 40,000–50,000 kg of body wastes a day into the sewers and streets. Cf. Victor Davis Hansen, *The Western Way of War: Infantry Battle in Classical*

Greece (London: Hodder and Stoughton, 1989) 197–209, on the problems of disposal after battles (e.g. sheer mass, need for haste, decomposition and disfigurement, smell, bloody soil).

20 Hopkins (1983), 6–8, remarks that gladiatorial shows perhaps happened regularly only a few times per year, but 'frequency and significance are not Siamese twins'. Regulations about numbers and expense were evaded, and 'Gladiatorial shows suffused Roman life.'

21 On the hierarchy of the arena, see, most recently, Edmondson's excellent summary (1996) 95–8; and see further below.

22 See discussions in Ville (1981) 228–55; Robert (1940) 283–302; Schneider (1918); Lafaye (1896); and more popular treatments by Grant (1967) 28–35; and Auguet (1972) 19–45. Wiedemann (1992), 102–27, updates such treatments. Coleman (1990), 54–6, 61–2, offers an excellent summary typology of punishments by degree of survivability. As 'direct' death penalties *summa supplicia* (beasts, crux, fire) 'afforded no chance of survival' (55). Damnation to a gladiatorial or venatorial *ludus* was an 'indirect' death penalty 'whereby offenders were condemned to performances that might offer a chance of temporary survival, depending on skill and luck, but would in the end usually prove fatal'. Such penalties, with death as 'likely but not inevitable', were seen as 'providing a public service in the form of entertainment' (56). In fatal charades 'mitigated' penalties offered victims the possibility of survival if they burned their hand, performed self-castration, or wore the *tunica molesta*: 'self-inflicted torture might plausibly rank equal in entertainment value to the high-risk (but not necessarily fatal) category of gladiators and *venatores*'. For their cooperation the victims gained some hope, but their bodies were 'marked' by their punishment. Cf. Coleman's suggestion (1993), 62–3, that the aquatic performance of the myth of Leander in Titus' games in AD 80 was a mitigated punishment.

23 Ps. Quint. *Decl. Maj.* 9.5, 9.8, 9.12: a rich young man was captured by pirates and sold, like a bad slave, to a gladiatorial trainer, who equipped him for the arena with training, weapons, and armor. Cicero, *Sest.* 64.135, criticizes Vatianus for improperly taking gladiators from slaves who were condemned by their masters to workhouses or prison rather than from the slave market. Vitellius rejected his young favorite and sold him to a travelling gladiatorial trainer: Suet. *Vit.* 12. *Damnati ad arenam* became 'penal slaves' or 'slaves of the penalty' (*servi poenae*); if slaves they were no longer anyone's property, and if free they immediately lost their freedom, citizenship, and ability to inherit; see Bauman (1996) 122–3 and Garnsey (1970) 164–5 on *Dig.* 48.19.12 and 29. Wiedemann (1992) 105: 'The criminal condemned *ad ludos* was a socially "dead man" who had a chance of coming alive again.' If a man survived he could be discharged from fighting (*rude donatus*) at the end of three years and set free at the end of five: Paulus *Sent.* 5.17.2(3), 5.23.4; cited by Hopkins (1983) 24. Further on the distinction between condemnation to death and to the arena, see below.

24 Suetonius, *Calig.* 30.3, Loeb, relates an incident: 'Once a band of *retiarii* in tunics, matched against the same number of *secutores*, yielded without a struggle; but when their death was ordered, one of them caught up his trident and slew all the victors. Caligula bewailed this in a public proclamation as a most cruel murder, and expressed his horror of those who had the heart to witness it.' See further in ch. 5 below.

25 Cf. Plin. *HN* 8.16, 8.36. On *venator* versus *bestiarius*, see G. Lafaye, 'Venator', *Dar.–Sag.* 5 (1914) 709–11; Ville (1981) 88–90.

26 Edwards (1993), 98–136, offers insights into Rome's ambivalence about actors and the theater. As she demonstrates, 118, 123–6, actors were supposedly base and obscene *infames*, and they were socially and legally marginalized as 'the

inversion of the soldier-citizen' (131) and the 'antithesis of (Ro)manhood' (136); but, 127–31, actors were also celebrities patronized by emperors, and members of the elite sometimes appeared on stage. Theaters, 110–19, were sites of social tension, political arenas, where social hierarchy and political authority were displayed but also challenged. Wistrand (1992), 30–40, 56, contrasts Roman authors' acceptance of arena violence with condemnations of theatrical performances (*scaena*) for their association with vice (*vitium*), the antonym of moral stature (*virtus*). Further on actors, now see W. D. Lebek, 'Moneymaking on the Roman Stage', 29–48, in Slater (1996).

27 Ville (1981) 329–44, esp. 344, discusses the paradoxical social position of gladiators and stresses the profound 'ambivalence' of the gladiator as virtuous fighter, executioner, and walking dead man. Romans identified with gladiators just as the Balinese, as discussed by Geertz (1974), identified with their fighting cocks: the fighters were symbolic expressions of both the Romans' self-image and their image of the 'other' – of barbarism or inhumanity. As Geertz, 7, explains, 'In identifying with his cock, the Balinese man is identifying not just with his ideal self, or even his penis, but also, and at the same time, with what he most fears, hates, and ambivalence being what it is, is fascinated by – The Powers of Darkness . . . In the cockfight, man and beast, good and evil, ego and id, the creative power of loosened animality fuse in a bloody drama of hatred, cruelty, violence and death.'

28 Hopkins (1983) 1–3, 5, 29. Barton (1993), 14–16, 20–2, also sees the amphitheater as a battlefield in the heart of town wherein gladiatorial combats, as a form of simplified, purified soldiering, recalled the romanticized single combats of the early Republic. Oakley's discussion (1985) of traditions of single combat helps explain the appeal of the gladiator as soldier; on the importance of individual action even after the transition to hoplite warfare emphasized corporate solidarity and military discipline, see his 405–7. Like fighting cocks or pit bulldogs, the gladiators came to represent or symbolize their masters and fans, providing vicarious self-validation of Roman militarism and machismo.

29 Willing to die with integrity: e.g. Sen. *Dial.* 2.16.2, *Ep.* 30.8; Cic. *Phil.* 3.14.35, *Tusc.* 2.17.40–1 (in note 89 in ch. 2 above concerning Cannae); cf. Tert. *De spect.* 12. Epictetus, *Diss.* 1.29.37, claims that imperial gladiators, resentful if not selected, offered prayers and pressured officials to be allowed to fight. Seneca praised gladiators for their willingness to face death, their fortitude, and their desire for glory, but he had contempt for timid gladiators. Pliny, *Pan.* 33.1, claims that in Trajan's games even slaves and criminals showed a desire for praise and victory, and thus inspired Romans to endure honorable wounds and to disdain death. On the educational value of gladiatorial spectacles, i.e. as an inspiration to military virtue, as a theme in Seneca and works of the first century AD, see Wistrand (1990) 33–5; Wistrand (1992) 14, 28, 75–9. Ville (1960), 299–307, shows that pagans later responded to Christian criticisms of games with similar arguments about their military value.

30 On gladiatorial instruction for soldiers and the relationship of amphitheaters to military colonists, see ch. 2. Making an argument, however, for the gladiator as anti-soldier, J. Maurin, 'Les Barbares aux arènes', *Ktèma* 9 (1984) 103–11, feels that gladiators fighting with barbarian weapons symbolized types of barbarians, who stood in stark contrast to the Roman infantryman as a proper military model.

31 Wiedemann (1992), 34–8, sees the combats not as a public display of killing but as a 'demonstration of the power to overcome death' (35): dying by the sword the gladiator, in a sense, overcomes death, and the gladiators' deaths provide consolation for spectators gathered to honor the death of a great man

with games. Similarly, see Auguet (1972), 196–8, on elevation. Wiedemann, 38, suggests that the gladiator's demonstration of military virtue 'gave him a claim to be a Roman citizen'. He, 46–7, 90–7, feels that socially liminal gladiators might (47) 'pass from the social death of *infamia* back to life as part of the Roman community again'. However, see below on the persistent stigma associated with gladiators.

32 Plass (1995) quote at 89; 73: 'Prizes were awarded for what society rejected, since bloodletting in the arena was an aspect of social order by being something against which social order defined itself.' Similarly, Hornum (1993) 86: 'The gladiator and his activity in the *munus* were attractive not only for his honor and bravery in the midst of humiliation but as a vehicle for the preservation of state order.'

33 Barton (1993) 81. She, 62, 65–6, feels that the madness was shared by all classes, both sexes, and even emperors.

34 Barton (1993), 20, 35, 40–6 (see further below on oaths), builds on the idea of *devotio* as self-sacrifice in H. S. Versnel, 'Self-Sacrifice, Compensation, and the Anonymous Gods', in *Le Sacrifice dans l'antiquité* (1981) 135–94. The Roman general Publius Decius Mus in 340 BC in the Samnite Wars dedicated his body to the earth and the gods of the dead in return for the future victory of his troops; then he made a suicidal attack on his foes to save his own men by diverting the gods' anger onto the enemy; see Livy 8.9.9–10; on a similar *devotio* by Decius the Younger: 10.28.12–13. Barton (1993), 22, uses SHA *Max. et Bal.* 8.6–7 to suggest that soldiers were made to watch gladiatorial fights before campaigns to get used to the sight of wounds and blood; but Hornum (1993), 81–2, and Ville (1981), 288–90, reject the SHA's suggestion that, before setting out on campaign, emperors customarily gave games as a *devotio* directed against the enemy.

35 *Mali status* probably refers to disobedient, incorrigible slaves. Cf. Serv. *Ad Aen.* 3.67: *captivi* fought at funerals. Florus, 2.8.9, Loeb, cited by Barton (1993) n. 29 on 183, says that Spartacus honored his fallen officers with funerals 'like those of Roman generals, and ordered his captives to fight at their pyres, just as though he wished to wipe out all his past dishonour by having become, instead of a gladiator, a giver of gladiatorial shows'.

36 Ville (1981) 13. Ville, 423–4, remarks that death, not just skill, was crucial to the appeal of the shows. Rome used pariahs and malefactors for entertainment and moral edification. E.g. Diod. Sic. 36.10.2–3: after the end of the slave revolt in Sicily in 100 BC the proconsul Aquillius sent a thousand rebel slaves to Rome to be exposed to beasts. Cf. the modern punitive use of chain gangs or 'community service': convicts are selected for punishment, but their punishment can benefit society.

37 Compensation: Ville (1981) 365–6, 455; device: Karl Meuli, *Der griechische Agon: Kampf und Kampfspiele im Totenbrauch, Totentanz, Totenklage, und Totenlob* (Cologne: Historisches Seminar der Sporthochschule, 1968) 49. Marc Zvi Brettler and Michael Poliakoff, 'Rabbi Simeon ben Lakish at the Gladiator's Banquet: Rabbinic Observations on the Roman Arena', *Harv. Theol. Rev.* 83 (1990) 93–8, have revived and supported Meuli's idea with ethnographic parallels and with a passage from the Babylonian Talmud, *Gittin* 47a, in which a gladiator's last request, analogous to the elevating of victims via the banquet, is said to make the victim's blood 'sweet'. The costuming of Christians and other victims may suggest their elevation as sacrifices; see Coleman (1990) 66, 70.

38 It was offered to but refused by Christians. Tert. *Apol.* 42.5, Loeb: 'Nor do I recline to eat in public at the Liberalia which is the habit of the beast fighters taking their last meal'; cf. the *pultes pridianae* in *De spect.* 12.6. *Pass. Perp. et Fel.*

17.1: Christian *damnati* celebrated their last meal as an *agape* rather than as a *cena libera*; they told people who came to see them out of curiosity to take note of how they looked so that they would recognize them in the arena. Paul, I Cor. 15:32 (*Oxford Study Bible*; quoting the last sentence from Isa. 22.13), probably refers to *damnati ad bestias* being offered the meal: 'with no more than human hopes, what would have been the point of my fighting those wild beasts at Ephesus? If the dead are never raised to life, "Let us eat and drink, for tomorrow we die."' Petronius' allusions to the *cena libera* in narrating Trimalchio's banquet (*Sat.* 70–1, with the phrase *cena libera* used at 26.7) add to the scene as a contemplation of death; see Charles Saylor, 'Funeral Games: The Significance of Games in the *Cena Trimalchionis*', *Latomus* 46 (1987) 593–602, esp. 598–9.

39 Lucil. 4.2.172–5 (frag. 150, from Nonius 393.30; cf. Cic. *Tusc.* 2.41); see E. H. Warmington, *Remains of Old Latin*, Loeb (Cambridge, Mass.: Harvard U., 1938) 3:56–7. Lines 176–81 (from Cic. *Tusc.* 4.48) refer to Pacideianus' furor to kill his opponent; see Warmington, 58–9, cf. 114–15. Treggiari (1969), 141–2, suggests that gladiators were generally slaves under the Republic; she thinks it probable that gladiators used in political gangs (see her nn. 2–6) were freedmen (or future freedmen), but adds that freedmen gladiators 'are not directly attested for the republican period, though one known gladiator, Aeserinus, could have been a public freedman of Aeserina'. Barton (1993), 17, notes that Terence, *Phorm.* 964, in the second century BC first uses 'gladiator' as a literary metaphor: 'the spirit of the gladiator' as the equivalent of fierce or fearless.

40 On famous gladiators in political gangs, see ch. 2 above. Presumably well-known gladiators are named on Pompeian advertisements, e.g. *CIL* 4.1182 and 4.2508. See Sabbatini Tumolesi (1980) 116–19, 139–41, 147–50. Trimalchio (Petron. *Sat.* 52.3) had fights between the famous gladiators Hermeros and Petraites depicted on cups; and Petraites was possibly connected with names on some glass cups with gladiator scenes; see H. T. Rowell, 'The Gladiator Petraites and the Date of the Satyricon', *TAPA* 89 (1958) 13–24. On Petraites, see n. 4 in ch. 4 below.

41 Cic. *Phil.* 2.29.74, a metaphorical use of gladiatorial retirement; see Ville (1981) 325–9.

42 Suet. *Aug.* 45.3, *Ner.* 4. Augustus (Suet. *Aug.* 45.3) also increased the privileges of various types of professional entertainers. On the meaning of *sine missione*, see Wiedemann (1992) 119; Ville (1981) 403–5; and the remarks of D. Potter in reviewing Wiedemann in *JRS* 84 (1994) 230–1.

43 See K. Hopkins, 'Structural Differentiation in Rome 200–31 B.C.: The Genesis of an Historical Bureaucratic Society', 63–79 in I. M. Lewis, *History and Social Anthropology*, ASA monograph 7 (Tavistock: U. London, 1986). Usually applied to political and administrative changes as societies make the transition to a market economy, the pattern of 'the institutionalization of spheres of conduct which had previously been relatively undifferentiated' can be applied to the victims of the arena. As Emily Gowers, *The Loaded Table: Representations of Food in Roman Literature* (Oxford: Clarendon Press, 1993) 50–1, explains, Livy, 39.6.7–9 (cf. Plin. *HN* 9.67), dates the beginning of all Roman sin, including the arrival of cooks in Rome, to 187 BC. Also on cooks and supposed moral decline in the second century, see Edwards (1993) 177–8.

44 Florus, 2.8.8, Loeb, reflects the ideology of debasement and elevation in comments on Spartacus: 'the man who, from being a Thracian mercenary, had become a soldier, and from a soldier a deserter, then a highwayman, and finally, thanks to his strength (*in honorem virium*), a gladiator'. Florus, 2.8.14, adds that Spartacus died bravely 'as became a general (*quasi imperator*)'.

45 *Infamia* as a moral stigma and a legal status of diminished rights for citizens:
A. H. G. Greenidge, *Infamia: Its Place in Roman Public Life and Private Law*
(Oxford: Oxford U., 1894); John Crook, *Law and Life of Rome* (Ithaca: Cornell,
1967) 83–5; Adolf Berger, *Encyclopedic Dictionary of Roman Law* (Philadelphia:
American Philosophical Society, 1953) 500. *Infamia* applied to *auctorati, lanistae*,
actors, criminals, spendthrifts, and debtors. On the *infamia* of gladiators: Ville
(1981) 339–43; Wiedemann (1992) 28–9; H. Aigner, 'Zur gesellschaftlichen
Stellung von Henkern, Gladiatoren und Berufsathleten', 201–20, esp. 205–11,
in I. Weiler, ed., *Soziale Randgruppen und Außenseiter im Altertum* (Graz: Leykam,
1988). Athletics and gladiatorial combats were contrasted by goals and participants. Crook, 271, cites *Dig.* 11.5.2.1, a *senatus consultum* allowing betting on
athletic contests 'which are done for virtue', but not on other games. Crook,
163, also cites *Dig.* 9.2.7.4: 'If someone kills another in a wrestling match or
the pancratium or boxing, if it is in a public contest no Aquilian action lies,
because the damage is held to have been done for the sake of glory and valour,
not with the intent to injure. But this is not true of a slave, because it is freeborn people who go in for contests. It applies, however, to a *filius familias*.'
The stigma persisted in Christian circles: Hippolytus *Apostolic Tradition* 16: all
those who are *infames* by Roman law, including gladiators, were denied baptism;
see Rouselle (1988) 103–4.
46 Barton (1993) 12. Barton, 13, collects these and other comments, e.g. Calpurnius
Flaccus, *Decl.* 52: 'There is no meaner condition among the people than that
of the gladiator.' Tacitus, *Ann.* 1.76.3, criticizes Tiberius' son Drusus for his
excessive enthusiasm for gladiatorial bloodshed, however cheap the blood
(*quamquam vili sanguine*).
47 *Sest.* 64.134. The war against Spartacus was ridiculed and despised at first as
merely a matter of slaves and gladiators: App. *B Civ.* 1.118; Florus 1.4.7.5,
2.8.12.
48 Seneca classes *lanistae* with panderers: *Controv.* 10.4 (33),11; they might gain
wealth but they were contemptible: *Ep.* 87.15 (cf. *Ben.* 6.12.2). Isidorus, *Etym.*
10.159, says that *lanista* means 'executioner' in Etruscan. Juvenal, 3.29–40,
associates *lanistae* with people who contract themselves to clean out cesspools,
furnish funerals, sell slaves, and 'carry corpses to the pyre'. Juvenal, 3.153–9,
is indignant that sons of gladiators, pimps, and prostitutes were turning up in
front-row seats at the theater. Martial, 11.66, insults a man as an informer, a
cheat, a pimp, and a *lanista*.
49 Gaius *Inst.* 1.13–15, 25; see Jane F. Gardner and T. Wiedemann, *The Roman
Household: A Sourcebook* (London: Routledge, 1991) no. 5, pp. 24–5. *Dig.*
22.5.21.2 (Arcadius Charisius, ca. AD 300): when courts were forced to accept
gladiators as witnesses, their evidence was not to be accepted unless they were
subjected to torture (i.e. like slaves).
50 Sen. *Controv.* 10.4.18 (cf. 5.33): '[the rich] throw into the gladiatorial schools
all the best looking, the most fit for combat'; cited in Barton (1993) 80.
Wiedemann (1992) 105: 'A brave fighter might rise from the dead and re-join
the society of the living. That was . . . the gift of society as a whole: of the
Roman people, present in the amphitheatre.'
51 Status and hierarchy from slave to free and from *tirones* to *primi pali*: Lafaye
(1896) 1590–1; Ville (1981) 306–11, 334–9; Brown (1992) 184–6; Edmondson
(1996) 95–6. D. S. Matz, 'Epigraphical Evidence Relating to the Roman
Gladiatorial Establishment' (Ph.D. Diss., U. Minnesota, 1977) 135–7, esp.
112–18, like Wiedemann (1992) 117–18, discusses *CIL* 6.631 (= *ILS* 5084),
which lists thirty-two members (recruits and veterans) of a gladiatorial guild
(*collegium*) dedicated to the god Silvanus and organized into groups of ten

(*decuriae*). As Balsdon (1969), 291, notes, recruits (*novi auctorati, tirones*) were accepted at least as young as 17 (*ILS* 5107). On sixteen gladiatorial types (e.g. *retiarii, murmillones*), each with specialized equipment and instruction, see Lafaye (1896) 1583–90; Robert (1940) 64–73; Friedländer (1965) 4:258–67. Gladiators could be promoted within the school, e.g. from *primus palus* to *epistates*: see *IGRR* 1.207; cf. *ILS* 5103 (= *CIL* 6.10175); cited by Aubert (1994) 365. Edward Peters, *Torture* (New York: Basil Blackwell, 1985) 182–5, could be talking of gladiators when he notes that torturers in the modern era are generally recruited from the lower classes, their training includes self-abasement and abuse, there is an operative hierarchy of skills and privileges, and there is also psychological reinforcement among colleagues.

52 See J. H. Oliver and R. E. A. Palmer, 'Minutes of an Act of the Roman Senate', *Hesp.* 24 (1955) 320–49, on the so-called *senatus consultum de pretiis gladiatorum munuendis* from the joint reign of Marcus Aurelius and Commodus (AD 177–80). Two inscriptions, the Aes Italicense (here = I) from Italica in Baetica in Spain (*CIL* 2.6278 = *ILS* 5163) and the Marmor Sardianum (here = S), from Sardis in Asia (*ILS* 9340) fragmentarily preserve senatorial *acta*. Recorded were an imperial *oratio* and then the first senatorial response, which suggested amendments. To ease the burdens on the upper class of providing gladiatorial shows, the *acta* set expense limits on types of shows as well as price limits for the sale of types of gladiators. It also had special provisions of relevance to Gaul; see ch. 8 below.

53 Cf. Apul. *Met.* 4.13: a Greek *munerarius* assembled 'gladiators of the best bands (*gladiatores isti famosae*)'. See Ville (1981) 251–2. The old expense limit of 30,000 HS on commercial spectacles put on for profit (*munera assiforana*) was retained: I 29–35.

54 Of these common gladiators or *gregarii* (I 36, Oliver and Palmer trans.) 'one who may be rated "superior among the gregarii" (*melior inter tales*) [should] fight in a team under a standard for 2,000 HS'. I 59–61 concerns the buying and reselling of gladiators by provincial priests. On the role of the imperial cult and its provincial high priests, who were obligated to put on *munera* and kept families of gladiators and *bestiarii*, see Ville (1981) 188–93, 206–8, 212–13; Price (1984) 89, 104. Priests replaced gladiators as necessary and sold off survivors to successors. On the reselling of gladiators at Rome: Dio, 59.14.1–4, says that at the end of games Caligula would sell his remaining gladiators by public auction, forcing senators and knights to buy them at high prices. Suet. *Calig.* 38.4: once a certain Saturninus dozed at an auction, nodding his head, and 'bought' thirteen gladiators for 9 million HS.

55 Investments: Martial, 5.24.9, says that the gladiator Hermes brings wealth to the seat-contractors. Seneca, *Ben.* 6.12.2, compares the *lanista* to a farmer who feeds and cares for his flock, only to slaughter and skin the *optima boves*. Discussions of living conditions suggest that gladiators lived simply but probably better than the lowest citizens: see Wiedemann (1992) 112–17; Ville (1981) 301–29; Balsdon (1969) 296–8. Food: Juvenal, 11.20, satirically refers to the mixed scraps of food (*miscellanea* of the *ludus*); Gowers (1993), 111, 197, explains that 'miscellany' was originally a dubious plate of leftovers eaten by gladiators. Cf. Ps. Quint. *Decl.* 9.5: a gladiator's diet was disgusting, but strengthened the body. Housing: Scobie (1986) 427; Ville (1981) 298–301. Doctors cared for gladiators: Scribonius Largus 101; Plin. *HN* 26.135; Sen. *Helv.* 3.1; *ILS* 5119 (*in medicina decessit*); 5152 (*medicus* of the Ludus Magnus). See John Scarborough, 'Galen and the Gladiators', *Episteme* 5 (1971) 98–111.

56 Bathroom: cf. below on suicides. Scobie (1988), 200–1, notes that gladiators in the *ludus* at Pompeii lived under austere conditions, but they were not

guarded or completely disarmed. Lentulus Batiatus at Capua abusively kept Spartacus and others in confinement until the time for their combats, not because they had misbehaved but simply out of cruelty: Plut. *Crass.* 8.1.

57 Suetonius, *Claud.* 21.5, says that Claudius counted out gold coins at gladiatorial shows. *ILS* 5163.45–6 stipulates that of the prize money (set by local custom: S 5–7) free gladiators get one-quarter and slave gladiators get one-fifth. Further references to prizes: Wiedemann (1992) 122.

58 As Wiedemann (1992), 115, notes, laws (e.g. *Dig.* 38.1.37pr.) restricting actors and professional *bestiarii* from attaining legal privileges granted to the fathers of two legitimate children would exist only if such persons were assumed to have families. Plutarch, *Mor.* 1099B, comments that some married Greek gladiators on the eve of a fight would give their wives to friends; some would manumit their slaves. Juvenal, 6.216–17, suggests that *lanistae* and gladiators could make their wills as they pleased. Cf. *damnati ad metallum*, who had no right to make or benefit from a will; see Garnsey (1970) 131–2.

59 Petron. *Sat.* 45.11–12, Loeb: 'He produced some decayed twopenny-halfpenny gladiators, who would have fallen flat if you breathed on them; I have seen better ruffians turned in to fight the wild beasts . . . they were all flogged afterwards. How the great crowd roared at them, "Lay it on!" They were mere runaways, to be sure.' Wistrand (1992) 24: 'What people absolutely did *not* want to see were coward gladiators running away instead of fighting; those who tried were promptly punished.' Cf. SHA *Gal. Duo* 12.3–4: people were shocked when Gallienus in jest honored a *venator* with a garland after he repeatedly failed to kill a bull.

60 Fans called to Claudius to bring on Palumbus, 'the Dove': Suet. *Claud.* 21.5. Spectators shouted out instructions, often helpful ones, to gladiators: Tert. *Ad Mart.* 1.2. Suet. *Calig.* 35.3: Caligula complained that Romans gave more honor to gladiators than to emperors. Titus was partial to Thracians, but he bantered with the crowd and let them influence a gladiatorial show: Suet. *Tit.* 8.2. The most prominent groups in sources are fans of Myrmillones (*scutularii*) and of Thracians (*parmularii*); see Ville (1981) 443–5. On fans in the later Empire, see C. Roueché, *Performers and Partisans at Aphrodisias in the Roman and Late Roman Periods* (London: SPRS, 1992) esp. 79–80.

61 Suetonius, *Claud.* 21.5, says that Claudius granted freedom to a chariot-fighter (*essedarius*) when his four sons pleaded for his release. Fronto, *Ad M. Caes.* 1.8.2, Loeb, tells Marcus Aurelius that using oratory is 'doing the same as you do when, at the people's request, you honour or enfranchise those who have slain beasts manfully in the arena; criminals they may be or felons, yet you release them at the people's request'. See other examples in Plass (1995) n. 1 on 243.

62 E.g. Grant (1967) 96–7; Barton (1993) 48; Ville (1981) 303, 330–1, 344; Hopkins (1983) 21–3; Wiedemann (1992) 26; Gunderson (1996) 144–5.

63 Graffiti proclaiming gladiators' erotic powers: e.g. *CIL* 4.4289, 4342, and 4345; also 4.4353, 4356 (*ILS* 5142d), 8916, and 4397. Juvenal, 6.82–113, condemns such liaisons and feigns indignation about a noble woman, Eppia, taking off with the scarred gladiator Sergius. Messalina intervened to spare her defeated lover-gladiator against the wishes of Claudius and the crowd: Dio 60.28.2. Cf. Mart. 5.24.10: 'Hermes cura laborque ludiarum'. The professional names of some gladiators (e.g. Eros, Narcissus) are suggestive; see Robert (1940) 301 and his 'Monuments de gladiateurs dans l'orient grec', *Hell.* 8 (1950) 44–6. Hopkins (1983), 22, notes that *gladius* was slang for penis and that, according to Festus 55L s.v. *caelibari hasta*, it was customary for a new bride to have her hair parted with a spear, at best one which had been dipped 'in the blood of a defeated and killed gladiator'. Plass (1995), n. 2 on 206, suggests that

gladiatorial combats ritually reaffirmed communal vitality and that the instruments of violence acquired procreative potency. On the blood of gladiators as a potion, see ch. 6 below.

64 The skeleton of a rich woman with gold jewelry was found with some eighteen skeletons in the excavation of the armory of the gladiatorial barracks at Pompeii; see A. Mau, *Pompeii: Its Art and Life* (London: Macmillan, 1899) 157–8. E.g. Hopkins (1983) 23; Mitchell (1991) 166; Hönle and Henze (1981) 17–18; and Gunderson (1996) 143 use this to suggest the psychosexual appeal of gladiators. Even Wiedemann (1992), 115–16, suggests that she may have been the wife or lover of one of the gladiators. Perhaps, however, she was simply fleeing, took shelter, and was trapped by the ash storm. Richardson (1988), 85–6, noting the great number of skeletons, including those of children and even dogs, and the great amount of portable wealth found in the gladiatorial *ludus*, suggests that the site was used as an evacuation center.

65 At a wanton banquet arranged by Tigellinus as part of Nero's spectacles in AD 64 the masses were allowed to drink, eat, and debauch: slaves debauched mistresses (Dio 62.15.5, Loeb) 'and now a gladiator would debauch a girl of noble family before the eyes of her father'. Q. Curtius Rufus, possibly the historian of Alexander, was said to be the son of a gladiator: Tac. *Ann.* 11.21; Plin. *Ep.* 7.27.2. Cf. Plut. *Galb.* 9.2: the freedwoman mother of Nero's praetorian prefect, Nymphidius, was supposedly seduced by the gladiator Martinus and then married him for his fame. Cf. stories about Commodus below in ch. 7.

66 Mitchell (1991) 67–8, 74–80, 103–11, 138. As Mitchell, 74, says: 'The roughest, toughest and meanest man, the expert practitioner of violence, will always seem more attractive to the masses than a cultivated man-about-town or dandy ... In a land of servitude and dependence, the guapos embodied a much-valued air of personalized power and autonomy.'

67 Mitchell (1991) 57–67, 154–75, quote at 165. Mitchell, 53, points out that picadors, not matadors, are the popular villains of the bullring: the picador is 'the man most accused of being a butcher, an executioner, or something even more insulting'. Cf. Barton (1993) 65–6, 81 on the appeal of the forbidden.

68 Edmondson (1996), 96, suggests, from results at Pompeii, that senior gladiators were often spared when defeated by junior opponents because spectators respected fighters of higher status.

69 Suetonius, *Iul.* 26.2, Loeb, comments on Caesar's arrangements for a gladiatorial show for his daughter Julia: 'He gave orders too that whenever famous gladiators fought without winning the favour of the people, they should be rescued by force and kept for him.' The tale of Eppia and Sergius in Juvenal 6 (above in n. 63) suggests discharge, possibly for wounds.

70 Balsdon (1969), 301–2, suggests that few men fought more often than once a year, and cites *ILS* 5090, 5107, 5112–15. Wiedemann (1992), 120, assumes a minimum of two fights a year. Inscriptions: see Ville (1981) n. 211 on 320–1; and Wiedemann (1992) 121; both of whom cite *ILS* 5113 (= *CIL* 10.7297), from Sicily, recording that a certain Flamma died at 30 having fought thirty-four fights, including twenty-one wins, nine draws, and four defeats which he survived (*missus*).

71 Mart. *Spect.* 29.3 on Priscus and Verus; cf. 5.24.7, 'Hermes trained to win but not to kill (*vincere nec ferire doctus*).'

72 *CIL* 10.6012 = *ILS* 5062: *occidid(i) xi gla(diatores) prim(arios) Camp(aniae)*.

73 Gaius *Inst.* 3.146, cited in Lafaye (1896) 1576.

74 Cf. Minturnae above in n. 3. Results painted on walls at Pompeii: e.g. *CIL* 4.8055: the freedman Oceanus, who had won thirteen times, won; and the freedman Aracintus, who had won nine times, lost; *CIL* 4.8056: the freedman

112

Severus, who had won thirteen times, lost; and Albanus, a freedman of Scaurus, who had won nineteen times, won. As Balsdon (1969), 337–8, notes, an announcement of a gladiatorial show at Pompeii, *CIL* 4.2508, gave names and records of gladiators who were to fight, and later the results were added: three killed, six spared, nine victorious.

75 The best recent discussion of gladiators' chances of survival is in Wiedemann (1992) 119–22, with bibliography, who, 120, suggests by comparison that three out of five people at Rome died before they reached their twenties. For a discussion of the problems of estimating life expectancy from epigraphy, see K. Hopkins, 'Graveyards for Historians', 113–26; and Pierre Salmon, 'Les Insuffisances du matériel épigraphique sur la mortalité dans l'antiquité romaine', 99–112, both in Hinard (1987a). More broadly on trying to calculate life expectancy in the Roman Empire, see Parkin (1992) 71–8, 84, 92, who estimates the average life expectancy at birth of the Roman population as in the range of twenty to thirty years; those who survived to age 5 might on average live another forty years.

76 Ville (1981) 318–25; Clavel-Lévêque (1984a), n. 256 on 203, estimates the odds of survival as one in seven in the first century but worse later.

77 A *collegium* of retired gladiators in Rome is mentioned in the epitaph of a retired gladiator at Ancyra: *ILS* 7559; Robert (1940) 263 and no. 90. Wiedemann (1992), 118, also notes a reference to a *collegium* of *bestiarii* at Rome in *ILS* 5148.

78 Sen. *Ep.* 70.19: even 'men of the meanest lot (*vilissimae sortis*)', 22: even 'the most despised of men (*contemptissimis*)', 25: 'even the lowest class of slave', 26: 'abandoned and dangerous men (*perditi quodque noxiosi*)'. See Wistrand (1990) 39–40.

79 Seneca, *Ep.* 70.20, Loeb, sees the act as 'an insult to death', but Plass (1995), 106, feels that it was more likely one of despair than heroism.

80 Sen. *Ep.* 70.22–3; he was detained in a *ludus* but, as Ville (1981), n. 21 on 236, points out, he was a *damnatus ad bestias*. Cf. *Ep.* 70.26–7: a barbarian killed himself with the sword which he had been given to fight with in a naumachy.

81 Diodorus Siculus, 36.10.2–3 (noted above in n. 36), reports that in 100 BC captive rebel slaves from Sicily committed mass suicide at public altars at Rome to avoid being forced to do combat against beasts. In the late fourth century AD Symmachus, *Ep.* 2.46.2, notes that twenty-nine Saxons strangled each other rather than appear in his son's show. Van Hooff (1990), 16–17, discusses all these examples of suicides to avoid death in the arena; he notes Seneca's interest in advocating death before dishonor, but, as he says, 87, 'in the last resort all suicides are committed because hope has been lost'.

82 Sen. *Ep.* 4.37.1. Petron. *Sat.* 117.5–6, Loeb: Eumolpus' co-plotters swear a *sacramentum* to obey him 'to endure burning, bondage, flogging, death by the sword, or anything else that Eumolpus ordered. We pledged our bodies and souls to our master most solemnly (*religiosissime*), like regular gladiators (*tanquam legitimi gladiatores*).' Cf. Sen. *Ep.* 71.23; Juv. 11.5–8. Horace, *Sat.* 2.7.58–9, repeats the terms with reference to an *auctoratus*. On the public declaration, see below.

83 Barton (1994) 52; on the terminology, cf. Thome (1992) 86–7. As Barton (1993), 14–15, explains, one put one's life 'on deposit' with the gods of the underworld: n. 12 on 14: 'If one broke one's oath, one's honor and one's life were forfeit; one became *sacer* (sacred) and liable to execution as a *piaculum*, or expiatory sacrifice, to the offended gods.' On the oath, see Ville (1981) 246–9; Barton (1993) 14–17, with detailed notes, and other bibliography in Barton (1994) n. 66 on 66.

84 Barton (1994) 52–4; cf. her n. 82 on 68, on theories of sacrifice applied to gladiators. On the importance of volunteerism for turning slaughter into sacrifice, see Versnel (1981) esp. 145–8. Sacrifice always implies consecration, but the victim must not be forced to offer his neck or the spirit of the unwilling victim would seek vengeance. Such a sacrifice might threaten the community: see Henri Hubert and Marcel Mauss, *Sacrifice: Its Nature and Functions*, trans. W. D. Halls (Chicago: U. Chicago, 1964) 9, 30, 33, 79.

85 On *devotio* see above and Barton (1993) 40–6. Barton (1993), 15, notes, however, that, while the oath bound gladiators to the gods, unlike the *devotio* of a general or the oath of a soldier or martyr, nothing was demanded or guaranteed in return. Similarly on *devotio*: Barton (1994) 53–4. See cautionary points below on *auctoramentum* versus *sacramentum*.

86 The Aes Italica of around AD 177 states that an *auctoratus* had to announce his intention to fight before the Tribune of the Plebs; *auctorati* began at a legal price set at 2,000 HS, but if they reentered the profession after being released, they could earn up to 12,000 HS (I 62–3). Also, I 60 mentions the use of *auctorati* as well as normal gladiators by provincial priests. Robert (1940), 32–3, 267, reconstructs the procedure: a volunteer gave his name to a *munerarius*, his age and physical ability were checked, and, if he was accepted, a contract was made and the oath taken. Further on *auctorati*, see Ville (1981) 246–55; Wiedemann (1992) 106–9.

87 Bloodlust: e.g. Tert. *Ad Mart.* 5.1 (men of privilege become gladiators or fight beasts); Manil. *Astron.* 4.225. Profit: e.g. Tiberius persuaded some retired gladiators to appear by paying them 100,000 HS each: Suet. *Tib.* 7.1. Financial pressures: see Balsdon (1969) 289–90; Wiedemann (1992) 108.

88 E.g. Hor. *Epist.* 1.18.36; Sen. *Ep.* 19.13; Juv. 11.8–9, 19–20. Juvenal, 8.183–210, condemns nobles who voluntarily debased themselves as actors and gladiators in the praetor's games; particularly scandalous is the participation of a Gracchus (8.199–210) as a *retiarius*, thus helmetless and recognizable to all – and a cowardly one at that, who shames his opponent by fleeing.

89 Barton (1993) 35. On the literary condemnation of prodigals, usually children of the rich who squandered inherited resources, who sometimes became gladiators and ruined their reputations by their public degradation, see Edwards (1993) 178–80. Lucian, *Toxaris* 57–60, tells a romantic tale of a Scythian, robbed and penniless, who in a theater, after a *venatio* and the execution of criminals in chains (see figure 3), accepted an open challenge to duel against a gladiator for money. He received the sum before the fight and asked his friend to bury him if killed; although wounded he won and was dismissed. See M. Kokolakis, 'Gladiatorial Games and Animal Baiting in Lucian', *Platon* 10 (1958) 333–44.

90 Barton (1993) 15–17, unique: n. 13 on 15. Lafaye (1896), 1574–5, distinguishes the *auctoramentum*, as a legal contractual declaration, from the traditional oath; see further in Antonio Guarino, 'I *gladiatores* et l'*auctoramentum*', *Labeo* 29 (1983) 7–28.

91 Cicero, *Fam.* 10.32.3, from Asinius Pollio, says that as quaestor in Spain in 43 BC Balbus forced a captured Pompeian soldier named Fadius into a gladiatorial *ludus*; he won two combats without pay (*gratis*), but when he refused to take the oath (*auctorare sese*) Balbus had him burned to death. Barbara Levick, 'The *Senatus Consultum* from Larinum', *JRS* 73 (1983) 97–115 at 110, feels that the crucial distinction is that the fighter refused to enter a contract and accept pay as a gladiator. Cf. Ville (1981) n. 9 on 230–1.

92 See Robert (1940) 285–97, esp. 285–7, who suggests that monuments and epitaphs mentioning wives indicate that these buried gladiators were free; but cf. Ville (1981) 240–6.

114

93 Ville (1981) 227, 255. Incomplete inscriptions of two gladiatorial *familiae* at Venusia, *ILS* 5083/5083a (= *CIL* 9.465–6), show eighteen slaves and nine or ten recruits or apparently free men. Wiedemann (1992), 107, contrasts this with *ILS* 5084, the list of thirty-two members, all slaves, of an association of imperial gladiators of AD 177 dedicated to Silvanus (noted above in n. 51). Cf. *familiae* in *ILS* 5060, 6296.

94 Famous references to women in the arena include: Mart. *Spect.* 5; Tac. *Ann.* 15.32; Suet. *Ner.* 12.2, *Dom.* 4.2; Juv. 1.22–3, 6.246–7, 265–7; cf. Ville (1981) 263; Levick (1983) 99, 106–7; Balsdon (1969) 290–1; Wiedemann (1992) 112. On the arena's appeal for women: Barton (1993) 26, 66.

95 Wiedemann (1992), 102, feels that free volunteers are overemphasized 'precisely because they were unusual'. Hornum (1993), n. 27 on 86, comments: 'At any rate, even if the freeborn combatants were as numerous as the slaves, this does not negate the games as a context for punishment of insolent slaves, criminals and prisoners of war, both in the outright executions and in the combats.'

96 Owners could not force manumitted gladiators back into combat: *Dig.* 38.1.38 (Callistratus); cited in Wiedemann (1992) 122. Nevertheless, a retired gladiator (*rudiarius*) might fight again: Tert. *De spect.* 21; Suet. *Tib.* 7.1 (noted above in n. 87); Ovid *Tr.* 2.17.

97 Barton (1993), 27–9, 36–8, 46, sees volunteering as a compensatory reaction to the world of inescapable degradation in the Civil War era, but the Gracchan legislation shows *auctorati* earlier: the Acilian Law excludes from equestrian extortion juries anyone who has or shall have contracted himself and fought for pay; Johnson et al. (1961) Doc. 45.6,8; Wiedemann (1992) 29. Citing two Atellan farces of uncertain date (perhaps of the second century) entitled *Pomponius auctoratus* and *Bucco auctoratus*, and also Cic. *Orat.* 3.86 citing Lucilius' mid-second-century reference to a Q. Velocius who fought as a Samnite as a boy, Wiedemann (1992), 109, suggests that *auctorati* existed by the second century BC and included some equestrians and even senators by the first century BC.

98 *Tusc.* 2.41; on the passage, see Barton (1993) n. 38 on 22; Wistrand (1992) 77–8. Commenting on Scipio's gladiatorial show at New Carthage in 206 BC in honor of his dead father and uncle, Livy, 28.21.2, Loeb, contrasts the participants with the gladiators of his own day: 'The exhibition of gladiators was not made up from the class of men which managers are in the habit of pitting against each other, that is, slaves sold to the platform and free men who are ready to sell their lives. In every case the service of the men who fought was voluntary and without compensation.' Note that the fighters were Celtiberians; some were sent by their tribal chiefs as examples of native valor, while some came to settle personal disputes or rivalries.

99 Edmondson (1996) 83, but see his qualification on this below; Wiedemann (1992) 28–30, quote at 29. Wiedemann notes that *Dig.* 38.1.37pr. (Paulus) (an edition of the Julian Papian laws) denies to 'those who hired themselves out to fight in the arena' the usual right of freedmen with two legitimate children born in freedom to be exempt from further economic obligation to their former owners.

100 When Glabrio, a consul in AD 91, aroused the anger and jealousy of Domitian for his prowess in the arena, the emperor, ironically, could justify having him put to death, in part, for the crime of fighting against beasts: Dio 67.14.3.

101 Dio 43.23.5: knights in single combat in Caesar's games of 46 BC; Suet. *Iul.* 39.1: senators too.

102 See Edmondson (1996) 104, 106–8, citing *Dig.* 3.1.1.6, 3.2.2.5 and recent

scholarship. Similarly, Gunderson (1996), 136–42, explains that, despite prohibitions, members of the elite might be drawn to perform in the arena to demonstrate military virtue; it was important that upper-class combatants fought for glory and not money, and their fights were probably not to the death. When two knights fought in Drusus' games in AD 15 and one was killed, Tiberius forbade the killer ever to fight again: Dio 57.14.3. In 29 BC the senator Quintus Vitellius fought in the arena in Octavian's show for the dedication of the Temple of Caesar: Dio 51.22.4; cf. 53.1.4. Cf. testimonia on *munera pro salute* in Hornum (1993) 82–3. Dio, 56.25.8, says that equestrian gladiators' fights were eagerly watched, even by Augustus and praetors in charge of the events.

103 On the decrees, and on the elite in the arena, prohibited but sometimes allowed or forced, see Levick (1983) 97–115; W. D. Lebek, 'Standeswürde und Berufsverbot unter Tiberius: Das SC der Tabula Larinas', *ZPE* 81 (1990) 37–96; Ville (1981) 246–70; Barton (1993) 25–7. Earlier prohibitions threatened offenders with *atimia* (loss of elite rights but not of citizenship), but the *consultum* of AD 19 perhaps went further; see ch. 4. Newbold (1975), n. 10 on 591–2, lists testimonia in Dio concerning twenty instances of men or women of the senatorial or equestrian ranks appearing, sometimes under the emperor's compulsion, in public performances.

104 There was also a ban against free females under 20 or free males under 25 pledging themselves as gladiators (*auctorare*), unless so consigned by Augustus or Tiberius (lines 17–18).

105 Dio, 48.43.3, mentions a law of 38 BC prohibiting any senator from fighting as a gladiator. The condemnation of men who compromised their freedom and voluntarily worked for wages was an ancient literary commonplace; see M. I. Finley, *The Ancient Economy* (Berkeley: U. California, 1973) 65–9, 73–6.

106 The phenomenon persisted. Vitellius forbade the practice again: Tac. *Hist.* 2.62; SHA *Marc.* 12.3 records a senator's remark that many praetors had fought in the arena. Wiedemann (1992), 110–11, notes that various emperors underwent instruction in gladiatorial weapons as youths, but these should not be confused with professional gladiators.

107 Suet. *Ner.* 12.1: in AD 58 Nero made 400 senators and 600 knights fight and perform in the arena. Dio 59.10.1–4, Loeb, notes that Caligula forced many men to fight as gladiators, 'and thus put many people to death, among others twenty-six knights, some of whom had devoured their living, while others had merely practised gladiatorial combat'. Cf. Yavetz (1988) 114–15, on the crowd's appreciation of the forced debasement of members of the elite by emperors. On emperors who forced spectators into the arena, see ch. 7 below.

108 Pliny, *Pan.* 81.1–3, trans. Anderson (1985) 101–2, applauds native hunting traditions, saying that once hunting was training for youths and future generals, an honorable way to keep wild beasts from the fields and to assist farmers. He praises Trajan for hunting alone in the wild, for expending effort and enjoying the chase as much as the kill; and he contrasts Trajan's hunting with Domitian's mere slaughtering of tamed beasts brought to him. Cf. Dio Chrys. *Or.* 3.135–7. Further on Hadrian and hunting: Aymard (1951) 523–36.

109 Suet. *Dom.* 19; Aymard (1951) 194. In AD 66 when Nero tried to impress him with a show at Pozzuoli, Tiridates of Armenia from his seat shot and killed bulls and other beasts with arrows: Dio 62(63)3.2. According to Suetonius, *Ner.* 53, Nero planned to pretend to be Hercules: he had a lion trained so that he could kill it in the arena with a club or by strangling it.

110 Estate: SHA *Comm.* 8.5, Loeb: 'He was also called the Roman Hercules, on

the ground that he had killed wild beasts in the amphitheater at Lanuvium; and, indeed, it was his custom to kill wild beasts on his own estate.' In arena: SHA *Comm.* 12.12, Loeb: 'He also killed with his own hand thousands of wild beasts of all kinds, even elephants. And he frequently did these things before the eyes of the Roman people.' Dio 73(72).10.3, Loeb: 'all alone with his own hands, he dispatched five hippopotami together with two elephants on two successive days; and he also killed rhinoceroses and a camelopard'. Dio 73(72).19.1: he entered the arena to kill domestic animals brought to him.

111 Dio 73(72).18.1. Dio explains that the arena was divided into four quadrants so that Commodus could spear the beasts more easily at close range. Herodian, 1.15.1–4, sees Commodus as a hunter with talent but not courage, and he reports, 1.15.5, suspicious claims about Commodus' skill – that he decapitated ostriches in full stride with arrows with curved tips, that he used a spear to save a *venator* from a leopard, or that he killed a hundred lions with a hundred shots. Cf. claims about the 'sporting Pharaohs' of the eighteenth dynasty in Decker (1992) 154–62.

112 On Commodus and other emperors as gladiators, see ch. 7 below. Anderson (1985), n. 10 on 171, seeing 'no reality behind the symbolism', rejects Aymard's attempts, (1951) 537–58, to present Commodus' hunts as symbols of virtue. As Anderson comments, 148, using Amm. Marc. 31.10.18–20, when Gratian (AD 375–83) later killed beasts in public he reminded army officers of Commodus: 'the Romans, though they expected their leaders to possess the manly qualities of the hunter, and also to provide for the destruction of wild beasts as a public spectacle, preferred the emperor himself to hunt like a gentleman, not like a circus performer'.

113 As Edmondson (1996), 96–7, explains, even types of executions reflected a social hierarchy: decapitation by the sword was less demeaning than death by crucifixion or fire, which were less demeaning than being thrown to the beasts. As he says: 'The normal result was death in all cases, but the niceties of social stratification had to be preserved even in death. Stratification provided structure even in the deracinated world, the demi-monde, of those who performed in the arena.'

114 On executions in the arena, see Ville (1981) 235–8; Wiedemann (1992) 68–97. Like announcements at Pompeii (e.g. *ILS* 5063/5063a), Apuleius, *Met.* 4.13, distinguishes *noxii* from gladiators and *venatores* in listing preparations for a *munus* in Greece. Suetonius, *Ner.* 12.1, notes that in a gladiatorial show in Nero's amphitheater no one was allowed to be killed, 'not even *noxii*'. Balsdon (1969), 288–9, sees two classes of gladiators, those with and those without hope of surviving: 'For gladiators proper – the criminals condemned to death hardly deserve the title – there was hope, however slender.' Similarly, Lafaye (1896), 1573, calls the modern application of the name gladiator to all *damnati ad gladium* an 'abuse of language'.

115 Bauman (1996) 158 and n. 36 on 203, on Ulpian, *Collatio leg. Mos.* 11.7.4, clarifies the distinction: a sentence of *ad gladium* meant certain death within a year, but *ludi damnatio* did not necessarily mean certain death, for those sentenced to the games might in time be restored to freedom or be released from the games. As Bauman suggests, Ulpian was probably referring only to gladiatorial games.

116 Cf. Suet. *Claud.* 25.2 concerning masters who killed slaves rather than abandoning them on the Tiber Island. Although Antoninus Pius forbade the deliberate killing, cruel punishment, and obscene abuse of one's own slaves, masters still had the right to punish their own slaves. Constantine forbade

117

killing one's own slave but did not penalize accidental death caused by normal punishment. See Alan Watson, *Roman Slave Law* (Baltimore: Johns Hopkins U., 1987) ch. 8, 'The Punishment of the Slave', 115–33; Robinson (1995) 43–5; Robinson, 'Slaves and the Criminal Law', *ZRG* 98 (1981) 213–54; Wiedemann (1992) 73–7.

117 *Dig.* 48.8.11.1–2, Modestinus 6 *reg.*; cf. Apion in Gell. *NA* 5.14.27; see Robinson (1995) 43. SHA *Hadr.* 18.7–9; cf. *Dig.* 11.4.5: Hadrian forbade masters to kill slaves or to sell them to *lanistae* without giving a reason.

118 Torturing of slaves was common in legal interrogations, and in the famous case of the death of the urban prefect in AD 61 (Tac. *Ann.* 14.42–5) all the household slaves were executed for failing to defend their owner at the risk of their own lives. See ch. 5 below on punishment of slaves at Puteoli.

119 As Lintott (1968), 49, says, Romans could be callous and indifferent to physical suffering – especially of beings regarded as inferior; and, 42, 'A captured enemy had, of course, neither status nor rights.' Brown (1992), esp. 186, 207–8, explains that mosaics emphasize the emotional distance between empowered viewers and viewed, the distance of patron and audience from 'legitimate victims of institutionalized violence'. On attitudes in law, see below. Wiedemann (1992), 146–50, explains that Christian critics focus on the viewers or producers, not on the pagan victims; they were not against the cruelty of the games or executions as institutions.

120 On the passage see Wistrand (1990) 35–7, and his conclusion, 42, that Seneca 'is for the death penalty and advocates public executions as terrifying warnings to enhance the respect for law. He criticizes executions that aim at nothing else but satisfying the sadistic demands of the spectators to be entertained.' Wistrand (1992), 16–20, reiterates his proper interpretation of Seneca's attitudes.

121 As the Magerius mosaic from Smirat in Tunisia clearly shows, the point was to honor the editor of the games: Dunbabin (1978) 85; Brown (1992) 198–200. SHA *Aurel.* 37.2 notes that a conspirator involved in the murder of Aurelian near Constantinople was tied to a stake and exposed to beasts, and marble statues showing the execution were established along with other statues honoring Aurelian. Depictions of spectacular executions of *noxii* in art are neither rare nor sympathetic: see Brown, esp. 185, 194–7; Potter (1993) 66–9; Vismara (1990) esp. 42–60; idem, 'Sangue e arena: Iconografie di supplizi in margine a: *Du châtiment dans la cité*, *DArch* 5.2 (1987) 135–55; and H. Leclerq, 'Ad Bestias', Cabrol-Leclerq, *Dict. d'arch. chrétienne* 1 (1907) figs 88, 91–2. On terracotta vases: G. Lafaye, 'Criminels livrés aux bêtes', *Mémoires de la Société Nationale des Antiquaires de France* (1893) 97–116; M. Pottier, 'Sur quelques documents céramiques du musée du Louvre', *CR Acad. Inscr.* (1913) 444–7. From near Sousse in Tunisia and now in the Louvre (CA 2613), a terracotta depicts a woman on a bull attacked by a leopard, with a male figure in front (see figure 4); ill. in Wiedemann (1992) fig. 7; Vismara (1987) 141–2, fig. 10. Reliefs with *noxii*, e.g. from Sardis, Ephesus, Smyrna, should not be misinterpreted as gravestones: Lafaye (1914) 707–8; Robert (1940) 90–2 and pl. 24 (reliefs from Sardis), and several of his articles in *Hell.*, e.g. 3 (1946) pl. 12; 7 (1949) 141–5, pl. 22.2; 12 (1954) pl. 23.2. Worthy of note, a relief from Hierapolis depicts three chained prisoners (see figure 3), one of whom is identified as Appas, presumably to declare the removal of a notorious criminal; Robert, *Hell.* 8 (1950) 72, pl. 24. Potter (1996), 153, suggests that this naming of a prisoner is apparently unique in known execution monuments.

122 Brown (1992) 194–6, fig. 9.5; cf. S. Aurigemma, *I mosaici di Zliten*, Africa italiana II (Rome: Società editrice d'arte illustra, 1926) 180–97. Aurigemma,

244–8, dates this to the Flavian era, but Dunbabin (1978), 235–7, suggests the late first or very early second century; D. Parish, 'The Date of the Mosaic from Zliten', *Ant. af.* 21 (1985) 137–8, prefers a third-century date. On whether the victims were Garamantes who attacked the frontier in AD 70, see Aurigemma (1926) 269–78, but cf. Dunbabin (1978) 235–6.

123 Brown (1992) 196–7, fig. 9.6; Dunbabin (1978) 66–7, pls. 50–1; Coleman (1990) 54, pl. II (Zliten), III (El Djem). See below: ch. 6 (on *ad bestias*), chs. 5 and 8 (on procedures).

124 On commodification, Clavel-Lévêque (1984b), 194–6, cites Josephus as an example of the empire-wide supply of slaves and captives for arenas. Josephus, *BJ* 7.23–4, 37–8, 40, 96, also notes Titus' use of Jewish captives as gladiators and as *damnati ad bestias* in shows at Caesarea, Berytus, and elsewhere in the East. Coleman (1990), 54–7, also discusses Rome's supply of 'dispensable' criminals and captives; 54: 'prisoners-of-war, no less than captured beasts, are among the spoils of empire that can be displayed as proof of the success of the imperial venture, and to entertain loyal subjects'. Coleman, 63: 'from the Roman point of view, a condemned criminal was a commodity whose punishment might fulfil a social need'.

125 *Dig.* 48.19.31pr. (Modestinus) ('sed ei eius roboris vel artificii sunt, ut digne populo Romano exhiberi possint'), cited by Hopkins (1983) 10; Ville (1981) n. 24 on 238. Millar (1992), 194, suggests that condemnation to the beasts or *ludus* 'no doubt [owed] something to the need of the emperors for a ready supply of victims'. *Dig.* 48.19.29 (Gaius): delays in executions *ad bestias* were allowed (i.e. for preparations for shows). Pliny, *Ep.* 10.31.2, mentions men sentenced to the mines and arena (*in ludum*) who had improperly become public slaves.

126 Of course, Romans were hardly unique in their inhumanity to criminals and the dregs of society. In third-century BC Alexandria vivisection was supposedly performed on criminals provided from prison by the kings: Celsus *Med.* 1, Proem 26; Tert. *De anim.* 10.30; see L. Edelstein, *Ancient Medicine* (Baltimore: Johns Hopkins U., 1967) 249–50; J. T. Vallence, 'Vivisection', *OCD*[3] (1996) 1610. In Britain the Anatomy Act of 1832 ordered that unclaimed bodies of those who died in workhouses were to be made available for dissection. See Ruth Richardson, *Death, Dissection and the Destitute* (London: Routledge, 1988), on this and other ways in which rituals of death reflect tensions between rich and poor.

127 Prices: cf. below. *Damnati* not sent to Rome were sold locally for shows: Apul. *Met.* 10.23: a murderess was bought by her owner from a prefect to mate with an ass in the arena. Conditions of purchase and time limit: Paulus *Sent.* 5.17.3; cf. Balsdon (1969) 288–9; Wiedemann (1992) 77, n. 55 on 99.

128 Androcles: Gell. *NA* 5.14.29–30; Ael. *NA* 7.48. Cf. Jennison (1937) 68; Ville (1981) 115–16, 238–9; Wiedemann (1992) 75, 78, 89, 167. Seneca, *Ben.* 2.19.1, tells a similar tale of a *bestiarius*, formerly a kindly animalkeeper, exposed to beasts in the arena: a lion recognized him as a friend and saved his life by joining him against the other beasts. Apuleius, *Met.* 4.13, however, shows that criminals condemned to the beasts were to have no chance of reprieve.

129 H. J. Leon, 'Morituri Te Salutamus', *TAPA* 70 (1939) 46–50. Coleman (1993), 73, avoids calling naumachies 'mock' naval battles 'because, although these conflicts were not taking place in an actual theater of war, they were in grim · earnest in the sense that people were meant to get killed'. Land battles: e.g. Domitian's mass battle at the Circus Maximus in AD 89, probably with Dacian prisoners of war: Dio 67.8.2; Claudius staged the conquest of a British

town in the Campus Martius, probably with British prisoners of war: Suet. *Claud.* 21.6. With references to the naumachies of Caesar, Claudius, and Nero, Coleman (1993), 67, suggests that it was standard practice to use prisoners of war and condemned criminals in naumachies. Dio, 48.19.1, specifies that Sextus Pompey used prisoners of war for a fight to the death in his naumachy in the sea off Sicily in 40 BC. Josephus, *AJ* 19.7.5 (trans. W. Whiston), says that Herod Agrippa commemorated the new amphitheater at Berytus with a combat between two armies of 700 men each, using up all the condemned men he had and having them all killed at once: 'that both the malefactors might receive their punishment, and that this operation of war might be a recreation in peace'.

130 This was a battle between Sicilians and Rhodians using 19,000 men and probably 100 warships: Tac. *Ann.* 12.56; Suet. *Claud.* 21.6. Dio, 61(60).33.3–4, records the event with *aspazometha*. Coleman (1993), 70–1, sees the naumachy as 'effectively an extension *en masse* of the gladiatorial duel, and thus a form of "indirect" death penalty'; but she notes that Claudius intended 'that there be massive casualties' and that in Domitian's naumachy 'virtually everyone perished' (Dio 67.8.2).

131 After an interval of some time a second spectacle was held, and this time a show of gladiators fought an infantry battle on floating platforms: Tac. *Ann.* 12.57.1.

132 Leon (1939) 50. Plass (1995), n. 1 on 243, here sees a 'second game of clemency within the primary game'.

133 On *trinqui* and Christians, see ch. 8 below. M. Aurelius personally had reservations about spectacles, especially blood sports. *Med.* 1.5: Aurelius was praised as a youth by his tutor for not being a partisan of the Greens or Blues any more than a member of groups of gladiatorial fans. *Med.* 6.46: amphitheater shows were repetitive and tedious. Dio 72(71).29.3–4: he was against such bloodshed and watched gladiators only with blunted weapons, and tried to control their expenses. SHA *Marc.* 11.4: he was careful about public expenditures and 'limited gladiatorial shows in every way', but he acknowledged their importance and arranged them. SHA *Marc.* 23.4–5, Loeb; also 17.7: 'And while absent from Rome he left forceful instructions that the amusements of the Roman people should be provided by the richest givers of public spectacles, because, when he took the gladiators away to the war, there was talk among the people that he intended to deprive them of their amusements and thereby drive them to the study of philosophy.' Cf. Sabine Schmidt, 'Mark Aurel und Spectacula', *Stadion* 10 (1984) 21–43.

134 Millar (1992), 195, suggests that the emperors deprived the *fiscus* of incomes not in the sense of removing all taxes on the sale of gladiators – the usual interpretation – but rather only in the sense of reducing the prices allowed and thus reducing taxes and the profits of the *lanistae*.

135 Economy: SHA *Marc.* 21.6–9; cf. 23.5, which says that, because of pressures on the frontier and the economy, the emperor trained slave volunteers for military service (21.6, cf. above on Cannae in ch. 2), turned gladiators (the *Obsequentes* or Compliant Ones) and bandits into soldiers, and auctioned off palace furnishings to raise funds. With the best fighters recruited for war, he had to resort to *noxii* more and more for spectacles. Wiedemann (1992), 134–5, feels that Aurelius' moral arguments mask fiscal motives, i.e. aiding provincial notables and demonstrating the need for fiscal retrenchment.

136 What follows is largely based on Robinson (1995); Bauman (1996); Nippel (1995); Garnsey (1970); Cantarella (1991); Ville (1981) 232–40; Crook (1984); MacMullen (1986a) and (1986b); articles in *Châtiment* (1984); W. Kunkel,

An Introduction to Roman Legal and Constitutional History, trans. J. M. Kelly (Oxford: Clarendon Press, 1966); and Berger (1953).

137 Coleman (1990), 44–9, surveys Rome's penal aims in comparison with modern attitudes, noting the prominence of retribution (the principle of *talio*), humiliation, and deterrence (of potential offenders; cf. *Dig.* 48.19.15.20) rather than correction or prevention (e.g. via incarceration). Rome sought to achieve such aims via aggravated executions in public settings before audiences, as in arena punishments. Similarly, Bauman (1996), 38–42, 80–2, 161–4, 156–9, shows that Romans, both the masses and the intellectuals, saw punishments as *exempla* (Gell. *NA* 7.14.4) – a form of deterrence (*poenae metus*) in the interest of the community (*utilitas publica*). E.g. in the preamble to his Edict on Prices (*ILS* 642 = *CIL* 3.2.824ff.; Johnson et al. (1961) no. 299) Diocletian justifies the death penalty for infractions by saying that from the time of early Rome penalties and fear have been the best way to guide people to act properly. Cf. Plut. *Mor.* 561c–d on the idea that public punishments and executions deter crime and restore order to the community.

138 Robinson (1995) 15: 'Equality before the law was not a Roman concept.' MacMullen (1986a), 147, declares that 'Among Romans everything depended on status.' He cites Callistratus, in *Dig.* 48.19.28.16: 'Our ancestors in every sort of sentence dealt more harshly with slaves than with freeborn and with men of ill repute than those of good repute.'

139 Pliny, *Ep.* 9.5, warning that equal treatment is unfair, applauds the provincial administration of Calestius Tiro for preserving distinctions of class and rank. As Garnsey (1970), 1, notes from Gell. *NA* 7.14.3, punishment justifiably sought 'the preservation of honour, when the dignity and prestige of the injured party must be protected, lest, if the offence is allowed to go by without punishment, he be brought into contempt and his honour be impaired'. Ulpian, *Dig.* 48.19.9.11, declared that there were different penalties and that not all men should suffer the same penalties.

140 See W. K. Lacey, '*Patria Potestas*', 121–45, in Beryl Rawson, ed., *The Family in Ancient Rome* (Ithaca: Cornell U., 1986); Y. P. Thomas, '*Vitae necisque potestas: le père, la cité, la mort*', in *Châtiment* (1984) 499–548.

141 On the development of the judicial systems: Bauman (1996) 9–34, 50–64; Robinson (1995) 1–14; Garnsey (1970) 153–72; Kunkel (1966) 60–71.

142 On exile and interdiction from fire and water as legal options, see Bauman (1996) 12, 14–18, 26–30; Garnsey (1970) 118–21.

143 Garnsey (1970) 5–6, 13–100, and his 'Why Penalties Became Harsher: The Roman Case, Late Republic to Fourth-Century Empire', *Natural Law Forum* 13 (1968) 141–62 at 157. *Dig.* 48.19.13: judges imposed any sentence they wished 'within the limits defined by reason'. However, Bauman (1996), 136–9, cautions that a judge's discretion was limited by any specific statements of penalties in imperial rescripts.

144 E.g. Suet. *Claud.* 14, Loeb, says that as a judge Claudius changed punishments if he thought them too lenient or severe: 'overstepping the lawful penalty, he condemned to the wild beasts those who were convicted of especially heinous crimes'. Cf. Bauman (1996) 70–6, on Claudius' undeserved reputation for cruelty and inconsistency as a judge.

145 Garnsey's (1970) study of discrimation and the dual-penalty system discusses forms of corporal and capital punishment; but Bauman's recent study, (1996) 124–36, qualifies Garnsey on points and in tone. E.g. Garnsey, 103–4, 221–79, feels that severe penalties originally intended for and reserved for slaves and aliens became applied equally to common citizens; but Bauman, 133–6, rejects the idea of a significant coalescence of slave and free penalties under the

Principate. Finding the evidence for an assimilation of the status of slave and *humilior* inadequate, Bauman concludes, 140, that equalization of penalties for slave and lowly free criminals is 'largely a myth'. Also, Garnsey (1970), 153–72, argues that the dual penalty system did not first emerge around the time of Hadrian, as many works suggest, on the basis of *Dig.* 48.19.15. Garnsey, 171–2, holds that the imperial constitutions did not create the dual system; they just confirmed earlier privileges of status. Bauman, 124–7, however, feels that significant penal differentiation by status was not a major factor until the second century and was significantly entrenched under the Severans.

146 E.g. for various crimes classed as homicide the original penalty had been deportation and forfeiture of property, but in the classical period the penalty was death for the better classes and crucifixion or the beasts for lower classes: Paulus *Sent.* 5.23.1–2. Penalties for sedition similarly varied by rank from deportation to an island to crucifixion and the beasts: Paulus *Sent.* 5.22.1; cf. 5.26.2; see Robinson (1995) 43, 46, 80. On parricide see ch. 7 below; on treason, see below.

147 As in the case of the Catilinarians (Cic. *Cat.* 4.10), however, citizens could lose their right of appeal and trial by acting manifestly as enemies of Rome; see Bauman (1996) 45–8.

148 See Robinson (1995) 12–13 on appeals and safeguards against abuses.

149 See excellent summaries in Robinson (1995) 74–8; Crook (1984) 252–5; Erich S. Gruen, *Roman Politics and the Criminal Courts, 149–78 BC* (Cambridge, Mass.: Harvard U., 1968) 259–60; Barbara Levick, *Tiberius the Politician* (London: Thames and Hudson, 1976) 180–200; A. W. Lintott and J. P. V. D. Balsdon, 'Maiestas', *OCD³* 913–14. In detail, see Bauman (1996) passim, R. Bauman, *The Crimen Maiestatis in the Roman Republic and Augustan Principate* (Johannesburg: Witwatersrand U., 1967), R. Bauman, *Impietas in Principem: A Study of Treason against the Roman Emperor with Special Reference to the First Century AD* (Munich: Beck, 1974). Introduction in 246 BC: see Bauman (1967) 28–9, (1996) 13.

150 Cic. *Inv. rhet.* 2.17.53: 'Maiestatem minuere est de dignitate aut amplitudine aut potestate populi aut eorum quibus populus potestatem dedit aliquid derogare.' E.g. anyone who abused, hurt, or killed a plebeian tribune was accursed and his property was consecrated to Ceres: Dion. Hal. *Ant. Rom.* 6.89.3. Dio 44.6.2: when Caesar was granted the sanctity of a tribune anyone who insulted him by deed or word was to be declared 'an outlaw and accursed'.

151 Robinson (1995) 49–51; Crook (1984) 250; Ramsay MacMullen, *Enemies of the Roman Order: Treason. Unrest and Alienation in the Empire* (Cambridge, Mass.: Harvard U., 1966) 35–8 (on writers), 131–3 (on magic, divination, and astrology). On the role of the emperor as judge, especially concerning treason, see Millar (1992) 516–27.

152 As a member of the Second Triumvirate Augustus had a suspected traitor, a praetor with a tablet under his toga, seized and executed: Suet. *Aug.* 27.4.

153 Sen. *Ben.* 3.26.1, Loeb. Suet. *Tib.* 58, Loeb, claims that Tiberius condemned a man for removing the head of a statue of Augustus to replace it with that of another, and that it was treason to beat a slave or to change one's clothes near a statue of Augustus, or 'to carry a ring or coin stamped with his image into a privy or brothel, or to criticize any word or act of his'. Aelius Saturninus was thrown off the Tarpeian Rock in AD 23 for his poems: Dio 57.22.5; and Sextius Paconianus was strangled in prison for a lampoon: Tac. *Ann.* 6.3.4, 6.39.1. Tacitus, *Ann.* 3.49–3.51.1, writes that the knight Caius Lutorius Priscus, charged by an informer, was convicted by the senate in AD 21 and

immediately executed for a poem slightly insulting to Tiberius; cf. Dio 57.20.3. On such incidents, now see the balanced account in Bauman (1996) 58–64, who qualifies the image of Tiberius in Tacitus, explaining exaggerations concerning punishments for words and poems, and noting the role of the senate, the detrimental influence of Sejanus, and the increase of abuses in Tiberius' later years. Bauman feels Tiberius should largely be exonerated but admits that the potential for abuses did increase. On Tiberius and treason, see further below in ch. 7.

154 E.g. Dio, 58, frag. 2, Loeb, says that Tiberius put to death a man of consular rank for carrying a coin with the emperor's image while he used a latrine; cf. previous note on Suet. *Tib.* 58. Seneca, *Ben.* 3.26.1–2, tells a story that a praetorian named Paulus escaped the trap of a notorious informer and was saved from charges of treason when his slave stopped him from relieving himself at a banquet while wearing a portrait ring of Tiberius; noted by Levick (1976) 194. Cf. Suet. *Poet.* (*Vita Luc.*), Loeb, pp. 502–3: when Lucan recited a verse by Nero while relieving himself in a public latrine the other occupants fled, apparently afraid of being associated with treason. On the story that Titius Sabinus was executed in AD 28 when agents got him to cast aspersions on the imperial regime and his words were recorded by eavesdroppers, see Bauman (1996) 62 and n. 59 on 179. Epictetus, *Diss.* 4.13.5, suggests that Rome's secret police in plain clothes apparently tricked commoners into seditious statements and then led them away in chains to execution. On secret police: MacMullen (1966) 164–5; W. G. Sinnigen, 'The Roman Secret Service', *CJ* 57 (1961) 65–72.

155 Domitian saw non-support of his favorite Thracian gladiators as treason; see Bauman (1974) 163–5. Suetonius, *Dom.* 10.1, says that when a spectator criticized Domitian's biased supervision of matches, the emperor had him dragged into the arena, forced to wear a placard declaring that he was a fan of Thracians and spoke ill of the emperor, and then had him torn to pieces by dogs. Cf. Plin. *Pan.* 33.4, trans. and cited in Bartsch (1994) 32:

> How open now are the enthusiasms of the spectators, how carefree their applause! No one is charged with treason for hating a gladiator, as used to happen; no one is transformed from spectator into spectacle and atones for his wretched pleasures with hook and flames. Domitian was a madman and ignorant of true honor, who gathered charges of treason in the arena and thought he was being looked down on and despised unless we venerated his gladiators too.

Note that Suetonius, earlier in *Dom.* 10.1, adds that when Domitian killed Hermogenes of Tarsus for allusions in his *History*, he also had the scribes who wrote out the work crucified.

156 On accusers and rewards, see Robinson (1995) 78, 99–101, and n. 126 on 153 with testimonia (e.g. Tac. *Ann.* 3.37, 4.31); and Bauman (1996) 109, n. 43 on 178. Bauman, 61, 69, feels that the account in Tacitus, *Ann.* 4.29.1–2, of a mob threatening a failed accuser with the dungeon, the Rock, and the sack, is an example of black comedy.

157 As noted by Coleman (1990) 46, Seneca, *Clem.* 1.20.1, says that the emperors' chief motivations in punishment of crimes were retribution and revenge. Peters (1985), 6–7, observes that even modern states with great resources and centralized power structures paradoxically feel very vulnerable to foreign and domestic threats, and therefore justify extraordinary measures in matters seen to be of national security.

158 Garnsey (1970) 35, 74–5, 105–7, 111, 141–4. If linked to conspiracy, magic became punishable by death; see MacMullen (1966) 95–127. Tacitus, *Ann.* 2.27, 32, mentions one magician thrown off the Tarpeian Rock and one beaten to death in public in 'the traditional punishment'. On conspirators thrown off the Tarpeian in Dio and Tacitus, see Bauman (1996) 60–1.

159 *Dig.* 48.18.10.1; *CTh* 9.5.1; see Robinson (1995) 13, 78. On Roman torture, see Peters (1985) 18–36, who approaches torture as a legal and public issue; 3: torture is 'torment inflicted by a public authority for ostensibly public purposes'.

160 On the benefits of suicide, see Bauman (1996) 74–5 and ch. 4 below; on applications and implications of *damnatio memoriae*, see ch. 7 below.

161 Livy, 3.58.6–9, suggests that the practice was used in the early Republic: in 449 the decemvirs Appius Claudius and Oppius killed themselves in prison before trial, but the tribunes confiscated their property. Discussing the confiscation of *bona damnatorum*, the property of persons condemned on criminal charges, from the Republic to the treason trials of the Empire, Millar (1992), 163–74, notes the relative ease with which emperors and provincial governors could indulge in condemnation and confiscation of property. On the post-mortem trial and confiscation of the property of Sejanus and his followers, see Dio 58.15.41, and further in Levick (1976) 189; cf. the post-mortem trial of Antistius Vetus under Nero: Tac. *Ann.* 16.10–11. Cf. chs. 4 and 7 below.

162 Suet. *Dom.* 12.1–2, Loeb: 'The property of the living and the dead was seized everywhere on any charge brought by an accuser. It was enough to allege any action or word derogatory to the majesty of the prince.'

163 See Robinson (1995) 16, 21, 77–8, with legal testimonia (e.g. *Dig.* 58.4.11).

164 Constantine: *CTh* 9.24.11; see MacMullen (1986a) 147–66, esp. 153–8; Grodzynski (1984) 373–82.

165 MacMullen (1986a), 165, disagrees with Garnsey (1968) 141–62, who, 147–8, 158, ties harsher penalties to increasing absolutism.

166 As noted above, some emperors were notorious for forcing spectators and even men of status into the arena. Caligula had a physically large man, a centurion named Proclus, forced into two bouts and then executed: Suet. *Calig.* 35.2; Dio 59.10.4. Caligula applied *summa supplicia* to *multos honesti ordinis* not just for serious crimes but for criticizing his shows or not swearing by his genius: Suet. *Calig.* 27.3; Dio 59.10.4. A knight thrown to beasts professed his innocence, so Caligula had his tongue cut out: Suet. *Calig.* 27.4. Claudius so enjoyed *venationes* and *meridiani* that he went early and stayed after midday; he sometimes forced arena attendants and carpenters to fight if their props malfunctioned, and he even forced one of his pages into the arena in his toga: Suet. *Claud.* 34.2. Cf. other incidents in chs. 6 and 7 below.

167 *Dig.* 47.14.1.3, Ulpian 8 *de off. proconsulis*, cited by Robinson (1995) 26, says that execution or the mines were the usual penalties for aggravated rustling but that the courts at Rome sent rustlers to the beasts. Lucian, *Alex.* 44, tells a story of slaves who, on the basis of an accusing oracle by the pseudo-prophet Alexander, were tried for killing their master's son and thrown to beasts by the magistrate of Galatia. The boy later returned home unharmed. Josephus, *BJ* 7.446, says that Catullus, governor of Libyan Pentapolis, used a minor sedition as a pretext to kill 3,000 wealthy Jews; he felt safe in doing so because he added their confiscated possessions to the emperor's revenue.

168 Wiedemann (1992), 140–1, properly notes that 'The unjust condemnation of the innocent was a required theme of rhetorical invective.' However, legal abuses were not mere rhetorical fabrications any more than fatal charades were mere theatrics. Existing in all cultures, the potential for abusive violence is

124

increased by excess latitude in military or judicial discretion, but also by simple over-exposure to violence and the resulting sense of banality and unreality in response to human suffering. See Hannah Arendt, *Eichmann in Jerusalem: A Report on the Banality of Evil* (New York: Viking, 1963).

169 G. W. Bowersock, *Martyrdom and Rome* (Cambridge: Cambridge U., 1995) 18, sees the enthusiasm for spectacles in Asia Minor as possibly contributing to the phenomenon of martyrdom: 'Pressure on the part of local authorities to find victims over and above the criminals who would normally be provided for a show must have been unusually great.' Judges could impose arbitrary and diverse penalties on Christians in the first and second centuries; see ch. 8 below.

170 E.g. Piso sent some to Clodius for beast shows, and Caelius asked Cicero to send him some: Cic. *Pis.* 89; cf. *Fam* 8.4.5. See n. 125 above on *Dig.* 48.19.31. On the judicial power of provincial governors, especially over peregrines, see P. Garnsey, 'The Criminal Jurisdiction of Governors', *JRS* 58 (1968) 51–9; MacMullen (1986a) 149–50; Lintott (1968) 36–8. SHA, *Avid. Cass.* 4.1–5, claims that a governor of Syria burned and drowned various criminals, mutilated deserters, and crucified undisciplined men. More reliably, see: Suet. *Galb.* 9.1, 12.1; Sen. *Ira* 1.18, 2.5.5; Philo *In Flacc.* 78f.

171 In early Rome, from their establishment in 290–287 (Livy *Per.* 11), the *triumviri* or *tresviri capitales* ran the prison, supervised executions (*Dig.* 1.2.2.30), and adjudicated crimes by the poor, slaves, and non-Romans. References in Plautus suggest that they had extensive jurisdiction over runaway slaves or slaves found loose at night, and apparently they could imprison free men as public enemies after the laying of appropriate charges; see Lintott (1968) 102–6; Bauman (1996) 17–18, n. 30 on 167. Nippel (1995), 22–6, however, doubts that the *tresviri* fulfilled any general police function or exercised summary criminal jurisdiction over ordinary citizens and slaves.

172 The urban prefect, with perhaps 3,000 men, was responsible for public order; the prefect of the watch (*vigiles*) led men forming a fire brigade, a supplemental police force and night watch; both worked together closely with the praetorians. See Bauman (1996) 50, 100–14; Crook (1984) 71–2; Robinson (1995) 10–11; Garnsey (1970) 95, 98; Edward C. Echols, 'The Roman City Police: Origin and Development', *CJ* 53 (1958) 377–84; John E. Stambaugh, *The Ancient Roman City* (Baltimore: Johns Hopkins U., 1988) 124–7. The prefect of the watch, attending to theft, burglary, and lesser crimes, was normally limited to giving non-lethal beatings; see Bauman (1996) 103, 112; but Crook (1984), 72, notes a case, from *Dig.* 12.4.15, of the prefect of the watch executing a slave burglar. Nippel (1995), 90–8, admits that the criminal jurisdiction of the prefects increased over time, but he doubts that they were active in *ex officio* prosecution of ordinary crimes; cf. his 'Policing Rome', *JRS* 74 (1984) 20–9.

173 Urban violence, seen by Nippel (1995) 45 as popular justice, was sometimes directed against urban and praetorian prefects. E.g. Plut. *Galb.* 17.4; *Otho* 2.2; Tac. *Hist.* 1.72: masses in the circus and theater call for the death of Nero's Tigellinus. Later, crowds in the circus and theaters compelled Otho to order Tigellinus' death (he committed suicide). Similarly, in AD 189 riots forced Commodus to acquiesce as a crowd dragged and beheaded the corpse of the praetorian prefect Cleander, who was hoarding grain: Dio 73(72).13.1–6; SHA *Comm.* 7.1; Hdn 1.12–3.

174 Under the Empire the urban prefect, aided by the urban cohorts, could inflict summary (non-capital) punishment to keep order at the games; see Balsdon (1969) 266.

175 Bauman (1996) 159: 'One of the main reasons for that volume [of juridical material on the punishment of *humiliores*] is that the suppression of crime was not always the main consideration. The demands of the games made a constant supply of victims imperative.'

176 As Crook (1984), 72, notes, the first reference to the urban prefect having criminal jurisdiction applies to Nero's reign.

177 As Grodzynski (1984), 362–3; and Bauman (1996), 134–5, explain, Roman law (*Dig.* 48.19.1) recognized that financial penalties could not be exacted from slaves and the indigent to recompense the state for their injurious crimes, so discretionary punishments were used to exact the debt upon their bodies. Ville (1981), 228–40, sees a shift from captives to more use of volunteers and *damnati* from the legal system. Similarly, Coleman (1990), 54–7, 72, feels that the available supply of victims as a commodity influenced the scale of shows, and that legal sources helped increase supplies. Coleman, 45, suggests that 'the demand for brutal public entertainment will be seen to act as a "market force" in the selection of punishment at Rome'. Similarly, Callu (1984), 341, notes that victims condemned to the arena provided a more spectacular punishment than fire or crucifixion; he suggests that punishments did not always suit the crime or the status of the criminal: 'Il faut trouver des condamnés pour l'arène, quel qu'ait été le crime.'

178 Hornum (1993). Some competitors in the games may have invoked Nemesis against overly successful or arrogant rivals to assist their own victory, but this formed only a minor element of the cult.

179 Hornum (1993), 15, traces the relationship of Nemesis to the Roman emperors back to Julius Caesar (see App. *B Civ.* 2.90), and he notes that Pliny (*HN* 11.251.3–4) 28.22.5–6) places a cult of Nemesis on the Capitoline by AD 77. It would thus have been close to the Carcer, the Temple of Concord, the Tarpeian Rock, and other sites associated with social order.

180 Hornum (1993) 78–90, quote at 90. Nemesis was depicted iconographically as trampling prostrate foes or as holding a wheel (or scales or a measuring rod) of justice. Issues of imperial coins used images and epithets to tie Nemesis to the emperor, to imperial victory, and the peace it brought; see Hornum (1993) 24–41, 62–70, Appendices 3–4.

181 Under the Empire the army remained closely associated with amphitheaters and games. Amphitheaters were often built near garrisons, with soldiers involved in the construction, and military units had close ties with the emperor cult and its games. Moreover, military camps were used as imperial prisons for local criminals, who might be sent to shows in Rome or used in shows at a local amphitheater. See P. Le Roux, 'L'Amphithéâtre et le soldat sous l'Empire romain', 203–15, in Domergue et al. (1990).

182 Virgil's underworld (*Aen.* 6.430) includes a category of souls of those falsely condemned (*falso damnati*) and executed for crimes they did not commit; see Alan E. Bernstein, *The Formation of Hell: Death and Retribution in the Ancient and Early Christian Worlds* (Ithaca: Cornell U., 1993) 65–8. Tertullian, *De spect.* 19, Loeb, claims that innocent men were condemned to the arena even for non-capital crimes through the vindictiveness of judges: 'Certain it is that innocent men are sold as gladiators for the show, to be victims of public pleasure.' Likewise, Lactant. *Div. inst.* 6.20.

183 Bauman (1996) 163. Bauman's detailed study takes a sympathetic look at punishment at Rome in theory and in practice, in literary and legal sources. He notes some ameliorating concerns (e.g. 6–8, 18–20, 26–9, 78–86 and passim) about humanity, clemency, and fairness (*humanitas, clementia, aequitas*), and some positive reforms did limit the use of the death penalty via the

option of exile (or of allowing the condemned the choice of type of death
(*liberum mortis arbitrium*) to avoid public shame (*contumelia*) (36–7, 54)) and
control accusers and charges of treason; but ultimately (141–64) he admits
that Roman attitudes to punishment focused on public interest rather than
humanity.

184 MacMullen (1986a), 151, notes a trend from decreasing enthusiasm for gladiatorial combats to an increased taste for public executions and judicial
brutality in the later second and early third centuries AD.

185 As Ariès (1982) 11–12, cf. 44–5, says of medieval attitudes to men killed
by criminal action: 'The victim cannot be exonerated; he is inescapably dishonored by the vileness of his death . . . The death of condemned prisoners was
shameful by definition. Until the fourteenth century, they were denied even
religious reconciliation: They were damned in the next world as well as in
this one.'

4

DEATH, DISPOSAL, AND DAMNATION OF HUMANS: SOME METHODS AND MESSAGES

The Shades are no fable: death is not the end of all, and the pale ghost escapes the vanquished pyre.

(Propertius 4.7.1–2, Loeb)

Roman death: rites and rights, hierarchy and the hereafter

That we are all equal in death, that death is the great leveller, was a popular idea with Sceptics and Epicureans; but in Rome individuals were not truly equal in death – in how they died (or were killed), how their remains were treated, how (or if) they were remembered in this world, or how their souls fared in the afterlife. Ancient cemeteries show that the kingdom of the dead was not an egalitarian realm. The archaeology of death is necessarily predisposed to the more substantial monuments of the elite, and obsequies invited conspicuous consumption and displays of status.[1] A Roman cemetery might contain monumental mausoleums, *cenotaphia* (garden tombs), or tombs of officials decorated with scenes of games they had given,[2] humbler burials in *columbaria* (sepulchers with niches for urns) and catacombs, and unmarked mass burials of the dregs of the city.[3] Just as burial rites and monuments reflected the privileges, pretension, and piety of Romans who died normal deaths,[4] the victims of spectacles at Rome were not equal in life, in death in the arena, or after death beyond the arena.

Ancient death must be approached as 'a protracted social process', not a simple event.[5] As Polybius (6.53–4) recounts, the deaths of prominent Romans called for an elaborate funeral with a procession, death masks (*imagines*) and a funeral oration to link the dead and the living, the past and the present, and to show the status and continuity of the family. We hear far less of the deaths and burial of the loved ones of common people, but they too deserved rites (e.g. the last kiss, closing of the eyes) and needed disposal.[6] For family members, especially heads of households, attention to family tombs and funerary rites was a sacred duty, for denial of burial,

128

grave, and rites meant the end of the family.[7] As Toynbee explains, 'All Roman funerary practice was influenced by two basic notions – first, that death brought pollution and demanded from the survivors acts of purification and expiation; secondly, that to leave a corpse unburied had unpleasant repercussions on the fate of the departed soul.'[8]

Sacred custom told Romans not to molest corpses (beyond stripping armor), to permit burial by relatives or others claiming the body, and failing that, to provide minimal burial. Properly, burial meant that the body was covered and no bone showed above the ground, but for ceremonial or minimal burial the sprinkling of three handfuls of dirt sufficed.[9] Such obligations applied to victims of accident, premature deaths, and honorable foes, that is to say foes killed on the battlefield – not unransomed or surrendered captives.[10] Out of pity and to avoid pollution, even slaves were usually – but not always – permitted proper burial.[11]

With a few exceptions, burial sites had to be outside the city. Ancient custom and repeated legislation, at Rome as in Greece, forbade burying (by cremation or inhumation) or dumping bodies within the boundaries of the city. The XII Tables order: 'A dead man shall not be buried or burned within the city' ('hominem mortuum in urbe ne sepelito neve urito'). An expansion of this is found in the Charter of the Colonia Genetiva Julia of 44 BC: 'No person within the boundaries of the town of the colony or within the area marked by the plow [pomerium] shall introduce a dead person, or bury, or cremate the same therein, or build therein a monument to a dead person.'[12] This ban on intramural burial probably arose more from Roman religious concerns about pollution within the city's sacred boundaries than from pragmatic concerns about unhygienic contamination and disease.[13]

Most Greeks and Romans accepted some idea of the soul and some at least a shadowy sort of afterlife. The finality of death, the belief that the dead just die and decompose, was known but not widely accepted. As Hopkins put it, 'Burial did away with the corpse, but not with the dead.'[14] Some intellectuals rejected the possibility of post-mortem suffering, but the majority of Romans, like Greeks, believed that the soul or spirit retained its identity and memory – and also the marks and mood of the moment of death.[15] Separated from its body, the soul could not know physical pain but, since it remained individual and conscious, it could suffer psychologically, enduring the shame of a dishonorable death or the longing for vengeance.[16] Greeks and Romans believed that the restless souls of murdered men lingered on earth tormenting their murderers or urging relatives to fulfill their duty of blood-vengeance. The untimely dead could be especially restless if they received improper or no burial.[17] Virgil immortalizes the Roman pathos for the tortured souls of an unburied friend or relative, e.g. Aeneas' steersman Palinurus, who was murdered on the shores of Lucania and left unburied. Just before Aeneas sees Palinurus on the banks of the

129

Styx in the underworld, the Sibyl explains that the ferryman Charon rejects the souls of the unburied.[18]

An anonymous lyric poem from a late second-century AD papyrus from Egypt describes a terrified man descending to Hades and seeing bodies of the unburied dead unable to cross the river encircling Hades. Dogs had come to feed on the corpses lying all over the path (lines 5–6). At the Shores of Ugliness,

> there lay a vast plain, full of corpses of dreadful doom, beheaded or crucified. Above the ground stood pitiable bodies, their throats but lately cut. Others again, impaled, hung like the trophies of a cruel destiny. The Furies, crowned with wreaths, were laughing at the miserable manner of the corpses' death. There was an abominable stench of gore.[19]

Images of damnation beyond death extended from the capital to the fringes of the empire.

Like Greeks, Romans felt that the boundary between the dead and the living was porous, that heroes could descend to Hades and that ghosts could visit the living to deliver messages and to exact vengeance by haunting. Scorned and suicidal, Dido threatens Aeneas that her ghost will haunt him all over the world and that vengeance will comfort her in the underworld.[20] Critics of the idea only prove that the masses believed in the interpenetration of the dead and the living.[21] Notions of the soul and the afterlife were shadowy, but traditional Roman religion believed in ghosts, demons, and spirits who were to be pitied or feared, and either appeased or expelled.[22] As Pliny (*HN* 28.4.19) said, everyone feared spells and curse tablets. The Greek and Roman practice of curse tablets, the magical custom of cursing a foe or rival by writing his name on a tablet and dedicating it to a god or demon, reveals a prevalent belief in spirits and demons, and in the ability to damn. From the over 1,500 curse tablets found in the Mediterranean area from the time of Homer to the Christian era, testimonia crossing all lines of class, gender, and culture, Gager concludes: 'First and foremost, it is now beyond dispute that nearly everyone – 99 percent of the population is not too high an estimate – believed in their power.'[23] Invoking the dead to incite chthonic powers, curse tablets show that damning satisfied emotions of hate and revenge or the desire to hurt a rival or enemy.[24]

For the Romans the dead were gone, but they were still with them. Belief in the existence and threatening power of dead spirits is also shown by burial rites, attention to tombs, and epitaphs and sepulchral warnings written as if spoken by the attentive dead.[25] Even ancestral ghosts (*manes paterni*) were seen as fearsome gods demanding attention. In the Parentalia festival, families made obligatory offerings to their dead at tombs, and at the Lemuria individual households and the whole state performed rituals of appeasement and lustration to the spirits of the restless dead in general.[26] In the Compitalia festival the Lares Compitales, ghosts of the crossroads who could be good or dangerous, were appeased with offerings of wool effigies (Dion. Hal. *Ant. Rom.* 4.14.3). Numerous ghost stories show a common belief that spirits of persons who were killed violently or died prematurely could trouble the living, especially their murderers.[27] According to the Younger Pliny (*Ep.* 7.27), his friend Athenodorus said that he had been visited by a ghost who told him to dig up a spot in his garden; when he found the remains of a murdered man and buried the bones properly, the ghost never returned. Although Romans were not consistent in their beliefs, the manner of death and disposal of arena victims would have been of concern to most killers and killed. Abuses could cause spiritual discomfort, exclusion, wandering, and haunting.

In the Roman world denial of even minimal burial was regarded as an abuse of decent humans, as a form of damnation beyond death, but it was acceptable when criminals' acts put them beyond the protection of any law. Ancient custom said that a traitor should not be mourned, and Roman stories of post-mortem insults, as a horror but also as a punishment and deterrent, were also cast back into the era of the monarchy and even earlier.[28] In the *Aeneid* Virgil's Homeric model obliged him to pick up the theme of corpse abuse, but Virgil also reflects the horrors of the Civil Wars and the arena. When Aeneas killed Tarquitus he spoke words of hatred: 'No loving mother shall lay thee in the earth, nor load thy limbs with ancestral tomb. To birds of prey shalt thou be left; or sunk beneath the flood, the wave shall bear thee on, and hungry fish shall suck thy wounds.'[29] Livy vilifies Tullia, wife of Tarquinius Superbus, for her association with the murder and abuse of her father King Servius (1.48.7). Influenced by the avenging ghosts of her sister and former husband, she drove her carriage over the corpse of her father (to whom Tarquin denied funeral rites (1.49.1)), thus committing a 'horrible and inhuman' crime; and she also defiled herself with the blood and even carried blood back to her house.[30] When forced to flee after the speech of Brutus, Tullia was (1.59.13, Loeb) 'cursed wherever she went by men and women, who called down upon her the furies that avenge the wrongs of kindred'.

Rome sanctioned denial of burial and rites in certain cases, notably those of persons who committed suicide by hanging themselves;[31] and tradition credits the introduction of corpse abuse as coercion for the living to the era of the monarchy. In what Van Hooff calls the 'historical "charter myth"' for the Roman abhorrence of suicide by hanging, Pliny says that when citizens committed suicide to escape the exhausting work of constructing sewers under Tarquinius Priscus, 'the king devised a strange remedy . . . He crucified the bodies of all who had died by their own hands, leaving them to be gazed at by their fellow-citizens and also torn to pieces by beasts and birds of prey.'[32] Saying (from Cassius Hemina) that the king was Tarquinius Superbus and adding that the laborers hanged themselves, Servius states that the ancient priestly books ordered that the bodies of suicides by hanging were to be cast out unburied (*insepultus abiceretur*).[33] The prospect of being shamed in death remained an effective coercion. Recall that the rebel soldiers from Rhegium in 270 BC were not only executed at Rome: 'And they did not receive burial, but were dragged out of the Forum into an open space before the city, where they were torn asunder by birds and dogs.'[34]

Sources ascribe many examples of corpse abuse and denial of burial to the late Republican era of proscriptions and civil wars.[35] They especially note examples of severe corpse abuse – the mutilation of a body to a point where it could not be recognized for burial in this world or for reception into the underworld,[36] perhaps because such insults were done to officials and citizens and not just to commoners. During the reign of terror of Cinna and Marius in 87 BC equestrians and senators were killed, senators were decapitated, and, according to Appian, 'No one was permitted to give any of the dead burial, and birds and dogs tore apart the bodies of such distinguished men.'[37] Adapting ritual patterns of punishment, abuse, denial of burial and purgation,[38] the proscriptions of Sulla, Octavius, and Antony were pseudo-legal purges driven by personal vengeance.[39]

Denial of burial appears in official documents and imperial policies. Note the terms of the Paphlagonians' oath of loyalty to Augustus, probably very similar to the oath administered throughout Italy earlier:

But if I do anything contrary to this oath . . . I myself call down upon myself, my body, my soul, my life, my children, and all of my family and property, utter ruin and utter destruction unto all my issue and all my descendants, and may neither earth nor sea receive the bodies of my family or my descendants, or yield fruits to them.[40]

Suetonius says that after Philippi Octavian abused the corpse of Brutus by decapitation, and that, when a distinguished prisoner asked for a decent burial, he was told that that was up to the carrion-birds.[41] Clearly Augustus and his subjects understood denial of burial as a supplementary punishment for disloyalty and treason.

The reign of Tiberius notoriously revealed Roman attitudes to suicide, treason, and denial of burial. At Rome suicide was acceptable or even admirable under certain conditions (e.g. to avoid dishonor, for the good of the community, to make a personal statement of philosophical or political integrity, or because of insufferable pain or mental or physical decay); but suicide did not allow individuals to escape responsibility for crimes and it might be taken as an admission of guilt.[42] In Tiberius' reign of terror there were many coerced suicides because, unless there was a suicide, conviction

132

for treason brought confiscation of property (the denial of any will) and denial of burial. Tacitus claims that in AD 33 when a knight, Vibulenus Agrippa, charged with treason, drank poison in the senate, he was hurriedly carried out by the lictors to prison, where, already dead, he was hung by the neck.[43] Tacitus explains the appeal of suicide:

> For these modes of dying were rendered popular by fear of the executioner and by the fact that a man legally condemned forfeited his estate and was debarred from burial; while he who passed sentence upon himself had his celerity so far rewarded that his body was interred and his will respected.[44]

By Roman law even criminals were to be permitted burial if they were executed *capite*, but traitors were an exception.[45] Even the mourning of traitors was criminal.[46] In the game of Roman political life, homicide, suicide, and denial of burial were not out of bounds.[47] Emperors always knew how to honor or insult the dead.[48]

Abuses against citizens of status were seen as atrocities, but spectacular executions of *noxii* in arenas were both legal and popular. Normal execution, as a privileged form of quick, unaggravated death restricted to *honestiores*, was distinct from deaths in the arena, which (in theory) involved condemnation for heinous crimes endangering the state's moral or religious stability. Out of wrath, or to establish a public warning for potential offenders, punishment was taken beyond death to despoiling the corpse, and even further.[49] Denial of burial was a symbolic extension of legal condemnation into ritual damnation – not a Christian Hell with divine judgement but a humanly induced, forlorn disquietude for the offender's spirit. With parallels in other cultures, abuse and denial of burial were intense insults stemming from deep-seated emotions of fear, disgust, and hate.

Death as a spectacle in some other pre-modern societies

Every people, the proverb has it, loves its own form of violence.
(C. Geertz, 'The Balinese Cockfight' (1974) 27)

Interpreting punishment as a juridical-political reactivation of the power of a sovereign against insult and attack, Foucault points out that the symbolic power of the beaten and broken body of the victim extended to the treatment of the corpse. He describes an execution at Avignon followed by post-mortem mutilation and dismemberment. The condemned was blindfolded and tied to a stake, a confessor gave him a blessing, the executioner killed him with a blow to the head by a bludgeon, the *mortis exactor* cut his throat with a large knife and severed the sinews near his heels, and then he opened up the stomach, took out the heart and organs, cut them up, and put them on hooks for display.[50] Many victims were similarly executed and abused in medieval and even modern Europe as public executions persisted as popular spectacles.[51] There are Roman parallels, but also significant exceptions: death in the arena seldom came so quickly and Roman *noxii* received no blessing – Roman sentiment was inconsistent with 'May God have mercy on your soul.' The enormously powerful symbolism of the abused and unburied corpse was more obvious, and it had more sacral connotations, in pre-modern societies: it communicated pathos or punishment depending on the relationship of the viewer to the viewed, the potential burier to the potentially (un)buried.

Ancient Assyria used inscriptions and reliefs to publicize its use of mutilation, corpse abuse, and denial of burial as spectacles of imperial intimidation. Assyrian kings repeatedly boasted of successfully completing their religious duty to wage wars, and of having built piles of corpses and decapitated skulls, of floods of blood, of dismemberments, impalements, and the skinning of foes. For example, King Sennacherib (704–681 BC) declared:

> I cut their [the enemies'] throats like lambs. I cut off their precious lives (as one cuts) a string. Like the many waters of a storm, I made (the contents of) their gullets and entrails run down upon the wide earth. My prancing steeds ... plunged into the streams of their blood as (into) a river. The wheels of my war chariot, which brings low the wicked and the evil, were bespattered with blood and filth. With the bodies of their warriors I filled the plain, like grass. (Their) testicles I cut off, and tore out their privates like the seeds of cucumbers.

Ashurbanipal (668–627 BC) declared:

> Their dismembered bodies I fed to the dogs, swine, wolves, eagles, to the birds of heaven and the fish in the deep ... What was left of the feast of the dogs and swine, of their members ... I ordered them to remove from Babylon, Kutha and Sippar, and to cast them upon heaps.

Assyrian vengeance and abuse of enemies extended even to their dead:

> The sepulchers of their [the Elamites'] earlier and later kings, who did not fear Assur and Ishtar, my lords, (and who) had plagued the kings, my fathers, I destroyed, I devastated, I exposed to the sun. Their bones (members) I carried off to Assyria. I laid restlessness upon their shades. I deprived them of food-offerings and libations of water.[52]

There is no doubt that the Assyrians and other Near Eastern peoples performed such acts, nor is there doubt that the fear thus inspired bolstered their empire.

Like Rome, ancient Greece had popular conceptions of souls and the afterlife, and normal social conventions applied to the burial of even marginal members of society.[53] Leaving someone unburied, especially intentionally, was usually seen as an atrocity.[54] Acting beyond the limits of human society and custom, Achilles angered the gods by abusing and denying burial to Hector, who had died honorably in battle.[55] In the underworld Agamemnon is angry because Clytemnestra had not only killed him but had not closed his eyes and mouth in death, denying him the usual ritual (*Od.* 11.424–6).[56] Witness the collapse of burial customs as a dehumanizing effect of the plague at Athens, and the horror of leaving unburied companions in the departure scene at Syracuse in Thucydides.[57]

Greek legend, law, and practice, however, show that in crises and certain contexts norms could be completely reversed. Actions that would be horrendous crimes if committed against decent people in normal society were accepted as traditional punishments imposed on noxious criminals (tyrants, traitors, and murderers). When the last of the Kypselid tyrants at Corinth was killed, his house was razed, his property was confiscated, his corpse was thrown unburied over the border, and the bones of his ancestors were dug up and cast out as well.[58] Under a famous curse for their religious crime, the living members of the Athenian Alkmeonidai were exiled and the bones of their dead were dug up and cast out.[59] Sophocles' *Antigone* and Euripides' *Suppliant Women* poignantly depict the emotional power of denial of burial.[60] Athens and Sparta both legally sanctioned and carried out the denial of burial of traitors and heinous criminals, throwing them in pits or ravines or throwing their remains beyond their borders.[61] Pre-Roman Greece, however, had no institutionalized program of spectacles regularly producing numerous, noxious corpses.

Spectacles of death including the public, brutal abuse and killing of captives figured prominently among the Maya, Aztecs, and other Amerindian cultures. Despite early misperceptions of the ancient Maya as peaceful farmers led by refined astrologers, it is undeniable that they were aggressive warriors who staged spectacles of death.[62] In their wars the Maya captured live prisoners, especially enemy kings, for elaborate public executions and sacrifices at public ceremonies including religious festivals, 'sports', and building dedications. Mayan art shows that warfare and human sacrifice were rituals essential to heir designations and to upholding kingship.

> Accession rituals . . . required the offering of at least one human captive. Such offerings not only satisfied the constant demands by the gods for repayment of the blood debt incurred by man at his creation but tested the mettle of the new king as well . . . To be a king, he had to take captives in war. Once made king, he was

135

in jeopardy of becoming the most valued booty of his enemy. To sustain his rule, a king would not only have to fight off his foe, he would also attempt to capture and humiliate his enemy.[63]

Scenes of the display of captives are much more common in art than scenes of death: captives were stripped of battle dress and weapons and then shamed in public with torments and humiliations (e.g. minimal clothing, binding, being dragged by the hair) before their execution.[64] Just as the Mayan royal family and nobles performed excruciating rituals of auto-sacrifice and blood-letting upon themselves (e.g. letting blood drip from pierced lips or penises) as offerings to ancestors and as a way to gain public merit and respect, the Maya bled and mutilated captives even more than the Aztecs did.[65] Their blood and flesh were offered to the gods and to ancestors in sacrifices commemorating battles and consolidating the power of kings.[66]

Aztec rites included elaborate human sacrifices (mostly of captive warriors and tribute slaves) on pyramids in the center of communities, e.g. to honor a new king or to dedicate a building project, or in regular sacrifices at four seasonal festivals.[67] Captives were maintained and displayed in the community, then paraded through the streets in costume to the top of the pyramid and placed over a stone altar. After sacrificial excision by priests with obsidian knives, the victim's heart and blood were offered to the Sun and other deities and placed in special deposits. Next, in a gesture combining pragmatism with added insult, the body was thrown down the steps. Then victims were decapitated and their skulls were displayed conspicuously to prove the imperial power of the king, and at the base of the pyramid old men took the headless corpse for dismemberment and distribution.[68] Possibly as an incentive to Aztec warriors to fight well, at least three of the limbs of each victim went to the Aztec warrior who captured the man, to be eaten in ritual cannibalistic feasts.

In a now largely discounted ecological, functionalist interpretation, Michael Harner suggests that, because the area lacked large animals, human sacrifice was a way of acquiring needed protein.[69] Clendinnen admits that,

> Surprisingly, the mode of the disposal of the bodies remains mysterious. We are usually told that skulls were spitted on the skull racks, limbs apportioned for ritual cannibalism, and the trunks fed to the flesh-eating birds and beasts in Moctezoma's menagerie, but such disposal techniques would clearly be inadequate. The bodies were perhaps burnt, although during their stay in the city Cortés and his men make no mention of any pyres or corpse-laden canoes, the detritus of human killings being confined, in their accounts, to the temple precincts. The land-locked lakes, precious sources of water and aquatic foods, offered no solution, so this large empirical matter remains unresolved.[70]

136

Disposal by dumping in pits perhaps was possible, but this has not been suggested or investigated.[71]

A more agonistic spectacle of death, Mayan and Aztec rubber ballgames were held prominently on special courts found in temple complexes (with room for large crowds of spectators) close to temples, palaces, and skull-racks at many sites, notably at Chichén Itzá in Yucatan and at the Aztec capital of Tenochtitlan.[72] The games are well documented by accounts by sixteenth-century Spanish clerics, Mayan and Aztec artifacts, reliefs and paintings emphasizing death and sacrifice, and Mayan literature. Much skill might be displayed as, without using hands, the teams had to keep the ball in motion without touching the ground as they tried to make contact with markers or rings to score points. Ballgames were often played by Mayan nobles or professionals for display, sport, or wagering, but war captives were also forced to play ritual games.[73]

The sacred book of the Quiché Maya, the *Popol Vuh*, shows that the ball-game had cosmological symbolism in Mayan mythology In this complex epic two sets of brothers played ball against the gods of the underworld. The first set lost and were decapitated. The second set, the Hero Twins, won the game but let themselves be sacrificed. Their bones were ground up and cast into a river, but they reappeared in the underworld, dismembered their enemies, and then became heavenly bodies (the sun and the moon or Venus). Mayan rulers perhaps dressed as the Hero Twins for the game, and the ballgame as a public spectacle reenacted on one level the capture of foes in war, and on another level a victory over death, darkness, and the underworld. 'It allowed the king to reign both as athlete and warrior. Blood sacrifice, the mortar of Maya dynastic life, was offered at the same time that the enemies of the kingdom were extinguished.'[74]

The ballgame was also the central part of an elaborate ritual starting with the display, humiliation, and torture of captives. Captives were later forced to play the ballgame as a preliminary and something of a selection process for human sacrifice. For captives this was a zero-sum or terminal game in which winning was everything – the existence of victors demanded the existence of losers.[75] Despite earlier confusion, clearly it was the losing players, if captives, who were decapitated; winners simply delayed their death. As Schele and Miller explain,

> Losers were sacrificed: their hearts were offered to the gods and, occasionally, their decapitated heads were placed in play. Time and again in depictions of the ballgame, images of human skulls are substituted for balls. It was a gruesome game played for the highest stakes – the players' lives.[76]

Depictions at Chichén Itzá, Copan, and Tikal show another stage (or vari-ation) of the spectacle of death. Here, losers were taken to a temple and bound and trussed up in the shape of a ball; they were thrown down long flights of stairs adjacent to the ballcourts to their deaths. Their decapitated skulls could be displayed nearby, and human bones found in wells and ritual receptacles represent votive deposits to the gods after sacrifice.[77]

Aztecs also practiced a ritual of torture by fire and a form of gladiatorial sacrifice. In a sacrifice to the fire god bound victims were thrown into a fire, only to be hooked out, badly burned but still alive, to face heart excision.[78] In the 'Feast of the Flaying of Men' for the festival of Tlacaxipeualiztli specially selected victims were individually tied to a sacrificial stone, termed the gladiator stone by the Spaniards, and put on display. The victim was given pulque (an alcoholic beverage) to drug him, four cudgels for throwing, and a club edged with feathers rather than blades. Perhaps the illusion of giving the victim a chance was arranged to elevate him into a more worthy sacrifice.[79] He fought four warriors with flint weapons. Clendinnen explains how the warriors were not supposed to shorten the spectacle with a quick kill. Their concern was

> to give a display of the high art of weapon handling: in an exquisitely prolonged performance to cut the victim delicately, tenderly with those narrow blades, to lace the living skin with blood (this whole process was called 'the striping'). Finally, the victim, a slow-carved object lesson of Mexica supremacy, exhausted by exertion and loss of blood, would falter and fall, to be dispatched by the usual heart excision.

The victim's blood was offered to the gods (by being put on the mouths of stone idols in temples) and the usual dismemberment and distribution followed.[80] The captor of the victim provided a cannibal feast for his family but abstained from the flesh himself because of his identification with his captive as a reflex of himself.[81]

To explain the cooperation of victims in most of the sacrifices Clendinnen points to the conditioning of the victim by preparations, rehearsals, and honors, and she notes the importance of the shared value system of warrior captive and captor in aiding a virtuous performance.[82] The Mexica had an 'arsenal of victim management, from the potent psychological force of special selection, of habituation through rehearsal, of admiration', a 'weakening of autonomy' through pampering to a 'heightening of awareness through dance and battle and drink'.[83]

Characteristic features of the abuse and sacrifice of captives by North American Indians, especially Hurons and Iroquois, are well documented. After his account of the Huron Feast of the Dead with its rituals of mourning, burial, grave goods, and funeral games, Francis Parkman adds a description of the Huron sacrifice of an Iroquois captive witnessed by Jesuit missionaries in 1637. The captive's hands had been mutilated, but he was received with formal hospitality (e.g the best food) at the Huron village. According to custom, he was given to be adopted into a family that had lost a relative in battle; but, because his hands were so torn and crushed that he would never have the use of them again, that family gave him over to be sacrificed by fire. That family still tended to him, and a sister of the slain Huron wept for him. According to custom, the Iroquois captive gave a 'farewell feast' for the Hurons and declared: 'Do your worst to me. I do not fear torture or death.' At night-fall the chief told the crowd to perform their roles well because the Sun and the god of war would be watching. Goaded by torches, the victim was forced repeatedly to run through eleven fires. Both mocking and complimenting the victim for his ordeal, the Hurons kept the victim alive and conscious as long as they could, and when he died near dawn, portions of his flesh were eaten.[84]

Over a century before Parkman, Father Joseph François Lafitau wrote about such torments and offered perceptive comparisons to antiquity. Of the constancy and heroism of captives, Lafitau writes: 'This heroism is real and the result of great and noble courage. What we have admired in the martyrs of the primitive church which was, in them, the result of grace and a miracle, is natural to these people and the result of the strength of their morale.'[85] Lafitau's observations go past the point of death: 'The cruelty of these inhuman creatures still pursues these unfortunates after their death. Some strike on the bark sheets of the lodges to force the dead man's soul to quit the village, in order that the wandering shades may not frighten them by appearing to them in the form of furies'[86] Discussing South American tribes and their more extensive cannibalism of captives, Lafitau also mentions a 'kind of charnel house' in villages where the skulls and bones of victims were displayed as trophies.[87] Finally, Lafitau offers, for his time, some enlightened comments on Amerindian cruelty:

> In fact what do they do more than the Greeks and Romans used to do formerly? What more inhumane than the heroes of the Iliad? What more barbarous than the gladiatorial combats and [their treatment] of slaves or the treatment of the wild beasts by these same slaves who made so much blood run in the Roman arenas? This people nevertheless, who had carried the perfection of all the arts, and of all the sciences capable of making manners gentle, and of culture as far as the borders of its empire, took its greatest delights in the inhumanity of combats of this sort; it made the charms of the great repasts consist in the view of these bloody spectacles and took a singular pleasure at the arena in giving the decisive signal for the life or death of the unfortunate being who had some disadvantage, although he pled for pardon.[88]

Even this brief survey demonstrates that Assyrians utilized the public display and denial of burial of dead enemies, that Greeks accepted the abuse and denial of burial of certain noxious persons, and that Amerindian ritual killings and human sacrifices were public and spectacular. Sacrificial rituals included degrees of care before the killing, as well as decoration or costuming of the victims, and some variations suggest contests or scapegoats. The killing, even of captive foes, by Aztec priests was quick, but the subsequent corpse abuse included rolling of the torso down the steps, mutilation, decapitation, and dismemberment. Hearts were offered to the Sun, heads were displayed, and parts were consumed; but Aztec cannibalism, epiphenomenal and limited, was probably intended as a further insult or a way to take on the virtues of the foe. The Maya, Hurons, and other groups also consumed blood and flesh from victims, but they first inflicted more aggravated forms of torture and death (e.g. fire, beating, mutilation). Showing that elements of Roman spectacles of death were not unique, such comparisons help frame the question of options of disposal.

NOTES

1 Toynbee's essential work (1971), including 'Funerary Rites', 43–61, esp. 43–50, notes class distinctions; cf. types of tombs from *columbaria* (113–16) and catacombs (234–44) to the monumental tomb of the Cornelii Scipiones (103–4, 113). Other useful works: Hopkins (1983), 'Death in Rome', 201–56; Hinard (1987a); H. von Hesberg and P. Zanker, eds., *Römische Gräberstraßen* (Munich: Bayerische Akademie der Wissenschaften, 1987), including N. Purcell, 'Tomb and Suburb', 25–41; Morris (1992); A. C. Rush, *Death and Burial in Christian Antiquity* (Washington, DC: Catholic U. of America, 1941); Franz Cumont, *Lux Perpetua* (Paris: Geunther, 1949); Franz Cumont, *After Life in Roman Paganism* (New Haven: Yale University, 1922); C. W. Bynum, *The Resurrection of the Body in Western Christianity, 200–1336* (New York: Columbia U., 1995) 51–8. Good, brief introductions include: Glenys Davies, 'Burial in Italy up to Augustus', 13–19, in R. Reece, *Burial in the Roman World* (London: Council for British Archaeology, 1977); Balsdon (1979) 252–7; Susan Walker, *Memorials to the Roman Dead* (London: British Museum, 1985). Tacitus, *Ann.* 16.16, on his duty to record deaths, comments that the illustrious dead deserve to be mentioned in history just as they are distinguished from the common dead in their burial rites ('ut quo modo exsequiis a promisca sepultura separantur'). Purcell (1987), 26–8, 31–2, shows that elaborate tombs, including the mausoleums of Augustus and Hadrian and the tombs of the Scipios and the Caecillii Metelli, were placed strategically to be seen from the Tiber or from major streets.
2 At Pompeii the famous tomb of Umbricius Scaurus had a stucco relief with gladiatorial fights and a *venatio* to commemorate games that he had given. An inscription names the *lanista* and says that the gladiators came from an imperial school at Capua; see Mau (1899) 410–12; Ville (1981) 201–12; Wiedemann (1992) 17.
3 As Purcell (1987), 33, notes, funerary architecture and style were related to 'status, honor, display, and benefaction'. Even in *columbaria* the size and decor of urns showed status, and catacombs (before Christian egalitarianism) also show grades of status. Even humble burials and burial clubs involved some resources: Purcell, 38–40. On burials of the poor: Toynbee (1971) 101–3; J. Le Gall, 'La Sépulture des pauvres à Rome', *BSAF* (1980–1) 148–52. Hopkins (1983),

207–17, discusses the high value which Roman society set on proper burial, the importance of individualism in death, and the dehumanizing anonymity of mass graves. Cf. ch. 5 below.

4 Social-climbing ancients might indulge in excessive or inappropriate self-promotion via games and monuments. Hor. *Sat.* 2.3.84–7: a miser ordered that if his heirs did not record the size of his fortune on his tomb, they were condemned to give a gladiatorial show with a hundred pairs of fighters and a vast feast for his townsfolk. In Petronius, *Sat.* 45.6, Loeb, a character antici-pates impressive games to be put on by a certain Titus: 'If he spends four hundred thousand, his estate will never feel it, and his name will live on for ever.' The pre-need arrangements of the gauche and pompous Trimalchio for his funeral and the care of his grave reveal a common Roman perception that people could influence their status and care after death. His will (*Sat.* 71.6–9) specified the erection of a ridiculous monument with a statue and scenes of the fights of a famous gladiator (Petraites; cf. n. 40 in ch. 3 above) to bring him life after death (*post mortem vivere*), plus a garden, plus a flattering inscription; also a freedman was appointed to care for the tomb and prevent defilement (e.g. by defecation).

5 Hopkins (1983) 217. Recent studies of death have been influenced by a model of the tertiary structure (separation, liminality, aggregation) of rites of passage; see von Gennep (1960). Excellent broad treatments include S. C. Humphreys, 'Death and Time', in Humphreys and King (1982) 261–83; and Metcalf and Huntington (1991), esp. 'Death as Transition', 79–130, with valuable discussion of von Gennep and R. Hertz. For a sophisticated treatment of the problems of interpretation, see Morris (1992), 'The Anthropology of a Dead World', 1–30. Morris, xiii, argues that 'by studying all aspects of death rites as integrated parts of ritual statements about the actors' perception of the world we can reach a new understanding of ancient social structure'. He explains social structure, 3, as consisting 'of taken-for-granted norms about the roles and rules which make up society – relationships of power, affection, deference, rights, duties and so on'.

6 Funerary rites: Toynbee (1971) 43–61. On the importance of proper burial, preparing the corpse, and the problems of moving corpses, see various essays in Hinard (1995), esp. Nicole Belayche, 'La Neuvaine funéraire à Rome ou "la mort impossible"', 155–69. For comparisons of pagan and Christian practices, see Rush (1941) 91–273. Funeral processions: Toynbee (1971) 46–8; Rush (1941) 187–235. Funeral masks: Plin. *HN* 35.6; cf. Florence Dupont, 'Les Morts et la mémoire: Le Masque funèbre', in Hinard (1987a) 167–72. In Juvenal, 3.260–7, Loeb, the soul of a poor man, who was killed and crushed beyond recognition by an overturned wagon full of marble, sits, 'a new arrival, upon the bank, and shuddering at the grim ferryman; he has no copper in his mouth to tender for his fare, and no hope of a passage over the murky flood, poor wretch (*infelix*)'. Similarly, Propertius, 2.13, 19–20, 23–4, contrasts the ceremonies of rich and poor men. On removal of corpses of the indigent, see ch. 5 below.

7 Van Hooff (1990) 165: 'Having a decent burial was "vital" for ancient people; the condition in which they expected to exist after death depended on the *iusta* paid to them, i.e. on the way in which their body was carried out for burial, cremated and got a last, permanent dwelling in a tomb that was visited by the relatives who on solemn occasions recalled their dead to life.' Cf. H. Lavagne, 'Le Tombeau, mémoire du mort', 159–65, in Hinard (1987a).

8 Toynbee (1971) 43.

9 Cicero, *Leg.* 2.22.57, says that the essential rite was the throwing of a little earth on the corpse or, in the case of cremation, the cutting of a fraction of it

(*os resectum*) for burial later; see also Hor. *Carm.* 1.28.35. When the whole body was irrecoverable, a surrogate (e.g. an effigy, a finger) might be buried. On minimal rites, see Toynbee (1971) 49; F. de Visscher, *Le Droit des tombeaux romains* (Milan: Guiffrè Editore, 1963) 32–9.

10 Tacitus, *Ann.* 1.22, Loeb, shows the *ius generis*: during the mutiny in Pannonia on the accession of Tiberius in AD 14, a common soldier gave a speech against the governor, Junius Blaesus, and his use of gladiators as his personal guard. The soldier claimed, falsely, that his brother, an innocent man, was killed by the general's gladiators, and he expressed outrage that the corpse could not be found: 'The enemy himself does not grudge a grave!'

11 Domestic slaves were considered members of the *familia* and its cult, and therefore eligible for cult considerations and burial. If the slave had not joined a burial club, the master might arrange a niche in a *columbarium*. Freedmen also might be included in a family tomb. The rules of a burial club from Lanuvium of AD 136 (*CIL* 14.2112 = *ILS* 7212, in Hopkins (1983) 213–15) include provisions for rites over an imaginary body when a slave member's owner refused to hand over the body for burial. Exposed babies never accepted into a family were an exception; see ch. 7 below.

12 XII Tables 10.1, 10.10; Cic. *Leg.* 2.23.58; *Dig.* 47.12.3.5, Ulpian 25 ad ed.; *CTh* 9.17.6; see O. F. Robinson, 'The Roman Law on Burials and Burial Grounds', *The Irish Jurist* 10 (1975) 175–86, at 176, 182. Charter of Urso (*Lex coloniae Genetivae*): *CIL* I² 594 = *ILS* 6087, trans. Johnson (1961) Doc. 114.73. Paulus, *Sent.* 1.21.2–3, trans. Jo-Ann Shelton, *As the Romans Did: A Sourcebook in Roman Social History* (Oxford: Oxford U., 1988) 97: 'One is not allowed to bring a corpse into the city lest the sacred places in the city be polluted. Whoever acts contrary to these restrictions is punished with unusual severity. One is not allowed to bury or cremate a body within the walls of the city.' Servius, *Ad Aen.* 6.154, says that early Romans buried relatives in their houses so that the spirits (*lares*) of the family could be cared for in the house, but later Romans feared being near the dead and wanted a sense of separation. In later times, the cult of the saints, depopulation, and the Gothic threat led to burials and reburials within the walls; see Ariès (1974) 15–18; J. Osborne, 'Death and Burial in Sixth-Century Rome', *EMC/CV* 3.2 (1984) 291–9.

13 Toynbee (1971) 48: 'Sanitary precautions and fear of defilement readily explain the law.' In agreement with Le Gall (1980–1) 148, Scobie (1986), 409, argues that Roman leaders were largely indifferent to the health of the masses: 'The Romans were legally more concerned about the intramural burial of the dead than they were about the disposal of human and animal wastes within the city.' On concerns about public health versus sacral pollution, see ch. 5 below. Rome had other taboos about disposal: e.g. Pliny, *HN* 2.145 (cf. Plut. *Mor.* 665c), reports that it was unlawful to cremate a person killed by lightning, that custom required burial. Cf. below on those who died by hanging.

14 Hopkins (1983) 233. Toynbee (1971) 33–9, on Roman beliefs, explains, 34, that 'there persisted and prevailed the conviction that some kind of conscious existence is in store for the soul after death and that the dead and the living can affect one another mutually'. Toynbee, 35–6, 135, also notes that Romans developed notions of moral responsibility and judgement concerning the afterlife. Similarly: Dill (1956) 484–528. Richmond Lattimore, *Themes in Greek and Latin Epitaphs* (Urbana: U. Illinois, 1942), collects Latin epitaphs denying or expressing skepticism about life after death, 78–82, and others which express a belief in or a wish for it, 54–5, 59–65; he concludes, 264–5, 342, that belief in an afterlife (as a better existence, i.e. along Christian lines) was not common, clear, or strong. Bernstein (1993) feels that early Greece and Rome had no

widely accepted notion of hell, which he defines, 3, as 'a divinely sanctioned place of eternal torment for the wicked'. Although Virgil, Plato, and Plutarch wrote of a moral death with rewards and punishments, 50–83, Bernstein, 21–49, feels that most commoners regarded death as neutral, as morally undifferentiated.

15 The intelligentsia (e.g. Sen. *Dial. (Cons. ad Marc.)* 19.4; Juv. 13.48) decried the concerns of common Romans, but the intellectual fashions of the literati neither outweighed nor outlived traditional rites and fears. Lucretius, 3.862–9, protested that there is nothing to fear in death, for death ends all possibility of suffering: we cannot suffer once immortal death takes away mortal life. See Charles Segal, *Lucretius on Death and Anxiety: Poetry and Philosophy in De Rerum Natura* (Princeton: Princeton U., 1990), esp. 17–25, on Roman fears about death and the afterlife. Pliny, *HN* 7.188–90, Loeb, rejects belief in sensation after death and in the immortality of souls (189–90): 'These are fictions of childish absurdity, and belong to a mortality greedy for life unceasing … Plague take it, what is this mad idea that life is renewed by death?' Lucian, *Luct.* 2, and Plutarch, *Mor.* 1105a (cf. 1104b), agree that the common people still believed in Hades. As Bernstein (1993), 115–22, explains, in his philosophical works Cicero disputed common notions of ghosts (*Tusc.* 1.13.29) and the afterlife (1.13.30), and he rejected the masses' beliefs that ghosts were joined to their bodies (1.16.37) and that souls suffer in the underworld (1.46.111); but in his oratory he used the idea of retributive punishment in the afterlife for rhetorical purposes (e.g. *Phil.* 4.4.10, 14.12.32).

16 Bernstein (1993) 27–30, 65, 92–104: souls in the Hades of Virgil and Homer wear the signs of their lives and deaths, and they can feel great passions. Cf. Virg. *Aen.* 6.426–36 on the unhappy souls of infants, those condemned to death on false charges, and those who committed suicide. Garland (1985), 74, agrees that the dead in the Greek Hades are frozen for eternity in the condition in which they died.

17 E.g. Suetonius, *Calig.* 59, Loeb, reports that Caligula's corpse was only 'partly consumed on a hastily erected pyre and buried beneath a light covering of turf', and 'it is well known that the caretakers of the [Lamian] gardens were disturbed by ghosts, and that in the house where he was slain not a night passed without some fearful apparition'. Ultimately, his sisters returned, exhumed the body, cremated it fully, and entombed it properly. Tertullian, *De anim.* 56, agrees that, if no funeral rites had been performed, the soul of the dead man could not be received among the Shades but wandered homeless upon the earth. As *biothanati* the restless souls of the unburied flutter near the corpse; see Cumont's classic works: (1922) 64–9, (1949) 334–8. Further on the afterlife, ghosts, and demons, see Garland (1985) 92–4; Hopkins (1983) 226–35; Georg Luck, *Arcana Mundi: Magic and the Occult in the Greek and Roman Worlds* (Baltimore: Johns Hopkins U., 1985) 161–225.

18 *Aen.* 6.325–30; cf. Hom. *Il.* 23.71–4. The unburied must wait 100 years to pass over. When Palinurus tells of his murder and begs Aeneas for burial (cf. Virgil's Polydorus and Misenus), the Sibyl tells him to give up hope of crossing over but offers him the small consolation that he will receive a tomb and offerings.

19 D. L. Page, *Select Papyri*, vol. III: *Literary Papyri, Poetry*, Loeb (Cambridge, Mass.: Harvard U., 1950) 416–21; cited by Garland (1985) 76.

20 Virg. *Aen.* 4.384–7. Ghosts might return to visit family members (Apul. *Met.* 8.4), to seek vengeance (Cic. *Div.* 1.27.57), or to punish offenders (Suet. *Otho* 7.2). See Bernstein (1993) 84–106.

21 In Petronius, *Sat.* 115, even people who apparently disbelieve in the afterlife feel compelled to give burial even to people they dislike: Lichas is washed

ashore from a shipwreck and, before seeing who it is, Eumolpus and his friends lament the cruelty of death at sea. Even after seeing that it is the hated Lichas, they give him a cremation burial, lest wild beasts mangle the carcass.

22 As Toynbee (1971), 34–5, points out, Plautus' *Mostellaria* testifies to the belief that spirits of the dead can haunt the homes of the living. In Petronius, *Sat.* 61–2, a man tells a tale of a man turning into a werewolf in an area of graves. The narrator of a story, *Sat.* 63, in which witches steal a boy slave's corpse and replace it with a straw dummy, concludes that there are witches and that ghouls go walking at night.

23 John G. Gager, ed., *Curse Tablets and Binding Spells from the Ancient World* (Oxford: Oxford U., 1992) 244. Gager, 3, 21, 175, defines *defixiones* (Greek *katadesmoi*) as inscribed tablets, usually of lead, enlisting the supernatural agency of spirits, demons, and gods to influence the behavior and welfare of persons (or animals, notably racehorses) against their will. Curse tablets were placed in fresh graves (e.g. Gager's nos. 13–15, aimed at charioteers at Rome, are tablets from a fourth-century AD tomb on the Via Appia), wells, pits, springs, or rivers, or even in the floors of stadiums and racetracks near the starting gates; see Gager, 18–21. In other words, they were deposited near new souls, chthonic accesses, or sites of the intended harm or control. As Gager, 19, explains, those who died young or by violence were thought to have restless souls, which stayed near the grave, and thus would be suitable messengers to the gods and/or casters of spells for the gods. Gods, such as Jupiter, Pluto, Nemesis, and Mercury, however, were always involved.

24 Ibid., 23, 119–21: curse tablets 'worked', not in the rationalistic sense of demons affecting a target's behavior, but in the sense that ancients believed that they worked, and thus they gave emotional release or comfort to their users. They explained misfortunes and failures, and, if targets were aware of them, they might induce them to some actions. Cf. the suspicion that Piso caused Germanicus' death via a spell or curse tablet: Tac. *Ann.* 2.69. From the XII Tables on, Roman law prohibited practitioners of magic, curses, and binding spells precisely because they were believed to work and because they could be used by persons beyond the control of the state; see Paul. *Sent.* 5.23.15–18 = Gager no. 157 on 258–9; penalties varied by class and later included crucifixion or the beasts. On magicians as a threat to social order, see MacMullen (1966) 95–127. Despite prohibitions, curse tablets flourished even into the Christian era; see A. A. Barb, 'The Survival of the Magic Arts', in A. Momigliano, ed., *The Conflict between Paganism and Christianity in the Fourth Century* (Oxford: Oxford U., 1963) 100–25.

25 Once a grave was legally a grave (i.e. with the sacrifice of a pig: Cic. *Leg.* 2.22.57), violation of sepulcher (*violatio sepulchri*) was a criminal offense: Cic. *Leg.* 3; *Dig.* 47.12. A proper sepulcher became a *locus religiosus* under sacral law and was no longer the alienable possession of anyone: Gaius *Inst.* II.3, 6, 9 (confirmed in *CIust* 3.44.2). See Toynbee (1971) 50–1, 76, and nn. 273–6 on 296–7; Crook (1984) 133–8; Hopkins (1983) 247–55; de Visscher (1963) 65–82; M. Ducos, 'Le Tombeau, *locus religiosus*', 135–44, in Hinard (1995). *SEG* 8 (1937) 13, the controversial 'Nazareth' decree, probably by Augustus or perhaps Claudius, if genuine, orders the death penalty for persons caught disturbing graves; see de Visscher (1963) 161–95. A subcategory of *defixiones*, curses on gravestones, invoke harm on anyone who disturbs the burial; see Gager (1992) 177–8. Cf. *CIL* 6.36467 (= *ILS* 8184); Toynbee (1971) 76–7: a tomb inscription from Rome threatens any desecrator: 'I pray that he may, while alive, endure prolonged pains of body and that, when he dies, the gods of the lower world will reject him.' Further on laws against violation and reuse of sepulchers: see de Visscher (1963) 139–46; Robinson (1995) 39–40.

144

26 As Ovid, *Fast.* 5.479, notes, the first *lemur* was Remus. See Toynbee (1971) 35, 64, on *manes* and the prowling of 'apparently kinless and hungry ghosts, the *Lemures*, and the mischievous and dangerous *Larvae*', citing Cic. *Leg.* 2.9.22; Plaut. *Capt.* 598, *Cas.* 592, *Amph.* 777. On festivals of the dead, see Toynbee (1971) 61–4; Daniel P. Harmon, 'The Family Festivals of Rome', *ANRW* 2.16.2 (1978) 1592–603. Ovid, *Fast.* 5.419–44, describes the private rites of the Lemuria as an ancient and sacred custom. As Toynbee (1971), n. 263 on 296, cautions, Ovid is wrong in suggesting that the object was to cleanse the house of *manes paterni*. As in the state festival, the aim of the Lemuria was to dispel all and any *lemures* or kinless and hungry spirits; the Parentalia was the more familially oriented rite.

27 Gager (1992) 12: one of the fundamental characteristics of the 'spiritual world' of ancient Mediterranean culture is the belief that 'the spirit or soul of dead persons, especially of those who had died prematurely or by violence, roamed about in a restless and vengeful mood near their buried body'. Suetonius, *Ner.* 34.4, Loeb, says that Nero, his conscience troubled over his matricide, often said that he was hounded by his mother's ghost 'and by the whips and blazing torches of the Furies'. Suetonius adds that the Magi performed rites to summon and appease her spirit.

28 In her dissertation Katariina Mustakallio, *Death and Disgrace: Capital Penalties with* Post Mortem *Sanctions in Early Roman Historiography* (Helsinki: Suomalainen Tiedeakatemia, 1994), argues that the concept of *damnatio memoriae* (see ch. 7 below) was known in early Rome. She studies eight cases of shameful post-mortem punishments (e.g. denial of burial, destruction of the house, prohibition of the use of the *praenomen*) in the historiographical traditions of the early Republic (in Livy and Dionysius of Halicarnassus), concluding that such punishments were associated with aspirants to *regnum*. She explains, 10–13, 80–1, that such ultimate sanctions meant dishonor for the individual in the afterlife and for the family in the world of the living.

29 *Aen.* 10.557–60, Loeb. Cf. Hom. *Il.* 21.122–7 (similarly 21.201–4), R. Lattimore trans.: Achilles killed Lykaon and threw him into the Xanthos River, denying him burial:

> Lie there now among the fish, who will lick the blood away
> from your wound, and care nothing for you, nor will your mother
> lay you on the death-bed and mourn over you, but Skamandros
> will carry you spinning down to the wide bend of the salt water.
> And a fish will break a ripple shuddering dark on the water
> as he rises to feed on the shining fat of Lykaon.

At the end of the *Aeneid* Turnus asks Aeneas for the right of burial (12.932–4) before he is killed, but Virgil does not comment on the fate of his corpse. Farron (1985), 21–33, sees Aeneas' treatment of his victims as a reference to Octavian's Civil War atrocities; cf. ch. 2 above.

30 Brutus' speech (Livy 1.59.10) recalls Tarquin's slaughter of Servius and presents Tullia's act of driving her carriage over the dumped corpse of her father as a breach of sacred ties, one which the gods would punish.

31 Superseding Y. Grisé, *Le Suicide dans la Rome antique* (Paris: Les Belles Lettres, 1982), the authoritative study of ancient suicide is now that by Van Hooff (1990), who discusses the Roman taboo in 'The Rope of Ghastly Death', 64–72. Cf. Artem. 1.4, cited by Van Hooff (1990) 160–1, who says that a man's dream that he lost his name came true: he ended his life with a rope and his relatives did not name him at the death meals; i.e. families excluded from tribute in

their funerary rituals those members who hanged themselves. On suicide, also see J.-L. Voisin, 'Pendus, crucifiés, *oscilla* dans la Rome païenne,' *Latomus* 38 (1979) 422–50; J.-L. Voisin, 'Apicata, Antinous et quelques autres', *MÉFRA* 99.1 (1987) 257–80; Paolo Desideri, 'Il trattamento del corpo dei suicidi', 189–204, esp. 190–7 on hanging, in Hinard (1995). The rules of the burial club from Lanuvium of AD 136 (*CIL* 14.2112 = *ILS* 7212, mentioned in n. 11 above) excluded suicides from funeral rites; see Hopkins (1983) 213–15; Van Hooff (1990) 166; Voisin (1987) 262–6; Grisé (1982) 153–6. Cf. further below in ch. 5 concerning Sassina and Puteoli. As Toynbee (1971), 73, notes, the Catholic Church declared suicide a crime at the Council of Arles in 452, and the Council of Braga in 563 said that suicides must be denied burial rites; and in England a stake was place through their hearts and they were buried at crossroads until 1823.

32 *HN* 36.107, Loeb. See Van Hooff (1990) 17, 66, 164–6, quote at 164; cf. Grisé (1982) 127–32. Voisin (1979), 445–6, suggests that the story may have derived from Tarquin's punishment of those who refused to work by hanging them, and thus denying them burial, as was the case with those who committed suicide by hanging themselves. Superbus was also associated, probably anachronistically, with use of the 'sack' penalty; see ch. 7 below.

33 Serv. *Ad Aen.* 12.603. Servius cites Varro declaring that it was not proper that such suicides receive rites. Voisin (1979), 428–36, offers a religious explanation – that those who hanged themselves lost contact with Mother Earth, that burying them would be a sacrilege, and that their tortured spirits were doomed to wander the earth. Voisin, 446–50, further suggests, from Varro in Servius, that the custom of hanging puppets or effigies (*oscilla*) in trees was a rite of purification associated with the unquiet spirits of the unburied dead who were killed or killed themselves by hanging.

34 Dion. Hal. *Ant. Rom.* 20.16.2, Loeb; see also Polyb. 1.7.12; the incident is discussed above in ch. 2. Cf. Livy's account, 29.9.10, Loeb, of an incident in 205 BC at Locri in which the commander Pleminius punished some military tribunes with more than torture and death: 'Not satisfied with a penalty paid by the living either, he threw them out unburied (*insepultos proiecit*).'

35 In detail on the proscriptions, see F. Hinard, *Les Proscriptions de la Rome républicaine* (Rome: École française de Rome, 1985) passim, 104–10 on executions, 42–4 on legalization; similarly, see his 'La Male Mort: Exécutions et statut du corps au moment de la première proscription', in *Châtiment* (1984) 295–311, esp. 297–302 on legalization.

36 Hinard (1984), 301–5, associates the proscriptions of Sulla in 82 with 'la male mort' – the opposite of traditional burial rites, in which proscribed victims died spectacular and humiliating deaths and then their bodies were systematically abused by decapitation or mutilation with the goal, 309, of preventing burial and depriving the victim of any status in the world of the dead. Similarly, David (1984), esp. 173–5, sees corpse abuse as an insult and as a proof of a ruler's power.

37 *B Civ.* 1.73; Appian, *The Civil Wars*, trans. John Carter (London: Penguin, 1996). Ibid., 1.71: 'These events no longer aroused religious scruple, or human retribution, or fear of opprobrium; on the contrary, men turned to savage deeds, and from savage deeds to displays of sacrilege – merciless killing, decapitations of men already dead, and exhibition of the results to create fear or horror or a sacrilegious spectacle.' Plut. *Mar.* 44.6: headless bodies were thrown out onto the street and trodden upon. On the display of heads, see ch. 7 below.

38 Out of hatred of Pompeius Strabo, father of Pompey, people disrupted his funeral, insulted his corpse, and dragged it from its bier, but officials prevented

further abuse; see Plut. *Pomp.* 1.2; Vell. Pat. 2.21.4; Licin. 22–3, cited by Nippel (1995) n. 47 on 44.

39 Lintott (1968) 50: 'The belief in private revenge was so deeply embedded in Roman thought that it could not be excluded from politics.' Cf. J. W. Heaton, *Mob Violence in the Late Roman Republic 133–49 B.C.* (Urbana: U. Illinois, 1939) 40–1. Hinard (1984), 309–10, suggests that in the proscriptions of 43 there was no reward for killing or turning in the victims, less mutilation (simple executions by decapitation), and no denial of burial.

40 *OGI* no. 532 = *ILS* 8781; trans. N. Lewis and M. Reinhold, eds., *Roman Civilization: Selected Readings*, vol. I: *The Republic and the Augustan Age*, 3rd ed. (New York: Columbia U., 1990, orig. 1966) 589.

41 Suet. *Aug.* 13.1–2. Farron (1985), 26–7, feels that these and other rhetorical and inflammatory charges stemmed from anti-Octavian propaganda. Dio, 48.48.5, mentions similar false charges against Sextus Pompey. On heads, see ch. 7, and on possible denial of burial for *auctorati*, see ch. 5 below.

42 On legal testimonia (e.g. *Dig.* 48.21.3.2) and justifications and implications of suicide, see Van Hooff (1990) 37–9, 53, 69–70, 80–4, 90, 168–72; A. Wacke, 'Der Selbstmord im römischen Recht und in der Rechtsentwicklung', *ZRG* 97 (1980) 26–77; Grisé (1982) 247–70; Crook (1984) 275–6; Plass (1995) 84–5. As Van Hooff explains, Rome's main legal concern was whether suicide committed during or just before a trial could be counted as a confession, and the legal focus was on wealthy defendants whose property the state might confiscate. Both the legalities and the history are complex. In Republican Rome suicide committed during the trial of a serious case which might bring execution and confiscation might be taken as a confession; but in Cicero's day suicide before conviction aborted the criminal proceedings and prevented ignominy and confiscations: Cic. *Att.* 1.4.2; Val. Max. 9.12.7: Lucius Macer, on trial for extortion (as a form of treason) in 66 BC, committed suicide after sending a note to Cicero saying that his property could not be sold; Cicero pronounced no verdict.

43 Tac. *Ann.* 6.23.1–2. As Levick (1976), 188–9, notes, Dio, 58.21.2, records only the death of 'Vibullius'. Cf. Suet. *Tib.* 61.4, Loeb: 'Of those who were cited to plead their causes some opened their veins at home, feeling sure of being condemned and wishing to avoid annoyance and humiliation, while others drank poison in full view of the senate; yet the former were bandaged, and they were hurried half-dead, but still quivering, to the prison.' Cf. Dio's story, 78.20.4, Loeb, noted by Van Hooff (1990) 69, that when an assistant of the king of the Quadians hanged himself before he could be executed, the emperor had his corpse abused to make the Quadians believe that he had indeed been executed rather than committing suicide, for suicide was honorable among them.

44 Tac. *Ann.* 6.29.1–2, Loeb. In AD 33 Tiberius granted burial to Asinius Gallus, who starved to death (voluntarily or involuntarily), even though he was still under charges: Tac. *Ann.* 6.23; cf. Dio 58.3.3. Under Domitian those who committed suicide while awaiting trial were without legal heirs (Suet. *Dom.* 12.1), but Van Hooff (see n. 42 above) shows that second-century AD legal reforms increased the valid justifications for suicide and narrowed the conditions under which the state was able to confiscate the estates of suicides. In effect, suicide was to be taken as a confession only if no valid justification could be found.

45 Bodies of persons condemned to normal execution by the sword were to be released to relatives ('Corpora eorum qui capite damnantur cognatis ipsorum non neganda sunt'), but denial of burial was allowed in cases of *maiestas* as an extra punishment; *Dig.* 48.24.1 (Ulpian Bk. 9 *De Officio Proconsulis*); Berger

147

(1953) 377; Levick (1976) n. 51 on 283. Callu (1984), n. 107 on 338, notes that *Dig.* 48.24.3 allows the retrieval of bones and ashes after execution by fire. Suetonius, *Vesp.* 2.3, recounts that as praetor Vespasian, in order to curry favor with Caligula, suggested that the bodies of the conspirators Lepidus and Gaetulicus should be denied public burial 'as an additional punishment'. On treason and law, see ch. 3 above.

46 Suet. *Tib.* 61.2, Loeb: 'The relatives of the victims were forbidden to mourn for them.' For example, Cloatilla, wife of Scribonius, was prosecuted by the senate for having buried her husband even though he was condemned for involvement in Sejanus' conspiracy (Quint. 8.5.16). No mourning for Sejanus: Dio 58.12.4. Cf. examples in Levick (1976) n. 50 on 282, and in ch. 7 below. Enemies, traitors, *suspendiosi*, and those who killed themselves out of consciousness of their guilt were not to be mourned; see *Dig.* 3.2.11.3, cited by Van Hooff (1990) 69, 165.

47 Plass (1995), 81–134, interprets political suicide as socially sanctioned violence, a response to political disruption and a reaffirmation of security. He applies game theory to suggest rules and moves in the interaction between emperors and their opponents. Inducing or performing suicide in certain ways could be tactical moves to score points. Similarly, Plass sees denial of burial (and of wills and inheritances) as moves to show or oppose power. He explains, 84–5, that politicians could retain integrity in suicide and win, symbolically, by losing. Further on suicide as a political device, see MacMullen (1966) 75–94; Van Hooff (1990) 112–13; and M. T. Griffin, *Seneca: A Philosopher in Politics* (Oxford: Clarendon Press, 1976) 367–88.

48 E.g. Dio, 78.13.7, claims that Caracalla had the bodies of some of the most illustrious men he had killed cast out unburied. Caracalla's own corpse was brought secretly into Rome by night and cremated, possibly to protect it from abuse; see Dio 79(78).9.1; Aur. Vict. *Caes.* 21.6; cited by Morris (1992) 54–5. He showed honor to Sulla by repairing his tomb 'because he was emulating his cruelty'.

49 For Romans not all deaths were the same, nor were all disposals. The nature of a person's dying or being killed had consequences for the nature of his or her afterlife. As Van Hooff (1990), 77, says of various methods of suicide: 'In antiquity the appearance of the mortal remains has everything to do with the way and degree in which one is supposed to live in the hereafter. The art of dying should be a worthy fulfilment of life.' Romans, especially the elite, were preoccupied with status, dignity, shame, and loss of face. They fully appreciated the significance of corpse abuse via violation of the integrity of bodies and of damnation via denial of burial rites.

50 On public executions as ritualized spectacles with emotionally intense popular involvement and moral approval, see Foucault (1977) 32–69, esp. 47–51. Foucault, 51, comments: 'In the explicit reference to the butcher's trade, the infinitesimal destruction of the body is linked here with spectacle: each piece is placed on display.'

51 John Lofland, 'The Dramaturgy of State Executions', 275–325, in Horace Bleackley, ed., *Executions Viewed Historically and Sociologically* (Montclair, N.J.: Patterson Smith, 1977), discussing procedures in England around 1700, notes that modern state executions in the West impersonalize, privatize, and make covert the act of killing.

52 Assyrian texts are from Daniel D. Luckenbill, *Ancient Records of Assyria and Babylonia*, 2 vols. (Chicago: U. Chicago, 1926–7), vol. 2, sections 254, 795–6, 810. These and similar claims are quoted in Erika Bleibtreu, 'Grisly Assyrian Record of Torture and Death', *Biblical Archaeology Review* (January/February 1991) 52–61; and in Jasper Griffin, *Homer on Life and Death* (Oxford: Clarendon

Press, 1980) 45–6, who suggests that reports of Assyrian atrocities influenced motifs of mutilation of corpses and denial of burial in Homer's *Iliad*. Cf. n. 55 below. Cf. I Sam. 17.44–6: Goliath cursed David by his gods and threatened to give his flesh to the birds of the air and the wild beasts of the field, and David replied that he would cut off Goliath's head and give the corpses of the Philistine army to the birds of the air and the beasts of the field.

53 Souls were thought to linger near the body during putrefaction and near the tomb later. Inconsistently, souls were also thought to descend to Hades. As Garland (1985), 76, comments: 'Such inconsistencies should come to us as no surprise: afterlives, after all, are not the creatures of logical positivists.' The classic study is Erwin Rohde, *Psyche*, 5th ed., trans. W. B. Hillis (London: Macmillan, 1925, orig. 1897); accessible modern studies include Donna C. Kurtz and John Boardman, *Greek Burial Customs* (Ithaca: Cornell U., 1971); J. Bremmer, *The Early Greek Concept of the Soul* (Princeton: Princeton U., 1983); and Garland (1985). On the archaeology of Greek burial rites, see Ian Morris, *Burial and Ancient Society* (Cambridge: Cambridge U., 1987), esp. 29–43, who suggests the emergence of a new social structure in the eighth century with a new emphasis on the city state as a community of citizens.

54 Aelian, *VH* 5.14, says that Athenian law required that anyone who saw a corpse had to put earth on it, even if the person was a stranger. See Garland (1985) 101–3. Cf. n. 82 in ch. 5 below on the Athenian *koprophoroi*.

55 Hector begs for burial (*Il.* 22.337–44) but Achilles says that Hector despoiled the corpse of Patroclus, and now he will be unburied: dogs and birds will tear him shamelessly, but Patroclus will get a grand burial. On the contrast between ideal heroic death and the horror of an abused, unburied corpse exposed to carrion beasts, see Griffin (1980) 44–9, 115–19, 137–8, 160–1; J.-P. Vernant, 'La Belle Mort et le cadavre outragé', 47–76, in Gnoli and Vernant (1982). Charles Segal, *The Theme of the Mutilation of the Corpse in the Iliad* (Leiden: Brill, 1971), suggests that the theme of abuse shows not so much primitivism as the destructive passions unleashed by war. Segal, 30–2, sees an enlargement of the mutilation theme in *Il.* 21 when the Xanthos or Skamandros River, in support of the Trojans, criticizes enraged Achilles for filling his stream with the bodies of slain Trojans (21.214–21). Achilles had denied burial for Lykaon among others, but he agrees to drive his foes out of the river and onto the plain before continuing his slaughter. Later Xanthos wants his tributary Simoeis to help him kill Achilles and cover his body with sand to prevent the Greeks from giving him burial rites (21.305–23), but Athena and other gods help Achilles and force Xanthos to desist.

56 Garland (1985), 93–5, discusses Greek notions of the 'murdered dead' and their angry, vengeful spirits as a category of the 'unquiet dead'. As chthonic deities the Furies may have embodied the curses of the murdered, unavenged dead. Garland, 94, 163, also notes the Greek practice of *maschalismos* mentioned in tragedy, in which a murderer cuts off extremities from the corpse of the victim, either to prevent vengeance or to add further humiliation; cf. Rohde (1925) 582–6; Van Hooff (1990) 162–3.

57 Thuc. 2.52.4 (plague), 7.75.1 (Syracuse). Proper burial in the family burial-ground and tending to ancestors' tombs were considered fundamental to the family. Euripides' Medea gains additional revenge against Jason by monstrously refusing to let him know where she will bury the children and thus preventing him from performing his obligatory and comforting mourning rites. Cf. W. K. Lacey, *The Family in Classical Greece* (Ithaca: Cornell U., 1968) 80–1, explaining the impact of the failure of the Athenian generals to retrieve the bodies of the dead at Arginusae.

58 W. R. Connor, 'The Raising of the House in Greek Society', *TAPA* 115 (1985) 79–102, at 81, cites (Ephorus frag. 60 in) Nikolaos of Damascus (*FGrH* 90 F60). Connor, 83, admits that the story may not be historical but says that it would have been fabricated along the lines of traditional punishments.

59 Thuc. 1.126.11–12; Hdt. 5.71; Plut. *Sol.* 12.3. As a convicted traitor Themistocles was denied burial in Attica, but Thucydides, 1.138.6, reports rumors that relatives secretly brought back and buried his body; cf. Plut. *Them.* 22.4–4.

60 Aesch. *Sept.* 1013–24: Thebes orders that Polyneices be dishonored as a traitor, that his corpse be cast out unburied, without obsequies, to be torn by dogs and birds. By one tradition, Kreon also refused to let the families of those who attacked Thebes bury their dead, so Theseus buried them at Eleusis; but the Thebans denied this: Plut. *Thes.* 29. 4–5; Paus. 1.39.2.

61 On throwing bodies off cliffs, into the sea, beyond the boundaries, etc., see Parker (1983) 33–48, esp. 43–7; Cantarella (1991) 91–105. Athens: Xen. *Hell.* 1.7.22: by Athenian law temple robbers and traitors were to be denied burial in Attica and to have their property confiscated. Plutarch, *Phoc.* 37.2–3, Loeb, says that after the execution of Phocion by hemlock, 'his enemies, as if their triumph were incomplete, got a decree passed that the body of Phocion should be carried beyond the boundary of the country, and that no Athenian should light a fire for his obsequies'. Cf. Plutarch's remark, *Them.* 22.2, Loeb, that at a site in Melite in Attica in his day 'the public officials cast out the bodies of those who have been put to death, and carry forth the garments and the nooses of those who have dispatched themselves by hanging'. Further on suicide as miasmatic in Greece, see Van Hooff (1990) 162–3. Plato, *Leg.* 9.873b, 874b, said that murderers and parricides should be cast out unburied. See *Resp.* 4.439e (cited above in n. 4 in ch. 1) on executions and corpses outside the North Wall at Athens; Garland (1985), 95, suggests that the pit (*barathron*; cf. Hdt. 7.133) may be the long depression beside the Northern Long Wall near the so-called Hill of the Nymphs. At Sparta the worst criminals were thrown into the Kaiadas (Thuc. 1.134.4; Strabo 8.5.7; Paus. 4.18.4); on a pit found filled with skeletons, see P. G. Themelis, '*Kaiadas*', *AAA* 15 (1982) 183–201; Morris (1992) 71–2.

62 Detailed studies include: Linda Schele and Mary Ellen Miller, *The Blood of Kings: Dynasty and Ritual in Maya Art* (New York: George Braziller and the Kimbell Art Museum, 1986); E. Boone, ed., *Ritual Sacrifice in Mesoamerica* (Washington, D.C.: Dumbarton Oaks U., 1984), including Linda Schele, 'Human Sacrifice among the Classic Maya', 7–48; Linda Schele and David Friedel, *A Forest of Kings: The Untold Story of the Ancient Maya* (New York: William Morrow, 1990).

63 Schele and Miller (1986), 'Warfare and Captive Sacrifice', 209–22; quote at 220.

64 Schele in Boone (1984) 7–48, with 43–5 on humiliations.

65 Schele and Miller (1986), 216–18, note that captives of the Maya were tortured and mutilated without mercy: they suffered beatings, cuts, disembowelment, burning by fire, scalping, and forms of protracted bloodletting such as having the ends of their fingers cut off. At 218: 'In contrast, the quick deliberate heart excision practiced by the Aztecs can be regarded as a merciful act.'

66 Schele in Boone (1984), 7–11, notes that most victims were decapitated, but variations included heart excision, disembowelment, shooting with arrows, beating with thorny branches, and being thrown from heights. See further on Mayan sacrifice in B. Brundage, *The Jade Steps* (Salt Lake City: U. Utah, 1985) 88–90, 155–78. Plass (1995), n. 14 on 187, compares the smearing of victims'

blood on the mouths of Mayan idols (as the Aztecs also did, see below) with the offerings of the blood of arena victims into the mouth of a statue of Jupiter Latiaris (discussed in ch. 2 above). Recent finds show that the Moche peoples of Peru, for a long period of time and over a wide area, also practiced a sacrificial ceremony in which bound war captives had their throats cut and their blood was ritually consumed in ceremonial goblets. This was probably part of the state religion and it was performed in major ceremonial complexes with multiple pyramids. See Christopher B. Donnan and Luis Jaime Castillo, 'Finding the Tomb of a Moche Priestess', *Archaeology* 45.6 (Nov.–Dec. 1992) 38–43.

67 Discussions of Aztec sacrifice rely on the sixteenth-century accounts of natives' testimony by Fr. Bernardino de Sahagún, *Historia general de las cosas de la Nueva España*, 4 vols., ed. Angel María K. (Mexico City: Parrúa, 1956) (see Fr. Bernardino de Sahagún, *The Florentine Codex: General History of the Things of New Spain*, 12 books in 13 volumes, trans. Arthur J. O. Anderson and Charles Dibble (Santa Fe: School of American Research and U. Utah, 1950–82)) and first-hand accounts by Bernal Díaz, *The Conquest of New Spain*, trans. J. M. Cohen (Harmondsworth: Penguin, 1963). The best recent discussion, heavily used here, is Inga Clendinnen, *Aztecs: An Interpretation* (Cambridge: Cambridge U., 1991) 87–110. Other studies: Michael E. Smith, *The Aztecs* (Oxford: Blackwell, 1996) esp. 221–7; Davies (1981) 198–241; Georges Bataille, *The Accursed Share: An Essay on General Economy*, vol. 1, *Consumption*, trans. Robert Hurley (New York: Zone Books, 1988) 45–77. Arthur Demarest, 'Overview: Mesoamerican Human Sacrifice in Evolutionary Perspective', in Boone (1984) 227–34, notes that human sacrifice changed ideologically from a legitimation of individual personal power in the Classic era to legitimation of the states, the polity as a whole, in the Post-classic era of regional competition. The Aztecs represent the height of this trend to using the militaristic cult of human sacrifice in increasing numbers in an age of expansionism and interpolity competition. Rome knew a similar shift from the triumphs and *munera* of individuals in the Republic to those of the emperor as the state under the Empire. Plass (1995), 22–4, sees Aztec sacrifices as comparable to Roman *munera* as political intimidation and as responses to concerns about danger; in both cases brutality kept vulnerability at bay, but, Plass suggests, Aztec sacrifice was more essentially religious and cosmic in scope.

68 Clendinnen (1991), 89, describes the ritual of sacrifice. The account of the Spaniard Díaz, op. cit., 386–7, who witnessed an Aztec sacrifice of captives on a temple-pyramid at Tenochtitlan (Mexico City) in 1521 provides details:

> we saw our comrades who had been captured in Cortes' defeat being dragged up the steps to be sacrificed. When they had hauled them up to a small platform in front of the shrine where they kept their accursed idols we saw them put plumes on the heads of many of them; and then they made them dance with a sort of fan in front of Huichilobos. Then after they had danced the *papas* [priests] laid them down on their backs on some narrow stones of sacrifice and, cutting open their chests, drew out their palpitating hearts which they offered to the idols before them ... Then they kicked the bodies down the steps, and the Indian butchers who were waiting below cut off their arms and legs and flayed their faces ... Then they ate their flesh with a sauce of peppers and tomatoes.

That victims were even kept in cages and fed carbohydrates to be fattened, however, is a European misconception. The 'fattening coops' were a Spanish interpretation of the holding cages; see Clendinnen (1991) 89.

69 Michael Harner, in 'The Enigma of Aztec Sacrifice', *Natural History* 86.4 (April 1977) 46–51, and 'The Ecological Basis for Aztec Sacrifice', *American Ethnologist* 4 (1977) 117–35, proposed that ecological circumstances and problems of food supply led to extensive cannibalism, practiced under the guise of sacrifice. Rather than the usual estimate of 20,000, Harner favors an estimate of 250,000 victims of Aztec human sacrifice per year in the fifteenth century. Thence Marvin Harris, *Cannibals and Kings: The Origins of Culture* (New York: Random House, 1978) 105–10, accepts the idea of a state system of redistribution of human protein related to the depletion of the Mesoamerican ecosystem. However, scholars generally reject Harner's theory and put Aztec concern for piety above their need for protein. E.g. Davies (1981), 14, 235–8, noting that commoners were not normally allowed to eat human flesh, rejects the idea of cannibalism as fundamental to the Aztec diet. Again, in 'Human Sacrifice in the Old World and the New: Some Similarities and Differences', in Boone (1984) 211–16, Davies sees Aztec cannibalism as a ritual and not a pragmatic, materialistic act. He comments, at 214, that: 'The eating of the victim is mainly, if not solely, an alternative method of disposal. Anthropophagy is a natural consequence of theophagy, the eating of the deity, that serves in so many religions as a means of uniting man and gods.' Against Harner, see Marshall D. Sahlins, 'Culture as Protein and Profit', *NYRB* 23 (Nov. 1978) 45–53; Barbara J. Price, 'Demystification, Enriddlement and Aztec Cannibalism: A Materialist Rejoinder to Harner', *American Ethnologist* 9 (1978) 98–115.

70 Clendinnen (1991) 91. That torsos were taken away to the Royal Zoo to be consumed by birds, snakes, and other carnivores, as suggested by Harner, 'Enigma of Aztec Sacrifice', 49, is unlikely. Davies (1981), 235, argues that the victims, as the property of the god to whom they were sacrificed, would not be treated as offal and thrown to animals. Moreover, there were too many victims for the zoo, and there were no zoos in the provinces. Davies suggests rather that the torso, with the vital organs associated with the victim's soul, would have been eaten.

71 Cf. nineteenth-century European accounts of mass human sacrifices in Dahomey (modern Benin) in West Africa. The 'Annual Custom' sacrificed perhaps 500 to honor the ghost of the previous king and the 'Grand Custom' used perhaps twice as many to honor a new king, with perhaps 40,000 assembled spectators. In this non-cannibalistic culture the victims were later thrown into pits and exposed to dogs and vultures. See Davies (1981) 141–65, citing A. B. Ellis, *The Ewe-speaking Peoples of the Slave Coast of West Africa* (London: Chapman and Hall, 1890) 123.

72 See David Wilcox and Vernon Scarborough, eds., *The Mesoamerican Ballgame* (Tucson: U. Arizona, 1990); G. Van Bussel et al., eds., *The Mesoamerican Ballgame: Papers Presented to an International Colloquium* (Leiden: Brill, 1991). The clear discussion in Schele and Miller (1986) 241–54, with further bibliography, is largely followed here.

73 Schele and Friedel (1990) 126. Many spectators gambled on the outcomes, often for high stakes, and professional ballplayers, according to Schele and Miller (1986) 243, were seen as 'unsavory types'.

74 Schele and Miller (1986) 253. The myth is summarized in Schele and Miller (1986) 243–54, and Schele and Friedel (1990) 74–5, using the translation by Dennis Tedlock, *Popol Vuh: The Definitive Edition of the Mayan Book of the Dawn of Life and the Glories of Gods and Kings* (New York: Simon and Schuster, 1985).

75 Schele and Miller (1986) 241: in the Precolumbian ballgame 'human sacrifice was overt rather than suppressed. Just as in warfare, the Precolumbian ballgame makes death the final step in play, defining victory or defeat in stark

terms.' Like the Roman arena, the ballcourt was a liminal place of confrontation, between life and death, this world and the underworld. As Schele and Friedel (1990) 76, put it, the ballgame 'was the arena in which life and death, victory and defeat, rebirth and triumph played out their consequences'.

76 Schele and Miller (1986) 243.

77 Recent reports include: George E. Stuart, 'Mural Masterpieces of Ancient Cacaxtla', *Nat. Geog.* 182.3 (Sept. 1992) 120–36; Michael D. Lemonick, 'Secrets of the Maya', *Time* 142.6 (Aug. 9, 1993) 44–50.

78 Clendinnen (1991) 97.

79 The combat is described by Harris (1978) 100, using Sahagún's account, and discussed by Clendinnen (1991) 94–6. Davies (1981), 208, 239, 269, 276, sees parallel rituals among the Tsimshians of Alaska and the Tupinambas of Brazil. Harris (1978), 102, notes that the Iroquois sometimes tied prisoners to stakes and gave them a club to defend themselves, and that sometimes prisoners were kept alive and treated well for extended periods. Harris, 102–3, also notes that the Tupinamba of Brazil allowed prisoners some element of dodging of blows and self-defense before their death, and sometimes prisoners were well treated and given privileges before they were killed. Like the the Roman gladiators with their ambivalent status, such victims were accepted and cherished but also hated and cursed.

80 Clendinnen (1991) 95.

81 See further in Clendinnen's 'The Cost of Courage in Aztec Society', *P&P* 94 (Feb. 1982) 44–89.

82 Clendinnen (1991) 96–7, 103–10. There were occasional breakdowns, e.g. some victims cried or panicked; and sometimes victims bought and offered by the featherworkers were so eager to die that they leaped off the pyramid, but such suicides by captives were rare. Clendinnen, 105, explains that at the Toxcatl festival a beautiful captive was selected to be the image of the god Tezcatlipoca for a year. Instructed by priests, he was adorned with costumes and jewelry; he enjoyed open hospitality and spent his days relaxing and playing flutes. As the next festival drew near he was given four 'wives', enjoyed public banquets, and then walked up the pyramid, stepping on his flutes, to be sacrificed. Victims to be sacrificed to the fire god also were given 'pleasure girl' companions, 103, 108. On the victim as both sacred and cursed: Bataille (1988) 51–2, 59–61.

83 Clendinnen (1991) 103.

84 Francis Parkman, *The Jesuits in North America* (Boston: Little, Brown, 1963, orig. 1867), Feast of the Dead, 159–68, sacrifice, 168–71, based on the *Jesuit Relations* for 1637. Similarly, captives of the Iroquois had to run gauntlets, had their fingernails pulled out, had limbs cut off, were decapitated or burned at the stake. Remains were eaten, and warriors sought the privilege of eating the heart of a brave prisoner to absorb his courage; see Harris (1978) 60, 102–3; Lewis M. Morgan, *League of the Iroquois* (New York: Corinth Press, 1962). Clendinnen (1991), 87–8, n. 1 on 321–2, notes similarities between Aztec and North American Indian ritual violence. From Anthony F. C. Wallace, *The Death and Rebirth of the Seneca* (New York: Knopf, 1970) 104–7, she recounts a missionary's story of a Seneca captured (also in 1637), pampered, and treated as a family member by the Hurons, and then tortured by fire and blows with communal and female participation throughout a night, singing his warrior cry, then burned at the stake with heated axe heads the next day, with his hands, feet, and head cut off and given to certain individuals as promised.

85 Joseph François Lafitau, *Customs of the American Indians Compared with the Customs of Primitive Times*, ed. and trans. William N. Fenton and Elizabeth L. Moore, 2 vols. (Toronto: The Champlain Society, 1977. Originally published 1724 as

Moeurs des sauvages amériquains. comparées aux moeurs des premiers temps). I thank Dr Ingomar Weiler for recommending this work of early comparative ethnography. Using the writings of the Jesuit Brébeuf (on whose death in 1643, see ch. 8 below) and others, Lafitau recounts the slow and progressive burning and mutilation of captives by Iroquois, 155–7, as part of 'Torture of Captives by North and South American Indians', 155–71; quote at 158.

86 Ibid., 157; a comparison of ancient and Amerindian beliefs about souls follows, 235–45.

87 Ibid., 170, discussing South American torture of captives, 164–71. His 'Different Ways of Disposing of Bodies', 224–35, ranges from the ancient Near East to the Americas.

88 Ibid., 161–2. Cf. George Catlin, *Letters and Notes on the Manners. Customs and Conditions of the North American Indians*, 2 vols. (New York: Dover, 1973, orig. 1844) 2:240:

> cruelty is one of the leading traits of the Indian's character; and a little familiarity with their modes of life and government will soon convince the reader, that *certainty* and *cruelty* in punishments are requisite (where individuals undertake to inflict the penalties of the laws), in order to secure the lives and property of individuals in society.
>
> In the treatment of their prisoners, also, in many tribes, they are in the habit of inflicting the most appalling tortures, for which the enlightened world are apt to condemn them as cruel and unfeeling in the extreme; without stopping to learn that in every one of these instances, these cruelties are practiced by way of retaliation, by individuals or families of the tribe, whose relatives have been properly dealt with in a similar way by their enemies, and whose *manes* they deem it their duty to appease by this horrid and cruel mode of retaliation.

154

5

DISPOSAL FROM ROMAN ARENAS: SOME RITUALS AND OPTIONS

> No loving mother shall lay thee in the earth, nor load thy
> limbs with ancestral tomb. To birds of prey shalt thou be
> left; or sunk beneath the flood, the wave shall bear thee on,
> and hungry fish shall suck thy wounds.
>
> (Virgil *Aen.* 10.557–60, Loeb)

Rituals of death and removal

Death was not the last act in the arena. Ancient art depicts the collection
and deaths of animals, and even the brutal punishment of *damnati*, but
most works stop short of the actual killing (and hence short of the removal
and disposal) of gladiators. The moment of decision was the height of a
gladiatorial combat, the peak of spectator empowerment, the scene to immor-
talize.[1] Providing the shows was more glamorous than cleaning up after
them, but self-advertisement sometimes extended to the indecorous task of
disposal. The suspense and the sport ended with death, but the violence,
the involvement of the spectators, and the spectacle were not over.

A summary account of the pomp and circumstance of the arena, 'a day
at the spectacles', covering the preparations, the preliminaries, and the
conduct of the actual combats or killings, seems de rigueur for works on
Roman life.[2] Auguet also gives an embellished reconstruction of post-
mortem rituals and removal of defeated gladiators:

> a personage who seemed as if he had been removed from the wall
> of an Etruscan tomb entered the arena; he was clothed in a close-
> fitting tunic and wore long boots of supple leather. His face was
> not altogether human. He had a nose like the beak of a bird of
> prey and held a long-handled mallet in his hand. He was the
> Etruscan Charon, preceded by a Hermes Psychopomp, brandishing
> a red-hot caduceus which he applied to the flesh of the vanquished
> man to make sure that he was really dead and not merely uncon-
> scious or wounded. Then, this proof established, Charon took
> possession of the dead by striking him with his mallet. As soon as

155

> Hades, according to the most archaic rites, had been assured of its prey, the *libitinarii* bore the corpse away ... on a stretcher ... towards the Porta Libitinaria, situated on the main axis of the amphitheatre opposite the one through which the gladiators entered. It is so called after the goddess Libitina, who presided at funerals and pleased no one.[3]

Like Gérôme's paintings, such reconstructions weave together the scattered testimony of artistic and literary sources.[4] Many elements, however, come from Christian accounts of executions of *noxii*, not proper gladiatorial combats, which, as we have seen (in ch. 2 above), took place at different times of the day and involved different procedures and equipment.

As in Roman society at large, methods of removal and disposal varied according to the victim's status. In the arena gladiators were spared and marched out through the Gate of Life (Porta Sanivivaria), or they accepted quick and honorific death by the coup de grâce. Gladiators who fought and died well were carried out through the Gate of Death (Porta Libitinaria) on stretchers or biers.[5] In stark contrast, victims in *meridiani* usually faced certain death and received further insults. After public confirmation of their death, their bodies were apparently abused, mutilated, and dragged off by hooks. Both symbolic and efficient, hooks added insult and provided a way to avoid personal contact with an obscene body.[6]

The famous Zliten mosaic from Tripolitania (Libya) of perhaps the late first or second century AD is a crucial piece of evidence. The Zliten and other mosaics present gladiatorial combats and executions (and hunts) in the same arena, but this is an artistic device to depict a sequence of spectacles over one or more days. To stage all the elements of a full *munus* simultaneously would be chaotic and dangerous, as well as an inefficient use of resources. In the Zliten mosaic the distinction between true gladiators in the north and south friezes and beasts and *damnati* in the east and west friezes is striking (see figure 1, a and b). Set off by herms, musicians, and elaborate death carts, gladiators fight one-on-one duels or stand in *missio* postures, while *damnati* and animals are jumbled together, without *missio* scenes, and set off by leaping animals at the corners. As elite fighters, gladiators were separated as main attractions, and dead gladiators were carried out.[7] Being dragged out by hooks was a post-mortem abuse inappropriate for elite gladiators who had fought and died well.

The suggestion that Charon and Hermes attended to dead gladiators is based on a Christian commonplace. Probably writing from autopsy at Carthage, and predisposed to stress idolatry and Roman religious insincerity, Tertullian (*Apol.* 15.4, Loeb) notes depictions of gods by masked men in the amphitheater: 'But you really are still more religious in the amphitheater, where over human blood, over the dirt of pollution of capital punishment, your gods dance, supplying plots and themes for the guilty ("saltant dei vestri argumenta et historias noxiis ministrantes") – unless it is that often the guilty play the parts of gods.' He continues (15.5): 'We have laughed, amid the noon's blend of cruelty and absurdity, at Mercury using his burning iron to see who was dead. We have seen Jove's brother, too, conducting out the corpses of gladiators, hammer in hand.' ('Risimus et inter ludicras meridianorum crudelitates Mercurium mortuos cauterio examinantem, vidimus et Iovis fratrem gladiatorum cadavera cum malleo deducentem.') Tertullian's *Ad Nationes* (1.10.47) adds that Dis Pater with his hammer leads the funeral procession or obsequies ('Ditis pater, Iovis frater, gladiatorum exsequias cum malleo deducit'), and that Mercury has a winged cap and a heated wand to test bodies. Tertullian refers to dead 'gladiators', but he uses the term loosely. For Tertullian arena victims were either martyrs or gladiators, either virtuous, passive Christians with the hope of salvation, or vulgar, combative heathens damned by their depravity. The context here is clearly executions in *meridiani*, the midday games with *noxii*, not gladiatorial combats.

Certainly, chthonic associations with the arena were strong. Before combats new gladiators were flogged by *larvae*, representing demons or malicious spirits of the dead,[8] and the image of Mercury as Hermes Psychopompus, the conductor of souls, is well established.[9] The identification of the other arena god as the Etruscan Charon, an identification based on associating Tertullian's mention of a hammer with scenes from Etruscan art, is not secure, however.[10] As noted above (in ch. 2), fourth-century Etruscan tomb paintings do depict a sinister, hawk-nosed figure with a hammer, but continuity from fourth-century BC Etruscan tombs to second-century AD practice need not be assumed. Scholarship has shifted away from crediting Roman *munera* to Etruscan origins, and the Etruscan Charon should not be forced into the amphitheater (at Rome or Carthage).[11] Although later Christians interpreted gladiatorial fights as sacrifices to Charon, Tertullian, who knew the works of Suetonius and Varro, explicitly identifies the arena 'gods' as Dis Pater and Mercury, not Charon.[12] There may be an Etruscan parallel, but the 'god' here is Dis, a major Roman, rather than a lesser Etruscan, god.[13]

The dramaturgy of death in *meridiani* was a ritualized version of the traditional execution procedure transposed to the arena as the games expanded and used more and more condemned men. *Noxii* were killed in public to spread the responsibility and to provide a lesson for the community, and executioners and attendants were perhaps masked to assume personas. Deaths had to be verified, for (as noted above in ch. 3) according to law and the terms of purchase, *noxii* were to be killed within a time limit. Moreover, attention was paid to religious concerns – of the dead or of – collectively – the killers.[14] Rome went to ritual lengths to claim and lead away these noxious souls because they were dealing with the undesirable and disquieted souls of men killed horribly and involuntarily (except for Christian martyrs:

157

see ch. 8 below) – reluctant *damnati*, not willing gladiators. As infernal and psychopompic gods, Dis Pater and Mercury, the coroner and priest of the arena, confirmed the deaths publicly by fire and hammers,[15] and claimed and took away the hostile souls of Rome's victims. Getting the bodies and souls out of the arena, however, just began the process of disposal.

We know that human casualties were taken from the arena to the *spoliarium*, a place whose location and identification remain uncertain. Etymologically, a *spoliarium* should have something to do with *spolia*, the spoils of war, the stripped arms of the defeated enemy, which were displayed in triumphs and votive games. The *spoliarium*, then, should be a place for stripping arms,[16] but it housed another function not implied in its name. Seneca (*Ep.* 93.12, Loeb), on the quality versus the length of human life, comments:

> Do you regard as more fortunate the fighter who is slain on the last day of the games than one who goes to his death in the middle of the festivities? Do you believe that anyone is so foolishly covetous of life that he would rather have his throat cut in the dressing-room than in the amphitheater (*iugulari in spoliario quam in harena*)?

Seneca does not specify gladiators, just men who die in games, but the *Augustan History* refers to throwing the corpse of Commodus, 'the gladiator', into the *spoliarium*.[17] Along with *noxii*, unsuccessful gladiators who were denied *missio* and received the coup de grâce in the arena, plus those who were unconscious, incapacitated, or killed outright in the combat, apparently had their throats routinely slit to confirm death and prevent deception.[18] Some handling and undressing (or redressing) of the body are standard mortuary practices, but Rome was not venerating these dead. Rather Rome was retrieving resources (arms and armor) for future shows and ensuring that the spectacle had successfully completed one of its original functions. Victory and *missio* (and these only for gladiators) were the only normal ways to escape alive.

A martyrological passage suggests that Christian victims had their throats cut in or beneath the arena of the amphitheater at Carthage:

> [Saturus] was thrown unconscious with the rest in the usual spot to have his throat cut (*ad iugulationem solito loco*). But the mob asked that their bodies be brought out into the open (*in medio*) that their eyes might be the guilty witness of the sword that pierced their flesh. And so the martyrs got up and went to the spot of their own accord as the people wanted them to . . . Saturus, who being the first to climb the stairway (*prior ascenderat*) was the first to die.[19]

David Bomgardner has argued that *solito loco* refers to a subterranean cross-vaulted chamber at the west end of a tunnel under Carthage's amphitheater.

158

He identifies this as a *spoliarium* 'where the dead and dying were dragged to be dispatched, then stripped for burial'.[20] A subterranean chamber would fit the reference to stairs, but the actual chamber was rather small.[21] There is no textual reference to a *spoliarium* at Carthage, and other scholars have interpreted the passage differently. The 'usual place' may have been near the edge of the arena, the stairs may have led to a raised platform in the midst of the arena, and the crowd may have demanded that the final killing be done not at the 'usual place' but on that platform.[22]

Many amphitheaters (e.g. at Capua, Puteoli) have chambers similar to that at Carthage, and the Colosseum has large subterranean rooms in wedge-shaped annexes at either end of the main axis; but Dio (73(72).21.3) refers to the carrying out of Commodus' helmet through the Porta Libitinaria, implying that at Rome the dead were taken out, not down. Furthermore, the listing of the *spoliarium* in a late Roman 'List of Offices' (the *Notitia Dignitatum*) puts it in Regio II (the Caelian), not in III with the Flavian Amphitheater, which suggests a separate facility (see map 1).[23] From Praeneste a municipal inscription honors a magistrate for giving a gladiatorial show and for 'constructing a *spoliarium* on land purchased at his own expense', again suggesting an independent building or facility.[24] Rome's *spoliarium* should still be quite near to the Colosseum, but references tie it to the Ludus Matutinus, the training facility for beast-fighters. A doctor of the Ludus Matutinus commissioned an inscription for himself, a *lanista*, a *retiarius*, and a *curator spoliarii*.[25] The existence of a curator suggests that significant functions and more than a room were involved. The curator probably had a staff of slaves, some to strip and transport bodies, others to keep order and record the dispatching of bodies.[26] For now it remains unclear how many *spoliaria* Rome had, as rooms, buildings, or sites; each of the imperial gladiatorial schools may have had such a room, but there was probably a central site.

After the spectacle the living and the dead – with differing degrees of dignity or abuse, and by different gates or routes – proceeded out of the arena or were taken to the *spoliarium* to be stripped.[27] Throats of all corpses were probably routinely cut to insure that no gladiator tricked his way out of the profession and to confirm that *noxii* were truly dead. With characteristic attention to detail, Rome had an official to supervise these operations. For the dead the *spoliarium* was a place of last judgement and a final clearing house; those worthy of some dignity and peace were separated from those worthy of further insult and enduring torment. At most, however, the still enigmatic *spoliarium* was a temporary morgue for corpses on their way to some form of ultimate disposal elsewhere.[28]

Some options: burial, pits, exposure, crucifixion, fire

Spectacles of death held at various sites throughout the city left Rome with the problem of what to do with literally tons of human and animal flesh.

159

As an extension of the whole spectacle, the treatment and disposal of the corpses and carcasses were related to Roman customs and feelings about the victims. Again and again history shows that animal and human life can be cheap and killing can become easy, but, as the Nazis learned in the Final Solution, disposal can be difficult.[29] The Nazis and Rome (on a much smaller scale) had a similar problem but different options for disposal. The Romans did not share the Nazis' desire to conceal disposal and limit public knowledge of their atrocities. For Rome both the killing, as a performance, and the disposal, as a display, were to be seen. The size of shows, the resources, the facilities, and the enthusiasm of the spectators grew with the Empire, but the justifications for killing and the solutions for disposal adhered to ancestral customs (*mos maiorum*).

In spectacles the means of death and the means of disposal usually differed. Romans were creative in arranging diverse and, for them, entertaining deaths, but there were only so many options for ultimate disposal of bodies. Conceivably, corpses and carcasses could have been inhumed, cremated, exposed (to carrion animals or the elements), eaten, or dumped in pits or bodies of water.[30] Disposal was a matter of both logistical and religious concern, and each possible method of disposal had implications for Roman attitudes toward the victims. For the Romans, the social order was constructed and communicated in this world, and it could be extended into the next.

The simplest and most humane option concerning humans was for Rome to provide proper burial or to allow corpses to be claimed and buried by normal private means. This happened in the case of many true gladiators (i.e. from whatever source, slave or free, trained under a *lanista* or at an imperial school to a level of skill and specialization, and bound by oath to fight until dead, freed, or the fulfillment of their contract). Inscribed tombstones, many with carved reliefs, show that professional gladiators were generally allowed and sometimes provided with decent burial (see figure 2).[31] Corpses could be claimed and buried by owners or editors, relatives, burial clubs, or fellow gladiators.[32] The editor of a show might provide a multiple burial, a polyandria, with a monument, perhaps to honor the gladiators but more probably to commemorate his own generosity.[33] Many individual burials arranged by relatives and friends are known from epitaphs, mostly of the second and third centuries AD. Epitaphs often list the gladiator's name, style of fighting, and number of combats, as well as the name of the person who arranged the burial.[34] Beginners appear – not cheap *noxii* but *tirones* who had been in training in some specialized style of combat; but a newcomer's best hope was probably his colleagues or a self-serving owner.[35] Most of the gladiators recorded in epitaphs tend to be successful ones who had lived long enough with enough success to become free, develop friendships and marry or cohabit, save money, and make funeral arrangements.[36] Proper burial, and especially individual commemoration through

160

an epitaph, indicates a certain level of resources and status. Some fighters'
epitaphs proclaim their status as '*lib.*', which probably means freedman
rather than freeborn.[37] If a slave gladiator survived to manumission, and
especially if he then contracted to fight again as a veteran *auctoratus*, he had
ample opportunity to arrange and fund his burial. Prone to superstition,
gladiators would make arrangements as soon as they could.[38] Burial clubs
of gladiators venerated certain gods, but primarily served to provide an
economic and efficient guarantee of decent burial.

The *senatus consultum* from Larinum of AD 19 raises the possibility that
auctorati (contract gladiators) of senatorial or equestrian rank were denied burial. The fragmentary inscription mentions only one penalty for members of
the elite who performed on stage or in the arena: after a lacuna, line 5 says
that they were not to *libitinam haberet*. The phrase is not otherwise attested
and its meaning has been debated, but Levick sees denial of decent burial as
a possibility. Denial of burial is well attested for certain crimes, and *libitina*
must have something to do with funerals or burial.[39] It is noteworthy that,
as well as being non-retroactive (i.e. not applying to those who had performed
prior to the edict), the penalty did not apply to the male or female children
of an actor, gladiator, *lanista*, or procurer. A senatorial denial of burial to
auctorati would represent an inversion of the 'inverse elevation' of gladiators:
gladiators of lowly origins might elevate themselves and earn burials and
epitaphs, but elite Romans who debased themselves in the arena might end
up unburied. The Roman spectacles allowed 'worthless' humans to elevate
themselves, and they also provided punishment for Romans who immorally
debased themselves across proper class lines.

Municipal charters discriminated politically against *auctorati* and *lanistae*,
and the rules of some municipal cemeteries prohibited burial of *auctorati*.
An inscription from Sassina in Umbria records that one Horatius Balbus
donated a public cemetery with plots 10 feet square to his township, and
it stipulates the exclusion of contract gladiators, those who had hanged
themselves, and those who followed some immoral trade for profit ('extra
au[ct]orateis et quei sibi [la]queo manu attulissent et quei quaestum spurcum
professi essent').[40] Achieving no elevation or redemption as gladiators,
auctorati remained alienated in society and ostracized in death. Ville feels
that the inscription explicitly denies the cemetery only to free contract
gladiators, and that there was no need to forbid slaves. Unfortunately, some
works repeat Ville's misleading suggestion (from this inscription) that
corpses of servile gladiators were thrown onto refuse heaps.[41] Gladiators,
even servile ones, might be allowed burial – if someone wished to provide
it and if the cemetery was open to such burials – but the stigma of *infamia*
followed *auctorati* beyond death.

Performance and not just legal status affected the likelihood of burial.
Proper burial seems to have been a privilege acquired over time by elite
gladiators, one earned individually by successful performance.[42] The earliest

gladiators were complete social outsiders without rights or privileges, nameless slaves and captives, possibly disposed of on the pyres of noble Romans.[43] Over time, however, by their contribution to society, gladiators earned privileges, a chance of survival, and even fame and wealth. They became specialized and professionalized providers of mass entertainment, a growing social need in the era of 'bread and circuses'. Barton's 'elevation' and Wiedemann's 'resurrection' went beyond death when gladiators gained the privilege of marginal but decent burial. The epitome of Ville's 'ambivalence' is that socially alienated gladiators might be integrated into (at least the edges of) society after death.

Voluntarism and complicity were crucial to gladiatorial virtue and hope. Even under duress, the *sacramentum* may have been essential for the possibility of burial. In the hierarchy of the arena, gladiators who fought and died well were the ideal, and Romans were angered and disgusted when a gladiator's training and courage fell short, when a fighter did not accept death well, resisted the death blow, or begged for mercy. Then spectators turned into adversaries and demanded that those who died poorly suffer excessive mangling and stabbing.[44] Failed, unredeemed gladiators who did not live – and die – up to expectations reduced themselves, like enemies and captives devoted as *sacri* to chthonic deities, to the status of *noxii*.[45] Therefore they got certain death, mutilation, hooks, and denial of rites. Most gladiators died well out of training and esprit de corps, but, realistically, also because the alternative was worse.[46] Just as soldiers would rather die on the battlefield than face abuse as prisoners, and just as political victims committed suicide for the sake of the family estate, gladiators died well in part to gain a glorious, untormented death and burial rites.

The disposal of gladiators was a significant symbolic act, but not a logistical problem for Rome. The disposal of *noxii*, however, presented a significant logistical and symbolic problem. Only with skill could a victim's status be offset with hope and privileges. Arguably, the vilest men, as gladiators, had the best chance of survival and decent burial, while other *damnati* – some of them perhaps good men condemned for political reasons, innocent victims of reigns of terror, or pious followers of illegal cults – had no hope of life or decent treatment. Most *damnati* went straight and soon to the beasts or the *meridiani* unless, when sorted, they showed signs of special training or potential. *Noxii*, whose lives and deaths suggested neither virtue nor skill, were abused and damned. Purchasers of condemned convicts were contractually bound to have them killed by a deadline, but there was no clause concerning provision of burial. Did anyone bother to provide decent burial for the thousands of Dacians killed in Trajan's games? Most of the dead probably had no one to claim or bury them – or people were prohibited from doing so. Many arena victims were condemned for some form of treason, and such condemnation brought infamy, ignominy, and denial of even the most basic rites.

Compared to the substantial evidence for gladiator burials, the disposal of pagan arena *noxii* remains a puzzle. Clues may lie with what happened to people of similarly humble status who died or were executed outside the arena. Familiar with medieval and Biblical 'potter's fields' for paupers and criminals,[47] scholars tend to dismiss the indelicate question of disposal of both arena corpses and carcasses by suggesting that they were deposited in pits or potter's fields (*carnaria* for beasts, *puticuli* for humans) – some dumps in the area of the Esquiline outside and east of classical Rome (see map 1), where they were exposed to the elements and to carrion animals (dogs and birds).[48] Suburban dumping of corpses is attested for paupers and slaves, but this was not the only answer for disposal of *noxii* at Rome.

Some inscriptions from Puteoli and Cumae are crucial to understanding the possible use of the Esquiline for burials and disposal. A *lex locationis* of the colony of Puteoli specifies the contractual duties of the public under-taker concerning burials and executions.[49] Prices and services are listed, with rates per mile and a standard distance of five miles (I 5,23,14). A prohibition against abandoning corpses is to be enforced with a fine of 60 HS per corpse (I 29–II 2). The contracting undertaker (*manceps*) is to keep a staff of thirty-two workers, who are to be of sound body and free of marks (*neve stigmat(ibus) inscrip(tus)*).[50] Forbidden to reside within a certain distance of town, the workers may enter the city only on official business (II 3–4) and they must wear a special cap in town. They may not attend the public baths after the first hour of daylight. The inscription (II 8–14) goes on to detail the contractor's responsibilities concerning punishments. For a fee (4 HS each), an owner could have his slave punished privately (II 8–10) and the contractor was to supply the equipment (posts, chains, ropes, and flog-gers). The contractor (II 11–14) was also to carry out punishments or torture (*supplicia*) ordered by the magistrate, again supplying the equipment (nails, pitch, wax, etc.), but this time without charge.[51] Particularly interesting is the stipulation (II 13–14) that 'Again, if he is ordered to drag away the corpse with a hook (*unco extrahere*), the work-gang is to be dressed in red and ring a bell (*cum tintinnabulo*) while dragging away the body *ubi plura cadavera erunt*.'[52] Bodel feels that, although vague, this last phrase suggests a site, and that accordingly 'at Puteoli during the late Republic the bodies of those deprived of a proper burial were deposited in a specified area and left to rot'.[53] Puteoli was probably typical in having such a site.[54]

A section, possibly taken from an earlier law, declares that funerals of decurions and of those who died prematurely (*funera acerba*) get the highest priority (II 15–21).[55] This accords with honors for officials and with concerns about disquieted souls. Suicides by hanging (*suspendiosum*) are to be removed within an hour of their being reported, and corpses of slaves within two hours of daylight (II 22–3).[56] Unless the contractor is negligent in his duties, he has a monopoly on all such matters of burial and disposal, and those making other arrangements are to be fined (III 1–4).

These arrangements for disposal are strikingly detailed. The official under-taker is apparently responsible for the disposal of corpses of both the normal and the abnormal dead (e.g. abandoned, premature, suicides, slaves, execu-tions at the edge of town).[57] There is no explicit reference to arena spectacles, but ritualistic aspects relating to fear of pollution (e.g. stipulations concerning hooks and dragging of *damnati*, residence, timeliness, costume, and bells) are reminiscent of both the ritual in the arena and an execution ritual in the Forum at Rome (see ch. 7 below). The actual site of disposal is, probably though not certainly, some form of mass grave or dump. As Bodel suggests, Puteoli and other colonies probably followed the model of Rome in arranging sites and procedures of disposal by establishing funerary headquarters at suburban groves of Libitina, the goddess of funerals (see below).

The history of the Esquiline area at Rome and its relationship to disposal and Libitina are indeed complex. The Campus Esquilinus outside the Esquiline Gate included a public cemetery housing both humble, common graves for the dregs of Rome and *columbaria* and impressive tombs for indi-vidual burial.[58] This area was used for executions, burials, and disposal of all kinds of refuse, possibly including arena victims, but most of the site was covered and closed to disposal early in the first century BC. Similar activities shifted to an area of the Esquiline south of the Gate in the first century BC before part of the Esquiline was reclaimed by Maecenas for his famous gardens, the Horti Maecenatis.[59]

In the 1870s Lanciani found several hundred man-made pits (of 4 by 5 m by 10 m deep) near the northwest corner of the Piazza Vittorio Emanuele (i.e. outside the Agger (embankment) and the Esquiline Gate).[60] Lined with tufa, the pits were separated by a travertine channel. Lanciani excavated some seventy-five of these and he describes the discovery in dramatic terms:

> In many cases the contents of each vault were reduced to a uniform mass of black, viscid, pestilent, unctuous matter; in a few cases the bones could in a measure be singled out and identified. The reader will hardly believe me when I say that men, beasts, bodies and carcasses, and any kind of unmentionable refuse of the town were heaped up in those dens.[61]

Following Lanciani's assumption, these vaults or pits have commonly, but apparently incorrectly, been associated with Horace's potter's field and what Varro calls *puticuli*:

> Outside the towns there are *puticuli* 'little pits', named from *putei* 'pits', because there the people used to be buried in *putei* 'pits'; unless rather, as Aelius writes, the *puticuli* are so called because the corpses which had been thrown out *putescebant* 'used to rot' there,

164

in the public burial-place which is beyond the Esquiline (*ibi cadavera proiecta, qui locus publicus ultra Esquilias*). This place Afranius in a comedy of Roman life calls the *Putiluci* 'pit-lights', for the reason that from it they look up through *putei* 'pits' to the *lumen* 'light'.[62]

Horace's classic description of a public cemetery or potter's field must refer to a different part of the Esquiline (*Sat.* 1.8.8–22, Loeb): 'Hither in other days (*prius*) a slave would pay to have carried on a cheap bier the carcasses of his fellows, cast from their narrow cells. Here was the common burial-place (1.8.10 *commune sepulcrum*) fixed for pauper folk ... Here a pillar assigned a thousand foot frontage and three hundred of depth, and provided that the graveyard should pass to no heirs.' This is now a wholesome place for a walk along the Agger, but formerly, one (1.8.16) 'looked out on a ground ghastly with bleaching bones [i.e. shallow or no burial, or disturbed burials]'. Horace also characterizes the Esquiline as a spot frequented by witches performing black magic, invoking the spirits of the dead, and collecting ingredients for potions.[63]

Reviewing Lanciani's work, Pinza rejected the identification of such pits as *puticuli*. Bodel accepts Pinza's demonstration that the site of Lanciani's pits was covered with a layer of debris in a levelling of the area in the late Republic before Maecenas' establishment of his gardens.[64] Bodel is uncertain if Lanciani's pits are indeed *puticuli*, but in any case clearly the area outside the Esquiline Gate had been used for 'mass disposals of human carcasses in the most informal fashion'.[65] Dumping in such pits, open to the elements until covered over when full, would not constitute the provision of even minimal burial.

In a separate find on the Esquiline at the corner of Via Carlo Alberto and Via Ratazzi just north of the Esquiline Gate, Lanciani in 1876 discovered a mass grave in part of the moat (*fossa*) of the ancient embankment (*agger*), with a mass of human remains 160 feet long, 100 wide, and 30 deep. When the earth above collapsed and the remains were exposed, they crumbled to dust but smelled badly enough that Lanciani gave his workers a break. Lanciani estimated that the ditch contained some 24,000 bodies from the late Republic, and his cross-section shows bones of domestic animals in the same zone as the human remains.[66] There is uncertainty as to the status of those dumped. Plague victims is a strong possibility, or Bodel sees a simple overflow from the area of the pits.[67]

Lanciani and others probably felt that executed criminals and captives ended up in pits and mass graves like those he found because the Esquiline was tied to undertakers (see below) and because it was known as a place of execution.[68] Traditionally, executions and disposal were probably carried out in the area outside the Esquiline Gate, and there were still executions on the Esquiline after Maecenas' reclamation. Tacitus (*Ann.* 2.32.3, Loeb) ties the Esquiline to traditional forms of execution: under Tiberius the senate expelled astrologers and magicians from Italy; one was thrown from the Rock, another was executed 'by the consuls outside the Esquiline Gate according to ancient usage (*more prisco*) and at the sound of the trumpet'. Under Claudius foreigners who usurped the rights of citizens were to be executed *in campo Esquilino*, and Nero ordered the execution of a consul-elect in 'a place set apart for the execution of slaves (*locus servilibus poenis sepositus*)', which Hinard takes as the Esquiline.[69]

After centuries of use, the burning of bodies and the dumping of refuse in the Esquiline cemetery was regulated in the early first century BC as the city grew. In the area of the main railroad station and southwest of the Castra Praetoria some 400 feet from the Servian Wall, Lanciani found in situ facing toward the city two of a probable line of travertine terminal stones (*cippi*) with inscribed sanitary regulations. A third stone was found in 1942 during the construction of the station. The stones mark an area of about 200 m along the *agger* roughly from the Esquiline Gate to the Viminal Gate. According to the inscription, the praetor L. Sentius on the orders of the senate forbade the construction of places for burning corpses, the dumping of *stercus* (excrement in its primary sense, any undesirable product to be discarded), and the abandoning of corpses between the line of the stones and the city.[70] A private graffito in vermilion on one stone urged people to carry dirt a long way off, lest they suffer harm ('stercus longe aufer ne malum habeas').[71] As Bodel points out, the area covered by Sentius' edict was much bigger than the 60 square meters of Lanciani's 'puticuli' or Horace's potter's field (ca. 295 by 88 m), so the intent must have been to protect an entire region in which dumping and fires had become a 'pernicious nuisance'. Such a nuisance, in fact, that the area was probably covered over close to the time of the edict.[72]

Bodel has recently compared the testimony of these terminal stones to that of the enigmatic Lex Luceria from Apulia, a local ordinance probably from the third century BC, which prohibits the dumping of dung, the abandoning of corpses, and the performance of rites to honor the dead. Bodel has convincingly reinterpreted the reference to *in hoce loucarid* in the first line of this text. He sees this not as a sacred law against the pollution of a sacred grove but as a civil law established to mark off an area, a grove of Libitina in the middle of a graveyard, as public land for the use of undertakers, and to end dumping and burials in the area.[73] The word *lucar* was known to have something to do with public revenues allocated for public entertainments and something to do with revenue associated with the goddess Libitina. Bodel explains that, unlike sacred groves which were not revenue producing, groves of Libitina were established by the state and produced revenue from death taxes or the sale of funerary contracts to undertakers, and such revenue could be used to subsidize public entertainments. The prohibitions against rites and abandoning of corpses show that the area had been used as a cemetery and that dumping had become a problem.

The law then closed a section of a cemetery, Bodel explains, making it a *lucus Libitinae*, a place of business established by the state for the use of private contractors undertaking funerary concessions.[74]

Also relevant, a travertine block inscribed on both faces, found in situ in the pre-Augustan layer (covering Lanciani's 'puticuli') just outside the Esquiline Gate, bears the text of a *senatus consultum* protecting an area belonging to the Pagus (district, canton) Montanus.[75] Permanent and temporary crematoria (*ustrinae, foci ustrinae causa*) are forbidden. Bodel suggests that there was no provision against dumping corpses because the area was no longer used for the informal dumping of the poor in pits. He further suggests that specified regions of the *pagus* were entrusted to undertakers under the supervision of the plebeian aediles, and that this *senatus consultum* was posted at the headquarters of the Libitinarii, the funeral undertakers.[76] Generally located on the Esquiline outside the Agger, and probably in this area, the Lucus Libitinae housed the headquarters of the *libitinarii* of Rome, where funerals were arranged and equipment for funerals could be bought. The site had a temple dedicated by Augustus to the Roman funerary goddess Libitina, who was associated with Venus or Proserpina.[77]

According to Bodel's convincing reconstruction of the history of the public burial ground outside the Esquiline Gate, 'During the third and second centuries [BC] the corpses of paupers, criminals and some slaves were unceremoniously heaped along with other refuse in pits similar to or identical to those excavated by Lanciani.' With increasing population and needs, the garbage and human refuse spilled over to an area including the territory to the north toward the Viminal Gate. Even the moat (*fossa*) outside the embankment (*agger*) near the Esquiline Gate was used and filled. By the early first century the problem was getting out of hand, so the praetor's edict prohibited dumping and oversaw the termination of the zone. At the same time, restrictions on the construction of new crematoria reduced the risks of fire. Probably at the same time, Lanciani's pits were buried under a layer of rubble. Years later but before Maecenas, a *senatus consultum* again banned burning and dumping in the regions of the Pagus Montanus; no reference was made to the dumping of corpses, probably because there were no longer mass burials in the area.[78]

When the area near the Esquiline Gate was closed, the need for such an area continued and shifted south. Bodel and Häuber agree that Horace's boneyard (*commune sepulcrum*) seen from the Servian rampart was an area south of the Esquiline Gate around the so-called Auditorium of Maecenas.[79] New mass graves established there after the Social War became filled and were a public nuisance by the time of Maecenas. In 35 BC Maecenas covered this area to the south with his estate, the Horti Maecenatis (see map 1), which did not extend north to the Esquiline Gate. Finally, the area of the Esquiline between the Servian Wall and the line of the Aurelian Wall was reclaimed as a quarter with streets and sewers and made into the fifth Region of the city.[80]

As we have seen, officials prohibited indiscriminate dumping of refuse and bodies, which was a serious, continuing problem for Rome, especially in the streets and at the edge of town.[81] Laws forbidding the throwing of excrement, corpses, and animal skins into the streets were clearly broken.[82] Ancient literature speaks with horror of carrion animals, birds and dogs, feeding on exposed, unburied, or inadequately buried corpses. Martial writes of a dying derelict who hears dogs howling in anticipation of eating his corpse and tries to keep birds of prey (*noxias aves*) at a distance by flapping his rags at them.[83] Seneca compares a legacy-hunter sitting at a patient's bedside to a vulture, and Suetonius tells of a stray dog picking up a human hand at the crossroads and dropping it before Vespasian.[84] Nero's horse was frightened by the smell of a corpse thrown into the road near the Praetorian Camp at the northeast edge of the city.[85] Perhaps the most notorious example of 'dumping' was the exposure of unwanted infants.[86] Obviously, the normal demographic pressures of Rome and the recurrence of disastrous pestilences made heavy demands on all means of disposal.[87]

Bodel makes a strong argument, consistent with his interpretation of the Lex Luceria, that the problem of dumping was a matter of urban maintenance, secular law, and civic regulations, and not of sacral law, *mos*, and the *pax deorum*. The areas of dumping on the Esquiline were on public land (*loca publica*), not *loca religiosa*. He suggests that the XII Tables may show religious as well as civic concern about burials but that by the late Republic public welfare was the primary consideration.[88] However, ancient religious sensibilities must not be underestimated. Normally laws restricted the use of land once tombs were established and the land thus became a *locus religiosus*. Bodel admits that popular belief held any burial site to be *privata religio*, but he shows that the state had full jurisdiction over public land.[89] To whatever degree Rome's concerns about dumping were pious or pragmatic, the Esquiline and the suburbs had enough problems without the addition of arena victims.

Clearly there were executions in the area of the Esquiline, and the corpses may have been buried, dumped, or exposed nearby. Dumping on the Esquiline was primarily a way to dispose of the indigent and the abandoned dead of Rome.[90] Neither ancient texts nor Lanciani connect the Esquiline to arena spectacles. Moreover, torture, execution, abuse, and disposal were not confined to the suburbs. From Rome's earliest days such things took place in the Forum, and as the spectacles grew they were transposed to arenas in the heart of town. The more spectacles of death were concentrated within the city, and the more the city expanded, the less likely was it that deposition on the Esquiline or similar fields would be used for arena disposal.[91] Pits could provide a symbolic casting out, along with non-provision and probable prevention of burial by relatives, but the lustral quality of pits could be outdone. Other options must be considered, including crucifixion and fire.

Understandably, discussions of crucifixion often focus on the Christian Gospels and the debated historicity of the accounts of the death and disposal of Jesus,[92] but executions in Judea were perhaps adapted to local Jewish customs. Archaeology shows that death might be hurried and corpses of crucified men might be taken down at night and allowed burial in Judea,[93] and in Italy the case at Puteoli suggests that corpses were removed 'if an order was given'. Victims of crucifixion died slow, agonizing deaths,[94] and they were guarded – certainly until dead and probably longer.

Crucifixion should be seen as a form of exposure to the elements and beasts, for, outside Judea, it is unlikely that most corpses were taken down, let alone buried after crucifixion. In Petronius' story of the widow of Ephesus the governor of a Greek province ordered that some thieves be crucified near the tomb where a widow was mourning her buried husband. A soldier assigned to watch the crosses, 'to prevent anyone taking down a body for burial', of course, became preoccupied with the widow. While the soldier neglected his watch, the parents of one of the crucified men took down his corpse at night and gave it burial rites. The next day, seeing one of the crosses empty, the guard feared punishment, but he and the widow conveniently found a replacement.[95] Usually, then, to prolong the message of deterrence, corpses were simply left to suffer excarnation via animals and decay. This horrid but probably effective custom seems to have continued at medieval gallows.[96]

At Rome the burning of flesh could serve various functions: sacrifice and cooking, proper cremation as a form of burial, and also torture, execution, and corpse abuse. Until the early second-century AD shift to inhumation, the normal (individual) burial method at Rome was cremation. Tacitus (*Ann.* 16.6) calls it the Roman *mos*. An expensive but conspicuous burial custom, cremation was also appealing because it meant that the body could not be disturbed (by animals or foes).[97] Of old, Rome banned intra-urban cremation. There were exceptions, notably spontaneous mob outrages and planned imperial honors; but for religious and practical reasons, to prevent pollution and to avoid fires, cremation was normally done outside the city.[98] Even after the development of a fire brigade (by Augustus) and some building regulations, Rome remained something of an enormous tinderbox.[99] Funeral pyres invited disaster.

Noting that population pressures and the impracticality of pits may have led to change in public burial practices, Bodel suggests that mass crematoria may have replaced mass inhumation in the first century AD.[100] He suggests that Martial's reference to *infelix rogus* may indicate that the bodies of the poor were routinely destroyed in public crematoria.[101] Martial refers to four branded slaves carrying a common corpse (*vile cadaver*) in a narrow *sandapila* in the north end of the city – 'the pauper's burying-ground receives a thousand such (*accipit infelix qualia mille rogus*)'.[102] *Rogus* normally means 'funeral pyre', but Martial may be using the term figuratively.[103] This corpse was common, cheap, or poor (*vile*), not *noxius*, and mass crematoria seem impractical on various grounds.

Medieval history may have led Lanciani and nineteenth-century Europeans to see pits as Rome's solution to disposal of masses of the poor and criminals, and images of the crematoria of Nazi death camps may have inclined more modern scholars to assume such facilities at Rome; but the evidence for mass cremations of the poor and of criminals is very limited. Fire hazards and problems of transportation also apply. Moreover, as was the case at Puteoli and in the Roman arena, some corpses, those of the hated and dangerous and not the defenseless and humble dead, were singled out to be dragged with hooks and disposed of in an insulting manner.

Certainly fire was a legal and spectacular means of torture, abuse, and aggravated execution. Torture by burning was thought appropriate to induce testimony from slaves, even though that testimony might be unreliable. Similarly, fire and hot irons were used in the arena to provoke men and beasts to fight, and also to confirm the deaths of victims. Famous fatal charades actualized the burning of the hand of Scaevola, and sources refer to the *tunica molesta*, an inflammable garment worn by incendiaries, parricides – and even paid volunteers, who for a certain sum agreed to run a set distance in this burning coat.[104]

In contrast to cremation (a holocaust or nearly total consumption) as a form of burial, victims and corpses were sometimes burned, partially or fully, as a form of insult and abuse but not as a final means of disposal. As a legal term *crematio* technically meant, not full cremation, but execution by fire, a punishment reserved for the lower orders and increasingly used under the Empire.[105] Suetonius says that the soldiers' cremation of the body of Tiberius prevented the crowds from abusing it with 'the ignominy of an Atellan half-burning'.[106] Even with death by fire, disposal remained a problem. The sordid but certain truth is that flesh, being mostly water, is not very flammable by itself.[107] Funeral pyres were stuffed with papyrus to achieve the necessary large, hot fire, but accidents are recorded.[108] In the arena humans burned at the stake had to be smeared with tar or to have wood or some other fuel piled around them. Even then, however, disposal was needed.[109]

As discussed below (in ch. 8), fire was certainly used for torturing and killing Christians and for abusing and insulting their corpses; and martyrology provides abundant references to the burning of bodies, in part because the image suited the apocalyptic tone of such literature. Death by fire and burial by cremation were abhorrent to early Christians because, following Jesus' example, they preferred whole inhumation. Tertullian (*Apol.* 50.3, Loeb) says that Christians were called '"faggot-fellows" and "half-axle men" because we are tied to a half-axle-post, and faggots are piled round us, and we are burnt'.

Martyrology evokes images of bodies 'consumed' by flames, but torture and 'slow burning' were the norm. Lactantius recounts gory but graphic orders for execution by fire under the late Empire:

For people of no rank (*humiliores*), the penalty was burning. Maximian had first permitted this form of execution against the Christians, issuing instructions that, after being tortured, the condemned should be burnt with slow fires. When they had been bound fast, a gentle flame would first of all be applied to their feet, long enough for the skin on their soles to be contracted and torn from their bones. Next, torches which were first lit and then put out were applied to each limb in turn, so that no area of the body was left unaffected. During all this, their faces should be splashed with cold water and their mouths moistened in case their throats got parched with dryness and they breathed their last too quickly. Death would finally supervene when, over the greater part of the day, their skin had been burnt off them, and the force of the fire had penetrated to their most vital parts. Then a pyre was made and the already burnt bodies were burnt again; their bones were collected, ground to powder, and tossed into the rivers and the sea.[110]

Fire was used to torture and kill, but when used as a means of disposal it involved a second complete burning of the dead remains, and even then, as in normal cremation burial, some limited remains (bones, ashes) required disposal.[111] This would apply to animal as well as human flesh, but there is no indication that animal flesh from the arena was disposed of by incineration.

With traditional purificatory qualities, fire was a dramatic and effective means of torture and execution, but the need for fuel and the fire hazards involved made fire too inefficient, expensive, and dangerous to be a significant means of arena disposal. Rome needed, and had, a simpler and more satisfying system of waste disposal.

NOTES

1 Ville (1981) 423–4; Brown (1992) 202–7. The famous Bourghese mosaic is exceptional in showing an arena littered with bodies.

2 E.g. Carcopino (1975) 262–4; Balsdon (1969) 298–301; Friedländer (1965) 2:60–1; Lafaye (1896) 1593–6. For excellent discussions of elements (e.g. *pompa*, salute, *habet*, thumb gesture, *missio*, coup de grâce, etc.), see Ville (1981) 386–430; and Wiedemann (1992) 92–7.

3 Auguet (1972) 53–6, quote at 55, apparently embellishing Lafaye (1896) 1596. Animals were probably dispatched and removed, with less ceremony, by slaves (or possibly horses) using hooks.

4 See illustrations of Gérôme's arena paintings (e.g. *Pollice Verso*, *Ave Imperator*, *Martyrs' Prayer*, *Retrieving the Beasts*) in Golvin and Landes (1990) passim. E.g. Gérôme puts the salute from Claudius' naumachy in an amphitheater, and confuses the hook removal of *noxii* with gladiators.

5 Stretchers (*sandapilae*) for gladiators: Ps. Quint. *Decl. Maj.* 9.6. Pliny, *HN* 37.11.45, mentions amber-trimmed stretchers under Nero. Martial, 8.75.16, making a pun on 'dead Gaul', associates *sandapila* with gladiators. On differential body removal, see Ville (1981) 376–7; on gates, see Golvin (1988) 323.

171

Porta Libitinensis or Libitinaria: SHA *Comm.* 16.7; Dio 73(72).21.3: the door 'by which the dead are usually removed'. The gate for victorious gladiators was the Porta Sanivivaria: *Pass. Perp. et Fel.* 10.13; cf. 20.7.

6 E.g. in Apuleius, *Met.* 10.29, a man turned into an ass was to mate with a noxious woman in a show, but he did not want to 'pollute' his body thus. On *contagio sceleris*, the notion of sacral-magical infection by contact with a contaminated person, see Thome (1992) 77 and n. 23 on 94–5. The hooks used in dragging are not to be confused with the hooks used in the eastern Empire that were inserted into the mouths of convicts at trials to prevent them from verbally abusing authorities; on such hooks see Potter (1996) 151, with references. Further on hooks and dragging, see below in ch. 7.

7 See Aurigemma (1926) 147–72, 180–97, and figs. 151–9, 162–5, 177; Brown (1992) 194–7, 205–7; Dunbabin (1978) 66. Wiedemann (1992), 118, feels that the height of the carts suggests that they were designed as operating tables as well as stretchers. On *noxii* in art see ch. 3 above.

8 Seneca, *Apocol.* 9.3, Loeb, mentions a proposal that anyone improperly declared a god 'be delivered over to the bogies, and at the next public show be flogged with a birch amongst the new gladiators (*inter novos auctoratos*)'. Demons: cf. Suet. *Ner.* 34.4 above in n. 27 in ch. 4. Coleman (1990), 67, suggests that the amphitheater might be seen as the 'threshold of the underworld'.

9 Mercury and souls: e.g. Sen. *Apocol.* 11, 13; Hor. *Carm.* 1.10.17–18. Commodus entered the arena in the guise of Mercury: Dio 73(72).17.3–4. Ville (1981), 378–9, suggests that Mercury was not introduced earlier than the end of the first century AD; and he notes a depiction of Mercury and a body on a curse tablet from the amphitheater at Carthage; cf. A. Audollent, *Defixionum Tabellae* (Paris: Fontemoing, 1904) no. 246. On Mercury in North African venatorial mosaics, see Brown (1992) 198–9, n. 30 on 211.

10 Charon: e.g. Lafaye (1896) 1593, 1596; Schneider (1918) 783; and Friedländer (1965) 2:41, and most sources thereafter, but not Balsdon (1969) 301. Franz de Ruyt, *Charun, démon étrusque de la mort*, Études de philologie, d'archéologie, et d'histoire anciennes, I (Rome: Institut historique belge, 1934) 23–34, discusses scenes of Charon in Etruscan art, and, 191–2, sees an association, via the mallet, with the Etruscan Charon.

11 Ville (1981), 2, rejects the identification of Dis with the Etruscan demon Charon. Cf. Hopkins (1983) 4: 'Pluto or Charon'; Barton (1993) 62: 'the lurid costumed Charons at the gladiatorial games'; Wiedemann (1992) 85 and 155: 'Charon, the Etruscan Mercury'.

12 Quoted in n. 26 in ch. 2 above concerning the festival of Jupiter Latiaris, Prudentius, *C. Symm.* 1.379–98 (cf. Aur. Vict. *Caes.* 11.8), condemns *munera*, mentions a parade (*pompa*), and says that Charon by murder receives offerings that pay for his services as guide. Like the Charon in Virgil, *Aen.* 6.298–315, this fourth-century Charon is clearly Hellenized. Prudentius does not explicitly put Charon in the arena, but some scholars, e.g. Clavel-Lévêque (1984b) 201, see both Charon and Dis there. See further in Ronnie H. Terpening, *Charon and the Crossing: Ancient, Medieval and Renaissance Transformations of a Myth* (Lewisburg, Pa.: Bucknell U., 1985).

13 When executions moved to the arena the victims remained *sacri*, so it was appropriate that a chthonic god, Dis more authoritatively than Charon, claim his property in the arena.

14 Modern executions are still heavily ritualized concerning the preparation of the condemned, the role of witnesses and executioner(s), the verification and announcement of death, and the burial of the remains by the family or the state. See Colin Turnbull, 'Death by Decree', *Natural History* 87 (May 1978) 52–66.

15 Cf. the use of sacrificial mallets: Suet. *Calig.* 32.3. To double-check death, dead popes are tapped thrice on their foreheads and their baptismal name is called out thrice (as an *acclamatio*); see Toynbee (1971) n. 119 on 288; de Ruyt, op. cit., 236.

16 Recall that Livy (ch. 2 above) says that Campanians used captured fancy Samnite arms for their gladiators. *OLD* s.v. and S. B. Platner and T. Ashby, *A Topographical Dictionary of Ancient Rome* (London: Oxford U., 1929) 494, both see a *spoliarium* as a site where corpses of gladiators were stripped of their equipment, but *OLD* sees 'a place in an amphitheater' and Platner–Ashby see 'a building'.

17 SHA *Comm.* 18.3, 5, 19.1, 3 ('gladiatoris cadaver in spoliario ponatur'); also the corpse is to be cut or mangled (*lanietur*); see further in ch. 7 below. Cf. Suet. *Claud.* 34.1, which probably refers to the coup de grâce, not throat-slitting in the *spoliarium*.

18 Lactantius, *Div. inst.* 6.20, cited by Friedländer (1965) 2:61, says that crowds demanded that bodies of victims (clearly gladiators denied *missio* and given the death blow) be abused (*dissipari*) to confirm that death was not merely pretended. *Confectores* are known from martyrology; see ch. 8 below. On undertakers (*libitinarii*) and the disposal of *noxii*, see below.

19 *Pass. Perp. et Fel.* 21.6–8, trans. Musurillo (1972); on the events, see further in ch. 8 below.

20 David L. Bomgardner, 'The Carthage Amphitheater: A Reappraisal', *AJArch.* 93 (1989) 89–90, 102, quote at 89; a subterranean gallery led from this chamber to the west, and cemeteries also lay to the west of the amphitheater. See his figs 1.5 and 10. Auguet (1972), 215–16, suggested that the *spoliarium* at Carthage was the lower hall at one end of the axis of the amphitheater near the Porta Libitinaria; but cf. Golvin (1988) 34. Auguet, 114, suggested that bodies of *venatores* killed in combat were sent to the *spoliarium*, citing finds of curse tablets invoking misfortune on the hunters, but Bomgardner feels that the curses came from a pit in the arena.

21 Bomgardner (1989) 102, fig. 10, gives dimensions of ca. 2.0–2.3 by 5.6 m for the chamber, including two niches (ca. 0.8 by 2.3 m) in its opposite walls. The niches were 'large enough for a body to be laid out', but the chamber's capacity was quite limited.

22 Coleman (1990), 59, feels that customarily victims mauled by beasts were thrown on one side of the arena to be dispatched by having their throats cut (i.e. to confirm their death), but that on this occasion the crowd asked for the dispatching to be done out in the open so that they might see the victims' faces. Brent D. Shaw, 'The Passion of Perpetua', *P & P* 139 (1993) 3–45, at 10, suggests that victims mounted a platform, as depicted in the mosaic at El Djem. Petronius, *Sat.* 45.6, Loeb, writes of a gladiatorial show that will have a 'butchery done in the middle (*carnarium in medio*), where the whole audience can see it'. Scobie (1988), 210–11, explains that normally in an amphitheater there was a wooden fence with a net away from the base of the podium for security reasons. The fence allowed good viewing except for a 'dead' or 'blind angle' at the base of the podium. Possibly crowds asked that gladiators be centered for the *missio* scene and that victims also be put in plain view for the *confector*.

23 Although the Colosseum was in III, the *armamentarium* and *samniarium* (where weapons were stored and maintained) are listed with the *spoliarium* in II. Golvin (1988), 151, 336, suggests a location to the west of the Colosseum in one of the annexes. Similarly, Richardson (1992), 366, suggests that 'one common dressing room for the amphitheater' was on the Colosseum square, 'just inside the boundary of Regio II'.

24 *CIL* 14.3014 = *ILS* 6252: 'ludum gladiatorium omni impensa sua, ita spoliarium a fundamentis exstructum ornatumque pro nitore civitatis'. See Ville (1981) 297, who feels that a mutilated inscription found at Rome, *CIL* 6.1744, probably refers to this munificence.

25 *CIL* 6.10171; see Ville (1981) n. 172 on 299, n. 96 on 273, n. 125 on 281; but cf. Sabbatini Tumolesi (1988) 17.

26 The *cryptarius* in *CIL* 6.631 and 3713 probably attended to the subterranean passages and galleries; see Ville (1981) n. 185 on 304.

27 Only proper gladiators had body armor and needed to be stripped and sorted according to performance. As Seneca shows (above in ch. 3), *damnati* in *meridiani* sometimes had weapons but not armor. Like weapons, clothes showed status (or some role), but public nudity was an insult.

28 An analogous site was the Carcer, a temporary holding area for foes to be disposed of elsewhere; see ch. 7 below.

29 Grant (1967), 8, exaggerated the Roman case in suggesting that Nazism and Roman gladiators were 'the two most quantitatively destructive institutions in history'. Colin Wells, *The Roman Empire* (Glasgow: Fontana, 1984) 278, says that the amphitheater housed 'institutionalized terror on a scale unknown in the modern world, except in Soviet Russia'. He also compares the desensitizing effects of overexposure to brutality at martyrdoms and in Nazi death camps. Eichmann and others approached disposal with military or industrial efficiency and even took pride in their system of mass destruction. Compared to Rome, the Nazi crime was greater in extent, shorter in duration, had an ethnic focus, and could better use fire and ditches. Unlike the attempted secrecy of the Nazis, Rome's methods of death and disposal added to the 'institutionalized terror'.

30 Arguing that the fate of the dead body does not matter, Lucretius (3.888–93, Loeb) surveys methods of disposal:

> For if after death it is an evil to be mauled by the jaws and teeth of wild beasts, I do not see how it should not be unpleasant to be laid upon the fire and to shrivel in the hot flames, or to be packed in honey and stifled, and to be stiff with cold lying upon a slab of cold marble, or to be buried and crushed under a weight of superimposed earth.

Minucius Felix, *Oct.* 11.4, Loeb, lists options: corpses may be 'torn to pieces by wild beasts or drowned in the sea, or buried in the ground, or consumed in the flame'. Metcalf and Huntington (1991), 24, explain that, in addition to burial, corpses 'are preserved by smoking, embalming or pickling; they are eaten – raw, cooked, or rotten; they are ritually exposed as carrion or simply abandoned; or they are dismembered and treated in a variety of these ways'. For a broad survey of disposal as a universal problem underlying the folklore of 'revenants' (the 'undead'), see P. Barber *Vampires, Burial, and Death: Folklore and Reality* (New Haven: Yale U., 1988), 166–77, who discusses several options: cremation, burial, covering the body with rocks or brush, disposal in water, excarnation (allowing scavengers to eat the flesh), embalming, and mummification.

31 Numerous examples are collected and discussed by Wiedemann (1992) 114–16, 120–2; Ville (1981), esp. 240–55, 329–32; Balsdon (1969) 296–302; Robert (1940) 42–51, 287–302; and Lafaye (1896) 1591–2. Memorials of gladiatorial *familiae* and of shows given by high priests of the imperial cult might include reliefs of gladiators with inscribed names in the nominative, but these were normally not epitaphs or funeral *stelai*; see Robert (1940) 56–64; Roueché (1992) 61–4 and nos. 13–37; but cf. Wiedemann (1992) 17.

32 In rare instances emperors intervened personally. E.g. Caracalla forced the gladiator Bato to fight three men in succession on the same day, and when the third man killed Bato, the emperor honored him with a brilliant funeral: Dio 78(77).6.2.

33 E.g. Constantius, a *munerarius* at Tergeste (modern Trieste), donated a mass grave for all the day's gladiators in gratitude for the honor of giving the games and as self-advertisement of his own generosity: *CIL* 5.563 (cf. 9.465–6); cited in Lafaye (1896) 1591. As Lafaye points out, however, no important man made room for a gladiator in his own family tomb.

34 On gladiatorial epitaphs as indications of ethnicity: Ville (1981) 264–7; Wiedemann (1992) 113–15. On inscriptions and types of gladiators, now see Sabbatini Tumolesi (1988) nos. 63–100.

35 E.g., as Wiedemann (1992), 121–2, notes, the gladiators of the family of Gaius Salvius Capito buried at Venusia (*ILS* 5083/5083a (= *CIL* 9.465–6) discussed in n. 93 in ch. 3 above) included *tirones* who died before their first official fight as well as veterans who died after several fights.

36 E.g. the veteran *murmillo*, Marcus Ulpius Felix, originally from Gaul, died at the age of 45 and was buried (probably at Rome) by his wife and son: *ILS* 5104 (= *CIL* 6.10177 = 33977); Sabbatini Tumolesi (1988) no. 73. Wiedemann (1992), n. 54 on 15, collects examples of epitaphs set up by wives.

37 The epigraphical debate is long and complex: Robert (1940), 287–92, feels that *lib.* = *liber* (i.e. a free *auctoratus*), and Balsdon (1969), 302, agrees; but Ville (1981) 242–5, following Mommsen and Dessau, feels that *lib.* = *libertus* (i.e. a manumitted freedman gladiator). Ville feels that the epitaphs of slaves are indicated by reference to an owner or the absence of a reference to freedom. Ville's position seems best: an epitaph is a context for declaring achievement and elevation (e.g. a slave earning freedom), not for admitted self-debasement (a freeborn man accepting gladiatorial infamy). Cf. E. A. Meyer, 'Explaining the Epigraphic Habit in the Roman Empire: The Evidence of Epitaphs', *JRS* 80 (1990) 74–96, esp. 78–81, on testamentary privilege as a benefit of the acquisition of Roman citizenship.

38 Jerome's *Life* of Saint Hilarion the Hermit (*Vita Hilarion* 7 of around 390; J.-P. Migne, *PL* 23.32) includes a story that Hilarion had a vision of a gladiatorial fight with the loser asking him to give him a burial; cited by Friedländer (1965) 2:80; and Wiedemann (1992) 159.

39 See Levick (1983) 103–5 and the discussion in ch. 3 above. See ch. 4 above on justifications and implications of denial of burial, and see below on Libitina.

40 *CIL* I² 2123 = *CIL* 11.6528 = *ILS* 7846 = *ILLRP* (Degrassi) 662 = *ROL* IV, no. 106 on 50–1; probable date before 80 BC. See Purcell (1987) 37–8; cf. a similar benefaction at Tolentinum (*CIL* 9.5570 = *ILS* 7847); John Bodel, 'Graveyards and Groves: A Study of the Lex Lucerina', *AJAH* 11 (1986, special issue, publ. 1994) 1–133, at 34–5, n. 137 on 105. On the exclusion of those who committed suicide by hanging, see Van Hooff (1990) 67, 165; cf. further above in ch. 4. On tombs and euergetism, see Veyne (1990) 109–17; Pauline Schmitt-Pantel, 'Evergetism et mémoire du mort', in Gnoli and Vernant (1982) 177–88.

41 Ville (1981) 339–41, 462–3. Cf. Scobie (1986) 419: 'It also seems that the corpses of gladiators of servile status were thrown on garbage heaps, though the evidence for this is so far confined to Sassina.'

42 On the Roman notion that burial, monuments, and epitaphs were rewards for merit, see Lattimore (1942) 223 with examples of the use of *b(ene) m(erenti)*.

43 The original gladiators, *busturarii* who supposedly fought near the tomb (see Ville (1981) 25), were perhaps thrown onto the pyre, as Achilles sacrificed the

Trojan captives, but in Virgil Aeneas' main concern is sacrificing the blood of captives.

44 See Barton (1993) 22–4, citing Cic. *Mil.* 34.92; Sen. *De ira* 1.2.4, *Ep.* 82.12, *Tranq.* 11.5, shows that there were different deaths in the arena and a hierarchy of empathy in reaction to them. On failed gladiators, also see Wiedemann (1992) 38–9.

45 On gladiators, *devotio*, and *sacri*, see Barton (1993) 40–6; cf. ch. 3 above.

46 Even if a gladiator was not spared in the arena, his form of death, a quick blow to the neck decided after an appeal to the people and performed by an expert, was a privilege not granted to others who died aggravated, insulting deaths.

47 As Bodel (1986), 81, notes, 'potter's field' as a place to dump the corpses of strangers comes from Matt. 27.5–8 concerning Judas' blood money. On the Old Testament's Gehenna, a gully outside Jerusalem where bodies of executed criminals and unattended corpses were dumped, see Bernstein (1993) 169–72. As Ariès (1982) 56–9, or (1974) 18–22, explains, in medieval Europe great common graves (*fosses aux pauvres*) up to 30 feet deep and 15 by 18 feet in area were dug in courtyards between charnel galleries in the atria of church-yards. These common graves were filled with the dead, larger ones holding as many as 1,500 bodies. They were covered, but later old ditches were reopened and the bones were taken to charnel houses – galleries alongside churchyards above which ossuraries displayed bones as decoration. Note that Ariès (1982), 56, feels that use of these pits probably developed during epidemics and 'cannot go back much further than the sixteenth century'. These graves were associated with the poor and not the damned. See Ariès, 42–5, on the medieval practice of leaving the corpses of the excommunicated and the executed to rot unburied in fields or dumps; cf. n. 96 below on gallows.

48 *Carnaria*: Lanciani's term (see below); also in Pearson (1973) 21: unclaimed bodies were 'thrown into the *carnaria* along with dead animals and other refuse'. F. R. Cowell, *Everyday Life in Ancient Rome* (London: Batsford, 1961) 175, suggests that arena bodies were taken via carts and 'flung into a nameless common grave'. Cf. Plin. *HN* 35.49 on special carts used to take gladiators to the arena.

49 *AE* 1971 no. 88; no. 89 is a similar but more fragmentary text from Cumae. See discussions in L. Bove, 'Due nuove iscrizioni di Pozzuoli e Cuma', *RAAN* 41 (1966) 207–39; L. Bove, 'Due iscrizione da Pozzuoli e Cuma', *Labeo* 13 (1967) 22–48; Bodel (1986) 15–18, 72–80; Jean-Christian Dumont, 'L'Enlèvement du cadavre', 181–7, and François Hinard, 'La "Loi de Pouzzoles" et les pompes funèbres', 205–12, both in Hinard (1995). Bove (1966), 210, dated the Puteoli law to the late Republic or the time of Augustus; Bodel, 74–6, suggests a date closer to the time of Sulla.

50 Roman slaves, prisoners of war, and criminals (including those condemned to a gladiatorial school or the mines: *CTh* 9.40.2 (= *CIust* 9.47.17)) might suffer penal tatooing or branding; see Jones (1987) 145–55. Hinard, 'La "Loi de Pouzzoles"', esp. 206–7, 210–12, discusses the regulations concerning the personnel, relating concerns to the issue of pollution and not just hygiene. In discussing the possible site of the Lucus Libitinae at Puteoli he briefly, 209, draws parallels to the Esquiline at Rome, but see Bodel's detailed discussion below.

51 The details here (e.g. *crux*, fire probably for torture) indicate that those punished were slaves; see K. R. Bradley, *Slaves and Masters in the Roman Empire: A Study in Social Control* (Oxford: Oxford U., 1987) 122–3; F. de Martino, 'I "supplicia" dell'inscrizione di Pozzuoli', *Labeo* 21 (1975) 210–14. Bradley, *Slavery and Society*

at Rome (Cambridge: Cambridge U., 1994) 166, suggests that Rome had similar services and points out that Trimalchio had *tortores* on his household staff; see Petron. *Sat.* 49.6. On slaves as *noxii*, see ch. 3 above.

52 Trans. Gardner and Wiedemann (1991) no. 22; cf. Wiedemann (1992) 74–5.

53 Bodel (1986) 17, quote at 81; n. 229 on 117: the use of *ubi* for *quo* to mean 'to where' is colloquial; cf. Apul. *Met.* 9.39. Dumont, op. cit., 183, independently assumes that Puteoli had some dumping area where corpses were exposed. Cf. Gardner and Wiedemann (1991) no. 22, who take 'ubi plura cadavera erunt' as 'or bodies if there are several'. In personal correspondence, Wiedemann suggests that the use of the future tense (*erunt*) is hard to explain if one assumes a permanent dumping-ground for unburied cadavers. In the law from Cumae, in addition to references to *fossa*, *milliarum primum*, and *ustor*, there are references (Tab. A Col. I 3–10) to a *carnifex publice*, *pontem super cloaca{m*; and *conductor pontem*. Bodel (1986), n. 64 on 96–7, feels that II 10–21 concerns strangers without local connections who have died in the area; and Wiedemann (1992), 75, suggests II 3f. includes the provision: 'If the executioner (*carnifex*) acts in public or gives or wished to give a spectacle.' However, as Bove, 'Due iscrizione', 35, notes, the inscription is too fragmentary for a satisfactory interpretation.

54 In his work on surveying, Agennius Urbicus (*De controversiis agrorum* in *Grom. Vet.*, p. 86 La. = *Corp. Agr.*, p. 47 Th., cited by Bodel (1986) 81–3) notes that Roman towns had suburban sites for the disposal of indigents and for the punishment of *noxii*: 'habent et res p(ublicae) loca suburbana inopum funeribus destinata, quae loca †cula, culinas† appellant. habent et loca noxiorum poenis destinata.' The text is corrupt and Bodel, 82–3, discusses various interpretations of *cula* and *culinas* as places for funeral banquets, *ustrina*, or grave pits; but whether the reference is to crematoria or mass-grave pits is uncertain. Bodel, 36 and n. 50, also cites Frontinus, pp. 55–7 Lachmann ('inopum funeribus destinata . . . loca noxiorum poenis destinata') on such areas.

55 Bodel follows Bove, 'Due iscrizione', in taking *funus acervum* as *acerbum*, premature death. Dumont, op. cit., 185–7, with n. 19 on 185, discusses the issue, concluding that we cannot decide whether the reference is to the deaths of children or sons, either of which would be premature. Cf. Gardner and Wiedemann (1991) 25 and n. 7 on 26, who suggest that a 'mass funeral' would have had a higher priority.

56 *Suspendiosi*: see Van Hooff (1990) 67, and ch. 4 above. Dumont, op. cit., passim, stresses the problem of the pollution of the corpse and those who touch it as the main reason for the regulations concerning the personnel and the haste of removal. He suggests, 186, that there was less urgency with the corpse of a slave because it involved less pollution; cf. his 'La Mort de l'esclave', 173–86, in Hinard (1987a).

57 Further on the removal of abandoned corpses: Bodel, 33–5, n. 64 on 96–7, nn. 132–4 on 104–5. Hinard (1984), 301, without reference to Puteoli, suggests that a *carnifex* at Rome attended to corpses.

58 Cicero, *Phil.* 9.17, proposed state burial for Servius Sulpicius there; Horace, *Sat.* 1.8.36, refers to *magna sepulcra*; and Suetonius, *Vita Hor.* 65, Loeb, says that Horace was buried 'near the tomb of Maecenas on the farther part of the Esquiline Hill'.

59 R. Lanciani, *The Ruins and Excavations of Ancient Rome* (Boston: Houghton Mifflin, 1897, repr. New York: Bell, 1979) 409–12; Richardson (1992) 64–5. This cemetery was in use from the seventh to the first century BC, with a gap from the end of the sixth to the middle of the fourth century. See details in G. Pinza, 'Le vicende della zona Esquilina fino ai tempi di Augusto', *BCAR* 42

(1914) 117–75; M. Taloni, 'Le necropoli dell'Esquilino', in *Roma medio repub-blicana* (Rome: L'Erma di Bretschneider, 1977) 188–233; M. Albertoni, 'La necropoli Esquilina arcaia e Repubblicana', in *L'archeologia in Roma capitale* (Venice: Marsilio Editori, 1983) 140–55; Le Gall (1980–1) 148–52; and Ruth Christine Häuber, 'Zur Topographie der Horti Maecenatis und der Horti Lamiani auf dem Esquilin in Rom', *KJ* 23 (1990) 11–107. The most recent and important study, Bodel (1986), appeared in 1994 and is largely followed here.

60 See R. Lanciani, *BCAR* 2 (1874) 42–53, 3 (1875) 41–56; R. Lanciani (1897) 100, 409–12; and R. Lanciani, *Ancient Rome in the Light of Recent Discoveries* (London: Macmillan, 1888) 64–7, summarized in Hopkins (1983) 208–9; Bodel (1986) 40; Morris (1992) 42; and Platner–Ashby (1929) 435.

61 Lanciani (1888) 64–5; similarly, in *BCAR* (1897) 409–10.

62 *Ling.* 5.25, Loeb. Scholiasts on Horace (Porphyrio ad Hor. *Epod.* 5.100, Comm. Cruq. ad loc.) and Festus (241L s.v. *puticuli*) say that corpses of the poor and of cheap slaves were left to rot in such pits. Porphyrio, ad Hor. *Sat.* 1.8.11, says that there were public crematoria in the area. Richardson (1992), 323, points out that Varro and Festus were unfamiliar with this type of burial and spoke of it in the past tense, and that, while the common graves were trenches, the *puticuli* seem always to have been individual burials. It is also noteworthy that the pits contained common vases and lamps.

63 Hor. *Sat.* 1.8.19ff.: witches frequent the site at night 'gathering bones and harmful herbs'. Hor. *Epod.* 5.83–102, Loeb: witches are about to murder a kidnapped boy to get ingredients for a love potion when the boy swears vengeance:

> With curses I will hound you; by no sacrifice shall my awful execra-tion be warded off. Nay, even when, doomed to die, I have breathed my last, at night I will meet you as a fury; and as a ghost I will tear your faces with crooked claws, as is the Manes' power . . . The rabble, pelting you with stones on every side along the streets, shall crush you, filthy hags. Then by and by the wolves and birds that haunt the Esquiline shall scatter far and wide your unburied limbs . . .

64 Pinza, op. cit.; cf. G. Pinza, *BCAR* 40 (1912) 65, 82; also Taloni, op. cit., 188–96.

65 Bodel (1986) 40–2, quote at 42, 45–7.

66 See Lanciani in n. 60 above; cross-section noted by Bodel (1986) n. 165 on 110.

67 Hopkins (1983), 208–9, discusses the practicality of using pits during epidemics, and notes that, 'In such circumstances, cremation was too costly, because it consumed expensive fuel.' Livy, 3.6.2–3, records a plague as early as 463 BC, and there were frequent outbreaks in and around Rome from 181 to 71 BC, one plague lasting three years: Livy 40.19.3, 41.21.5; Val. Max. 1.8.2. Perhaps pits were dug on the Esquiline in the second century at the then edge of the city to deal with the problem, but by the time of the great plagues of the Empire the city had grown past the redeveloped Esquiline area. In the autumn of AD 65 some 30,000 deaths from plague were recorded at the Temple of Libitina: Suet. *Ner.* 39.1. In a pestilence under Commodus 2,000 people often died in Rome in a single day: Dio 73(72).14.3. On the identity of the diseases and mortality estimates at Rome, see William H. McNeill, *Plagues and Peoples* (New York: Anchor Press, 1976) 103–4. As Barber (1988), 140, explains, mass graves were space- and labor-efficient; they were a common

response in Europe in times of mass death when normal methods of disposal were insufficient.

68 Lanciani (1897) 409. On suggestions by scholiasts, see Nash (1961–2) 487. On possible use of executioner's pits in Roman Nubia and in the Romano-British site at Lankhills, Winchester, see Theya Molleson, 'What the Bones Tell Us', in Humphreys and King (1981) 27–8.

69 Claudius: Suet. *Claud.* 25.3; cf. Strabo 5.3.9; Nero: Tac. *Ann.* 15.60.2. See n. 54 above on Agennius Urbicus. Hinard (1987b), 113–15, sees the Esquiline as a place of execution for slaves and the lowly, and, using Horace, as a place of denial of burial and exposure. He interprets the Esquiline as a special magical area used to calm the fears of the Romans. He also suggests, 113, that the rebel soldiers executed in 270 BC in the Forum and exposed 'outside the city' (see ch. 2 above) were dumped on the Esquiline, but this seems logistically unlikely. Again, Hinard, 113–14, feels that those executed and denied burial on the return of Marius in 87 (App. *B Civ.* 1.73; see ch. 2 above) ended up on the Esquiline. We need not associate every unspecific reference to denial of burial with exposure on the Esquiline. See Hinard, 114–15, for a suggestion, based on an emendation of Plut. *Galb.* 28.2–3, that the Sessorium was a place where those put to death by emperors were punished.

70 On *stercus*: Bodel (1986) 30. Cf. Lanciani (1888) 64–6; Hopkins (1983) n. 11 on 210. *CIL* I² 838–9 = 6.31614–15 = *ILS* 8208: 'Nei quis intra terminos propius urbem ustrinam fecisse velit nive stercus cadaver iniecisse velit.' See the discussion in Bodel (1986) 42–4, fig. 1, and n. 166 on 110, who suggests a date early in the first century BC. Richardson (1992), 294, feels that the stones probably refer to Sulla's enlargement of the *pomerium*, which seems aimed at incorporating the Campus. A. E. Gordon, 'Seven Latin Inscriptions in Rome', *G & R* 20 (1951) 77–9 and pl. 105a, without substantiation, suggests that the inscription may refer to animals from the public games.

71 Graffito: on *CIL* 6.31615 = I² 839; cf. *ILS* 8207b (Verona); see Bodel (1986) 44; Robinson (1975) 181. Cf. praetors' actions that corpses should not be dumped on other men's land: *Dig.* 11.7.2.1.

72 Bodel (1986) 47.

73 Ibid., 7–13, 17–23. See his extensive bibliography in n. 5 on 86. Standard editions include *CIL* 9.782, *CIL* I² 401, and *ILS* 4912. On Libitina, see n. 77 below.

74 Ibid., 3–4, 64–8 and passim. Bodel, 65–6, suggests that Rome may have confiscated the territory of private grave sites at Luceria as had been done with the establishment of Latin colonies elsewhere. The ban on rites may represent Roman disrespect for enemies' graves.

75 Ibid., 47–50; on *CIL* I² 591 = *ILS* 6082; further bibliography in Bodel, n. 174 on 111.

76 Bodel (1986) 50, cf. fig. 1, adds that this is further suggested by the find of an inscription (*CIL* I² 989) concerning an association of flute-players (*collegium tibicinum*), often used in funerals, found not 15 m away.

77 King Servius is said to have instituted a death register: Dion. Hal. *Ant. Rom.* 4.15.5; cf. Suet. *Ner.* 39.1; but Parkin (1992), 38–9, cautions that references to lists kept at the Temple of Libitina should not be interpreted as any systematic registration of the dead in the Roman Empire. Plutarch, *Num.* 12.1–2, says that Libitina was a goddess of funerals with a grove at Rome where burial arrangements were sold; cf. *Quaest. Rom.* 23. Festus, 322L, puts a Temple of Venus in the grove. See Bodel (1986) 13–15 and n. 53 on 94; Scullard (1981) 177; Richardson (1992) 235; Platner–Ashby (1929) 319; Gerard Freyburger, 'Libitine et les funérailles', 213–22, in Hinard (1995). On the undertakers

(*libitinarii* or *vespilliones*) and their assistants (*pollinctores*), see Toynbee (1971) n. 131 on 290. Apparently public undertakers, usually four at a time, carried corpses of the poor on cheap biers (*sandapila*) during the night to some form of burial or disposal; see Toynbee (1971) 45–6, on Suet. *Dom.* 17.3. Domitian was given a pauper's burial: 'cadaver eius, populari sandapila, per vespilliones'); Mart. 2.81, 6.77; also see below on Mart. 8.75.9–10 on branded slaves.

78 Bodel (1986), paraphrased from 50–2, quote at 50.

79 Bodel (1986) 52–4; Häuber (1990) 98–101; see Bodel, fig. 3, from Häuber.

80 Lanciani (1897) 100, 409–12; Platner–Ashby (1929) 269. Richardson (1992), 200–1, suggests that the Agger in the area was probably absorbed into the Gardens as a promenade. Suetonius, *Ner.* 38.2, says that Nero watched the fire of 64 from a tower in the Domus Transitoria (Nero's first house, which was intended to join the imperial residence with the Gardens of Maecenas); cf. Dio 62.18.1; but Tacitus, *Ann.* 15.39, says that during the fire Nero sang of the destruction of Troy in his private theater. Propertius lived in the area: 3.23–4, 4.8.1–2. Richardson (1992), 64, suggests that 'the cemetery limit must simply have been moved beyond the new line'.

81 E.g. Papinian (*Dig.* 43.10.5) favors prohibiting dumping of dung, bodies, or animal skins, as well as public brawling, in city streets. See Scobie (1986) 407–18, expanded upon by Bodel (1986) 30–8. Scobie (1986), 416, 418, notes corpses dumped in the street as a health hazard; cf. his 415, on municipal trash heaps.

82 In the Table of Heracleia (Johnson et al. (1961) Doc. 113.7–13, 17) keeping the streets free of rubbish was the responsibility of various officials: aediles had general supervision of streets, quattuorvirs were in charge of cleaning the city streets, and duumvirs were in charge of cleaning streets outside the city walls within a mile of Rome. Cf. Athens, where city commissioners (*astynomoi*) supervised public slaves who removed bodies of those who died in the streets to purify the deme: Arist. [*Ath. pol.*] 50.2; [Dem.] 43.57–8. See E. J. Owens, 'The *koprologoi* at Athens in the Fifth and Fourth Centuries B.C.', *CQ* n.s. 33 (1983) 44–50.

83 Mart. 10.5.10–12; see the discussion in Scobie (1986) 418–20. Recall Horace on wolves and birds in n. 63 above. In Petronius, *Sat.* 116, Loeb, a local says that legacy hunting has made Croton 'like a plague-stricken plain, where there is nothing but carcasses to be devoured, and crows to devour them'. Cf. the Greek imprecation, 'to the crows' (*es korakas*): Ar. *Vesp.* 982, *Nub.* 123, 133.

84 Sen. *Ep.* 95.43; Suet. *Vesp.* 5.5. Scobie (1986), 420, feels that dogs, 'necrophagous scavengers', must have been a common sight on the Esquiline. Eusebius, *HE* 9.8.10–12, writes of dogs feeding on unburied corpses during a pestilence under Maximian. In Phaedrus, *Fab.* 1.27, a vulture chastises a dog for digging up human bones.

85 Suet. *Ner.* 48.2. Petronius, *Sat.* 134.1, associates Eumolpus' impotency with black magic or with taboos such as stepping in dung or on a corpse at a crossroad.

86 E.g. Juv. 6.603; cf. Artemidorus 2.9 for the association of the poor with dungheaps. Refuting charges of baby killing by Christians, Tertullian, *Apol.* 9.7, says that Romans kill children cruelly by strangling and drowning them or by exposing them to cold, starvation, and dogs; similarly, *Ad nat.* 1.15.3–4; Min. Fel. *Oct.* 30.2; Lactant. *Div. inst.* 6.20. Exposure, which was at the discretion of a Roman father's *potestas*, should not be equated with infanticide since exposure did not necessarily mean death. In summary see Parkin (1992) 95–8; Thomas Wiedemann, *Adults and Children in the Roman Empire* (London: Routledge, 1989) 36–9; for a thorough historical treatment, now see W. V. Harris, 'Child-Exposure

in the Roman Empire', *JRS* 84 (1994) 1–22. On continuities from Rome to the Renaissance, see John Boswell, *The Kindness of Strangers: The Abandonment of Children in Western Europe from Late Antiquity to the Renaissance* (New York: Vintage, 1990) 51–179, esp. 129–31.

87 Burial needs of Rome: Purcell (1987), 32–3, estimates that during the high Empire a million people lived within 25 km of the center of Rome, creating an average burial-space demand of nearly eight tombs per square km per year. Bodel (1986), 19, estimates the mortality rate at around forty per thousand annually, or 40,000 for a Rome of a million. He suggests, 41, that of the half-million population of first-century Rome, about forty per thousand died annually, i.e. 20,000 per year or fifty per day. Aside from visitors and pestilences, perhaps 5 percent of these, or 1,000 per year, were indigent and needed public facilities. Bodel, n. 54 on 94, discusses plagues (cf. n. 65 above) and notes that Livy (40.19.4, 41.21.6) twice remarks that Libitina had trouble handling all the funerals.

88 See Bodel (1986) 33–5 and nn. 132–3 on 104. He argues that by the early Empire educated men understood the threat to public health from such dumping, believing, for example, that bad air from putrid corpses caused contamination. Cf. Scobie (1986) 399–400; and Ralph Jackson, *Doctors and Diseases in the Roman Empire* (Norman: U. Oklahoma, 1988) 42–55, who see little official concern for public hygiene.

89 Bodel (1986) 39; cf. ch. 4 above on sepulchral laws.

90 There were other suburban dumps and *necropoleis* (e.g. on the Appian and Vatican), but urbanization and expansions of the *pomerium* increased the related transportation problems, and pits were an excessive attraction for carrion animals. The need for pits may have been reduced by the development of burial *collegia* and the use (even for slaves) of *columbaria*. On Nerva's establishment of a burial allowance for the plebs of Rome, see Hopkins (1983) 211. Le Gall (1980–1) suggests that after the closing of the Esquiline, humble but proper burials of the poor shifted to the banks of the Tiber, and he sees parallels in the provinces and at Ostia (Isola Sacra). On Bodel's suggested shift to crematoria, see below.

91 Dion. Hal. *Ant. Rom.* 4.13, noted by Purcell (1987) 30, comments on the urban sprawl at Rome already by the end of the second century BC.

92 For an excellent treatment, see E. P. Sanders, *The Historical Figure of Jesus* (New York: Allen Lane, 1993) esp. 249–75. Deut. 21.22–3: corpses of criminals were to be buried on the day of the execution to avoid an affront to God and a defilement of the land. Jews were usually executed by stoning, but crucifixion was used by some leaders during the Hasmonean period; see Joseph. *AJ* 14.380–1.

93 On the discovery of the tomb of a crucified man in the Jewish cemetery at a site northeast of Jerusalem, see Tzaferis (1985). The execution was relatively quick and the body was turned over to the family and received not only proper burial but elite reburial. Ossuary no. 4 from Chamber B of Tomb no. 1, inscribed with the name Yehohanan son of Hagakol, contained the bones of a man crucified in the first century before the destruction of Jerusalem in AD 70. Study of the bones shows that the man's feet were nailed to the cross through both heel bones; the nail hit a knot and bent. To remove the body the feet were amputated with an axe; the heel bones, nail and traces of wood were found in the ossuary. The man's forearms, not palms, were nailed. A small seat (*sedile*) supported his left buttock and his legs were bent up in a difficult position. As with the thieves with Jesus (John 32.19), his legs were broken by a blow to hasten death and allow burial on the same day.

94 Eusebius, *HE* 8.82, says that Egyptian martyrs were crucified upside down and kept alive until they starved to death on the cross. Seneca, *Dial. (Cons. ad Marc).* 20, says that crucifixions were done in various ways to increase pain. Tzaferis (1985), 49–50, explains that death could come in two to three hours via muscle spasms and asphyxia, but the agony was commonly prolonged by the Romans for two to three days. Cf. Hengel (1978) 29; Callu (1984) 336–7.

95 Petron. *Sat.* 111–12, Loeb. Pliny, *HN* 36.107, discussed in ch. 4 above concerning Tarquin's corpse abuse, suggests that crucified bodies ended up torn to pieces by wild animals and birds of prey. Callu (1984), 337, omits this reference, but he agrees that the bodies of victims remained on the cross until consumed by carrion animals. Voisin (1979) 440–3, with further bibliography, associates crucifixion, like suicide by hanging, with denial of burial; the victim loses contact with the earth, is denied acceptance in the realm of the dead below, and wanders the earth near the site of death.

96 Cf. Foucault in ch. 4 above. Ariès (1982), 43–4, explains: 'The bodies of those who had been executed were not taken down but remained exposed for months, even years.' Corpses hung from gallows, vulnerable to carrion birds, and body parts might adorn the gates of the city. Gallows, enclosed with walls, sometimes came to coincide with dumps for both bodies and garbage.

97 On the developments, see Toynbee (1971) 39–42; A. D. Nock's classic essay, 'Cremation and Burial in the Roman Empire', *Harv. Theol. Rev.* 25 (1932) 321–59; and Morris (1992) 31–69.

98 Cf. ch. 4 above. See Toynbee (1971) 48 on exceptions, such as the mob's cremation of the body of Caesar (Plut. *Iul.* 68.1) in the Forum. Cicero, *Leg.* 2.23.58, attributes the XII Tables' ban on cremation in the city to the fire hazard; cf. 2.24.61 on the ban in the XII Tables (10.9) on cremation within 60 feet of a building without the owner's permission. Dio 48.43.3, Loeb: a senatorial decree of 38 BC prohibited 'any burning of dead bodies from being carried on within two miles of the city'. Cf. *CTh* 9.17.6; and Bodel (1986) 33.

99 Nero's fire prevention legislation: Tac. *Ann.* 15.43; Suet. *Ner.* 16.1. Property in Rome brought good returns, but frequent fires made such an investment too risky: Gell. *NA* 15.1.3. On fire problems, see Z. Yavetz, 'The Living Conditions of the Urban Poor in Republican Rome', *Latomus* 17 (1958) 500–17, esp. 510–13.

100 Bodel (1986) 81–3, n. 194 on 114. Häuber (1990), 15, 65, notes the appearance of monumental *columbaria* along the Via Labicana-Prenestina around the time of Maecenas.

101 Bodel (1986), n. 194 on 114, also cites Luc. 8.736–8, but this concerns the humble cremation of Pompey's decapitated corpse in Egypt in the fashion of a pauper's funeral.

102 Mart. 8.75.9–10, Loeb. The location in Martial is near 'the Covered and Flaminian Ways' – a colonnade near the Mausoleum of Augustus. An injured Gaul convinced the slaves to drop the corpse and carry him, leading to Martial's witticism that the man could aptly be called 'dead Gaul' (*mortue Galle*, 16), probably a play on the insults used against gladiators (*mirmillones*) with Gaulish helmets in the arena; see Ville (1981) 408.

103 Juvenal mentions *furnacula* and abuse of Sejanus' statue, but Sejanus' corpse was not burned.

104 Distance: Mart. 5.1; Tert. *Ad Mart.* 5.1. Juvenal, 8.235, claims that Catiline deserved the *tunica molesta* for his incendiary plans. Martial, 10.25, mentions options presented to some *damnati* for the sake of entertaining the spectators:

182

he tells the reader not to be impressed with a criminal representing Mucius Scaevola who put his hand in a fire during a show. Apparently his only other option was to wear the *tunica molesta*. In other words, if the criminal would add to the show, he might survive minus his hand. Martial suggests that it would be braver to refuse than to burn his hand. On the same incident, this time praising the courage of the criminal, as a spectator to his hand's noble death, like the original Scaevola (see 1.21), see 8.30 and, similarly, Ter. *Apol.* 50.5. Further references to the *tunica*: Sen. *Ep.* 14.5; Tatian *Ad Gr.* 24. See Coleman (1990), 60–2, who sees these as 'mitigated punishments'; cf. Wiedemann (1992) 87 for a metaphorical interpretation.

105 Berger (1953) s.v. *crematio* (*exurendum damnari, igni necari*); Grodzynski (1984) 368–9. Cf. ch. 2 above.

106 Suet. *Tib.* 75.3. Similarly, the melting of the statue of Sejanus (and abuse of statues in general) was surrogate corpse abuse, whether by blows, hooks, fire, or casting into water. Juv. 10.61–4, Loeb: 'And now the flames are hissing, and amid the roar of furnace (*caminis*) and of bellows the head of the mighty Sejanus, the darling of the mob, is burning and crackling, and from that face, which was but lately second in the entire world, are being fashioned pipkins, basins, frying-pans and slop-pails!' Also, 10.81–2, figuratively of the purge: '"I hear that many are to perish."– "No doubt of it; there is a big furnace ready (*magna est fornacula*)."' Cf. ch. 7 below.

107 Cf. Hom. *Il.* 23.168–9: Achilles wrapped Patroclus' corpse completely with the fat of sacrificial victims, according to Hughes (1991) 52, to help the body to burn. Using forensic evidence, Barber (1988), 76–7, notes that full cremation is time-consuming and requires good ventilation and a large amount of fuel – especially without a special furnace. He cites one case of the use of 21 cubic meters of wood. He comments, 77: 'Cremation . . . is actually not tidy at all . . . It is both expensive and unpleasant – hence most common among the rich, who can afford the expense and oblige others to endure the unpleasantness for them.'

108 Mart. 8.44.14, 10.97.1; cited by Toynbee (1971) 49. Plutarch, *Ti. Gracch.* 13.5, tells of a diseased corpse erupting corrupt matter and extinguishing its funeral pyre. Pliny, *HN* 7.186, notes that when the corpse of Marcus Lepidus was thrown off its pyre by the force of the flames and the fire was too hot to allow it to be replaced, wood was piled about his naked corpse and his cremation continued.

109 Juvenal, 1.155–7, shows that victims burned at the stake were dragged away, leaving a furrow through the floor of the arena.

110 Lactant. *De mort. pers.* 21.7–11; J. L. Creed, ed. and trans., *Lactantius De Mortibus Persecutorum* (Oxford: Clarendon Press, 1984) 35. Slow burning to force Christians to recant: e.g. Lactant. *Div. inst.* 5.11.16–17; further below in ch. 8. Cf. torture by fire in ch. 4.

111 Callu (1984) 337–8, with testimonia from Euseb. *Mart. Pal.* in nn. 83 and 87 on 333, notes that victims were often just tortured with slow fire; they then had to be finished off and disposed of. He speculates, 338, that the charred bodies of victims not completely consumed by fire were crammed into mass graves ('dans des charniers réputés maudits'). Callu, n. 107 on 338, notes the reference in chapter 17 of the *Passion* of St Theodotus of Ancyra (discussed below in ch. 8) to a site outside Ancyra where convicts were beheaded, crucified, or burned at the stake, but he too is probably thinking of the Esquiline.

6

ARENAS AND EATING:
CORPSES AND CARCASSES
AS FOOD?

And I like eating what I go after.
(President George Bush, 1990)

The issue of disposal extends beyond pits, fire, and other usual answers. Another possibility to be considered, another way to dispose of human and animal flesh, is consumption or ingestion by humans or animals. Was any significant portion of the tons of human and animal flesh produced by Roman spectacles disposed of by being eaten by men or animals before or after removal from the arenas?

Anthropologically, the acquisition, sharing, and eating of animal (or human) flesh have always been profoundly symbolic. At the basest level, meat is meat, and some societies have practiced cannibalism as a gesture of triumph, a form of vengeance, or a way to absorb the strength of foes.[1] Greeks and Romans, however, made a clear distinction between animal flesh as a highly desired food and human flesh as potentially miasmatic and taboo as food.[2] As noted above, apparently some of the blood of men killed in the arena in certain festivals was sacrificed to Jupiter, and some Romans drank such blood as a potion believed to cure epilepsy.[3] There are pagan rhetorical references to (auto)cannibalism and to an omnivorous ogre, but we need not speculate that Romans intentionally and directly ate human arena flesh.[4] In response to Roman accusations that Christians were cannibalistic, and working within a broader discourse on human sacrifice, Christians charged Romans with indirect cannibalism; but Romans 'consumed' human arena victims only in a metaphorical sense.[5] Yet to what degree did Rome 'feed' Christians and others to beasts?

Ad bestias – consumption or abuse?

The common modern notion that starved carnivores feasted on and wholly ingested human victims in the amphitheater derives from Christian and literary images. As Jonah was swallowed whole by the beastly whale, only to be saved, Christian martyrs were said to be 'swallowed' by devilish beasts, thus securing the crown of heaven. Before his death at Rome in AD 107 or 109 St Ignatius of Antioch wrote that he eagerly longed for death: 'Suffer me to be eaten by the beasts, through whom I can attain to God.'[6] Salvian's fifth-century polemic against games charges that,

> the greatest pleasure is to have men die, or, what is worse and more cruel than death, to have them torn in pieces, to have the bellies of wild beasts gorged with human flesh; to have men eaten, to the great joy of the bystanders and the delight of onlookers, so that the victims seem devoured (*devorari*) almost as much by the eyes of the audience as by the teeth of beasts. That such things may take place the whole world is ransacked . . . and in order that the flesh of men may be devoured by wild beasts, the last secrets of the world of nature are revealed.[7]

Such fervent texts should not be taken literally. Christians were killed and destroyed in the arena, but they were not 'eaten up'. The deaths and the 'baptisms of blood' were spectacular – the eating was minimal.[8]

Figurative Christian accounts have led modern studies and translations to suggest that victims were 'devoured' or 'consumed'. Ancient art, however, shows live victims being attacked, bitten, mauled, and bloodied (see figure 1b) rather than victims' corpses being eaten whole. Pagan sources usually say that victims were torn, ripped, or mangled; suggestions that they were consumed are fewer and figurative.[9] Martial (*Spect.* 8, 12) mentions mythological charades in which men were torn by bears (using *lacerare*); e.g. a Laureolus is exposed to a bear and his limbs are mangled (7: *laceri membris*). Strabo (6.2.6) reports seeing the execution in the Forum of the robber Selurus, who was dropped into wild-beast cages; modern works say that he was 'devoured', but Strabo says that he was torn asunder (*diapasthenta*).[10] Compare the Christian writer Lactantius' charge (*De mort. pers.* 21.5–6) that Galerius, who 'never dined without human blood being shed', kept selected bears to whom men were thrown to be eaten bit by bit, with pagan Ammianus Marcellinus' report (29.3.9) that around AD 372 Valentinian I kept two savage man-destroying bears (*duas ursas saevas hominum ambestrices*) in cages near his bedroom, but that 'after seeing many people buried whom Innocence [one of the bears] had torn to pieces', he returned it to the wild. The stories are similar, but the pagan version mentions burial, not ingestion.

Even Christian sources reveal that the goal of throwing men to the beasts was mauling and mutilation. Tertullian (*De spect.* 12) says that shows came to include savage beasts tearing men's bodies to pieces (*dissiparentur*). Martyrs did not disappear into beasts' bellies; supposedly they were often not even touched. Eusebius (*HE* 8.7.1–2, Loeb) writes of Egyptian martyrs at Tyre attacked by leopards, bears, wild boars, and bulls goaded with hot irons:

> The man-eating beasts for a considerable time did not dare to touch
> or even approach the bodies of those who were dear to God, but
> made their attacks on the others [i.e. beast-handlers] who presum-
> ably were provoking and urging them on from the outside; while
> the holy champions were the only ones they did not reach at all,
> though they stood naked, waving their hands to draw them onto
> themselves (for this they were commanded to do).

When, via divine providence, repeated attacks by beasts did no harm to
the martyrs, 'Then at last, after the terrible and varied assaults of these
beasts, they were butchered with the sword' (8.7.6).[11] Not destroyed, let
alone eaten by the beasts, the victims had to be killed and disposed of.

Having beasts wholly eat victims in the arena simply was not an efficient
means of disposal. Aside from scavengers (e.g. vultures and hyenas, sometimes bears and wild boars, or the dogs and crows of Rome), most wild
carnivores normally do not attack humans and eat human flesh. Even ferocious beasts (e.g. lions and leopards) had to be specially trained, and probably
starved, to become 'man-eaters'.[12] Dio says that the unsqueamish Claudius
enjoyed watching humans killed by humans or torn apart (*analoumenoi*) by
animals, but he put to death a lion 'that had been trained to eat (*esthiein*)
men and therefore greatly pleased the crowd, claiming that it was not fitting
for Romans to gaze on such a sight'.[13] Apparently Claudius was a tradi-
tionalist who opposed the introduction of this novelty. Even trained beasts
were not always efficient or reliable. Although trainers provoked them with
fire and whips, and Christians, as instructed, invited them by gestures,
disoriented beasts sometimes might not attack the victims, or they might
turn on the staff of the arena.[14]

Were human arena victims – alive or dead – fed to beasts outside the
arena? Suetonius says that, having collected wild animals for a show, and
having found cattle or butcher's meat to be too expensive (*pecudes carius
. . . ad saginam ferarum*), Caligula selected criminals to be 'mangled'
(*laniandos*, i.e. 'eaten' in this context, instead of butcher's meat), ignoring
the charges and going from one bald man to the next.[15] Caligula's actions
are presented as extraordinarily vicious, implying that beasts normally ate
non-arena, non-human meat. Throwing men to beasts to be killed in a show
was fine, but only a monster would actually feed men to animals as food.[16]

Like fire and crucifixion, beasts gave Rome a spectacular means of torture
and death. Constantine ordered that an owner be accused of homicide if he
mangled his slave's body 'with the punishments reserved to the State, that
is by having his sides torn apart by the claws of wild beasts, or applying
fire to burn his body'.[17] Even if trained or starved beasts ate some of the
flesh after killing their victims, clearly most of the remains had to be
removed for disposal. Killed in arenas in the midst of downtown Rome,
victims could not be left to carrion animals, as perhaps was the case in the

186

prehistoric version of such punishments when outcasts were driven into the wilds and exposed to natural forces to be killed and eaten. Another possible solution to the disposal of human victims will be proposed in the next chapter, but for now the fate of the animal flesh invites discussion.

Hunting, games, and game

That countless thousands of animals, fierce and timid, carnivores and herbivores, from elephants to ostriches, were killed in spectacles at Rome is certain. Recall, for example, that Titus had 9,000 killed (5,000 wild, 4,000 domesticated) over 100 days at the dedication of the Colosseum in AD 80, and Trajan had 11,000 killed over 123 days in his Dacian triumph in AD 107.[18] Yet the question of what happened to the carcasses is seldom asked.[19] Studies generally overlook the possibility that Rome made some practical use of animal carcasses from the arena. As an imperial resource in economic and symbolic terms, live beasts had value as arena exhibits, and dead beasts still had not outlived their usefulness to Rome.

Logically, animal arena meat could have been fed to other carnivorous animals awaiting the arena, but we have no evidence of this.[20] Moreover, like most human victims, most animals were not maintained for long before the show. They were costly to keep,[21] and the *vivarium* or stockyards for animals brought to Rome for spectacles was meant only as a temporary holding area.[22] Most animals brought in for a show soon ended up dead – the problem of feeding them basically ended with the show.

Were the carcasses of beasts from the arenas (the Forum and Circus, and later the Colosseum) simply taken away and dumped in pits (*carnaria, puticuli*) at the edge of town, like the corpses of slaves and the destitute? Such an assumption could be inspired by Lanciani's discovery of the pits on the Esquiline containing the bones of both humans and animals, but those pits were closed and buried in the first century BC.[23] Archaeology has discovered the bones of domestic and foreign animals in the substructures and drains of amphitheaters at Rome and in the provinces.[24] Bones in the substructures probably date from shows of the late Empire, and bones in drains (as well as in substructures) show that not all carcasses (or not every part of them) were dumped in pits.[25] Other possibilities deserve consideration.

Throughout most of our existence, we humans have been hunters, killers and eaters of beasts and, at times, of our fellow man. As *homo necans*, when man destroys other creatures in nature, he feels an ageless sense of anxiety, an instinctual need to justify his killing.[26] In his long history of predation, early man killed to survive – to eat the meat of herbivores, to protect himself from carnivorous predators, and to protect his territory and later his fields and flocks from natural threats. Ancient man ate the meat of unthreatening animals to survive, and he believed that, by sympathetic magic, he became stronger and braver by consuming the fresh flesh of ferocious and powerful animals.[27] Hunting was for food (to acquire or to protect sources of food), not just fun or sport. It was not a waste, an abuse of nature, or an act of excessive bloodymindedness. For Greeks and Romans human flesh was forbidden, but most animal flesh, especially game from the hunt, was a symbolically charged and valuable commodity.[28]

Modern discussions of hunting in antiquity are primarily interested in hunting as a 'field sport' of the elite, a practice acquired by Romans largely from the Hellenistic world in the second century BC. Furthermore, when drawn to the hunts of the arena, some scholars have seen the *venationes* as a disassociated, violent, and vulgar phenomenon, as a foreign and imperial corruption, as perverse and wasteful – neither true hunting nor true sport.[29] Imposing a modern ideology of sport hunting upon the Romans, some studies have seen hunting in the wilds and hunting in the arena as completely unrelated.[30] Like British fox hunters, ancient Romans should have hunted in a 'sporting' fashion, and beasts should not have been simply trapped and slaughtered. Hunts in the wilds and in the arena may have been at opposite ends of the spectrum of Roman hunting, but they were related in the minds and customs of the Romans.[31]

Although studies influenced by modern notions of hunting have downplayed native Roman hunting traditions, like societies from the ancient Near East to modern America, Rome knew the overlapping development of subsistence hunting, sport hunting, and hunting as a spectacle.[32] The same Latin words, *venator* and *venatio* (hunter and hunt), cognates of the verb *venor, -ari* and the noun *vena* (blood vessel), were used of sporting hunts in the countryside and of spectacular hunts in the arena.[33] Early Rome did not leave behind as dramatic evidence of hunting as we find in Homer or in Mycenaean art; but, like other early peoples moving from a rural to a more urban existence, native Italians did hunt for meat and to defend their farms (e.g. against wolves). Comparative anthropology shows that sedentarization and the development of animal husbandry among populations do not mean the end of hunting. Hunting continues as an important symbolic activity, and game meat is relished.[34] Greeks in Magna Graecia to the south and Villanovans and Etruscans to the north had established hunting traditions long before Rome became a Republic.[35] Diminished over time by urbanization, the general area around Rome had been a rich hinterland for wildlife (e.g. boars, hare, deer), and rural hunting continued before, during, and after Roman history.[36] An enduring taste for game meat led to a commercialized version of the rustic hunt as hunting came to include the harvesting of game animals. The meat of wild animals, hunted at large or kept in game preserves associated with villas, continued to be sold at markets.[37]

Preserved in literature and ritual, the idea that Romans themselves might capture and eat wild animals was old and enduring.[38] Virgil has Aeneas hunt with Dido (*Aen.* 4.129–70), and Livy (1.4.8–9) claims that Romulus and Remus hunted animals in the woods before Rome was founded.[39] Like the Greek Artemis, Diana, goddess of boundaries and mistress of the beasts, both a protector and a hunter of wild animals, was a pre-Roman Latin goddess, and she was often associated with *venationes*.[40] In later art the analogy of rural hunts to urban beast spectacles is undeniable: mosaics intermingle scenes of farming, sporting hunting, rural meals, and the capturing of beasts for the arena.[41]

The roots of Rome's hunting spectacles, then, intertwined strands including native Italian subsistence hunting, ritualized animal baiting, Hellenistic-style grand, aristocratic sport hunting, and the spectacular (and spectatory) royal hunts of Near Eastern kings. However institutionalized, artificial and unsporting *venationes* may be in our eyes, Romans saw spectacular *venationes* in the arena as hunts, not as sacrifices. Early Christians might regard them, like all spectacles, as idolatrous sacrifices,[42] but the animals were 'game' rather than domesticated sacrificial victims.[43] The normal sacrificial sequence, notably the cutting of 'willing', flawless victims' throats, was not found at hunts. *Venationes* were held in the morning, before the main meal of the day, not because they were unpopular, but because morning was the traditional time for hunting.[44] The elements of the chase (e.g. dogs, spears, and hunters), the resistance of the beasts, the emphasis on using 'wild' and often dangerous animals, the care expended on scenery to suggest sylvan settings in arenas — all these show that the killing of beasts was meant as a re-creation of actual hunts.[45] The animals had little chance, but hunts were compelling, and the skills of the hunters impressed admiring urbanites.

What happened to the meat? The answer may be suggested by connections among traditions of hunting, animal baiting, animal spectacles, and the distribution and eating of meat. If, as argued below, arena meat was eaten by the people at Rome, this will be the final confirmation of the enduring nature of the *venationes* as ritualized hunts to provide food for the community or to protect the community's food supply.

Conditions and customs at Rome, and comparative anthropology, suggest that the Romans would not simply have dumped all the tons of animal flesh left after the spectacles. While probably more analogous than derivative, the bullfights of modern Spain offer a helpful comparison. The state bullfight (the *fiesta national de toros*) arose as an official institutionalization of rural fiestas in which bulls were brought into an enclosed space in the centers of towns and tormented and ultimately killed by masses of Spaniards.[46] Popular involvement by knowledgeable spectators still heavily influences the direction of bullfights, and crowds demand that matadors perform as sportsmen or artists and kill their bulls in the proper ritual manner. Crowds pressure judges to award bulls' ears to skillful and suicidally courageous matadors.[47] Respected and crucial to the spectacle, bulls are carefully bred and selected; but the numerous horses, who until recently died horribly in

189

the ring, evoked no sympathy.[48] Band music accompanies the fights, and as matadors circle the ring collecting flowers and other gifts, dead bulls are dragged across the arena and through a gate.[49] Most relevant here, none of the meat of the bulls, killed in the ring or later in the corrals, and butchered at or near the bullring, goes to waste. Formerly given to hospitals and poor-houses, it is now sold in the markets and butcher shops to be eaten by the people.[50] Similarly, livestock from modern rodeos, after some degree of abuse but not intentional killing in the arena, usually end up slaughtered for meat and by-products. Probably closer to the symbolic dimensions of Roman beast hunts, the owner of the victorious fighting cock in Balinese society, according to Geertz, eats the remains of the loser.[51]

The common people of Rome were pragmatic, demanding, and often hungry. In the late first century BC Rome was a city of perhaps a million souls with 200,000 or more on the grain-dole lists, and astute politicians and patrons were concerned with grain supplies and the threat of shortages and food riots.[52] The diet of the lowly Roman was protein-deficient, and festivals and public banquets were anxiously awaited.[53] Focusing on the elite and the nouveaux riches, the delicacies in Apicius' cookbook and the exotic meats in Trimalchio's elaborate, expensive, and yet gauche dishes in Petronius are not representative.[54] Most Romans were not fussy eaters, and wealthy Romans had adventuresome palates. Apicius includes recipes for wild game and a sauce for meat that smelled bad.[55] Horace claims that Rome's forefathers finished up boar meat even if it had gone bad.[56] Remember that *garum*, a sauce made from rotten fish, was the Roman's condiment of choice. Romans ate scavenger fish that fed on sewage in the Tiber,[57] and Roman potions included wild boar's dung, human blood, and more.[58] In a society resource-ful enough to use night-soil, to tax toilets, and to save urine for fullers, it seems probable that dead arena animals (their meat, hides, and horns) were utilized commercially for profit or symbolically for political effect.[59] If Caligula felt that butcher's meat was too expensive for arena beasts and fed them convicts instead, would that ingeniously exploitative megalomaniac, who sought popularity through games, have wasted arena meat? At least some of the animal meat from the beast spectacles could have been given to the people of Rome, both as a nutritional supplement and as a political device.[60] Common Romans were hungry and malnourished, and givers of games were unlikely to waste potential arena-meat gifts.

Spectacles and food: spectators and scrambles

In pagan (and Christian) minds spectacles were routinely associated with public banquets and distributions of food, including animal flesh (*viscera-tiones*).[61] In Greece public sacrifices on a large scale led to distributions of meat to citizens,[62] but this was not normally the case at Rome. Public banquets and distributions at Rome were associated more with *munera* and triumphs, that is, with the major occasions for beast spectacles.[63] Early leaders provided funeral banquets, and Sulla, Caesar, and other generals gave banquets and doles of meat at their triumphs.[64] Public banquets were a political device and a social obligation for the wealthy.[65] Cicero (*Off.* 2.57) complained that aediles squandered money on 'public banquets, doles of meat among the people, gladiatorial shows, magnificent spectacles, and wild-beast fights', but he knew that such things were politically advantageous.[66] Some emperors are said to have given banquets at which guests received not only regular meat but raw meat and live animals as meat-gifts.[67] Accustomed to fresh meat killed and butchered in the vicinity,[68] Romans may have been drawn by the sounds and smells of the arena, attending spectacles, as Greeks flocked to sacrifices, in anticipation of a meat meal. What would be stench to moderns used to plastic-wrapped supermarket meat, the smells of the arena would have evoked the excitement of early hunts and of later meat feasts, especially for the *plebs rustica*.

To add suspense and sport to banquets and spectacles of all kinds, Augustus and the Julio-Claudians popularized a variant on the patron's and politician's traditional distribution of gifts to clients and citizens. To the crowd they scattered tokens (*missilia*) or lots (*sortes*) redeemable for gifts, or they let the spectators scramble for the gifts themselves.[69] Some of Nero's notorious public entertainments had an agonistic, participatory flair.[70] At plays he threw presents to the people 'including a thousand birds of every kind each day, various kinds of food, and tickets for grain ... gold ... slaves, beasts of burden, and even trained wild animals'.[71]

During his 100-day spectacle in AD 80 Titus (Dio 66.25.4–5, Loeb) 'threw down into the Colosseum from aloft little wooden balls variously inscribed, one designating some article of food ... or again horses, pack animals, cattle or slaves. Those who seized them were to carry them to the dispensers of the bounty, from whom they would receive the article named.' Similarly, at the amphitheater Domitian distributed baskets of food, and scattered gifts to be scrambled for (Suet. *Dom.* 4.5; Dio 67.4.4). Of Domitian's largesse at the Saturnalia Statius says that early in the morning nuts, dried fruit, and cakes were showered on the crowd by means of a rope stretched across the amphitheater. Then a meal was served in the stands, with both the lowly and the elite sitting in places of honor, and with Domitian joining them. A spectacle (including female gladiators) followed until nightfall, and near nightfall a second scrambling was held: 'Amid the tumult dense clouds of birds swoop suddenly down through the air [flamingoes, pheasants, guinea fowl] ... Too few are there to seize them all, exultantly they grasp their fill and ever clutch fresh plunder.'[72] Of games honoring the northern triumph of Stella, Martial says that:

> Each day provides its own gifts, the cord's rich burden fails not,
> and full-laden spoil falls upon the people; now come in sudden

showers sportive tokens; now the bounteous ticket assigns the beasts of the arena (*nunc dat spectatas tessera larga feras*); now the bird is glad to fill a lap that gives it safety, and – that it not be torn asunder – wins, while apart, by lot its owner.[73]

Elagabalus also distributed tokens or chances before and throughout his reign; such scrambles were often meaty and sometimes dangerous, but they aided his popularity.[74]

Mass scatterings (*sparsiones*) and scramblings presented a significant opportunity for spectator involvement at spectacles.[75] At these surrogate assemblies people were not just passive spectators: they interacted with their leaders and became players in a communal sporting drama. Tokens perhaps assigned to spectators the meat of a particular beast being killed before their eyes. The spectacle was expanded up into the stands. A *sparsio* was a free-for-all communal contest.[76] You had to catch the objects, animals, or tokens. You had to participate to win. You had to be there.

The presentation of a 'hunt' may have presumed distribution, or distribution may have been a special bonus. The method of distribution can only be conjectured, but recall the reference to Titus' 'dispensers'.[77] At the Colosseum each spectator had a ticket with his seat assignment and thus an automatic token for claiming gifts. Martial (5.49.8–10) ridicules a certain greedy Labienus who used three disguises to enable himself to get three baskets of food at a show. Responsible for markets, games (under the Republic), and streets, the aediles attended to beasts en route to the arena; possibly they also attended to their disposal.[78] They may have contracted arena meat out to the meat processors who provided sausages for the eating houses, but emperors perhaps had them distribute meat to the people.[79] For effect, distribution of gifts was probably done in public, near or even in the arena. Perhaps gifts were on a 'first come first served' basis, enhancing the element of scrambling.

While meat distributions and the popularity of scrambles and giveaways at spectacles only suggest the use of arena meat as gifts of food for the masses, Christian sources explicitly claim that Romans ate arena meat. In response to Roman charges that Christian sacraments were cannibalistic feasts,[80] Tertullian charges Romans with indirect cannibalism, saying that they eat the flesh of beasts (herbivores and carnivores) soiled with human blood from the arena:

> [What of] those who dine on the flesh of wild animals from the arena, keen on the meat of boar or stag? That boar in his battle has wiped the blood off him whose blood he drew; that stag has wallowed in the blood of a gladiator. The bellies of the very bears are sought, full of raw and undigested human flesh.[81]

One obvious source for the assumption that arena meat was simply dumped, the Covenant Code (Exod. 22.31), commands Hebrews not to eat any flesh 'torn by beasts in the fields', but instead to throw it to the dogs. Christians were forbidden to attend spectacles, to eat sacrificial meat, or even to touch normal butcher's meat lest a trace of blood remain.[82] To bolster charges of pagan human sacrifices at spectacles Christians noted a practice abhorrent to them – the eating of animal meat from the arena, a practice which Romans perhaps took for granted.

Poor Romans were probably willing and eager to have any animal meat, even if it came from the arena. Clients might grumble, but they ate what they could get from their patrons.[83] In the arena, as in rural hunts, excited 'wild' beasts fought or ran to escape, and hence their meat would have tasted 'gamy', a desirable flavor.[84] Galen says that physicians assembled at the dissection of a large elephant and the heart was taken out by the imperial cooks.[85] Apuleius tells a story (*Met.* 4.13–14, Loeb) of a magistrate in Greece who assembled gladiators, hunters, convicts, and wild beasts for a show. Many great bears were collected, but arrived too soon and died of the summer heat. The carcasses lay in the street (4.14) and 'then the common people, having no other meat to feed on, and forced by their rude poverty to find any new meat and cheap feasts (*sordentia supplementa et dapes gratuitas*), would come forth and fill their bellies with the flesh of the bears'.[86] Without Judeo-Christian sensibilities, Romans probably found flesh torn by beasts in the arena acceptable. Casting it to the dogs outright would have been wasteful, and dumping it at the edge of town would simply have led to scavenging.[87] The paucity of meat in the normal diet of the urban plebs probably meant that almost every bit of edible non-human flesh was eaten up.[88] As in the third world of today, unless bound by ideologies or taboos, people in antiquity seldom wasted animal protein. Even in dangerously meat-rich modern America very little of the flesh of a butchered animal is rendered or sent to become dog food.

Given these considerations, some later accounts of the giving of arena animals to the masses seem less suspect. The *Historia Augusta* (SHA *Gord. Tres* 3.5–8, Loeb) says that as aedile (prior to AD 238) Gordian I gave twelve exhibitions of beasts, one per month. It mentions a picture of one of Gordian's hunts depicting over 200 stags, 30 wild horses, 100 wild sheep, 10 elks, 100 bulls, 300 ostriches, 30 wild asses, 150 wild boars, 200 chamois, and 200 fallow deer. 'And all of these he handed over to the people to be killed (*populo rapienda*) on the day of the sixth exhibition that he gave.'[89] Also, for a triumph at Rome in AD 281, Probus is said to have held a magnificent wild beast hunt 'at which all things were to be the spoils of the people (*populus cuncta diriperet*)'. The Circus, arranged like a forest, held 1,000 ostriches, 1,000 stags, 1,000 wild boars, plus deer, ibexes, wild sheep, and other grass-eating beasts. 'The populace was then let in, and each man seized what he wished (*rapuit quisque quod voluit*).'[90]

The *Historia Augusta* is hardly an unimpeachable source, so such numbers may be doubted; but the traditions of meat distributions and of baiting and hunting wild beasts are tied to games and festivals from earlier ages. Probus and Gordian probably just offered a variation: instead of a distribution after the hunt, they allowed the people to do the hunting and distribution themselves during (and contributing to) the spectacle.[91] They turned the problem of disposal into a positive demonstration of imperial largesse. Symbolically even better than bringing the game up to the spectators via tokens, such hunts brought the plebs down from the stands into the arena, reconnecting them to their rural past.[92] Irregular distributions of meat from the arena would not substantially reduce the needs of the masses, but, in symbolic terms, they meant that at times an unemployed plebeian could still put meat on the table.

To anthropologists and sociologists imperial largesse in the form of distributions of gifts of food evokes notions of potlatching (provision of ritual competitive feasts by leaders) or euergetism (public displays of generosity by wealthy individuals) as forms of competitive conspicuous consumption.[93] Like shared meals in general, feasting at festivals and spectacles meant incorporation, commensality, and communion.[94] Providing the hospitality appropriate to their social position, emperors used hunts to fulfill their obligation to feed and to amuse their people. Meter aside, Juvenal's *panem et circenses* (10.81) could have been *carnem et venationes*. It was the comfortable literati, not the destitute plebs, who – occasionally – criticized the arena. The plebs hated Tiberius for his economy, especially concerning shows, but they loved the irresponsible Caligula for his games and for his distributions of meat.[95] Arena meat had a history and an association with sport that the grain dole lacked.[96] More public and personal, meat given via the spectacles inspired more emotional gratitude.[97] Ancients would gladly have eaten wild game, especially if, as spectators, they were indirectly the hunter-killers. Beast spectacles linked the rustic past and the symbolic present of Rome, and game from the arena filled the belly and excited the spirit of the Romans.

Addendum: America

Lest such speculations seem irrelevant, consider that the symbolism of acquiring, eating, and sharing meat, especially that of hunted game, has persisted in American history from frontier hunts to Andrew Jackson's rustic presidential feasts to employers' distributions of Christmas turkeys to 'pork barrel' politics.[98] Frontier barbeques were practical and symbolic. Preserving large amounts of meat was difficult, fresh meat was preferred, and barbeque meals came with reciprocal obligations and implications for status.[99] The sportsman's code in America decrees that virtuous hunters eat part of their game, not just kill wantonly. In a long tradition of hunter-politicians, such as Teddy Roosevelt, Jimmy Carter, and now Bill Clinton, George Bush as president defended his quail hunts in South Texas as a male ritual, adding:

194

'And I like eating what I go after.'[100] Finally, American rodeos and fairs preserve rustic and robust traditions including turkey shoots, greased pig contests, and rattlesnake roundups. Also they often include calf scrambles in which youths in an arena try to drag calves into a marked area, and the winners get gift-certificates, tokens, redeemable for the purchase of calves.[101] Perhaps trying to understand the Romans – their hunts and their food, their games and their game – may help us better understand ourselves.

NOTES

1 See ch. 4 above. For general treatments, see Harris (1978) or R. Tannahill, *Flesh and Blood: A History of the Cannibal Complex* (New York: Dorset Press, 1975). For a counter-argument challenging the historicity of the practice, see W. Arens, *The Man-Eating Myth* (New York: Oxford U., 1979); but cf. the recent discussion by Lawrence Osborne, 'Does Man Eat Man?', *Lingua Franca* 7.4 (April/May 1997) 28–38.

2 Peter Garnsey, *Famine and Food Supply in the Greco-Roman World* (Cambridge: Cambridge U., 1988), 28–9, 35, notes that human flesh was the least desirable food (e.g. Ps. Quint. *Decl. Maj.* 12), but he cites examples of cannibalism in antiquity during famines and sieges (e.g. Caes. *B Gall.* 7.77). As early as Hesiod (*Op.* 276–80), the taboo against cannibalism was said to separate humans from animals. In Homer, Achilles' desire to eat Hector's flesh raw (*Il.* 22. 346–8), like the desire to abuse the corpses of enemies throughout the *Iliad*, was an expression of rage and the craving for vengeance; see Segal (1971) 38–41 and passim. On the themes of cannibalism and eating animal flesh raw in Germanic and Greek legend, see Griffin (1980) 19–21, who feels, 20, that 'Such terrible acts of cannibalism . . . represent in the *Iliad* a temptation which is avoided, something which would be too appalling to be actually allowed to happen.'

3 See ch. 2 above. Accusing pagans of drinking blood and of cannibalism, Tertullian, *Apol.* 9.10, Loeb, adds: 'Again, those who, when a show is given in the arena (*munere in arena*), with greedy thirst have caught the fresh blood of the guilty slain (*noxiorum iugulatorum sanguinem*), as it pours fresh from their throats, and carry it off as a cure for epilepsy – what of them?' Also on human blood as a cure for epilepsy: Min. Fel. *Oct.* 30.5; Plin. *HN* 28.1.2; Celsus *Med.* 3.23. Scribonius Largus, 17, says that fresh gladiator blood worked best. Plin. *HN* 28.34: game killed with a knife with which a man had been killed was a cure for epilepsy. Along similar lines, potions were made from criminals' blood and corpses from ancient Egypt to medieval Europe to nineteenth-century China; see Tannahill (1975) 34, 64–5.

4 Barton (1993), 51, cites Ovid's tale, *Met.* 8.738–78, that King Erysichthon, out of insatiable hunger, resorted to autocannibalism. Plutarch, *Cic.* 49.3–4, Loeb, doubts the story that, when Antony handed Philologus over to Pomponia, wife of Quintus, she punished him in dreadful ways and 'forced him to cut off his own flesh bit by bit and roast it, and then to eat it'. Cf. Suet. *Vit.* 14.2 and Tac. *Hist.* 1.44.1 for cannibalistic rhetoric and the rage of Vitellius and Otho. Suetonius, *Ner.* 37.2, Loeb, claims that Nero kept a glutton with an enormous appetite: 'It is believed that it was his wish to throw living men to be torn to pieces and devoured by a monster (*polyphago*) of Egyptian birth, who would crunch raw flesh and anything else that was given him.' Cf. Friedländer (1965) 4:8, with later examples. Cf. charges of cannibalism against Egyptians: Juv. 15.12, 78–83.

5 McGowan (1994) explains second-century charges of Christian cannibalism as examples of 'labelling', of using a symbolic stereotype to characterize social relations within the social construction of reality. Rather than merely confusing the eucharist with eating the body and blood of humans or misassociating Christians with supposedly 'historical' cannibals, within an existing discourse on cannibalism, Romans perceived Christians as threats to the social body, in part because they excluded themselves from socially constitutive practices (animal sacrifices, the emperor cult). Once seen as threats, Christians were associated with various elements already established in the social construction of cannibalism (434): 'To be "cannibal" meant to be lawless, primitive, foreign, immoral, secretive and violent.' On the metaphorical use of cannibalism in literature, also see Gowers (1993) 42, 189, 198–200. On 'indirect' cannibalism, see below.

6 *Ep. ad Rom.* 4.1–2, trans. K. Lake, *Apostolic Fathers*, Loeb, 2:231; see further discussion in ch. 8 below. Bowersock (1995), 6, 77–8, notes the metaphorical style of the text: e.g. 'food of beasts', 'wheat of God', the desire to be 'ground by the teeth of wild beasts' into the 'pure bread of Christ'. Early martyrs perhaps wanted to be 'swallowed whole' or 'entirely consumed' to preserve their somatic integrity for resurrection. On total consumption and total salvation, see ch. 8 below. Romans were perhaps receptive to the idea of total consumption of Christians by beasts at a symbolic level: beasts thus absorbed and disposed of miasmatic contaminations and threats to Roman society.

7 Salvian *De guber. Dei* 6.2.10, trans. E. M. Sanford, *On the Government of God* (New York: Octagon Books, 1966) 160. Sanford, n. 11 on 160, notes that Salvian's diatribe against the games 'has been one of the most quoted portions of his work'. At the end of the third century Arnobius, *Adv. nat.* 4.36, similarly condemned pagan games and the pleasure which spectators took in watching men devoured by beasts or killing one another.

8 Cf. *Pass. Perp. et Fel.* 8.21.1–2 (trans. Musurillo (1972) 129–30): not having been touched by the beasts, Saturus tells a soldier: '"I am going in there and I shall be finished off (*consummor*) with one bite of the leopard." And immediately as the contest was coming to a close a leopard was let loose, and after one bite Saturus was so drenched with blood that as he came away the mob roared in witness to his second baptism: "Well washed! Well washed!" For well washed indeed was one who had been bathed in this manner.' On Saturus, see n. 14 below.

9 On art, see ch. 3 above. Potter (1993), 66, n. 89 on 84, notes that ancient texts commonly say that androphagous beasts were used in arenas, but he cautions that 'it seems to have been the practice to allow the beast to bite, trample, gore, or . . . to have intercourse with, but not to kill, the victim'. Cf. the fictional account of the martyr Thecla, who jumped into a pool of supposedly man-eating fish: *Act. Paul. et Thec.* 21.

10 Cf. Hopkins (1983) 11, following Friedländer (1965) 2:72. Cicero, *Fam.* 7.1.3, quoted above in ch. 1, says that the sight of men 'mangled' by animals was not novel. In Apuleius, *Met.* 10.28, 34, a woman is condemned to be exposed to beasts to be destroyed and torn. Apuleius' suggestion, *Met.* 4.13 (cf. 6.31) that *noxii* were to be food for beasts (*suis epulis bestiarum saginas*) is figurative and ironic because the beasts (bears) themselves end up eaten (see below).

11 Similarly, Euseb. *Mart. Pal.* 6.7 and 11.30. Eusebius, *HE* 5.1.38, says that martyrs at Lyons (see ch. 8 below) were abused, then thrown to beasts, and then still later tormented with the iron hot seat: beasts neither killed nor ate them. At Lyons (*HE* 5.1.39) Blandina was tied to a post and exposed 'as meat' (*bora*), but none of the beasts touched her. As Wiedemann (1992), 89, notes,

the unwillingness of beasts to attack was taken as a sign of the martyr's innocence, a theme as old as the story of Daniel. Eusebius' use of 'man-eating beasts'
involves a metaphor of consumption; cf. *HE* 9.8.12: during plague and famine
'death devoured whole families'. Cf. Tac. *Hist.* 2.61: a rebel Boian was exposed
to wild beasts and they did not rend him (*non laniabatur*), so he was executed
before Vitellius. Tertullian, *De spect.* 23, Loeb, refers to 'him who pushes another
in front of himself to the lion – in case he is not quite murderer enough when
he cuts his throat afterwards'. Cf. Sen. *De ira* 3.43.2; *Act. SS. Tarachi, Probi et
Andronici* 10.

12 On training man-eaters, see Jennison (1937) 69, 86, 194–5. Novatian, *De spect.*
5.2, claims that cruel masters carefully trained wild animals to be more ferocious
as they punished victims before spectators.

13 Dio 60.13.4, Loeb. Dio, 72.29.3–4, says that M. Aurelius refused to watch a
lion trained to eat men and refused spectators' demands that the lion's trainer
be freed. Wiedemann (1992), 136, notes that the emperor still felt compelled
to agree to the demand that the lion be displayed in the arena.

14 Martial, 2.75.5–7, says that an enraged lion killed two young arena attendants.
Plut. *Brut.* 8.6–7: Megarians released caged lions intended for games, hoping
that they would attack assaulting Caesarian forces, but the lions turned on the
Megarians. Coleman (1990), 59, notes two failed attempts in the *Pass. Perp. et
Fel.*: a *venator* who had tied Saturus to a wild boar was himself gored by the
boar and died a few days later (19.5), and a bear refused to leave its cage to
attack Saturus even though the martyr was bound in stocks (19.6); finally he
was mauled, but even later his throat was cut (21.6–7). Cf. Euseb. *HE* 8.7.1–2
quoted above.

15 *Calig.* 27.1; cf. Lactantius on Galerius above. Callu (1984), 337 with n. 106, feels
that Caligula just 'rushed the stages' of a procedure in which beasts ate men in
the arena. Callu, n. 106, also cites Apul. *Met.* 6.32 (quoted in ch. 2 above), but
Apuleius is referring to worms ('cum vermis membra laniabunt'); further on
worms and punishment, see Callu, 354–6. Plass (1995), 48, comments: 'True or
false, the story measures the convertibility of life understood as a simple economic resource (in the food supply) into symbolic social values (entertainment
as a vehicle of unrestricted imperial power).' Tertullian's reference to criminals
being fed to wild beasts, *Apol.* 44.3, using *bestiae saginantur*, probably stems from
the passage in Suetonius. Dio, 59.10.3–4, tells a similar tale: in AD 38 Caligula,
during a scarcity of *damnati*, had commoners from the crowd seized and thrown
to the beasts, and he ordered that their tongues first be cut off so that their cries
should not disturb his peace. Cf. Suet. *Calig.* 27.4: Caligula threw a knight to
the beasts; when he protested his innocence, the emperor had his tongue cut off
and put him back in the arena. Suetonius, *Calig.* 27.3, also claims that Caligula
shut honorable men up in cages like animals. Cf. Pliny, *Pan.* 27.3, who praises
Trajan for feeding the children of citizens from his own resources and not, like
arena beasts, on the 'blood' of slaughtered men. Millar (1992), 169, explains that
the 'blood' here is a metaphor for the confiscated properties of persons condemned
by the emperor.

16 Cf. the possibly fictional story, flattering to Augustus, that Vedius Pollio wanted
to throw a live slave 'as food' to lampreys in his fish pond, but Augustus
prevented such an act of unprecedented cruelty: Dio 54.23; Sen. *De ira* 3.40,
Clem. 1.18.

17 *CTh* 9.12.1; Wiedemann (1981) no. 187.

18 Titus thus apparently killed on average 90 per day and Trajan killed on average
89.4 per day, possibly suggesting a practical limit to daily carcass disposal, or
perhaps mere coincidence.

19 Jennison (1937) and Aymard (1951) examine the collection and slaughter of an incredible number and variety of animals, but they pay scant attention to the final issue of disposal. Ann Hyland, *Equus: The Horse in the Roman World* (New Haven: Yale U., 1990) 249, raises but does not resolve the question: 'The slaughter was so enormous and so frequent that one wonders what happened to the remains. Obviously some were used as food to keep the next in line fit for exhibition, but the shambles outside the arenas must have been vast and not all the by-products capable of being used. It would not have been long before putrefaction set in and destroyed some useful parts.'

20 Rather, as noted above, Suetonius, *Calig.* 27.1, suggests that show animals were fed cattle or butcher's meat.

21 SHA *Aurel.* 33.4, Loeb: Aurelian's triumph in AD 274 included '200 elephants and 200 tamed beasts of divers kinds from Libya and Palestine, which Aurelian at once presented to private citizens that the privy purse might not be burdened with the cost of their food'.

22 Animals from overseas came in cages to the Tiber docks. Pliny, *NH* 36.40, tells of a sculptor at the docks studying a caged lion when attacked by an escaped leopard. On *vivaria* in towns, see Jennison (1937) 174–6; Scobie (1988) 200–3. Rome's *vivarium*, an enclosure for housing beasts waiting for shows, is described by Procopius, *Goth.* 1.22.10, 23.13–23; and *CIL* 6.130 (= *ILS* 2091; Sabbatini Tumolesi (1988) no. 11 on 26) mentions a *custos vivari* in AD 241; cf. *ILS* 5158 (*adiutor ad feras*); 5159 (*praepositus herbariarum*). Pointing out that the *vivarium* predates the Aurelian Walls, into which it was later built, Richardson (1992), 431–2, rejects earlier locations (e.g. E. Nash, *Pictorial Dictionary of Ancient Rome*, 2 vols. (New York: Praeger, 1961–2) 2:516 – outside the Porta Maggiore) and suggests that it was north of the Porta Praenestina.

23 See ch. 5 above. The bones in such pits may have been those of diseased animals, horses, and dogs. Although there were exceptions, the flesh of dogs was seen as taboo and that of horses was not generally eaten: S. Bökönyi, *Animal Husbandry and Hunting in Tác-Gorsium: The Vertebrate Fauna of a Roman Town in Pannonia*, Studia Archaeologica VIII of the Hungarian Academy of Sciences (Budapest: Akadémiai Kiadó, 1984) 12, 56. Hyland (1990), 249, agrees that horseflesh was not usually eaten, but notes that horses provided horsehair for ropes and helmet crests, leather, and hooves used as receptables in medicine kits. Further on horses, see n. 25 below.

24 Lanciani (1897), 373, after noting that the *venationes* of Anicius Maximus in AD 523 were the last recorded show in the Colosseum, comments: 'while repairing the drains and underground passages of the arena in 1878, we discovered a considerable quantity of bones, which were identified by Professor de Sanctis as pertaining to domestic animals, like bulls, horses, and stags. The discovery shows how insignificant the last shows must have been in comparison with those of the golden age.' More recent archaeology on the drains of the Colosseum in the 1970s has found and analyzed a quantity of bones of both domesticated (pigs, cattle, horses, even cats and dogs) and foreign or wild animals (lions, panthers, bears, stags, boars). The bones from domesticated animals, along with seeds of fruits and vegetables, may represent scraps from spectators' meals, but the exotic bones are possibly remnants of rough butchering of beasts on site after the shows. See G. Ghini, 'Prime indagini archeologiche', 100–5, in Reggiani (1988). On the eating of food in amphitheaters, see Dio 37.46.4 (Augustus commenting on a man eating in the stands), and Scobie (1988) 224–5. Early excavations in the arena of the Amphitheatrum Castrense (see map 1), the small amphitheater at the end of the Esquiline used for training and preparations for *venationes*, also yielded bones. Lanciani (1897) 385: 'Ficoroni

(*Roma antica*, p. 121) speaks of discoveries made towards 1740 by the prior of Santa Croce, concerning the crypts, which were full of "ossa di grossi animali"'.

25 The Roman amphitheater at the Guildhall site in London has yielded animal bones; see the discussion and bibliography in ch. 7 below. A. Grant, 'The Animal Bones', 137–8, in Michael Fulford, *The Silchester Amphitheater: Excavations of 1979–85*, Britannia Monograph Series no. 10 (London: Society for the Promotion of Roman Studies, 1989), discusses the discovery of animal bones (some sixty identifiable fragments) found in the silts and dumps used to raise the surface of the arena of the Silchester amphitheater in its stone phase in the early third century. These bones originally came from outside the amphitheater but may be related to its activities, probably hunts or equestrian events. Grant, 138, comments that horse flesh was not usually eaten (citing Toynbee (1973) 185) and was thus probably dumped in the vicinity of the amphitheater but the meat of any cattle or bulls used was 'certainly eaten', possibly being sold off after the show.

26 Burkert (1983), and most recently in his *Creation of the Sacred: Tracks of Biology in Early Religions* (Cambridge, Mass.: Harvard U., 1996), esp. 102–28, expands upon K. Meuli's theory that paleolithic hunters tried to expiate their guilt (i.e. a sense of responsibility and anxiety) through reparation rituals, which developed into sacrifices. The modern debate over hunting continues: is it sport or ritual, a brutal remnant of early primitivism, part of our heritage from frontier societies in a sylvan world? Cartmill (1993), passim, offers a cultural study of hunting as a mythic metaphor from the paleolithic era to modern times. He challenges the 'hunting hypothesis' (e.g. as in K. Lorenz, *On Aggression*, trans. M. K. Wilson (New York: Harcourt, Brace and World, 1966) and D. Morris, *The Naked Ape* (London: Cape, 1967)) that apes evolved into humans with the invention of tools and the start of killing, and that the early hunting of man as a killer ape imprinted fundamental patterns on human nature. Man's hunting may not be aboriginal and it may not be what made us human, but hunting traditions have undoubtedly influenced human cultures. H. Leon Abrams, Jr, 'The Preference for Animal Protein and Fat: A Cross-Cultural Survey', 207–23, in Marvin Harris and Eric B. Ross, eds., *Food and Evolution: Toward a Theory of Human Food Habits* (Philadelphia: Temple U., 1987), sees an evolutionary basis for the human preference for protein; 209: 'For more than 99 percent of this time span (3–4 million years) hominoid species depended on hunting and gathering food . . . Meat had been the mainstay of paleolithic mankind.'

27 Frazer (1957) 648–54. The fresher the blood or meat, even to the point of eating from a living body, the more potent the magic. By ancient tradition (Apollod. *Bibl.* 3.8.13.6; Schol. on Hom. *Il.* 16.37; Stat. *Achil.* 2.99–100), Chiron fed the young Achilles on the viscera of lions and wild pigs and the marrow of wild boars, bears, lions, and wolves, even before their death. See D. S. Robertson, 'The Food of Achilles', *CR* 54 (1940) 177–80.

28 For a detailed, structuralist discussion of meat as a cultural marker in Rome, see Mireille Corbier, 'The Ambiguous Status of Meat in Ancient Rome', *Food and Foodways* 3 (1989) 223–64. On the semiotics of food, including meat, see below.

29 E.g. Anderson (1985) is broad and perceptive, but he approaches ancient hunting, xi–xii, as the pursuit of a quarry for sport (i.e. recreation, although the game was generally eaten) and has little interest in hunting by professionals for profit, Roman beast spectacles, or fowling and fishing. As he admits, xii, 'If "sport" is narrowly defined as physical activity undertaken solely for amusement, few of the ancients qualify as sportsmen.'

30 E.g. Cartmill (1993), 30, defines hunting as 'the deliberate, direct, violent killing of unrestrained wild animals'. By the modern definition, the quarry

must be wild and free, unrestricted and able to flee. This excludes trapping, netting, sacrifices, canned hunts, and slaughter. In the seventeenth and eight-eenth centuries the term 'sport' was used to refer to fishing and hunting as genteel amusements or 'field sports'. A. J. Butler, *Sport in Classic Times* (London: E. Benn, 1930, repr. Los Altos: William Kaufmann, 1975), discusses only hunting (outside the arena), fishing, and fowling, all of which were to be done with proper sportsmanship. He comments, vi, that 'few can realise how near in spirit and in working were many of the forms of ancient sport to those of today'.

31 See ch. 2 above. Elitist writers praised recreational hunting or took note of the spectacles produced by the elite. While the plebs did not hunt for sport, they were not without a sense of hunting tradition. Prone to asserting Greek cultural influences, Polybius, 31.29.5–7, claims that Scipio Aemilianus was unusual in pursuing sport hunting along Greek lines; but, as Harris (1979), n. 2 on 20, sug-gests, Polybius probably exaggerated Scipio's fame as a hunter to flatter his hero and his own favorite pastime. Sallust's suggestion, *Cat.* 4.1, that agriculture and hunting were 'tasks fit only for slaves' (*servilibus officiis*) should not mislead us; he is condemning a pastime of the *nobiles* whom he hated (cf. Varro's criticism of boar hunting: *Sat. Men.* 161, 293–6, 361). Polybius' and Sallust's comments reflect biases for and against Greeks and nobles; see Aymard (1951) 54–63.

32 Cf. Decker (1992), 147–67, suggesting that hunting in early Egypt developed from an economic activity to a status demonstration and also a recreation or sport. To the Roman tradition Anderson (1985), 83, devotes but one sentence: 'No doubt in primitive Italy the herdsman battled to save his animals from wolves; the peasant proprietor avenged himself on the wild boars that trampled his field; and venison, or more often hare, was sold by the hunter.' Cartmill (1993) 42: 'Hunting was not a traditional Roman pastime. The Romans of the early republic had regarded hunting as a farm chore, like slaughtering hogs or killing rats . . . they did not practice it as a sport. Sportive hunting came to Rome as a rich man's affectation . . . it filtered into Roman life following Rome's victory over Macedon in 168 B.C.' Still valuable, Aymard (1951) pays at least some attention, 25–41, to native hunting traditions in Etruria and Latium; and he, 83, places the *venationes* within Rome's eclectic hunting traditions.

33 As Cartmill (1993), 41, 67, notes, *venationes*, the source of the modern word venison, originally meant 'game, meat gotten by hunting', but is now used only of deer meat.

34 Sedentary farmers and pastoralists continue to hunt to supplement and vary their diets, to increase their income, and to control pests and predators competing for resources. Susan Kent, 'Cross-cultural Perceptions of Farmers as Hunters and the Value of Meat', 1–17, in Susan Kent, ed., *Farmers as Hunters: The Implications of Sedentism* (Cambridge: Cambridge U., 1989) 7–9, suggests that meat and hunting are 'consistently and ubiquitously valued more than plants and gathering or farming' and that 'meat and its acquistion tend to have value disproportionate to their economic and nutritional contribution' because of the symbolic dimensions of acquiring hunted meat (i.e. for male identity and status). Such anthropological studies suggest that game is seen as a resource to be consumed publicly and communally.

35 See Bonfante (1986) 260–1; and Ellen Macnamara, *Everyday Life of the Etruscans* (New York: Dorset, 1973) 175–6.

36 Graeme Barker and Richard Hodges, *Archaeology and Italian Society: Prehistoric, Roman and Medieval Studies*, BAR-IS 102, Papers in Italian Archaeology 2 (London: British Archaeological Reports, 1981) 139–40. Recent archaeological

study of rural settlements has found evidence of hunting in the remnants of wild animal bones in votive deposits, trash dumps, and campsites. E.g. see Alastair Small, ed., *Gravina: An Iron Age and Republican Settlement in Apulia*, vol. 1: *The Site*, Archaeological Monographs 5 (London: British School at Rome, 1992), in which J. Watson's discussion of animal bones (ch. 8) shows that the community hunted hare, red deer, and roe deer. Bökönyi (above, n. 23), 96–100, examines the faunal material from the Roman site of Tác-Gorsium during the imperial era. While animal husbandry was far more important to the food supply of the town, like other sites, Tác-Gorsium showed the hunting and consumption of thirty species of wild animals: aurochs (wild cattle), red deer, roe deer, wild pig, brown hare, and wild birds.

37 Varro explains the Roman harvesting of wild animals (especially boars, roe deer, and hare) from game warrens and game preserves (*leporaria, therotrophia*) for consumption and for sale. He says, *Rust.* 3.3.1–8, that animal husbandry at villas consists of three branches (the aviary, the hare warren, and the fishpond) and requires fowlers, hunters and fishermen. Varro, 3.12.1–2, mentions game preserves of forty *iugera* or even four square miles with boars, deer, hares, and wild sheep. A famous passage, 3.13.1–3, describes a preserve near Tusculum where boars and roe deer came to be fed at the sound of a horn, a sight compared to the aediles' hunts in the Circus Maximus, but without African beasts. Hughes (1994), 96–8, surveys kinds of non-sporting Greek and Roman hunting for subsistence, commercial, and military purposes. Jennison (1937), 133–6, discusses hunting parks but spends more time, 99–136, on 'menageries' kept for pets and recreation.

38 Fresh meat, as from a hunt or from the arena, was desired and sometimes disguised as such: Horace, *Epist.* 1.6.56–61, writes of a man sending his servants, complete with hunting equipment, off to the meat market to buy a boar for dinner. Petronius, *Sat.* 40, describes Trimalchio's staging of a boar hunt at his banquet: the room was decorated with nets and hunting equipment, hunting hounds were let in, and a man in the costume of a hunter used a hunting knife to cut open a huge boar on a serving tray, releasing from its side live thrushes. The birds were immediately caught by fowlers and one was presented to each guest as a gift (40.7); cf. Plin. *Ep.* 5.2.1, cited by Corbier (1989) 238, on thrushes as gifts among nobles. See n. 65 below on Trimalchio and analogies to the arena. Pliny, *Ep.* 1.6, was pleased with his capture of three boars even though he simply waited, writing in his notebook, by the nets; Aymard (1951) 159–62. As Anderson (1985), 122–53, notes, hunting for sport gained popularity in the late Empire, but, 122, 'At all levels of society, the meat of hunted animals was still eaten.' Cf. the suggestion in SHA *Tac.* 11.4–5, Loeb, cited by Corbier (1989) 236, that the frugal emperor Tacitus, as well as bringing home sacrificial victims and having his household eat them, was devoted to hunting and supplied his table with game.

39 Virgil, *Aen.* 9.605, has the Italian Numanus boast that Italians are tough in part because their boys forgo sleep and wear out the woodlands for the sake of hunting. Virgil, *G.* 3.404–13, recommends carefully tending to hounds that assist the hunting of boars, hares, roe deer, and wild asses. On hunting in Virgil, see Aymard (1951) 108–28. Horace, *Carm.* 3.24.54–6, suggests a decline in Roman virtues, for freeborn youths cannot stay on a horse and are afraid to hunt.

40 E.g. Tert. *De spect.* 12.7; Cassiod. *Var.* 5.42.2; see Ville (1981) 332–4. On the association of Diana with *venationes* in inscriptions and sculpture, see Jacqueline Carabia, '*Diana victrix ferarum*', 231–40, in Domergue et al. (1990); in mosaics, see Brown (1992) 192, 197.

41 Supplying the arena with wild animals expanded the scope and scale of Roman hunting even more; see Toynbee (1973) 263–78. Third- and fourth-century mosaics from North Africa and Sicily combine scenes of hunting with nets and cages to supply the arena, grand hunting on horseback for sport, and ordinary hunting for meat and against vermin. See Brown (1992) 188, 197; Toynbee (1973) 25–6; Dunbabin (1978) 262; Anderson (1985) 141–7.

42 See Tert. *De spect.* 4–13. Symbolically hunts became struggles against the vices of Satan; see Wiedemann (1992) 154. Later Christians did not see arena hunts as pagan sacrifices, and Constantine's ban on blood sacrifice did not apply to hunts. Coleman (1996), 64–5, properly approaches *venationes* not as religious ritual sacrifices but as imperial spectacles.

43 Like Spanish matadors (see below), hunters may have received ritual portions of the animals they killed. Cf. Aïcha Ben Abed Ben Khader and David Soren, eds., *Carthage: A Mosaic of Ancient Tunisia* (New York: American Museum of Natural History and Norton, 1987) no. 49 on 184: a decoration on an unpublished third-century AD goblet in the Bardot Museum depicts a *venator* 'raising his right hand in a victory sign and holding in his left hand the carcass of an animal [apparently a hare] that he no doubt killed in the arena'. Cf. below on bullfights and on Balinese cockfights. Cf. the Greek custom that hunters dedicated part of their game, the firstfruits of the hunt, to appropriate deities (e.g. Artemis and Apollo); see Xen. *Cyn.* 1.6; Arr. *Cyn.* 33.1; and W. H. D. Rouse, *Greek Votive Offerings* (Cambridge: Cambridge U., 1902) 50–1. On the Roman side, Rouse notes, from Ath. 5.221f, that skins of African buffaloes were hung in the Temple of Hercules at Rome. Hercules was a god of *venatores*, and a *venatio* could account for the dedication of skins of African beasts at Rome.

44 The training school for beast-fighters was aptly called the Ludus Matutinus, and Claudius so enjoyed the hunts that he went to the arena at daybreak (Suet. *Claud.* 34.2).

45 Hunt settings: e.g. SHA *Prob.* 19.3, a forest in the Circus Maximus; Calp. *Ecl.* 7.70–3, on Nero's amphitheater. Cf. Plass (1995) n. 11 on 182: 'so far as bloodshed in the arena was another ritual of control, *venationes* were perfect (entertaining), unrealistic, and entirely safe hunts'.

46 See Mitchell (1991) with bibliography. Rejecting any historical tie of bullfights to Roman spectacles or to primitive communal hunts, Mitchell, 15–40, sees the roots in rural bull-baiting and animal-baiting traditions. One of the modern era's most articulate commentators on the thrill of blood sports, Hemingway (1960), 238, claimed to have seen over 1,500 bulls killed.

47 Mitchell (1991), 18, 21, also notes that at rural Spanish fiestas (*capeas*) bulls are tormented or fought by amateurs, and their testicles are awarded to the killer or the man who first touches the bull.

48 Hemingway (1960) 187, 220, 237, 248: a red-jacketed bullring attendant carries a special knife to finish off badly wounded horses in the ring. He administers a quick coup de grâce between the vertebrae at the base of the skull. Similarly, a broad-bladed knife was used to cut the spinal cord at the top of the neck and thus finish off bulls in the ring if they were hamstrung or too far gone to be killed properly.

49 On rituals, including the procession, the covering of dead horses with a canvas, the dragging away of carcasses by mules, and the smoothing of the sand by servants, see Gary Marvin, *Bullfight* (Oxford: Basil Blackwell, 1988) 31–4; and Hemingway (1960) 60, 96.

50 I thank Drs Colin Wells and Richard Mandell for independently suggesting a parallel to Rome. Hospitals: Hemingway (1960) 268. Mitchell (1991), 89, estimates that modern Spain houses some seven to eight thousand bullfights a year

killing approximately 25,000 bulls. Marvin, op. cit., 34, explains that after removal the carcass is cleaned and jointed into six parts; while the meat sometimes goes to charity, usually the impresario who bought the live bull sells the meat to offset his expenses. Mitchell, 69, feels that the main point of the killing was emotionalism, not utilitarianism; but Marvin, 61–2, 112, sees the slaughterhouse as a link between the bullfights and urban meat production: aspiring matadors used to practice killing bulls in slaughterhouses, and men caped bulls in informal fights in the corrals of the slaughterhouses.

51 Geertz (1974) 7: 'as is invariably the rule, the owner of the winning cock takes the carcass of the loser – often torn limb from limb by its enraged owner – home to eat'. Moreover, 8, the man who attached the spurs of the winning cock is awarded the spur-leg of the loser. The abuse of the losing cock by its owner compares with the corpse abuse of *noxii* and failed (not just defeated) gladiators, and the consumption of the carcass probably also has a parallel at Rome. In America cockfighting continues to be popular and legal in some states (e.g. New Mexico, Louisiana). At an illegal fight in Fort Worth in February 1996 police seized nineteen dead and eighty-five live birds; the humane society put down the live birds, leading to protests from a Texas organization of gamefowl breeders. However, after legal fights cock carcasses are sold to petfood companies or to local cattle ranchers who use them as bait in coyote traps; B. Shlachter, 'An Ancient Blood Sport', *Fort Worth Star-Telegram* (Feb. 18, 1996) A23, 27; H. Mullen, 'Blood and Feathers', *Dallas Observer* (June 6–12, 1996) 23–36. Modern sensibilities deter people from eating mutilated cock carcasses but, even in modern times, such protein is not simply dumped out as useless garbage. See further on America below.

52 On food supply and crises at Rome, see Garnsey (1988) 167–268. Defining his terms at 6, Garnsey at 14, states that 'famines' (catastrophic food shortages causing starvation) were rare, but 'shortages' (subsistence crises short of famine) were frequent and took place in at least one year in five in the period 123–50 BC. The Roman state had to intervene, mostly concerning the *annona*, to guarantee the availability of subsidized or free grain. David Cherry, 'Hunger at Rome in the Late Republic', *EMC/CV* n.s. 12 (1993) 433–50, similarly argues, 448, that many of the poor in late Republican Rome were 'probably underfed and undernourished much of the time'. As he notes, 433–4, ancient writers rarely mention chronic hunger because they were 'uninterested in the poor'; but Cicero, *Att.* 1.16.11, describes the plebs in 61 BC as pitiable and starving, and Dio, 48.18.1, says that many died of starvation during the shortages of the late 40s.

53 Donald V. Sippel, 'Dietary Deficiency Among the Lower Classes of Late Republican and Early Imperial Rome', *AncW* 61.1, 2 (1987) 47–54, at 53, concludes that the urban poor, living mostly on grain, suffered widespread nutritional deficiency (protein–calorie malnutrition).

54 On the semiotics of food as a literary subject, as a metaphor or aesthetic figure, and on its moral value in Roman literature and biography, see the excellent studies by Gowers (1993) and Edwards (1993). As places where the lower classes met and ate vulgar meat dishes (e.g. sausages, tripe, etc., called *offelae* or bites or mouthfuls), cookshops (*popinae*) were disdained in elitist literature; see Corbier (1989) 233, 240–5. On extravagant and even disgusting meals described in literature from a hostile perspective, see testimonia in Gowers, n. 21 on 7; and Friedländer (1965) 2:146–64. Edwards, 186–91, also discusses moralistic and philosophical attacks on enthusiasm for expensive and exotic foods as a form of prodigality; she explains that such criticisms were a way of defining and controlling the behavior of the elite. Barton (1993), 53, feels that, because

it had been overly satisfied over time, the Roman palate became harder to stimulate and 'surrealistic comestibles' were sought. She notes that Elagabalus' meals included camel heels, mullet beards, nightingale tongues, and more (SHA *Heliogab.* 20.5–7) and that Vitellius invented a dish, the Shield of Minerva, which included pike livers, pheasant and peacock brains, flamingo tongues, and lamprey spleen gathered from the edges of the Empire (Suet. *Vit.* 13.2). Gowers, 36, 207, sees the Shield of Minerva as 'an imperial conquest of the world in miniature'.

55 See B. Flower and E. Rosenbaum, *The Roman Cookery Book: A Critical Translation of The Art of Cooking by Apicius* (London: Harrap, 1958). Apicius, *De re coquinaria* 8.1–4, covers the meat of wild boar, deer, wild goat, and wild sheep. He includes a sauce, 8.4.2, for all kinds of game, and a sauce, 6.5.6a, for 'high' birds of any kind, possibly birds that ate carrion or fish, or simply bird meat that had spoiled. Apicius, 8.8–9, also covers hare and dormice. Romans had cleared farms of rabbits and dormice, developed a taste for them (e.g. Petron. *Sat.* 31.10), and ended up raising them to eat.

56 *Sat.* 2.2.89–92; cited by Horace as a display of moral integrity, according to Gowers (1993) 138. She, 18–20, notes references to food within moralistic myths of Rome's development from its simple pure past to decadent urban culture. Cf. Cicero's criticism of Piso's dinner parties (*Pis.* 67), in which he served rancid meat (*carne subrancida*), as, according to Edwards (1993) 201, 'a parody of traditional Roman frugality'.

57 On river-pike, wolf-fish, or sea-bass caught *intra duos pontes* (the Aemilian and the Sublician), downstream from the Tiber Island where the Cloaca Maxima drained from the market district, see Macrob. *Sat.* 3.16.11–16 and Lucil. 1176 M; cited in Balsdon (1969) 37, 39; cf. Gowers (1993) 215. Also see Hor. *Sat.* 2.2.31 and Juv. 5.103–8 on the eating of scavenger fish.

58 Dung: Plin. *HN* 28.237; on human blood see n. 3 above.

59 See Vespasian's witticism on taxing urine (i.e. from public toilets): Suet. *Vesp.* 23.3. Night-soil: Columella *Rust.* 10.85. On sewage wagons in Rome and on *stercorarii* who clean domestic cesspits, see Bodel (1986) 32–8; or Scobie (1986) 408, 413–14, who suggests that the contents of cesspits were sold by those who emptied them to farmers at the edge of town. Fullers' jars in streets to collect urine for mordanting dyestuffs: Mart. 6.93.1; Macrob. *Sat.* 3.16.15.

60 Another potential group of arena-meat consumers was the Praetorian Guard. As Corbier (1989), 226–30, explains, Roman soldiers regularly consumed meat, both from livestock and hunted game. Roy W. Davies, *Service in the Roman Army* (New York: Columbia U., 1989) 66, 188, 191–5, 205, notes that soldiers in the legions continued to hunt for both recreation and food; see further in his 'The Roman Military Diet', *Britannia* 2 (1971) 122–42. Even Persian kings did not waste food. Cf. Ath. 4.145e–f, Loeb, quoting Heracleides of Cumae's *Persian History*, on the dinners of Persian kings: 1,000 animals were killed daily including horses, camels, oxen, asses, deer, and various small creatures, as well as ostriches, geese, and cocks: 'And of these only moderate portions were served to each of the king's guests, and each of them may carry home whatever he leaves untouched at the meal. But the greater part of these meats and other foods are taken out into the courtyard for the body-guard and light-armed troopers maintained by the king; there they divide all the half-eaten remnants of meat and bread and share them in equal portions.' Similarly, 4.145f, Persians of high rank give the leftovers from their banquets, mainly meat and bread, to their slaves.

61 Tertullian, *De spect.* 27, Loeb, urges Christians to avoid the games as a poisonous delicacy from the devil; 28.1: 'Our feast, our marriage-festival, is not yet. We cannot take our place at table with them, because they cannot with us.' As

McGowan (1994), 439, notes, Pliny, *Ep.* 10.96, commented that the spread of Christianity in Bithynia had hurt the sales of meat of sacrificial victims. Whether original or not, the association between gladiatorial shows and banquets (see ch. 2 above) continued. Elegabalus often watched gladiators and boxers before banquets (*ante convivium*), and while eating lunch (*dum pranderet*) he exhibited *noxii* and hunts: SHA *Heliogab.* 25.7–8; cf. Lucius Verus' similar habit: SHA *Verus.* 4.8–9. According to Suetonius, *Cal.* 32.1, Caligula supposedly arranged torture and decapitations as entertainment for his dinners.

62 In Greece meat from a normal 'Olympian' sacrifice (*thusia*) in a festival might be sold, but it was generally given to citizens. Xenophon, [*Ath. pol.*] 2.9, claims that the masses favor frequent festivals and sacrifices for the sake of the victims allotted to them. Aristophanes, *Nub.* 386–7, associates the Panathenaia with indigestion. The hides from victims were sold by the state, and Panathenaic meat was distributed by demes in the fourth century; see Vincent J. Rosivach, '*IG* 2^2 334 and the Panathenaic Hekatomb', *PP* 56 (1991) 430–42; Vincent J. Rosivach, *The System of Public Sacrifice in Fourth-Century Athens* (Chico, Calif.: Scholars Press, 1994).

63 Some festivals (e.g. the Septimontium and Ludi Romani; see Cic. *De or.* 3.73) had meals (*epulones*), and a college of three priests, the *tresviri epulones*, was established in 196 BC to organize and supervise such meals; see Scullard (1981) 186–7. Normally, sacrificial meat, beyond the god's share, was eaten by priests or senators or sold by the quaestors to market vendors. See Veyne (1990) 220–1; Corbier (1989) 225, 230; J. Scheid, 'Sacrifice, Roman', *OCD*[3] (1996) 1345.

64 As Corbier (1989), 230 and n. 65–6 on 256, notes, the son of Q. Fabius Rullus provided a *visceratio* and *epulum* on the death of his father in the third century ([Aur. Vict.] *De vir. ill.* 32.4); on M. Flavius, see n. 66 below. As noted above in n. 86 in ch. 2, like others, Titus Flamininus in 174 BC gave funeral games with a banquet, a dole of meat (*visceratio*), theatrical performances, and a gladiatorial combat: Livy 41.28.11. Sulla and Caesar: Plut. *Sull.* 35.5; Suet. *Iul.* 38.2. Veyne (1990), 235–6, explains that triumphators were obliged to use some of their booty for the benefit of the people, and one method was to put on a public banquet (*cena popularis*) on the pretext of inviting a god to attend.

65 Plass (1995) 46–7: at banquets and *munera* the consumption of animal and human life had symbolic value for social recognition, and such extravagance was 'political capital'. On the analogy of banquets and games, see Saylor (1987), 593–602, who notes that Trimalchio wants his *epulum* recorded on his tomb with the fights of a gladiator: *Sat.* 71.6, 9. Saylor, 598, 601, sees *cena* (or *epulum*) and *munus* as the same thing in the minds of the guests (e.g. the dishes are served like events in the arena; cf. the dinner and *munus* in *Sat.* 45). Jones (1991), 185–90, also notes various allusions to the arena in the account of Trimalchio's banquet. Recently, on Trimalchio as a parody of Nero, see Bartsch (1994) 197–9. Competitive expenditure, especially on dinner parties (*convivia*), continued under the Empire as a politically valuable demonstration of liberality; see Edwards (1993) 186–8, 199–204; and Richard Saller, *Personal Patronage under the Early Empire* (Cambridge: Cambridge U., 1982).

66 As Veyne (1990), 220–1, notes, the earliest recorded *visceratio* was in 328 BC, when M. Flavius distributed a dole of meat to those who walked in his mother's funeral procession. Livy, 8.22.2–4, says that the meat caused Flavius to win the tribuneship, although he was absent, at the next election. Cicero himself, *Mur.* 77, associating banquets with games and gladiatorial displays as time-honored traditions, said that the people should not be denied the customary games, gladiatorial displays, and banquets if candidates provided them out of *liberalitas* rather than *largitio*.

67 At a fantastic banquet given by Lucius Verus, according to SHA *Verus* 5.1–3, Loeb, there were couches for twelve rather than the proper nine, and guests received presents including dishes, cups, wreaths, carriages with mules and drivers, and more: 'Furthermore, the comely lads who did the serving were given as presents, one to each guest; carvers and platters, too, were presented to each, and also live animals either tame or wild, winged or quadruped, of whatever kind were the meats that were served.' Returning to Rome in AD 202, Septimius Severus gave out largesse, including money, food, and spectacles: Dio 77(76).1.1–5. He celebrated the wedding of Caracalla and Plautilla, 77(76).1.2, Loeb: 'And we were all entertained together at a banquet, partly in royal and partly in barbaric style, receiving not only the customary cooked viands but also uncooked meat and sundry animals still alive'; and he put on a slaughter, 77(76).1.3–5, of some 700 beasts, 'both wild and domesticated', including bears, lionesses, panthers, lions, ostriches, wild asses, bisons, and sixty wild boars. Discussing these examples, Corbier (1989), 237–9, points out that the SHA or Verus was influenced by stories about Seleucid kings (i.e. that Antiochus VII not only fed his guest but sent them home with large quantities of uncarved meat, and that to celebrate his games at Daphne in 166 BC Antiochus IV gave gifts of uncarved meat and live geese, hares, and gazelles as well as wreaths, vessels, slaves, horses, and camels: Ath. 5.210d–e, 12.540a–c, quoting Posidonius). Corbier feels, however, that the structuralist opposition of raw versus cooked, connoting wild versus civilized, was not a major opposition in the Roman rhetoric of meat.

68 Scobie (1986) 420–1: 'Rome did not have a centralized slaughter-house from which meat was distributed to retail outlets.' Cf. Juv. 3.316 on sheep, pigs, and cattle driven live through the streets to city markets.

69 Augustus entertained Greek ephebes at his villa at Capri with a banquet and expected them to scramble for tokens good for fruit and sweetmeats: Suet. *Aug.* 98. As aedile in AD 13, Agrippa had tickets for gifts (e.g. money, clothes) scattered in the theater and he also let people scramble for gifts set out: Dio 49.43.1–4. Caligula scattered tokens for gifts of various kinds at theatrical shows, as well as giving a basket of food to every spectator: Suet. *Calig.* 18.2. Cf. Dio, 59.9.6–7, who says that Caligula distributed gifts to those who grabbed the tickets which he scattered at a gymnastic contest. As Edmondson (1996), 77, points out, Claudius' use of the term *sportula* (a small portion of food in a basket) to refer to brief, impromptu spectacles (Suet. *Claud.* 21.4) recalls the association of gift-giving with *munera*.

70 When the play, *The Fire*, was staged, actors were allowed to carry off the furniture of the burning house and keep it: Suet. *Ner.* 11.2. Scrambling for goods in a burning house sounds like a variation on volunteering for the *tunica molesta*. Dio, 62.15.1–6, Loeb (cf. Tac. *Ann.* 15.37), says that at a spectacle put on by Nero and Tigellinus, after a beast-fight, sea fight, and gladiatorial fight, the arena was flooded and set up with taverns and brothels. As noted in n. 65 in ch. 3 above, every man could take any woman he wished. The masses drank and 'wantoned riotously', some men and women died, and some women were 'seized and carried off'.

71 Suet. *Ner.* 11.2, Loeb. Cf. Dio 62(61).18.2: to spectators Nero threw out balls inscribed with the names of objects to be claimed by those who caught the balls.

72 Stat. *Silv.* 1.6.10–27 (rope and largesse), 43–4 (meal in the stands), 75–80 (birds); Friedländer (1965) 2:76; cf. Ville (1981) 151–2, and nos. 120–1. See Jennison (1937) 113–16, on eating ostriches and flamingoes. Apicius, Bk 6, has numerous recipes for ostrich, flamingo, peacock, and other birds; cf. Columella *Rust.* 8.8 on

raising pigeons for their meat. Cf. Trimalchio's distribution of live thrushes to his guests, noted in n. 38 above. Jones (1991), 194, sees Domitian's banquet as an example of 'theater-dinner' – meals given in theaters and other settings accompanied by visual entertainment, a variation of 'dinner theater' – the provision of visual entertainment at dinners. As he comments, 196–7, dinner theater and theater-dinner were 'complementary aspects of the same system of benefaction . . . On the public level, to offer the public both food and spectacle was to make one's generosity as conspicuous as it could be.'

73 Mart. 8.78.7–12, Loeb. J. F. Killeen, 'What was the *Linea Dives* (Martial, VIII, 78.7)?' *AJPhil.* 80 (1959) 185–8, suggests, from a painting from Pompeii, that the rope was a sort of hammock loaded with gifts and strung out above the audience. He also suggests that the rope was placed lower than the level where women sat so that they escaped the tumult that scrambles incited in the stands.

74 SHA *Heliogab.* 8.3, Loeb: when he entered the consulship in 220 or 222, Elagabalus climbed a tower and threw gifts (via tokens) to the crowd to be scrambled for: 'no mere pieces of silver and gold, indeed, or confectionery or little animals, but fatted cattle (*boves opimos*) and camels and asses and slaves, declaring that this was an imperial custom'. Cf. Hdn 5.6.9, Loeb: 'gold and silver cups . . . and every kind of domestic animal, except pigs'. Herodian, 5.6.10, adds: 'In the scramble lots of people were killed, trampled to death by one another or impaled on the spears of the soldiers.' As emperor, Elagabalus at his banquets gave chances inscribed on spoons for gifts ranging from ten camels to ten flies to ten ostriches. At his games he gave chances for items including ten boars or ten dormice; for performers, chances included prizes of 'a dead dog or a hundred pounds of beef': SHA *Heliogab.* 22.1–3; 22.4, 'All of this so pleased the populace that after each occasion they rejoiced that he was emperor.' Earlier, Hadrian in AD 119 had distributed gifts by throwing balls in the theaters and Circus. The nature of the gifts is uncertain, but Dio, 69.8.2, mentions them after noting that Hadrian had provided a show in which 200 lions were killed.

75 It is possible that leading citizens traditionally scattered gifts publicly as New Year's offerings; see H. Nibley, 'Sparsiones', *CJ* 40 (1944–5) 515–43. However, Coleman (1996), 53–5, finds a paradigm for distributions of largesse to a body of spectators in the Grand Procession of Ptolemy Philadelphus in Alexandria in 275/4. According to Athenaeus, 200b–c, that procession included a float decorated as a cave from which pigeons and doves flew out with ribbons tied to their feet to allow spectators to catch them. On such distributions in theatrical contexts, especially in Roman North Africa, see Coleman, 56.

76 Seneca, *Ep.* 74.7, claims that distributions caused disturbances in the stands, and some people left beforehand out of fear of injury. Scobie (1988), 218, via *Dig.* 18.1.8.1, notes that spectators sometimes sold balls to gamblers. Coleman (1996), 56, suggests that the elements of chance and risk (i.e. the tokens might bring gifts of different natures and value) appealed to the spectators' gambling instincts.

77 On *dispensatores*, best known concerning imperial distributions of money (*congiaria*), see Millar (1992), 136–7, who sees the giving of largesse via *missilia* as eccentric but 'still an expression, however crude, of the deeply-ingrained notion of the liberality of the monarch'.

78 *Dig.* 21.1.40, 42 (= Johnson (1961) Doc. 245 on 204): 'The aediles then say: "Let no one be found to have had a dog, pig, hog, boar, wolf, bear, panther or lion in any place where the public customarily walk, so as to be capable of damage or loss to anyone."'

79 Under the Republic, arena meat probably stayed the responsibility or property of the giver of the show. Later, with imperial usurpation of most games patronage, the emperor 'owned' this property. Juvenal, 12.102–7, shows that elephants were reserved for emperors and could not be owned privately. Imperial monopoly on elephants and lions: Ael. *NA* 10.1; *CTh* 15.11.1. Moreover, the fisc was used to benefiting from arena animals: *Dig.* 39.4.16.7 records a duty on the import of animals (e.g. lions, leopards) to Italy.

80 E.g. Tert. *De spect.* 19, *Apol.* 7.1. Cf. Euseb. *HE* 8.6.3: a metaphor of burning a martyr's body as 'if it were edible meat for the table'. Tatian *Ad Gr.* 23 (trans. A. Roberts and J. Donaldson, *The Ante-Nicene Fathers* (New York: Scribner's, 1925) 2:75): 'You slaughter animals for the purpose of eating their flesh, and you purchase men to supply a cannibal banquet for the soul, nourishing it by the most impious bloodletting.' Cf. above and McGowan (1994), who cautions, 415, that 'An accusation of cannibalism may be very poor evidence for the victuals normal to a group but may be good evidence for the relation between accuser and accused.'

81 Tert. *Apol.* 9.11, Loeb. Tertullian continues: 'Man's flesh goes belching, fattened on man's flesh. You who eat these things, how far are you from those Christian banquets?' Tertullian, 1.1, claims that 'some' (*illi*) of the magistrates, to whom the *Apology* is addressed, ate such meat. Other condemnations of eating meat at public meals apply to normal sacrificial victims (e.g. Tert. *De spect.* 13; Min. Fel. *Oct.* 12.5, 38.1), which Christians were forbidden to eat (1 Cor. 8, 10, Acts 15.20, 29), but the meat here is clearly from the arena; and it includes boars and stags, the two most popular game animals in Italy according to Anderson (1985) 93. Bynum (1995) 31–3, 41–3, 53–6, testimonia in n. 132 on 53–4, relates such charges (of indirect cannibalism) to 'chain consumption' arguments about bodily resurrection. Rouselle (1988), 118–19, accepts the historicity of the charges, and points to New World parallels to indirect cannibalism via beasts; see her n. 49 on 119. In a derivative passage, Minucius Felix, *Oct.* 30.6, Loeb, refers more generally to 'those of you who eat of wild beasts from the arena, fresh glutted with blood and gorged with the limbs and entrails of men'. Tertullian may have been referring to indirect cannibalism as part of 'human sacrifices' to Saturn at Carthage, but Minucius Felix wrote at Rome and used cultural references (e.g. infanticide) familiar to Romans. Arnobius, *Ad nat.* 2.39–43, charges that spectators at beast shows delighted in blood and dismemberment, ground their teeth, and ate pieces of beasts which had eaten humans. Cf. Athenag. *Resur.* 4 on the problem of fish, birds, and beasts who have preyed on humans and then been eaten by humans.

82 Gen. 9.3–4: every creature will be food for man, but never eat flesh with blood (i.e. life) still in it. Exod. 21.28 also prohibits eating the flesh of an ox that has gored a human to death, and Lev. 17.15 demands purification of someone who has eaten something which has been mauled by wild beasts. Lev. 17.11–14 allows hunting (of animals that may lawfully be eaten) as long as all the blood is poured into the dust (i.e. returned to God). Acts 10.11–13 permits the hunting and eating of all kinds of animals, freeing Christians from most Mosaic dietary restrictions (e.g. against pigs, camels, horses, etc.), but the ban on consuming blood (Acts 15.20, 29) still holds. Cf. Tert. *De spect.* 13, *Apol.* 9.13, and Euseb. *HE* 5.1.26 on the taboo against defilement by contact with the blood remaining in the animal after slaughter. Tertullian, *Apol.* 9.14, says that persecuted Christians were tested with blood sausages, which they could not eat; but *Apol.* 42.2 seems to suggest that some Christians did not refrain from the Roman meat market. As McGowan (1994), 437–8, explains, Christians' avoidance of sacrificial meals was central to the Roman view of them as a

208

foreign threat to the social order. R. Lane Fox, *Pagans and Christians* (New York: Alfred A. Knopf, 1987) 444, 455, notes that during the persecutions lapsed Christians were forced to offer pagan sacrifices and to eat of the roasted meat; see, e.g., Euseb. *Mart. Pal.* 9.2. Fox cites Cyprian, *De lapsis* 16, for the Christian notion that eating such meat meant consuming demons with it, which led to hallucinations and ill effects. On such dietary taboos and their origins, see Harris (1978) 127–38; M. Harris, *Cows, Pigs, Wars, and Witches: The Riddle of Culture* (New York: Vintage Books, 1984) 35–60; Peter Farb and George Armelagos, *Consuming Passions: The Anthropology of Eating* (Boston: Houghton Mifflin, 1980) 110–24; Mary Douglas, 'Deciphering a Meal', 61–81, esp. 71–9, in Geertz (1974); and Gillian Feeley-Harnik, *The Lord's Table: The Meaning of Food in Early Judaism and Christianity* (Washington: Smithsonian Institute, 1981, repr. 1994).

83 Martial, 3.60.7–8, contrasts the delicious turtle-dove put before his patron Ponticus with the magpie, found dead in its cage, set before the poet. On clients' cheaper or distasteful food (e.g. Plin. *Ep.* 2.6; Juv. 1.95–6, 115) and on the contrast between the host's and the clients' food in Juv. 5, see Gowers (1993) 211–19. References to food cannot simply be taken literally, but there is no doubt that the poor ate coarse food and that food was a significant gift.

84 Cartmill (1993), 104, notes that in modern Europe meat animals were tortured to death to make their flesh more tender and savory. On the distinctive and formerly prized flavor of 'dark-cutting' meat, due to reduced lactic acid, see H. McGee, *On Food and Cooking: The Science and Lore of the Kitchen* (New York: Scribner's, 1984) 96.

85 Gal. *On Anat.* 7.10, cited by Friedländer (1965) 2:66. The association of banquets with spectacles was turned inside out when elephants were presented dining formally in the arena; see Ael. *NA* 2.11.

86 In Petronius, *Sat.* 66.5–6, the mason Habinnas tells of a funeral feast for a slave in which the food includes entrails, sausages, peasants' bread, and bear meat. Habinnas' wife almost threw up on trying the main dish of bear meat, but Habinnas said that it tasted like roast wild boar; see Gowers (1993) 30–1.

87 Paleo-archaeology indicates that early man scavenged dead animals before he became a hunter; e.g. see M. H. Nitecki and D. V. Nitecki, eds., *The Evolution of Human Hunting* (New York: Plenum Press, 1987).

88 As Corbier (1989), 250, suggests, the ostentatious recipes found in Roman literature 'fundamentally opposed a popular cuisine that salvaged everything, the tripe, the blood (consumed as *sanguiculus* or black pudding) and so on'. Edward Champlin, 'The Testament of the Piglet', *Phoenix* 41 (1987) 174–83, at 174, notes, with Plin. *HN* 8.209 (on eating-houses), that the main meat consumed at Rome was pork, followed by beef and mutton, and that 'almost every part of the ancient pig was put to culinary use'. Juvenal, 11.79–81, refers to a ditch-digger's enthusiasm for pork tripe from cookshops. Apicius, Bk 7, has recipes for pig wombs, trotters, udders, skin, liver, stomach, kidneys, and lungs; Bk 2 has recipes for sausages, rissoles, and forcemeat, including the use of pig brains, stuffed wombs, and blood puddings (2.3.2). Scobie (1986), 419, suggests that dogs were used as a food source by the starving. Cf. Ar. *Eq.* 1397–9 on Athens.

89 The meat of many of these animals turns up in recipes in Apicius' Bk 8. Romans were enthusiastic about the taste of wild ass meat (Plin. *Ep.* 1.6), first served by Maecenas (Plin. *HN* 8.170), and the meat of donkey foals became fashionable (*HN* 8.68). Jennison (1937), 89, remarks on the large proportion of non-carnivorous animals in the list. Most sources were prone to emphasize the exotic and fierce animals in shows, or sometimes they give undetailed

numbers. E.g. as noted above in n. 11 in ch. 3, for his millenary games of 248, Philip the Arab 'presented or killed' countless wild and tame animals, beasts which Gordian III had intended for his triumph: SHA *Gord. Tres* 33.1–2. Note, however, that in Martial's *Spectacula* bulls and steers are the beasts most often mentioned, followed by boars and sows.

90 SHA *Prob.* 19.2–4, Loeb. Lions and leopards were killed on another day at the amphitheater: 19.5–6. Note the recurrence of the verb *rapere*, to carry off quickly by force.

91 Plass (1995), n. 21 on 198, accepts both examples as historical, suggesting that the spectators probably felt an excitement similar to modern fans 'storming the field after play concludes'. Wiedemann (1992), 13, 61, distrusts the SHA on these events, but he notes, 18, that coins advertise the munificence of some of these emperors: e.g. the Colosseum is shown on coins celebrating the millenary festival of Philip the Arab, and a bronze coin of Gordian III dating to AD 243 shows a fight between a bull and rhinoceros in the Colosseum. Friedländer (1965) 2:15–16, 42, 60, saw such distributions of arena animals as an occasional practice of the later Empire, but the SHA does not present it as an innovation. The idea of the plebs scrambling for meat must have been intelligible to the SHA's readers.

92 Rome retained in law the old idea that wild game was the property of its captor: *Dig.* 41.1.1. On legal issues concerning wild animals, including the responsibilities of the owner and the status of escaped animals, see August Menche de Loisne, *Essai sur le droit de chasse, sa législation ancienne et moderne* (Paris: A. Marescq Aîné, 1878) 13–36.

93 Anthropologists and sociologists, from Malinowski, Mauss, and Polanyi on, have elaborated on the symbolism of giving and sharing food, and the symbolism of meat is especially powerful. In general, see Farb and Armelagos (1980) 95–109, 144–57. As a gift, food establishes reciprocal obligations or social control; it creates bonds and defines status. McGowan (1994) 437: 'groups create and maintain boundaries by means of those with whom they choose to eat'. Lincoln (1985) 9: 'Of all human behaviors, there is nothing more conducive to the integration of society than the sharing of food, particularly a highly valued food such as meat. For commensality, a specialized form of gift exchange, facilitates the formation of *societas* by establishing a bond of sentiment and obligation among those who share a meal.' On Roman euergetism, see the classic study by Veyne (1990).

94 Seneca, *De ira* 2.8.2–3, remarks on the abnormal society of the gladiatorial school, where gladiators eat together and then fight each other. Recall that Statius, *Silv.* 1.6.43–4, emphasizes the communal aspect of Domitian's Saturnalian feast: although senators got larger baskets (Suet. *Dom.* 4.5), all classes were mixed together and the emperor joined them. Ville (1981), 434–5, accepts Statius' suggestion of a (temporary) social equalization during the meal; but Edmondson (1996), 95, feels that the passage 'owes more to the necessities of poetic patronage than to the realities of social practice'. On the dynamics of hierarchy versus equalization in communal meals, see Gowers (1993), 212, who feels that 'The communal meal, especially a public one, was above all a symbolic re-enactment of the social hierarchy.' Similarly, Douglas, op. cit., 61: 'If food is treated as a code, the message it encodes will be found in the pattern of social relations being expressed. The message is about different degrees of hierarchy, inclusion and exclusion, boundaries and transactions across boundaries.' As in distributions of sacrificial meat, sharing arena meat would suggest both solidarity or integration and social hierarchy (via the sequence of distribution on differential portions by quantity or quality).

95 On Tiberius' lack of enthusiasm for shows, see ch. 7 below. Josephus, *AJ* 19.1.16, trans. W. Whiston, notes that various groups were disturbed at Caligula's murder: 'the women and the youths had been inveigled with shows, and the fightings of the gladiators, and certain distributions of flesh-meat among them'. Corbier (1989), 230–2, suggests that the consumption of meat by the masses at Rome became routinized over time and that provision of meat by the state was justified. However unreliable, the story, in SHA *Alex. Sev.* 22.7–8, that the emperor Severus Alexander responded when the people complained about the price of meat, suggests popular and official concerns about the meat supply.

96 On the grain dole, see Garnsey (1988) passim; G. R. Rickman, *The Corn Supply of Ancient Rome* (Oxford: Oxford U., 1980); and Boudewign Sirks, *Food for Rome* (Amsterdam: J. C. Gieben, 1991). As Garnsey (1988), 214, explains, the grain dole, a food supplement rather than welfare since a ration was adequate only for two people, was only for the small portion of the population on the lists (the *plebs frumentaria*). Although only the very poor relied on it, it was likely to be taken for granted, and interruptions brought riots. In the third century Aurelian substituted baked bread for grain and added a portion of pork and oil, but only for the *plebs frumentaria*: SHA *Aurel.* 35.2, 48.1. Unlike the grain or money for the *plebs frumentaria*, distributions via scrambles were open to all spectators.

97 It was significant that the emperor presented or gave the games, that arena beasts were to be wild, and that the meat from the arena was to be fresh. Abrams, op. cit., 209, comments: 'in virtually all societies, meat and other animal products remain preferred foods. In most of the contemporary world, when people entertain guests for a meal, meat or some form of animal protein is usually featured as an expression of cordiality and friendship.' Gowers (1993), 38–9, sees triumphal imagery in literary descriptions of processions of dishes at meals, and she notes, n. 167 on 38, that *exhibere*, the standard term for serving food, was used of beast shows.

98 Like Rome, America experienced the development of subsistence, sport, and spectacular hunting. On the southern frontier meat hunting supplemented the food supplies of subsistence corn and hog farmers, but as areas developed cotton and cattle farming, and as communities became more hierarchical, the elite developed sport hunting, including turf sports and even fox hunting. Stuart A. Marks, *Southern Hunting in Black and White: Nature, History and Ritual in a South Carolina Community* (Princeton: Princeton U., 1991), discusses the ethnography and socioeconomics of indigenous sport hunting, its critics and defenders, and the influence of the encroachment of civilization on the tradition. He explains, 45, 63, 72, 175, 183–4, 218–19, 227, that the working class continued to see hunting as a positive male custom hallowed by tradition, but that more elitist recreational hunters came to disdain the meat or 'pot' hunter. Thad Sitton, 'East Texas Bear Hunts', *Texas Parks and Wildlife* (Feb. 1995) 42–5, explains that nineteenth-century bear hunts were of two types: bears were hunted as game (for meat, fat, and oil) in the late fall when they had become fat in the woods, and they were hunted as predatory varmints in the summer when they came out of the woods to prey on hogs in the uplands. Hunting vermin may have been a 'farm chore' for rustic Romans, but farm chores can lead to special meals. Texans, after early confrontations with rattlesnakes as verminous and venomous threats, ritualized the wearing of snake skin and the eating of snake meat, and came to acquire a taste for the meat. The ranch chore of castrating young male cattle led to the consumption of 'prairie oysters'. I thank my Texan student, Dewayne Quertermous, for some of these suggestions.

99 On the contrast between the emphasis on unprepared food in Rome and on the preparation of food in the USA, see Lowell Edmunds, 'Ancient Roman and Modern American Food: A Comparative Sketch of Two Semiological Systems', *Comparative Civilizations Review* 5 (Fall 1980) 52–68. In the modern West skill in preparation of food compensates for the absence of skill in acquisition or killing of animals for food. The emphasis on meat, fire, and the outdoors leads men to barbecue and participate in chili cookoffs.

100 Michael Satchell, 'The American Hunter Under Fire', 30–7, *US News and World Reports* 108.5 (Feb. 5, 1990) 34, refers to a study indicating that over 80 percent of Americans approve of hunting to put game on the table, but that 80 percent see hunting for trophies as wrong, and 60 percent disapprove of hunting merely for sport or recreation. Within the same article, Kenneth T. Walsh, 'George Bush: The Happy "First Hunter"', 33, quotes then President Bush. Before being elected, the last two governors of Texas, Anne Richards and George Bush Jr, went on heavily publicized dove hunts. Why is the flesh of wild game, or pseudo-wild game such as ranch-raised buffalo and farm-fed trout and catfish, popular in restaurants? Why is there a market for the killing of exotic and fierce animals in 'canned hunts'? On the positive side, some states including Texas have programs for distributing wild venison to the poor.

101 E.g. in the Fort Worth Stock Show; *Fort Worth Star-Telegram* (Tues. Jan. 31, 1995) Section A, p. 16. Begun in the Fort Worth Stock Show in 1987, this event has twenty-eight performances, 224 winners, 448 participants in all, and over $100,000 worth of prizes donated by sponsors. Each winner, who must catch and halter a calf and drag it to a target area in the arena, gets $500 toward the purchase of a heifer to be raised and shown at the next Stock Show. Like other rodeo events, this entertaining spectacle publicizes and promotes the skills of animal husbandry on the ranch.

7

RITUALS, SPECTACLES, AND
THE TIBER RIVER

To the Tiber with Tiberius! ('Tiberium in Tiberim!')
(Suetonius *Tiberius* 75.1)

We have seen that professional gladiators were definitely allowed the burial they had earned, that some arena refuse was possibly dumped on the Esquiline during the Republic, that fire, crucifixion, and beasts were means more of killing than of disposal, and that arena meat was probably distributed to the people of Rome. We have not yet, however, accounted for large quantities of human arena victims. This chapter will investigate the disposal of human victims via the Tiber River as a traditional and pragmatic custom. Although moderns have overlooked the idea, flowing water offered a logistically sensible and emotionally satisfying answer to the problem of disposal of corpses from arenas at Rome.

When Rome transposed theatrical abuse and ritualized executions of *noxii* to the arena on a spectacular scale, religious and practical problems about efficiency, haste, security, and disposal needed attention. Rome's wish to extend punishment and revenge by not providing – or even by preventing – proper burial rites left anxiety about hostile spirits. Rome easily assured itself that the killings were justified, but even the premature, violent deaths of worthless humans required some ritual removal and cleansing so that the spirits of the dead, which stayed near the body, would not trouble the living. Rome needed some means or rite of expelling those spirits and thus purifying Rome, and the ideal means were close at hand. Roman history and religion point to the Tiber River, more than to pits, beasts, and fire, as a traditional means of ultimate disposal (and of denial of burial) for victims. Examination of early executions and later spectacles, often taking place close to the river, indicates that the Tiber was repeatedly used to dispose of corpses. The Tiber River and its bridges were intimately related to old cults and rituals at Rome, and, as a traditional way to dispose of waste, the river offered expediency and purification.[1]

213

Water: punishment and purgation

Like fire, water had lustral or ritual cleansing properties that other means of disposal lacked.[2] From the great flood in Near Eastern tradition to baptism in Christian ritual, to Pontius Pilate's washing of his hands, water, representing the primordial waters of creation, was the great purifier of sins, guilt, and miasma.[3] From Moses to Romulus and Remus, water was a classic way to dispose of polluted objects, prodigies, and unwanted creatures – beings rejected from or never accepted into the community.[4] Salt water was best for the purification of accursed items, and the Tiber was seen as sending its contents to the sea.[5]

In religious terms, the early rampart (Agger) of Servius and the early religious boundary (*pomerium*) of Rome did not include or cross the Tiber, so the ban on intra-urban dumping was not broken.[6] Use of the Tiber to remove waste and restless spirits beyond the *pomerium* was an appropriate final phase in the damnation of *noxii* to the arena, which usually entailed denial of decent burial in addition to corporal abuse and death. Very simply, use of the Tiber was logistically pragmatic and symbolically reassuring: denial of burial thoroughly extended the process of damnation, and disposal by water cleansed the city and its people of filth and guilt. Throwing someone – or oneself – into the Tiber literally involved excommunication, expulsion, and expurgation.[7]

Rome's topography shows that sites of spectacles of death were often near flowing water. Beyond Rome executions and amphitheaters were usually found on the edge of towns, but Rome started with some executions in the Forum (see map 2) and the main spectacle sites remained downtown.[8] In practical terms, the deficiencies of pits and fire suggest that the use of the Tiber was necessary, especially with increased urbanization and expanded spectacles. The advantages of water over land transportation in antiquity are well known, and the ancient Tiber was a major, powerful river.[9] Hercules had to redirect a river to cleanse the Augean stables, but Rome had a cleansing river at hand. Cicero (*Rep.* 2.5–6, Loeb) said that Romulus was wise to place his city 'on the banks of a never-failing river whose broad stream flows with unvarying current into the sea'.[10] Accessible and efficient, the Tiber accommodated 3,000 Gracchans at once (see below), more than the human bulk of even an exceptionally destructive day of games. The image of bodies floating in the Tiber is revolting, but so is the image of thousands of creatures slaughtered in public for entertainment.

Legends and history show that the Tiber, which received the effluence of Rome's famous sewer system, was a customary, convenient, and quite polluted 'garbage dump'.[11] Tradition held that the Tiber Island itself was formed when, after the expulsion of Tarquin the Proud, people took a crop of ripe grain (grown on sacred ground, it was unusable for food) from the former tyrant's land in the Campus Martius, packed it into baskets, and

214

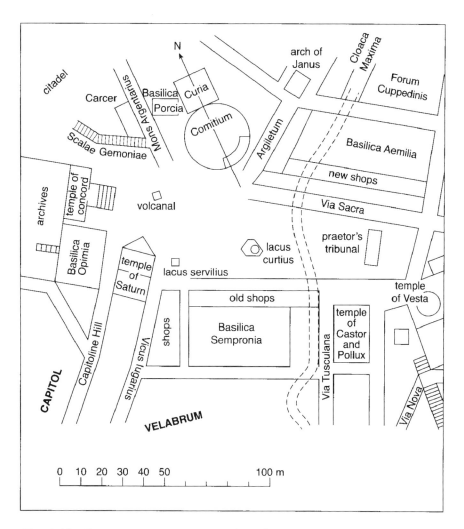

Map 2 The Roman Forum at the start of the first century BC

threw them into the Tiber, so that, along with the accumulation of other refuse, an island was formed.[12] When Sulla entertained the people with magnificent banquets there was excess food and every day 'great quantities of meat were thrown into the river'.[13] Nero (Tac. *Ann.* 15.18), trying to suggest a sense of security about the grain supply during the Parthian War in AD 62, threw into the Tiber the grain intended for the people, which had spoiled from being stored too long.

An intriguing possible connection between the Tiber, human sacrifice, and disposal emerges from a long-standing debate about the Sacra Argeorum.

215

What Plutarch (*Quaest. Rom.* 86) calls 'Rome's greatest rite of purification', this ritual may represent a parallel to the expulsion of hostile souls of the untimely dead via the Tiber. By ancient custom, effigies of men, bound hand and foot, were thrown from the sacred bridge (*pons sublicius*) into the Tiber each May. 'Argei' refers both to the effigies and the shrines (*sacraria*) involved in the rite (Livy 1.21.5). Pointing out that the rite follows immediately upon the conclusion of the Lemuria with its focus on spirits (*lemures*) and purification, Harmon argues that, 'The Argei rite is very similar to other purification rituals in which the Tiber merely carries away the sources of defilement.' Harmon feels that the pontiffs and Vestals, out of concern with the propriety of sacrifices, used a rite of sympathetic magic – effigies resembling corpses – to expel and exorcise hostile spirits, to release the land from any pollution and forestall the threat of retaliation by the spirits.[14] Holland offers another intriguing theory, relating the Argei to the Vestals' preparation of a special hand-ground bread: the chaff, as sacred, had to be disposed of by pit burial (i.e. covered, not just dumped) or by flowing water.[15]

Combining Harmon's theory (of a rite of purification in which the effigies represent the Lemures) with Holland's theory (on the role of the Vestals and the sacred spelt), B. Nagy ties both the Vestals and the Lemuria to a series of May rituals seeking the aversion and appeasement of spirits of the ancestral untimely dead as well as the purification of the city.[16] The *pater-familias* performed rites of appeasement for the family, and the Argei rite did so for the community at large. The Vestals gave offerings of spelt at the twenty-seven Argei shrines, immature grain being especially suitable for the Lemures as ancestral spirits of the untimely dead. The effigies, however, says Nagy, do not represent the Lemures but rather represent redemptive offerings to them. Nagy sees an early historical origin for the rite in the appeasement of the premature deaths of Romans by the sacrifice of appropriate victims, i.e. Greek enemies of the Etruscans who under the Etruscan monarchy were seen as foes and murderers of Romans. Over time effigies replaced the earlier actual human sacrifices, and the Romans continued the rite while becoming unsure of its origins.[17] Whether the rite's roots concerned Vestals or human sacrifice to the river spirits or to Lemures, it was related to some ritual cleansing or appeasement. It had something to do with potentially hostile spirits, with actual or surrogate human sacrifice, and with disposal or purification via the Tiber.[18]

Similarly intriguing, cleansing and punishment are associated with the Tiber in the *poena cullei*, a ritual execution, an aggravated punishment, and a denial of burial whereby parricides (probably killers of kinsmen) were tied in a leather sack and cast into a river.[19] As a public demonstration that a disturbing crime had been corrected, the punishment was probably introduced in the middle Republic (late third or early second century), but its first certain use in criminal law dates to around 101 BC (concerning a matricide).[20] Perhaps it was suspended between the 50s BC and the Principate of Augustus, but it is often noted under emperors such as Claudius.[21] Hadrian permitted *damnatio ad bestias* as a substitute for the sack 'if the sea were too far distant', but the use of the sack continued throughout the history of the Empire and was even expanded under Constantine.[22]

Hermaphrodites similarly were ritually drowned as prodigies, and at some point the sack penalty for parricides was aggravated even further with the addition of various animals to the sack. **M.** Radin sees the sack as

> plainly a *procuratio prodigii* – a disposal of a thing of evil portent . . . The perpetrator was not merely a criminal amenable to punishment, but a foul thing, unclean, causing the gods to withdraw their presence from a world he polluted, and requiring therefore hasty removal from the world in such a manner as to remove at the same time the miasma his body would inevitably spread.[23]

Having put himself beyond the bounds of human society, the victim was abused by animals as he died. Despised and vicious animals added to the punishment and also to the purification, by absorbing the miasma of the victim.

Executions and riots in the Forum

As a punishment, disposal via the Tiber was part of a traditional and legal execution ritual performed in and near the Carcer, Rome's oldest state prison.[24] Originally this was a short-term jail and a place of execution, usually by strangulation, for non-citizens, traitors, and foreign kings. As noted above, triumphs en route to the Capitol paused near the Carcer as the victorious general awaited word that one of his principal captives, paraded in the triumph, had been put to death in the prison or nearby.[25] Jugurtha, Vercingetorix, and other famous foes of Rome – with Cleopatra making herself an exception – were killed here.[26] The Carcer was located at north edge of the Forum at the foot of the east slope of the Capitoline to the right of the ascent from the Forum, between the Temple of Concord and the Curia, with a façade on the Mons Argentarius (see map 2).[27] Consisting of an upper and a lower chamber, the structure may go back only to the third century, but the use of the site for executions may be earlier. Sallust describes the lower, subterranean round chamber, the Tullianum, concerning the strangulation (by a noose) of the Catilinarian conspirators on the orders of the magistrates responsible for prisons and executions (*tresviri capitales*):

> In the prison, when you have gone up a little way towards the left, there is a place called the Tullianum, about twelve feet below the

surface of the ground. It is enclosed on all sides by walls, and above it is a chamber with a vaulted roof of stone. Neglect, darkness, and stench make it hideous and fearsome to behold.[28]

Too small to house any number of prisoners, this was just a holding area for the condemned.[29]

Numbers of prisoners under the Republic were small because Rome still allowed and preferred that citizens went into exile or committed suicide. Under the Empire prisons saw increased use for holding condemned persons for execution to prevent their escape.[30] Yet even then, like *vivaria* for beasts, and *spoliaria* for corpses, prisons were temporary holding areas. Rome did not believe in character redemption or the rehabilitation of felons via imprisonment.[31] Rome got on with procedures, enslaving, sending to the mines, or promptly executing persons who, in later societies, would usually be 'incarcerated'.

Ancient sources suggest that the name Tullianum came from its construction by Servius Tullius, but it probably derives from the spring (*tullius*) in its floor that emptied into a drain running to the southeast, probably into the Cloaca Maxima. Richardson comments:

> One is a bit surprised that the Romans should have chosen a place with a spring for their jail. It may be that originally criminals were condemned to death by starvation, and the spring functioned as the jug of water deposited with Vestal Virgins condemned for unchastity. Or it may be that the Carcer began its existence as a springhouse and was converted to use as a jail when the spring failed to produce an adequate supply.[32]

Such ties between water and places of killing, however, recur at Rome.

Under the Empire, after criminals were executed in or near the Forum their bodies were exposed for public viewing for three days on the 'Stairs of Mourning', the Scalae Gemoniae.[33] Richardson defines these as 'a flight of steps leading alongside the Carcer to the top of the Capitoline on which bodies of executed criminals were thrown for public exposure and disgrace'.[34] The topography is uncertain, but Valerius Maximus (6.9.13) specifies that the steps were in full view of the Forum. First mentioned during Tiberius' reign, the Scalae probably replaced the Gradus Monetae, which were destroyed when Tiberius enlarged the Temple of Concord, but there is no certain evidence that the Gradus Monetae were specifically used for exposure of corpses.[35]

It is well attested that executions in the area of the Forum, riots, proscriptions, and imperial treason trials often led to denials of burial and the dumping of corpses into the Tiber. As Lintott explains, when normal procedures proved inadequate to deal with crises, Romans resorted to violence in a characteristic fashion. Roman criminal law was modeled on ritualized self-help (*vim vi repellere licet*), and in some cases Rome went beyond the expediency of *ius* and *lex* to the emotionalism of *ultio*.[36] Scholars agree that the long tradition of disposal via the Tiber was intended to achieve denial of burial and purification by water.[37] Hinard and David suggest that early executions were held in the Forum, especially in the region of the Comitium, as a symbolically appropriate site, but that at the end of the Republic the traditional execution ceremony was replaced by a system in which exposure on the Scalae became the main public aspect of executions in the Forum as emperors used traditional sites (e.g. Carcer, Tarpeian) and symbolism to legitimize executions.[38] Under the Empire the people could be involved in a ritual of rejection; they could not save anyone, but they could participate (e.g. as witnesses or by abusing the corpse) before the corpse was dumped.[39]

Several incidents (and even witticisms) show that, after death and exposure in the Forum, bodies were dragged by hooks and thrown into the Tiber. Dio (61(60).35.4, Loeb) comments: 'Inasmuch as the public executioners were accustomed to drag the bodies of those executed in the prison to the Forum with large hooks, and from there hauled them to the river, he [Seneca's brother Gallio] remarked that Claudius had been raised to heaven with a hook.' Suetonius shows an impromptu application of the ritual to Vitellius:

> But they [soldiers] bound his arms behind his back, put a noose around his neck, and dragged him with rent garments and half-naked to the Forum. All along the Sacred Way he was greeted with mockery and abuse, his head held back by the hair, as is common with criminals ... Some pelted him with dung and ordure, others called him incendiary and glutton, and some of the mob even taunted him with his bodily defects ... At last on the Stairs of Wailing he was tortured for a long time and then dispatched and dragged off with a hook to the Tiber.[40]

When hooks or the Stairs are mentioned, dumping in the Tiber can be assumed.[41] Those who had become *hostes*, who threatened or insulted the people, were abused, killed, and disposed of without burial via the Tiber.[42]

In famous incidents, hatred or fear of the Gracchi lead to compounded insult and abuse.[43] In the attack on Tiberius in 133 BC over 300 were killed without trial by blows with sticks and stones, 'none by the sword' (Plut. *Ti. Gracch.* 19.6). Plutarch (20.2, Loeb) says that the conspiracy against Tiberius was a matter of hatred and anger, and that this is proven by the 'lawless and savage treatment of his dead body'. He notes that the senate denied Gaius permission to take his brother's body and bury it at night; he adds that the bodies of Gracchus and the other dead were thrown (Appian, *B Civ.* 1.16, says 'at night') into the river. Gaius later chastised the people for standing by and watching while Tiberius was beaten to death (Plut. *G. Gracch.* 3.3, Loeb) 'and his dead body was dragged from the Capitol through the midst of the city to be thrown into the Tiber'.

In 121 Gaius and 3,000 of his followers were also killed and their bodies were thrown into the Tiber.[44] Their property was sold and the proceeds confiscated by the public treasury, and Opimius offered a reward for the heads of Gaius and Fulvius.[45] Plutarch adds that the wives were forbidden to wear mourning and Gaius' wife was deprived of her dowry. Such treatment of the corpses and of their families reveals intentions beyond merely spontaneous homicide.[46] The systematic corpse abuse via decapitation, the denial of burial or any rites, the dooming of the family (no property, wife not to remarry), and the disposal by water all aimed at vengeance beyond death, at what imperial Rome called *damnatio memoriae*.[47] Such excessive violence went beyond the secular realm, and Rome took measures to restore the sacral order. After the atrocities, a lustration was performed for the city for the bloodshed, and the senate and Opimius restored the Temple of Concord (App. *B Civ.* 1.7.27), originally built in the Forum (symbolically close to the Carcer – see map 2) in 367.

Political violence and disposal by water

From Marius and Cinna on, in civil wars and proscriptions the Tiber received many more deposits. As Sulla approached Rome in 82 the younger Marius killed many of Sulla's supporters; the bodies were not spared but were dragged by the hook of the hangman. Appian comments: 'Their bodies were thrown into the Tiber, for it had now become usual not to bury the slain.'[48] When Sulla slaughtered 6,000 prisoners in the Circus Flaminius after the battle of the Colline Gate in 82 BC, what happened to the bodies, as the Tiber flowed nearby (see map 1)?[49] Sulla understood corpse abuse. Moved by hatred, he ordered that Marius' buried remains be scattered in the Anio River, and, presumably fearing similar abuse, he wanted his own body cremated.[50]

In one stage of what seems to have been a long history of Roman head-hunting, before and during Sulla's proscriptions, heads of senators were exhibited, fixed above and around the Rostra and the Lacus Servilius, a watering area or a depression in the ground, probably linked to the Cloaca Maxima passing below the Forum (see map 2).[51] According to Livy (2.19.1), in 88 BC the tribune P. Sulpicius was declared a public enemy and his head was exposed on the Rostra in the Forum. In the proscriptions of 43 (App. *B Civ.* 4.2.5–5.4.20) the triumvirs offered rewards for the heads of the proscribed, and Cicero's head and hand hung on the Rostra for a long time (5.4.20) as an insult to him after his death.[52] Heads from executions and even heads of victims killed elsewhere were brought to the Forum for abuse and display, as on an Aztec skull rack.[53] The fate of some heads is known,[54] but most perhaps were disposed of via the Cloaca Maxima. Displays and disposals of heads not only symbolized the defeat of an enemy in this world: the distancing of the head from the corpse meant that there could be no proper burial or peace in the afterlife.[55]

Concerning the public violence of 57 BC, Cicero speaks rhetorically of the Tiber filled with the bodies of citizens, of sewers similarly 'stuffed' ('corporibus civium . . . cloacas refarciri')', and of blood in the Forum being mopped up with sponges.[56] The assassins of Caesar (Suet. *Iul.* 82.4, Loeb), until halted through fear of Antony and Lepidus, intended to wash away his body and career – 'to drag his body to the Tiber, confiscate his property, and revoke his decrees'. In 44 BC when Amatius (Pseudo Marius) returned to Rome after the death of Caesar and was popular with the masses, Antony used the army to seize and murder him without trial. The body was dragged through the streets and thrown into the Tiber.[57] In 38 BC problems with the corn supply led to a famine and riot at Rome, and Octavius and Antony suffered stoning in their vain attempts to quiet the masses in the Forum. Antony called out the army and ordered a massacre. Soldiers took advantage of the situation to rob the corpses, which were then thrown in the Tiber.[58] Giving examples of Augustus' punishment of his slaves, Suetonius (*Aug.* 67.2, Loeb) says that, for their misbehavior during the sickness and death of Gaius Caesar, Augustus ordered that Gaius' tutor and attendants be 'thrown into a river with heavy weights about their necks'.[59] In these instances, when unfaithful or disruptive elements and supposed foes put themselves beyond the law and normal rights, defenders of order punished them with abuse and death, adding insult via the Tiber. Violence against enemies knew few bounds, but it followed ritual patterns.

The Tiber, execution, and corpse abuse are regularly conjoined under the Empire, especially concerning charges of *maiestas* and the suppression of the conspiracy of Sejanus. Dio (58.11.1–6, Loeb) reflects on human frailty as he describes how the people turned on Sejanus as he was being led to prison:

> For the man whom at dawn they had escorted to the senate-hall as a superior being, they were now dragging to prison as if no better than the worst . . . The populace also assailed him, shouting many reproaches at him for the lives he had taken . . . They hurled down, beat down, and dragged down all his images,[60] as though they were thereby treating the man himself with contumely, and he thus became a spectator of what he was destined to suffer. [When the senate condemned him] . . . he was executed and his body cast down the Stairway, where the rabble abused it for three whole days and afterwards threw it into the river. His children also were put to death by decree, the girl . . . having first been outraged by the public executioner on the principle that it was unlawful for a

virgin to be put to death in the prison. His wife Apicata was not condemned, to be sure, but on learning that her children were dead, and after seeing their bodies on the Stairway . . . she committed suicide.[61]

Tacitus (*Ann.* 6.19, Loeb) details the rage of Tiberius:

And as executions had whetted his appetite, he gave orders for all persons in custody on the charge of complicity with Sejanus to be killed. On the ground lay the huge hecatomb of victims (*immensa strages*): either sex, every age; the famous, the obscure; scattered or piled in mounds. Nor was it permitted to relatives or friends to stand near, to weep over them, or even to view them too long; but a cordon of sentries, with eyes for each beholder's sorrow, escorted the rotting carcasses, as they were dragged to the Tiber, there to float with the current or drift to the banks, with none to commit them to the flames or touch them.

There were to be no rites, no last farewells.[62]

Tiberius' reign of terror added to his unpopularity, but another factor, one more relevant to the plebs, was his negative policy on spectacles. Before becoming emperor Tiberius had given gladiatorial games (paid for by his mother and stepfather) in memory of his father and grandfather. As emperor he financed spectacles put on by his sons, and at the start of his reign he attended spectacles responsibly (e.g. to honor editors), but he lacked enthusiasm for shows.[63] Suetonius (*Tib.* 47.1) says that he hardly attended shows given by others and that as emperor he gave no public shows at all (*neque spectacula omnino*). Moreover, Tiberius reduced the cost of shows by limiting the number of pairs of gladiators, and after leaving for Capri in AD 27 he forbade hunting spectacles in the city of Rome.[64] Undermining his own image, Tiberius spurned the spectacular path to popularity.

At Rome the news of the death of the aged, parsimonious, and paranoid Tiberius was greeted with joy. Some people ran in the streets and, in what was probably a variation on a popular negative acclamation, cried 'To the Tiber with Tiberius!' ('Tiberium in Tiberim!') Others in the crowd wanted to use the hook and stairs or the ignominy of an Atellan half-burning.[65] A half-burning meant an incomplete releasing of the soul, thus dooming it to torment. Although he was cremated by the soldiers in a public ceremony, people offered prayers to Mother Earth and the Infernal Gods to give Tiberius no home below except among the damned. Such spectacular abuses were especially appropriate for an emperor hated both for not providing spectacles and for abusing his political opponents.[66] The Tiber was the final stage in an elaborate ritual of abuse and vengeance, denial and damnation, a ritual familiar to plebeians, senators, and emperors. Caligula, too, understood the significance of proper disposal and the ritual use of water. According to Suetonius, 'He banished from the city the sexual perverts called *spintriae*, barely persuaded not to sink them in the sea.'[67] Later, at Vespasian's funeral (Suet. *Vesp.* 19.2) a comedian in Vespasian's role made a morbid joke about how the frugal emperor might have responded to the expense involved, saying that they should save money and just 'throw me into the Tiber'.

Refuting charges that Christians are disloyal because they do not pay homage to emperors, Tertullian (*Apol.* 35.6–7, Loeb) makes an intriguing reference to the Tiber. He challenges the faithfulness of the Romans themselves, asking: 'does that Roman tongue spare any one of the Caesars? The Tiber shall be witness, and the training-schools of the beasts' ('Testis est Tiberis, et scholae bestiarum'). He continues on the fickleness of the mob in responding to any Caesar's largesse by shouting: 'Jupiter take our years to add to thine.' The reference to the Tiber and the schools of the beasts is perhaps a specific one to the reaction of the crowd to Tiberius' death, or possibly a mocking reference to the fate of sycophants who made vows for the health of Caligula and were then forced to fulfill those vows.[68] Given Tertullian's knowledge of spectacles and of Roman history, he may have been making a general reference to the punishment of traitors who speak ill of emperors.

Although it seems unlikely in most cases, disposal via drains and sewers – in addition to simply directly via the Tiber – is suggested by some ancient evidence, including Cicero's reference (*Sest.* 77, quoted above) to sewers 'stuffed' with bodies.[69] On his nocturnal rampages, Nero supposedly had a habit of beating men as they came home for dinner and 'stabbing any who resisted and throwing them into the sewers (*cloacisque demergere*)'.[70] As well as disposing of the body, Nero thus abused anyone who dared to defy him. The Cloaca Maxima of Rome had the capacity to handle bodies,[71] but lesser sewers feeding into it were smaller. Witness the story of Elagabalus' assassination:

> Next they [soldiers] fell upon Elagabalus himself and slew him in a latrine in which he had taken refuge. Then his body was dragged through the streets, and the soldiers further insulted it by thrusting it into a sewer. But since the sewer chanced to be too small to admit the corpse, they attached a weight to it to keep it from floating, and hurled it from the Aemilian Bridge into the Tiber, in order that it might never be buried. The body was also dragged around the Circus before it was thrown into the Tiber.[72]

For practical reasons, amphitheaters were commonly constructed with drains or channeled streams running under their main axes, and a great drain ran along the axis of the Colosseum with an outlet at the end of the gallery at the lowest level.[73] However, it seems unlikely that drains and sewers were extensively used for disposal of corpses from arenas. Heads of victims of proscriptions perhaps ended up in the sewers, but the bodies of *noxii* from spectacles were probably dragged by hooks, as of old, and thrown directly into the Tiber.

Possibly relevant to the question at hand, recent excavations at the Guildhall site in central London have found partial remains of a substantial amphitheater located about thirty meters from the southeast corner of Cripplegate Fort, a Roman fort established around AD 120. Expanding upon a timber phase built in 70/71, the 'masonry' rebuild of the amphitheater in around AD 125 included a masonry arena wall and a masonry entrance way flanked by two small side chambers, both with access onto the entrance and onto the arena. One chamber was perhaps a preparation area for gladiators and one was probably used to hold wild animals used in shows. The timber drainage system canalized a stream under the amphitheater and removed rainwater from the arena, emptying outside into the Walbrook stream and thence into the Thames. This system included a series of drains along the central axis and a series of associated perimeter gullies around the arena. Among other discoveries, excavators found the disarticulated bones of no more than twelve humans scattered spatially and chronologically in the drains and in related deposits. However, early suggestions that they represent the first discovery of amphitheater victims may have been premature, for the bones show no evidence of marks from weapons or animals. Since the average size of the drains was no more than 300 by 300 mm, they were not suitable for extensive arena disposal.[74] Whole bodies would have had to be removed and dumped elsewhere, but the Thames, like the Tiber at Rome, was an option.

Commodus the gladiator

Spectacles of death, damnation, and the Tiber overlap tellingly in the life and the death of Commodus, an emperor notorious for his irresponsibility and brutality.[75] Commodus' enthusiasm for spectacles of death seems to have been unrestrained. As noted above (in ch. 3), in private and in public, he killed animals, foreign and domestic, in large numbers, but without showing the proper virtues of a Roman hunter, by going out in the countryside to hunt in the Hellenistic mode, or the virtues of a *bestiarius*, by endangering himself in the arena. Commodus also seems to have been egotistical and sadistic in ordering executions,[76] but, thanks to admittedly hostile sources, he is most infamous as a 'gladiator'.

Said to have had his own room at the gladiatorial school, Commodus claimed to have fought 735 or even 1,000 fights,[77] but he was perverse even as a gladiator. Attended by the praetorian prefect, he fought left-handed as a *secutor* with blunted weapons.[78] He did not face true gladiators with deadly weapons, and even when slaughtering cripples he only allowed them to throw sponges.[79] Also, he demanded a million sesterces from the public fund for each show, making his entertainment a fiscal injury; and he had his inflated claims and titles inscribed in the public records. Rather than awaiting their response to his performances, he forced senators to applaud and to hail him as lord and victor. He once threatened them by holding up a severed ostrich head, and some, including Dio, avoided laughing – and death – by chewing laurel leaves. Many of the populace stayed away out of shame or in fear of the report that Commodus, playing Hercules hunting the Stymphalian birds, might shoot spectators.[80]

As a free man and an emperor, Commodus crossed the boundary between the empowered spectators and the powerless performers.[81] He threatened spectators and forced viewers into the arena,[82] and he even entered the arena personally and polluted himself by acting as a gladiator. Moreover, in the arena he was an embarrassment to the elite and a threatening tyrant to the masses.[83] Before his planned appearance in public to assume the consulship of AD 193, at which time he had intended to affront the dignity of the office by wearing gladiatorial armor, he was strangled by an athlete. He died the death of a *noxius*, not by accepting the coup de grâce like a true gladiator.[84]

The *Historia Augusta* (SHA *Comm.* 18.3–20.5, Loeb) gives at length (supposedly from Marius Maximus) what are said to be the acclamations of the senate upon Commodus' death and the judgement of the senate's decree (*sententiam senatus consulti*) demanding post-mortem abuse and *damnatio memoriae* for Commodus, as well as instructions from the pontifical college. Commodus had gloated in his power and mocked the senate, and the senators now wanted to mock him and abuse his defenseless body as he had abused the 'body' of the senate and the state. They declared (SHA *Comm.* 18.3–6, Loeb):

> The foe of his fatherland, the murderer, the gladiator, in the charnel-house let him be mangled (*hostis patriae, parricida, gladiator in spoliario lanietur*). He is foe to the gods, slayer of the senate . . . Cast the gladiator into the charnel-house. He who slew the senate, let him be dragged with the hook (*unco trahatur*); he who slew the guiltless, let him be dragged with the hook . . . He who spared not his own blood, let him be dragged with the hook.

The main repeated charges are: 'gladiator', murderer, enemy of the state and its gods, slayer of the senate and of guiltless citizens.[85] For such crimes, (19.1) 'Let the memory of the murderer and the gladiator be utterly wiped away. Let the statues of the murderer and the gladiator be overthrown. Let the memory of the foul gladiator (*impuri gladiatoris*) be utterly wiped away.' The senate also wanted Commodus' informers punished in spectacular fashion by lions and 'the club', again 'that we may be safe'.[86]

The acclamations continue (19.5–6): 'He who plundered temples, let him be dragged with the hook. He who set aside the testaments of the dead, let him be dragged with the hook . . . He who demanded a price for a life and kept not his promise, let him be dragged with the hook.' The senate repeatedly ordered post-mortem punishment for Commodus: 'let the body of the gladiator be dragged (*trahatur*) with the hook', 'mangled (*lanietur*) in the *spoliarium*', 'cast into the *spoliarium*'. Again with repetitions, as in a formal curse (19.2–3): 'In the manner of our fathers (*more maiorum*) let the slayer of the senate be dragged with the hook. More savage than Domitian, more foul than Nero. As he did unto others, let it be done unto him . . . let the body of the gladiator be cast into the charnel-house.' The text repeatedly mentions hooking, dragging and the *spoliarium*. The Tiber is understood, for it is mentioned earlier (17.4): 'The people and the senate demanded that his body be dragged with the hook and cast into the Tiber (*in Tiberim mitteretur*).' Once again, the Tiber was seen as the appropriate way to dispose of threats and contaminations.

The senate's rage went further: (19.9) 'The guiltless are yet unburied [i.e. because Commodus had denied burial]; let the body of the murderer be dragged in the dust. The murderer dug up the buried; let the body of the murderer be dragged in the dust.' Upon hearing that Commodus' body had been buried during the night, the senate cried out (20.2–5): 'With whose authority have they buried him? The buried murderer, let him be dug up, let him be dragged in the dust.' Cincius Severus said: 'Wrongfully has he been buried (*iniuste sepultus est*). And I speak as pontifex . . . the statues should be overthrown . . . they should be cast down. His name, moreover, should be erased from all public and private records.'[87] The *pontifex* and his college ordered the overthrow of Commodus' statues and the erasure of his name. The senate formally said that the 'gladiator' should have been dragged and cast out unburied into the Tiber, and thus excommunicated and damned.

Claiming autopsy (73(72).18.3, 21.2), Dio's account (74(73).2.2–4, Loeb) is briefer but similar:

> In this way was Pertinax declared emperor and Commodus a public enemy, after both the senate and the populace had joined in shouting many bitter words against the latter. They wanted to drag off his body and tear it limb from limb, as they did do, in fact, with his statues; but when Pertinax informed them that the corpse had already been interred, they spared his remains, but glutted their rage against him in other ways, calling him all sorts of names. For no one called him Commodus or emperor; instead they referred to him as an accursed wretch and a tyrant, adding in jest such terms as 'the gladiator', 'the charioteer', 'the left-handed', 'the ruptured'. To those senators on whom the fear of Commodus had rested most heavily, the crowd called out: 'Huzza! Huzza! You are saved; you

226

have won.' Indeed, all the shouts that they had been accustomed
to utter with a kind of rhythmic swing in the amphitheaters, by
way of playing court to Commodus, they now chanted with certain
changes that made them utterly ridiculous.

Dio clearly attributes the same tone and imagery to the reactions of the
senate.

The sources agree that the memory of the criminal, the murderer, and the
gladiator was to be utterly wiped away.[88] Denying him burial and abusing
his corpse with the hook was anticipated as 'joyful' to the senate, and the
pontifical college urged *damnatio memoriae* as 'needful'.[89] The senators' desire
for dramatically appropriate retributive vengeance is obvious: 'As he did unto
others, let it be done to him (*sic fecit, sic patiatur*).' The repeated justification
is security – 'that we may be safe'. For heinous crimes the threatening enemy
was to be punished, insulted, and cast out into the Tiber – damned to the
forlorn disquietude of a watery (non-)grave.

The senate's formal condemnation used traditional insults and called for
ancient procedures. Familiar motifs include: gladiator, parricide, *spoliarium*,
execution, dragging, hook, Tiber, denial of burial, *damnatio memoriae*.
Reviling Commodus as a 'gladiator', the senate's archaizing language refers
to the early, unelevated condition of gladiators.[90] A false and a failed 'gladiator' who had earned no elevation or redemption, Commodus deserved hooks,
abuse in the *spoliarium*, and denial of burial.[91] Note that Dio (74(73).2.3–4)
adds that Commodus' downfall was mocked with chanting similar to that
which he had demanded in the amphitheater. All this suggests the context
of spectacular punishments. The overlap of the vocabulary of the arena and
damnatio memoriae by the senate, the bastion of traditionalism, was not merely
rhetorical.[92] Like 'To the Tiber with Tiberius', the account shows that the
elite, masses, and historians knew the procedures. Abuse and denial were
public knowledge.

For centuries refuse and bodies, notably of those perceived to be conta-
minating or threatening the state, were dumped in the Tiber. Traditional
and convenient, this added the insult of denial of burial; the water removed
the pollution, and it offered purification against hostile spirits. Disposal via
the Tiber was a rejection of disruptive elements, a restoration of order, and
a lustration.[93] Topography, convenience, and legal/ritual continuity suggest
that the Tiber performed similar functions for the disposal of similarly miasmatic refuse from the games as damnation to the arena, over time, largely
replaced normal means of execution. Condemned *noxii*, pariahs and foes,
were killed in a public place as a spectacle, the dead were displayed and
denied burial, and disposal probably followed traditional lines. Completing
a ritual process, the Tiber bore arena corpses of *noxii* away from Rome and
prevented spiritual pollution and haunting by the souls of the untimely
dead, for whose violent deaths the Roman community was collectively

responsible. Further confirmation of the use of water to dispose of – and sometimes also to kill – victims comes from the writings and experiences of Christians.

NOTES

1 On the Tiber and the hydrography of Rome, see Joël Le Gall, *Le Tibre, fleuve de Rome dans l'antiquité* (Paris: Presses Universitaires de France, 1952; Le Gall (1953); L. A. Holland, *Janus and the Bridge* (Rome: American Academy in Rome, 1961); Caesare D'Onofrio, *Il Tevere* (Rome: Romana Società Editrice, 1980); Margaret Angela Brucia, 'The Tiber Island in Ancient and Medieval Rome', Ph.D. diss., Fordham U., 1990. As Barber (1988) shows, the disposal of the 'dangerous dead' (55) by throwing them into rivers and bodies of water (sometimes after burning, staking, etc.) was common in Russia and Slavic areas (30, 36, 44, 74); in folklore disembodied spirits cannot cross water, which has apotropaic powers (150, 181).

2 See Le Gall (1953) 57–82 on sacred water and its powers, esp. 74–7 on sanitary, ritual, and moral purification; and Holland (1961) 308 on the magic of living water. Cf. Parker (1983) 226–7; and Frazer (1957) 621–2, 711, on water as a common agent of purification. Hammurabi's Code prescribed testing those accused of sorcery by throwing them into a river: survival proved innocence, drowning proved guilt; see James B. Pritchard, ed., *The Ancient Near East: An Anthology of Texts and Pictures* (Princeton: Princeton U., 1958) 139, section 2.

3 After a normal Roman funeral the family returned home to perform a rite of purification via fire and water; see Toynbee (1971) 50. On the Roman belief in the Tiber's curative or purifying qualities (e.g. Hor. *Sat.* 2.3.290–2; Pers. 2.15–16; Juv. 6.522–6), see Brucia (1990) 25–7. On Tiberinus, the personification of the river, as a healer god, see Le Gall (1953) 68–74, 102.

4 Tales of unwanted babies cast out of communities onto hillsides for beasts or in baskets into rivers reveal an ancient custom of rejecting such beings but not directly killing them. Offspring of a Vestal, for example, were an abomination needing ritualized ablution. When Romulus and Remus were born to the ravished Vestal, her story about Mars as the father was discounted and Amulius ordered the children to be cast into the flowing river (*in profluentem aquam*: Livy 1.4.3). Livy, 36.37.2, says that in 191 BC when two domesticated cattle climbed up the stairway to the roof of a house, the haruspices ordered that they be burned alive and their ashes thrown into the Tiber.

5 Barber (1988), 170–1, explains that disposal by water, especially running water, affords quick removal with a minimum of handling. The most famous example is the placing of corpses in the Ganges River in India, providing both disposal and purification; see Barber, 77. Bodies do become buoyant with decomposition after a few days (Barber, 141–3, 147–51), hence the benefit of a powerful river headed to the sea.

6 Brucia (1990), 24–5, explains that the Tiber and the Tiber Island were not within Rome's walls until Aurelian's third-century AD walls, although Augustus did include them in his organization of Region Fourteen.

7 As Van Hooff (1990), 73, 75–6, 115, 151, demonstrates, committing suicide by jumping into water was presented as a desperate act of accepting a disgraceful end. E.g. Juvenal, 6.28–32, mocks a man for not avoiding his marriage by committing suicide by hanging himself, jumping from a window, or jumping from the Aemilian Bridge. To discredit Nero, Suetonius, *Ner.* 47.3, says that the emperor even considered jumping into the Tiber as one way of killing

himself. Cf. *CIL* 13.7070: a master's epitaph rejoices that the slave who murdered him ultimately committed suicide by jumping into the River Main.

8 Scobie (1988), 196, notes that the earliest combats in the Forum Boarium were near the Tiber: 'Spilt blood could ... be easily flushed into the Tiber from this site where presumably at least some cattle were slaughtered as well as sold.' Many arenas (e.g. the Forum, Colosseum, Circus Maximus; cf. the amphitheaters of C. Scribonius Curio and Statilius Taurus, the Saepta, the Circus Flaminius, and the naumachies of Caesar and Augustus, all in the Campus Martius) were near the Tiber, but then, of course, so was everything in early and downtown Rome. On the tie of the Circus Maximus to water and Consus, see Humphrey (1986) 61–2, 84–5, 94, 101, 127.

9 On the efficiency of sea over land transportation, e.g. see Finley (1973) 126–7.

10 L. A. and L. B. Holland, 'Down the Tiber on a Raft', *Archaeology* 3.2 (1950) 87–94, confirmed that the modern Tiber's current, though now slowed by time and accumulations in its bed, remains strong, even in summer. Pliny, *HN* 3.53–6, comments on the Tiber's many tributaries and its frequent floods at Rome (cf. 36.105; Hor. *Carm.* 3.29). Augustus established the *curatores alvei Tiberis* to attend to the Tiber's bed and flooding. Cf. Livy's remark, 2.5.3, that the Tiber usually flowed with a weak current in the summer, a remark made to add plausibility to the aetiological legend of the formation of the Tiber Island (see below).

11 On the metaphorical use of sewers as excretory parts of the 'body' of Rome, see Emily Gowers, 'The Anatomy of Rome from Capitol to Cloaca', *JRS* 85 (1995) 23–32. Hughes (1994), 162–3, notes that the Romans dumped 'every imaginable form of refuse' into the Tiber, that they did not drink from it, and that swimming in it must have been done upstream near the Campus Martius. On sewers and bodies, see below.

12 Livy 2.5.2–4; Dion. Hal. 5.13.1–4; Plut. *Publicola* 8.1–3. Brucia (1990), 6–17, feels that this tradition probably developed from an early taboo placed on the island because of its location in living water and its association with primitive Italian chthonic deities.

13 Plut. *Sull.* 35.1, Loeb: 'On consecrating the tenth of all his substance to Hercules, Sulla feasted the people sumptuously, and his provision for them was so much beyond what was needed that great quantities of meats (*opsa*) were daily cast into the river.' Unlike meat from *venationes*, the consecrated meat, an excessive quantity because even one-tenth of Sulla's wealth, bloated by civil war, was a great sum, became sacred to Hercules and had to be disposed of if unconsumed.

14 Daniel P. Harmon, 'The Public Festivals of Rome', *ANRW* 2.16.2 (1978) 1446–59 of 1440–68; quote at 1455. Plut. *Quaest. Rom.* 86: 'The Tiber carries away the source of defilement.' Frazer (1957), 647–8, sees the rite as a purification of demons; he also notes, 404–9, a modern Slavonic ritual in which effigies and puppets are thrown into waters during Lent to aid fertility and the return of spring and to prevent infection.

15 Holland (1961) 313–31. Cf. Le Gall (1953) on the Argei, 83–7, on similar rites, 78–82, 111, and on the Tiber as a means of disposal.

16 Blaise Nagy, 'The Argei Puzzle', *AJAH* 10.1 (1985) 1–27. Nagy discusses both theories (5–7) and sources (2–4; e.g. Dion. Hal. *Ant. Rom.* 1.38; Ov. *Fast.* 3.791–2 on the procession *ad Argeos*, 5.603ff. on rites, 5.621ff. on effigies; Varro *Ling.* 5.45ff.).

17 Ancient aetiologies also saw the effigies as substitutes for actual early sacrifices of Greeks or others disposed of in the Tiber; see Nagy (1985) 4–5. One famous ancient explanation is that Rome threw elderly victims, 60 and over, into the Tiber to save resources during famines (cf. Festus p. 452L; Ov. *Fast.* 5.633–4

and 623–4; Cic. *Rosc. Am.* 100; Livy 4.12.10–11 gives a version in which people facing starvation threw themselves in to commit suicide in 440–439 BC). See J. P. Néraudau, 'Sexagenarii de ponte', *Rev. Ét. Lat.* 56 (1978) 159–74; Van Hooff (1990) 168; or Wieslaw Suder, 'La Mort des vieillards', 31–45, esp. 36–8, in Hinard (1995). Balsdon (1969), 169, n. 2 on 392–3, favors the reasonable suggestion that the bridge was a bridge crossed by voters, and thus that the proverb meant that men over 60 should not vote. On Lactantius' charges (*Div. inst.* 1.21.6–9) that Maximian threw some elderly men into the Tiber, see O. Nicholson, 'Hercules at the Milvian Bridge', *Latomus* 43 (1984) 133–42.

18 Richardson (1992), 39, notes that the locations of the shrines, while obscure, were decidedly removed from temples, thus indicating that the spirits involved were dangerous: 'That the priests threw the dolls in the Tiber from the Pons Sublicius, therefore into the river at its greatest strength, suggests this was a rite of lustration.'

19 Debate on the crime of parricide and its punishment is extensive and continuing. See, e.g., J. D. Cloud, 'Parricidium, from the Lex Numiae to the Lex Pompeia de Parricidiis', *ZRG* 88 (1971) 1–66; M. Radin, 'The Lex Pompeia and the Poena Cullei', *JRS* 10 (1920) 119–30; D. Briquel, 'Sur le mode d'exécution en cas de parricide et en cas de *perduellio*', *MÉFRA* 92 (1980) 87–107; Y. P. Thomas, 'Parricidium, I, Le Père, la famille et la cité', *MÉFRA* 93 (1981) 643–715; A. Magdelain, '*Paricidas*', 549–71, in *Châtiment* (1984); Gruen (1968) 61–2; Cantarella (1991) 264–85; Robinson (1995) 13, 45–6, 67; and Bauman (1996) 30–2, 70–4, 128–9. The early Roman horror of parricide is evident in the story of Tullia's abuse of the corpse of her father Servius; see ch. 4 above. In early Rome parricide meant the intentional murder of a free man: XII Tables 9.4 (the so-called Lex Numae) ap. Festus p. 247L; see Cloud (1971) 3–12.

20 Discounting suggestions that Tarquin the Proud used the sack (Val. Max. 1.1.13; Dion. Hal. *Ant. Rom.* 4.62.4), Cloud (1971), 26–38, uses references in Roman comedy to date the institution of the sack before 191. Seeing an appropriate context in the religious hysteria in the wake of disasters in the Second Punic War, he suggests that sometime before 191 Lucius Hostius was the first person to suffer the sack for kin murder. First explicit use in the case of Publicius Malleolus around 101 for matricide: Livy *Per.* 68; Oros. 5.16.23; see Lintott (1968) 37–9, 41. Cicero's *Pro Sexto Roscio Amerino* relates how in 81 BC relatives of Sextus Roscius murdered the old man and threw him into the Tiber, and how they tried to seize the estate and protect themselves by accusing Sextus' son of parricide. Defending the son, Cicero (*Rosc. Am.* 30, 70–2; cf. *Orat.* 107) discusses the atrocity of parricide and the tradition and justification of execution by the sack and disposal by water, speaking as if the penalty was still in use. In the 50s Cicero (*Q Fr.* 1.2.5–7) was shocked when his brother in Asia sewed two Mysians in a sack for parricide and sought a third for the same punishment. As Lintott (1968), 37, explains, Cicero's concern was his brother's severity, not the plight of the victims. Cloud (1971), 47–66, suggests that Pompey's law on parricide, the Lex Pompeia de Parricidiis (*Dig.* 48.9.1), probably of 55 or 52 BC, defined parricide in terms of the murder of parents or close relatives, assimilated it with other forms of homicide, and suspended the sack and replaced it with *interdictio*; but see Bauman's cautions, (1996) 30–2, about whether Pompey changed the nature of the penalty.

21 Julius Caesar punished parricides with confiscation of their property (Suet. *Iul.* 42.3); Augustus tried to spare a man who had killed his father from the sack, which was only for those who confessed their guilt (Suet. *Aug.* 33.1). Claudius is said to have used and watched this form of execution; see Levick (1990) 117, 124, and Bauman (1996) 70–3, on Sen. *Clem.* 1.23.1 (claiming that Claudius

used the sack more times in five years than it had ever been used before) and Suet. *Claud.* 34.1. Dio, 61.16.1, says that people at night at Rome hung a leather bag over a statue of Nero to suggest that he should be punished for matricide; and Juvenal, 8.213–14, Loeb, suggests that the people of Rome would have given Nero more than one sack, not only for his parricides but also for a host of crimes, not the least of which was his performing on stage: 'Nero, for whose chastisement no single ape or adder, no solitary sack, should have been provided'. Suetonius, *Vit.* 6, records a general belief that Vitellius murdered his son then charged him with attempted parricide. Cf. below on SHA *Comm.* 18.10 (on *delatores*).

22 Hadrian: *Dig.* 48.9.9 pr. Cloud (1971) 50–1, citing literary references (e.g. Apul. *Met.* 10.8; Tert. *De anim.* 33.6; Lactant. *Div. inst.* 5.9.16), accepts that the sack was in use for murderers of parents and grandparents in the third century AD, and rejects the comment in Paulus *Sent.* 5.24 that seems to suggest that the sack was then obsolete. Robinson (1995), 47, accepts a suspension and return of the sack, seeing the return and the enclosure of the animals as inventions of the Christian Empire; cf. *CTh* 9.15.1 and references in her n. 80 on 128; but cf. Juvenal's reference to animals in the previous note. On Constantine's expansion of the punishment in 318/19 to all forms of parricide, see Cloud (1971) 56–8.

23 Radin (1920), 130, explains that in the sack penalty the prodigy's evil forces were to be neutralized by transferring them to certain animals, which were immediately killed. Cloud (1971), 31, agrees that this was a *procuratio prodigii* invented to remove the pollution of an unnatural crime against the community. Cloud, 35, and Wiedemann (1989), 38, note examples of disposal of hermaphrodites by dumping them in bodies of water, e.g. Livy 27.37.5–7 (at sea, ordered by the senate on the advice of Etruscan soothsayers), 31.12.8 (a 16-year-old boy). *Inst. Iust.* 4.18.6 specifies that the parricide is to be sewn in a sack with a dog, a cock, a snake, and a monkey, and that the sack is to be thrown in a nearby sea or river so that the dead victim be denied the 'light of heaven and the earth'. On the snake added to the sack as an infernal symbol, see Callu (1984) 355–6.

24 Livy, 1.33.8, says that Ancus Marcius built the Carcer in the center of town, just above the Forum, to stem the increase in crime with the growing population of Rome. It was still in use in the fourth century AD: Amm. Marc. 28.1.57. Christopher Hibbert, *Rome: The Biography of a City* (Harmondsworth: Penguin, 1985) n. 28 on 321, adds that 'Mamertine' was the medieval name for this ancient state prison, which was later converted into the chapel of S. Pietro in Carcere under the church of S. Giuseppi dei Falegnami. The Carcer in the Forum is not to be confused with a later military prison at Rome: *CIL* 6.531 (= *ILS* 3739) from the third century AD mentions a prison adjutant (*optio karc(eris)*) of an urban cohort.

25 See ch. 2 above. Cicero, *Verr.* 2.5.77, Loeb, mentions the execution procedure, saying that triumphing generals keep enemy leaders alive to lead them in the procession to let the people of Rome enjoy the spectacle (*spectaculum*): 'even they, as their chariots swing round to leave the Forum for the Capitol, bid their captives be led off to prison, and the day that ends the authority of the conqueror also ends the lives of the conquered'. Josephus, *BJ* 7.153–5, Loeb, records that in Titus' triumph after the fall of Jerusalem the procession ended at the Temple of Jupiter Capitolinus: 'for it was a time-honoured custom to wait there until the execution of the enemy's general was announced'. Simon son of Gioras, among the prisoners in the procession, was flogged and dragged by a noose 'to the spot abutting on the Forum, where Roman law requires that

malefactors condemned to death should be executed'. The news of his execution was met with universal acclamation and various banquets and celebrations followed.

26 E.g. Plut. *Mar.* 12.3–4, Loeb: after being exhibited in chains in Marius' triumph, Jugurtha went insane; he was thrown into the prison, where some persons tore off his tunic and others tore off his gold ear-ring with the lobe attached. He was 'thrown down naked into the dungeon pit' and after six days of hunger he 'paid the penalty which his crimes deserved'. Tiberius, concerning the Pannonian leader Bato in AD 12, broke the tradition of having enemy leaders strangled: Suet. *Tib.* 20.

27 Richardson (1992) 71, and figs. 19 (the Capitoline area) and 20 (a plan of the Carcer).

28 Sall. *Cat.* 55.3–4, Loeb. On the *tresviri capitales*, see ch. 2 above. Here, Sallust says (66.6), Lentulus was lowered down and strangled, ending his life 'in a manner befitting his character and his crimes'. Cf. the description of the foul conditions in the small underground dungeon at Alba Fucens, 'no larger than a nine-couch room', wherein criminals condemned on capital charges were held and into which Perseus of Macedon was thrown: Diod. Sic. 31.9.1–3, Loeb.

29 David (1984), 139–60, sees condemnation to the flooded chamber beneath the prison, like casting off the Tarpeian, as an abandonment to the gods. The symbolism included recurring motifs – darkness, wetness, and secret, sinister death in the shadows. David sees imprisonment in the Carcer as ambiguous for citizens: death was possible but not certain. Prisoners were executed unless an appeal (by the citizen's right of *provocatio*) led to popular intervention by the people's collective power of refusal. Non-intervention equaled the silent approval by the community of the deaths of public enemies.

30 See references, e.g. Tac. *Ann.* 6.3.5, 6.19.2, in Levick (1976) n. 58 on 284.

31 Ulpian, *Dig.* 48.19.8.9, sees imprisonment as a coercive detention rather than an official penalty; see Garnsey (1970) 145–50.

32 Richardson (1992) 71; cf. Varro *Ling.* 5.151; Festus 490L.

33 On this and other punishments and executions, see Hinard (1987b); and David (1984).

34 Richardson (1992) 345, with abundant testimonia. Platner and Ashby (1929) s.v.: 'a flight of steps leading up to the Capitoline past the Carcer, on which the bodies of certain criminals, who had been executed, were thrown and left exposed for a time – a frequent practice during the empire'. Tiberius exiled Agrippina the Elder to Pandataria Island, where she starved herself to death; Tiberius attacked her memory, getting the senate to add her birthday to the days of ill omen, and 'actually taking credit to himself for not having had her strangled and her body cast out on the Stairs of Mourning': Suet. *Tib.* 53.2, Loeb. See the metaphor in Tert. *Adv. Valent.* 36.1.

35 First mention: Val. Max. 6.3.3, 6.9.13. Richardson (1992), 182, 345, feels that it is probable that the stairs followed the course of the modern stairs leading down from the top of Via S. Pietro in Carcere, just northeast of the Temple of Concord, but cf. David (1984) 133.

36 See ch. 1 above on Lintott on justifiable violence in defense of the social order, and on cruelty, expediency, and hierarchical sympathy.

37 See Hinard (1987b) 119–21; and Le Gall (1953) 88–92 for examples and interpretations. Le Gall emphasizes the chthonic character of the Tiber; on the amphitheater as the threshold to the underworld, see Coleman (1990) 67.

38 David (1984) 167–74. Levick (1976), n. 51 on 283, feels that exposure on the Gemoniae was not invented by Tiberius (see below). Livy, 38.59.10, Loeb, on the trial of Lucius Scipio in 187 BC, says that Scipio Nasica claimed that

232

Lucius' foes, unable to seize his property, attacked his body and his honor. They prosecuted and insulted him: 'so that this most distinguished man might be shut up in prison (*in carcere*) among thieves of the night and brigands and may die in the darkness of a cell and then be cast out naked before the prison'. Cf. Ov. *Ib.* 163–5 mentioning execution, dragging, and hooks. David (1984), n. 188 on 172, however, rejects Livy's account as anachronistic.

39 David (984) feels that use of Tiber was ancient practice, attested for 206 (Polyb. 11.30), but that use of the stairs developed with the transition from Republic to Empire and invited more ritualized popular response, terror, and joy as a ritual of separation and rejection. Cf. Hinard (1987b), 118–19, 125, who suggests an unlikely shift of disposal to the Esquiline; cf. ch. 5 above. The greatest change, however, was the shift to spectacular arena executions.

40 *Vit.* 17.1–2, Loeb. Similarly, Tac. *Hist.* 3.84–5 (noted above in n. 2 of ch. 1 above); Dio 64(65).20.2–21.2. Tac. *Hist.* 3.85, Loeb: 'Finally, the soldiers drove him to the Gemonian stairs where the body of Flavius Sabinus had recently been lying . . . Then he fell under a shower of blows; and the people attacked his body after he was dead with the same base spirit with which they had fawned on him while he lived.' Cf. Juvenal on Sejanus below. Caroline A. Perkins, 'Vitellius the *Spectaculum*: A Note on *Histories* 3.84.5', *CB* 66.1–2 (1990) 47–9, suggests that Tacitus called Vitellius, deserted by the masses, a *foedum spectaculum* (84.5) as an ironic reference to his earlier sponsorship of spectacles. Galba was executed in the Forum and his corpse was similarly treated: Tac. *Hist.* 1.49; cf. other examples below. Nippel (1995), 44–6, sees such abuse of fallen emperors' statues and corpses as 'ritual punishments', with appropriate participation by crowds, which combined popular justice with official condemnation.

41 Hooks associated with jail and execution: Sen. *Ep.* 14.5. Germanicus' eldest sons, Nero and Drusus, declared public enemies by the senate on Tiberius' accusation, knew the custom. On the criminal island of Pontia, Nero was forced to suicide when an executioner, saying that he was sent by the senate, showed a noose for hanging and hooks for dragging his corpse to the Tiber: Suet. *Tib.* 54.2. Drusus was starved to death in a cellar of the palace, and both their bodies were chopped into so many pieces that Caligula later had difficulty in collecting them for burial (Suet. *Calig.* 15).

42 David (1984), 173–4, with abundant testimonia, explains that the verbal and physical abuse, which amounted to posthumous lynchings, helped legitimize executions: 'Le cadavre devenait un objet de spectacle.'

43 Testimonia on the Gracchi include: Plut. *Ti. Gracch.* 19.6–20.4, *C. Gracch.* 3, 13–17; App. *B Civ.* 1.16, 26; Vell. Pat. 2.6. Since Tiberius was not tried (except afterward in 132) or declared an enemy of the state, it was improper to execute him at all, let alone in the insulting manner of a non-citizen. Gruen (1968), 61–2, feels that most of the men killed were not Romans of status and that the numbers were exaggerated. On the supposed punishment of a certain Villius by being shut up in a vessel with snakes, Gruen suggests that Plutarch inadvertently included the execution of a parricide in his account of the political purge.

44 Plut. *G. Gracch.* 17.5; Vell. Pat. 2.6. Plutarch, *G. Gracch.* 18.1, says that Opimius was the first consul who arrogated to himself the powers of a dictator, and that he condemned to death without trial 3,000 Roman citizens. Foreshadowing Gaius' fate as he departs for the Forum, his wife Licinia fears that he will die like Tiberius, not gloriously in battle but via injustice at Rome: Plut. *G. Gracch.* 15.3, Loeb: 'If thy brother had only fallen at Numantia, his dead body would have been given back to us by terms of truce, but, as it is,

perhaps I too shall have to supplicate some river or sea to reveal to me at last thy body in its keeping.'

45 Plut. *G. Gracch.* 17.3–4; App. *B Civ.* 1.26. On heads, see below. People plundered their houses, conspirators were strangled, and Flaccus' son got to choose his own mode of death.

46 In contrast, Plutarch, *G. Gracch.*14.2–3, points out that Opimius and the senators made a great show of the body of Antyllius, murdered by supporters of Gaius, by carrying it on a bier through the Forum. Nippel (1995), 63–4, discusses the senate's imposition of posthumous sanctions in 121 against G. Gracchus (and his companions) and later in 100 against Saturninus, sanctions which included razing the houses of the seditious' leaders. Nippel, 64, explains: 'All these measures were intended to destroy the continuity of the culprits' family traditions by obliterating the places where their family gods and the portraits of their ancestors were kept, and preventing their relatives from fulfilling their religious duties towards them and displaying their familial traditions in funeral processions.'

47 See Levick (1976) n. 51 on 282–3; Berger (1953) s.v. *damnatio memoriae*: a disgrace inflicted on the memory of someone condemned to death and executed or already dead before the criminal prosecution was finished; *ignominia post mortem* for crimes against the state. Censures could include denial of mourning, erasure of one's name, and the holding of one's birthday accursed. In 30 BC Octavian was given honors for Actium and it was also voted to remove or destroy monuments commemorating Antony; even before news of Antony's death arrived, his birthday was declared accursed and his relatives were forbidden to use the name Marcus: Dio 51.19.3. Some emperors were officially damned (see n. 89 below on Domitian and Elagabalus), others unofficially. Dio, 50.4–56, notes that the senate wished to dishonor Caligula, but Claudius prevented an official decree; instead on his own he had images of Caligula removed at night. Although there was no official decree, the names of Caligula and Tiberius were not mentioned in the list of emperors recited in oaths or prayers.

48 *B Civ.* 1.88, trans. Carter, op. cit. in ch. 4, n. 37. Cf. Livy, *Per.* 86; plus other testimonia in Heaton (1939) 42–3; Hinard (1987b) 120 and (1984) 301; cf. ch. 4 above on denial of burial.

49 On the location, see Richardson (1992) 83; Hinard (1987b) 116. Plut. *Sull.* 30.2–3, Loeb: Sulla had the 6,000 collected in the Circus and ordered the senate to meet in the Temple of Bellona nearby in the Campus Martius; when the senators heard the shrieks of the captives being slaughtered, Sulla calmly told them not to be concerned, 'for it was only that some criminals were being admonished, by his orders'. Strabo, 5.4.11, says that Sulla had ordered that no prisoners should be taken, but some Samnites threw away their arms and some 3,000 or 4,000 were confined to the Villa Publica on the Campus Martius; three days later Sulla, showing a complete lack of respect for surrenderers, sent his soldiers in, slaughtered them all, and then began the proscriptions. Cf. Appian, *B Civ.* 1.93, who says that over 8,000 were killed, mostly Samnites.

50 Cic. *Leg.* 2.22.56–7. Pliny, *HN* 7.187, notes that Romans adopted cremation when they learned that bodies of men killed in distant wars were being disinterred; and he adds that Sulla, the first of the Cornelii to be cremated, asked to be cremated out of fear of reprisals for having dug up Marius' corpse. Lepidus and others wanted to deprive Sulla's body of funeral honors, but Pompey arranged proper cremation: Plut. *Sull.* 38.

51 The forces of Cinna and Marius had entered Rome in 87 BC and killed and decapitated the consul Octavius. According to Appian, *B Civ.* 1.71, his was the first head of a consul to be displayed in front of the Rostra in the Forum, but many

heads of senators followed. On Sulla's proscriptions: Cic. *Rosc. Am.* 89; Sen. *Prov.* 3.7.8; see further in Hinard (1985) 45–9 and (1984) passim. Sulla, Marius, and Cinna were notorious for this practice: e.g. Plut. *Sull.* 32.2, *Mar.* 44.3,6; Val. Max. 8.9.2. Lacus: Platner and Ashby (1929) 314; Nash (1961–2) 2:18–20; Richardson (1992) 232. For a detailed treatment, see J.-L. Voisin, 'Les Romains, chasseurs des têtes', in *Châtiment* (1984) 241–93. Voisin, 262–4, shows that Romans hunted heads (i.e. not simply decapitating bodies but transporting and displaying heads) from the early Republic to the late Empire. He suggests both change and continuity over time: a development from the decapitation of foreign foes by elite Romans to the decapitation of Roman citizens by lowly, obscure persons seeking a reward – a practice which spread (after its introduction in 121 BC) to head-hunting by cruel emperors, but one which kept a continuous emphasis on the heads of adult males of status.

52 Antony delighted in the death of Cicero: he had his hand and head cut off to add further humiliation: Plut. *Ant.* 20.2; Plut. *Cic.* 48.4–49.2; and he kept his head: App. *B Civ.* 4.20. Appian, *B Civ.* 3.26, trans. Carter, notes that Caesarian troops under Dolabella in 43 BC killed and decapitated Trebonius, and then threw his head 'like a ball from one to another across the town paving, laughing, until it was smashed to pieces. This was how Trebonius, the first of the murderers, was punished.'

53 Numerous examples of the claiming or display of the heads of political foes are collected by Voisin (1984). E.g. after the assassination of Caesar, a mob paraded the streets with the head of Helvius Cinna, mistaken for Cornelius Cinna, stuck on a spear: Suet. *Iul.* 85. After Philippi, Octavian sent Brutus' head to Rome to be thrown at the feet of Caesar's statue: Suet. *Aug.* 13.1. Under Tigellinus' influence, Nero at Rome mocked the heads of two dead men, one killed in Asia and one at Massilia: Tac. *Ann.* 14.57.4, 59.3. Dio, 60.16.1, Loeb, comments on the fate of suspected conspirators in Claudius' purge after the failure of the conspiracy of Scribonianus in AD 42: 'And when they were to die, the women, too, were led [from prison] in chains upon a scaffold, like captives, and their bodies, also, were thrown out upon the Stairway; for in the case of those who were executed anywhere outside the city, only the heads were exhibited there.'

54 Nero (Suet. *Ner.* 49.4) and Otho (Tac. *Hist.* 2.49) feared and Galba received such abuse. E.g. Plut. *Galb.* 28.2–3, Loeb: as the senate acclaimed Otho in AD 69,

> dead bodies, all in their consular robes, were strewn over the forum. And as for the heads, when they had no further use for them, that of Vinius was sold to his daughter . . . that of Piso was given to his wife Verania in answer to her prayers, and that of Galba was bestowed upon the servants of Patrobius. They took it, and after heaping all manner of insult and outrage upon it, cast it into a place called Sessorium, where those under condemnations of the emperors are put to death.

Suetonius, *Galb.* 20.2, remarks that after Galba was killed near the Lacus Curtius (a monument in the Forum with chthonic associations: see map 2 and Richardson (1992) 229–30), a common soldier cut off Galba's head, put it on a lance, and mocked it, but that eventually it was buried with the rest of the corpse.

55 Voisin (1984), 274, sees sacral overtones to head-hunting as a form of denial of burial: 'le décapité est ainsi privé de tout repos dans l'au-delà'.

56 Cic. *Sest.* 77; see Gowers (1995) 28, and Gowers (1993) 14–16, on this and

other metaphorical uses of the sewer as a 'waste-disposal unit' for political dumping. Further on sewers, see below.

57 Cic. *Phil.* 1.5; Livy *Epit.* 116. An anti-Antonian riot followed the murder; Antony dispersed it with troops, and had rebellious slaves crucified and freedmen thrown from the Tarpeian Rock. Antony similarly put down a riot in 47 with troops; 800 plebeians were killed and some of the leaders were thrown from the Tarpeian Rock: see App. *B Civ.* 3.3; Dio 42.29–33.

58 App. *B Civ.* 6.68; also see Vell. Pat. 2.77; and the similar account in Dio 48.31.6.

59 Suetonius, *Tib.* 62.2, Loeb, claims that at Capri Tiberius ordered that condemned men 'after long and exquisite tortures be cast headlong into the sea before his eyes, while a band of marines waited below for the bodies and broke their bones with boathooks and oars, to prevent any breath of life from remaining in them'. Cf. SHA *Avid. Cass.* 4.4, Loeb; cited by Callu (1984) 316: Avidius Cassius supposedly had criminals bound together ten at a time and thrown into rivers or the sea.

60 As Yavetz (1988), 27–8, 113, explains, crowds expressed their anger 'by committing atrocities on the corpses and smashing the monuments and statues of persons whom they hated'. Cf. the breaking of statues of Caligula on news of his murder: Dio 59.30.1a. In AD 20 crowds dragged Piso's statues down the Scalae Gemoniae but were stopped from shattering them by Tiberius.

61 Dio, 58.5.6–7, tells of omens of Sejanus' fate: his bodyguard had slipped earlier on the Scalae, and when Sejanus was taking the auspices 'many crows fell around him and cawed, then all flew off together to the jail and perched there'. Other omens, 58.7.1, concerned a statue of Sejanus; e.g. a rope was found coiled about its neck. On the executioner's violation of Sejanus' daughter before strangling her, also see Suet. *Tib.* 61.5 and Tac. *Ann.* 5.9. Cf. Juvenal's poetically graphic description (10.54–103, Loeb): Sejanus' statues are torn down and melted, and his body is abused. As noted in ch. 1 above, Sejanus was dragged by a hook (66–7) – 'a show and a joy to all!'. The mob claim that they never liked him, turning against him as they do against all condemned men (*damnatos*). Fearing implication in the conspiracy, men assert their innocence by abusing the corpse: 85–8: – 'Let us rush headlong and trample on Caesar's enemy, while he lies on the bank (*in ripa*)!' – 'Ay, and let our slaves see that none bear witness against us, and drag their trembling master into court with a halter around his neck.' On the suicide of Apicata, see Van Hooff (1990) 91, 151, and n. 40 on 273–4 on the testimonia.

62 Cf. Tac. *Ann.* 6.10: the mother of Fufius Geminus was executed for bewailing the death of her son. Suetonius, *Tib.* 61.4, says that as many as twenty a day, including women and children, were executed, flung on the Stairs, and dragged to the Tiber with hooks. Sejanus' friends, notably Sabinus – the first executed under Tiberius in AD 28 (Dio 58.1.3; Tac. *Ann.* 4.70), were similarly abused: Dio 58.12.1, 58.15.3; cf. 60.35.3. Bauman (1996), 63 and n. 61 on 179, however, warns that the reign of terror became a literary commonplace, and he notes that there were some deportations and even acquittals. For the touching story of Sabinus' dog attending his body and jumping into the river after it, see Plin. *HN* 8.145.

63 Games given: Suet. *Tib.* 7.1. Lack of enthusiasm: Dio 57.11.5–6. Tacitus, *Ann.* 1.54, 1.76, suggests that Tiberius simply did not like games personally. See Yavetz (1988) 106–13, on what he sees as the tragedy of Tiberius' unpopularity despite his efforts and benefactions to the people in non-spectacular ways. Yavetz, 108, admits that, because Tiberius gave an insufficient number of games at Rome, the people held him responsible for the amphitheater disaster at

Fidenae; see Tac. *Ann.* 4.62–3; Suet. *Tib.* 40; Dio 58.1.1a. Edmondson (1996), 84, agrees that Tiberius' attitude to games was a major cause of his unpopularity.

64 Shows: Suet. *Tib.* 34.1. Seneca, *Prov.* 4.4, heard a gladiator complaining that so few games were held when Tiberius was emperor that his youth was going to waste. Hunting spectacles: Dio 58.1.1a. Ironically, in his last year Tiberius himself threw darts at boars at garrison games: Suet. *Tib.* 72.2.

65 Suet. *Tib.* 47.1. On acclamations and the Tiber, see below on Commodus. Cf. Suet. *Calig.* 27.4: Caligula had burned alive in the arena a writer of Atellan farces because of a double entendre possibly intended to reflect on him.

66 Compare the case of Maximinus Thrax, discussed by T. W. Africa, 'Urban Violence in Imperial Rome', *Journal of Interdisciplinary Studies* 2 (1971–2) 2–21 at 17–19. In AD 238 a riot broke out on the rumor of the death of Maximinus, and the senate elected Gordian as emperor. Mobs overturned statues of Maximinus, lynched his associates, broke into houses, and abused people as informers, robbing and killing them. Herodian, 7.7.3–5, attributes the resentment of the masses to Maximinus' expropriation of public funds meant for games and entertainment.

67 Suet. *Calig.* 16.1, Loeb. Out of anger Caligula nearly killed his uncle Claudius when he had him thrown fully clothed into the Rhine: Suet. *Claud.* 9.1. At Lugdunum in Gaul Caligula organized a contest in the composition of elegies, and losers faced possibly being thrown (live) into the Rhone: Suet. *Calig.* 20. Cf. the anecdote that Claudius at court had the pleader Julius Gallicus thrown into the Tiber: Dio 61(60).33.8; see Duncan Fishwick, 'A Ducking in the Tiber (Dio 61[60],33,8)', *AJAH* 12 (1987, publ. 1995) 73–6. Aware of the symbolic significance of providing proper burial, Caligula aided his popularity by acting with propriety as a new emperor: he gave a funeral speech and a magnificent burial for Tiberius, he fetched the remains of his mother and brother Nero from Pandataria and the Pontian Islands, and he returned the ashes to Rome personally for burial in the imperial mausoleum: Suet. *Calig.* 15.1.

68 E.g. Suet. *Calig.* 27.2, Loeb:

> A man who had made a vow to fight in the arena, if the emperor recovered, he compelled to keep his word, watched him as he fought sword in hand, and would not let him go until he was victorious, and then only after many entreaties. Another who had offered his life for the same reason, but delayed to kill himself, he turned over to his slaves, with orders to drive him through the streets decked with sacred boughs and fillets, calling for the fulfilment of his vow, and finally hurl him from the embankment (*ex aggere*).

Like Dio 59.10.1–5, Suet. *Calig.* 27 abounds in beast references, some of which have been noted above: e.g. bald convicts are fed to beasts, honorable men are thrown to beasts or shut in cages like beasts, the manager of *munera* and *venationes* has his brains beaten out, a knight, with his tongue cut out to make him stop proclaiming his innocence, is thrown to beasts. Other vows: Suet. *Calig.* 14.2, Loeb: earlier, when Caligula fell ill, crowds gathered around the Palace: 'some even vowed to fight as gladiators, and others posted placards offering their lives' in return for his health. Dio, 59.8.3, tells of Afranius devoting himself and Atanius Secundus promising to fight as a gladiator; he says that Caligula compelled both to keep their vows, leading to their deaths. Wiedemann (1992), 8, notes that Persius, 6.48, mentions a man vowing a gladiatorial show with 100 gladiators in thanksgiving for Caligula's surviving an attempted conspiracy.

69 Cf. the disposal of Maximian's sycophants mentioned in n. 86 and St Sebastian, discussed in ch. 8. below

70 Suet. *Ner.* 26.1, Loeb. Tacitus, *Ann.* 13.25, recounts Nero's licentiousness and misconduct while disguised as a slave. He omits the sewer but notes, 13.25.3, that Nero began to take soldiers and gladiators with him to assist him if he met with serious resistance. Nero understood *damnatio memoriae*: Suet. *Ner.* 24.1, Loeb: while competing in contests for singers and heralds in Greece, 'To obliterate the memory of all other victors in the games and to leave no trace of them, their statues and busts were all thrown down by his order, dragged off with hooks, and cast into privies.'

71 Strabo, 5.3.8, says that veritable rivers of water passed through the aqueducts and sewers; washing the filth of the city into the Tiber, the sewers were large enough for wagons loaded with hay to pass through them. The Cloaca Maxima began as a stream and was channeled as a sewer under Tarquinius Priscus, but it still remained an open channel at the time of Plautus (*Curc.* 474); see Richardson (1992) 91–2. In 33 BC Agrippa cleaned out the sewers and sailed through the Cloaca Maxima underground into the Tiber: Dio 49.43.1; Plin. *HN* 36.104–8. As Scobie (1986), 413, 423, explains, Rome had only gravity sewers: they were 'flushed' to some degree by the overflow from fountains and from excess rainwater, but clogging was a problem; they might back up and flood the Forum, and they needed manual cleaning periodically. For futher bibliography on the sewer system, now see Gowers (1995) n. 11 on 24.

72 SHA *Heliog.* 17.1–3, Loeb, cf. summary restatement at 33.8; cf. Dio 80.20.2, 21.3; Zonar. 12.14; see Le Gall (1953) 89. Hinard (1987b), 120–1, suggests that the Aemilian Bridge was used routinely for disposals from executions in the Forum. SHA, *Heliog.* 17.5–7, Loeb, comments:

> After his death he was dubbed the *Tiberine*, the *Dragged*, the *Filthy*, and many other such names, all of which were to signify what seemed to have been done during his rule. And he was the only one of all the emperors whose body was dragged through the streets, thrust into a sewer, and hurled into the Tiber. This befell him as the result of the general hatred of all, against which particularly emperors must be on their guard, since those who do not win the love of the senate, the people, and the soldiers do not win the right of burial.

73 See the discussion of drainage from amphitheaters in Golvin (1988) 333–4; cf. 177 on the Colosseum. Richardson (1992), 7, comments on the hydrography of the Colosseum: 'a watercourse of some volume still runs in the lowest level of the excavations under the church of S. Clemente'. Ibid., 10: 'There is also an extensive drainage and sewer system following the main lines of the design and emptying under Via di S. Gregorio. This part of the amphitheater has received inadequate attention as yet.' On animal bones in the drains of the Colosseum, see n. 24 in ch. 6 above.

74 The finds are still largely unpublished, and I am grateful to Nick Bateman, director of the excavations for the Museum of London Archaeology Service, for his correspondence and for sharing with me a copy of his provisional statement, 'The London Amphitheatre: Excavations 1987–1996', forthcoming in *Britannia*. See his earlier summaries: 'The Discovery of Londinium's Amphitheatre: Excavations at the Old Art Gallery Site 1987–1990', *London Archaeologist* 6.9 (1990) 232–41; 'The London Amphitheatre', *Current Archaeology* 137 (1994) 164–71; and 'Guildhall: Beyond the Amphitheatre', *London Archaeologist* 7.10 (1994) 258–62. Cf. Wiedemann (1992) 45, 178; and Dominic Perring, *Roman*

London (London: Seaby, 1991) 61–3. Quantities of animal bones found in the
drains and related deposits within and around the amphitheater include the leg
bone (distal humerus) of a brown bear (found behind the masonry arena wall near
one of the side chambers) and the skull of a large bovine, possibly a bull (found
in one of the perimeter drains). The faunal remains have yet to be fully identified and analyzed.

75 As Dio, 73(72).10.2–3, Loeb, summarizes: 'Commodus devoted most of his life
to ease and to horses and to combats of wild beasts and of men. In fact, besides
all that he did in private, he often slew in public large numbers of men and
of beasts as well.'

76 E.g. he quickly condemned to the beasts anyone who ridiculed or disturbed
him in any way: SHA *Comm.* 10.2–3.

77 Dio, 73(72).17–21, Loeb, especially details Commodus' gladiatorial abuses.
SHA, *Comm.* 11.10–12, 12.10–12, 15.3–8, gives similarly scathing accounts.

78 Dio 73(72).17.2, Loeb: 'Moreover, he used to contend as a gladiator; in doing
this at home he managed to kill a man now and then ... but in public he
refrained from using steel and shedding human blood.' Herodian, 1.15.7, feels
that Commodus' combats in the arena lacked virtue because he did not fight
real enemies.

79 Dio 73(72).20.3, Loeb: 'he had once got together all the men of the city who
had lost their feet as a result of disease or some accident, and then, after
fastening about their knees some likenesses of serpent's bodies, and giving them
sponges to throw instead of stones, had killed them with blows of a club,
pretending that they were giants'. Also noted in SHA *Comm.* 9.6.

80 Dio 73(72).21.1–2, 20.2. Herodian, 1.14.9, mentions a statue of Commodus
with a strung bow set opposite the Curia to intimidate senators.

81 As Pliny's contrast of the spectacles of Trajan and Domitian makes clear, *Pan.*
33–5, an emperor was to show imperial generosity and justice in producing
inspiring spectacles with talented, equally matched combatants, and he was to
allow freedom of expression to the assembled spectators.

82 Cf. abuse of spectators by Caligula (Suet. *Calig.* 35.3; Dio 59.10.3–4; cf. Dio
59.28.11; Joseph. *AJ* 19.1.4: Caligula has soldiers kill protesters at the Circus)
and Domitian (Suet. *Dom.* 10.1; Plin. *Pan.* 33.4). Cf. ch. 3 above. As Brown
(1992), 184, explains, spectators were to feel distant and protected, and when
bad emperors threw spectators into the shows it was 'an especially disturbing
event. If the patron could ignore the boundaries between the viewer and the
viewed, the games ceased to function properly.' Similarly, Edmondson (1996),
83, says that such actions 'were reprehensible not just on moral grounds but
also because they threatened the social order of the amphitheatre and hence
Roman social order itself'.

83 Caligula fought a gladiatorial match with blunted weapons, and when his
opponent fell on purpose he stabbed him with a real dagger and ran about
with a victory palm-branch: Suet. *Calig.* 32.2; cf. Dio 59.5.4–5. Nero generally
performed in public in a more Greek vein, although Suetonius, *Ner.* 53, claims
that he once intended to emulate Hercules by killing a specially trained lion
in the arena in public; cf. Wistrand (1992) 25. Philostratus, *V A* 4.36, says
that Nero fought as a gladiator, but Miriam T. Griffin, *Nero: The End of a
Dynasty* (New Haven: Yale U., 1984) n. 36 on 247, notes that this is supported
by no other sources. One of the indictments of Didius Julianus was that he
had exercised with gladiatorial arms: SHA *Did. Iul.* 9.1. Like Nero in the
theater, Commodus in the arena presented 'the supreme anomaly', the 'supreme
breech of public norms': Plass (1995) 72, 74. Similarly, Wiedemann (1992)
131: 'The ultimate threat to established morality was for an emperor to appear

in the arena himself.' Commodus' actions prompted the explanation or slander that he was sired by a gladiator: SHA *Marc.* 19.7. Cf. Clavel-Lévêque (1984b), 198–201, who suggests that Commodus and other emperors who appeared in the arena were not just megalomaniacs pandering to the masses but leaders who understood the complex symbolism of gladiatorial combats. As Edwards (1993), 193–4, comments, emperors such as Commodus and Nero were condemned for their prodigal pleasures and for associating with gladiators and actors, but their enthusiasm for popular pleasures may have won them some popular favor.

84 Strangled: Dio 73(72).22.2–5. In Barton's terms, Commodus' fights and hunts involved skill but not *amor mortis*. He achieved no gladiatorial elevation because he faced no serious risk to his life; he fought inferior men and beasts, not equal opponents. Barton (1993), 31, cites Sen. *Prov.* 3.4: 'A gladiator reckons it ignominious to be paired with his inferior in skill and considers himself to have conquered without glory who has conquered without peril.' On the Roman concept of the equal opponent, see Barton, 28–30, 107–44, 184–5.

85 Cf. Dio 74(73).13.2–5: masses hostile to Didius Julianus after the murder of Pertinax reviled him as a stealer of the Empire and a parricide. Potter (1996) 132–41, esp. 139–41, with bibliography on Commodus in n. 45 on 141, discusses acclamations, or unified public chanting, at shows and trials. Such acclamations included the standard chants (e.g. parricide, to the *spoliarium*) found in SHA *Comm.* 18.3–19.9.

86 SHA *Comm.* 18.10, Loeb: 'Hearken Caesar: to the lions with the informers!'; 18.15: 'That we may be safe (*ut salvi simus*), cast informers out of the senate, the club for informers (*delatoribus fustem*)! While you are safe, to the lions with informers (*delatores ad leonem*)!' Informers were always hated as traitors. In AD 24 Vibius Serenus informed against his father, and the masses threatened him with jail, the Rock, or penalties for parricide: Tac. *Ann.* 4.28–9. Just as Trajan humiliated Domitian's informers, parading them through the arena onward to harsher punishments (Plin. *Pan.* 34.3), Titus properly had had informers scourged in the Forum and led in procession across the amphitheater; some were sold and others were deported to islands: Suet. *Tit.* 8.5; Mart. *Spec.* 4–5. When in AD 238 the senate condemned to death Maximian's informers and false accusers (cf. SHA *Max.* 15.1; Hdn 7.6), according to SHA, *Gord. Tres.* 13.8, Loeb, the people wanted more: 'But this . . . was not enough; the people decided that after they were put to death they should be dragged about and cast into the sewer (*in cloacam*).'

87 Recall that the senatorial decree of AD 19 (see ch. 5 above) apparently denied burial rights to *auctorati*. The supreme contract gladiator, Commodus deserved the supreme penalty.

88 These were not idle words. Witness the attempted erasure on line 6 of the Aes Italicense (see ch. 3 above) of the words *et Luci Commodi*. Note that Septimius Severus, wanting to present himself as a legitimate representative of the Antonines, later deified Commodus and attached himself to the Antonine dynasty: Dio 76(75).7.4; 77(76).9.4; SHA *Sev.* 10.3–6; Hdn 3.10.5.

89 As Levick (1976), 187, notes concerning the reign of Tiberius, savagery, *damnatio memoriae*, exposure on the Scalae Gemoniae, and denial of burial had all been ordered by the senate before in cases of aggravated treason. Cf. senatorial decrees of posthumous damnation for Domitian (Suet. *Dom.* 23.1; cf. Plin. *Pan.* 52) and Elagabalus (SHA *Heliogab.* 17.4); cf. the senate's declaration that Nero was a public enemy to be executed *more maiorum*, to be stripped, bound to a wooden fork (*furca*), and flogged to death: Suet. *Ner.* 49.2.

90 On emperors as performers, see n. 83 above. Wiedemann (1992), 177–8, sees

Commodus' self-presentation as Hercules and his antics in the arena as a symbolic claim to deserving deification, like Hercules, as the defender of civilization against beasts and criminals, as a creator of order and destroyer of barbarians, and as a hero conquering mortality. Wiedemann, 110: 'Like Hercules, Commodus wanted to do divine work on earth in order to achieve a place among the gods. Like Hercules, he was publicly reclassified as mad, but of course only after he had been assassinated.' Certainly gladiators were associated with Hercules, among other gods (e.g. Mercury, Mars), various emperors associated themselves with Hercules (see Wiedemann, n. 38 on 182), and most emperors from Augustus helped legitimize themselves with shows. Also, other emperors did appear in shows, but only Commodus performed as a *bestiarius*, a gladiator, and as Hercules (and Mercury) at spectacles. As Hopkins (1983), 20, suggests, 'Commodus' gladiatorial exploits were an idiosyncratic fall out from a cultural obsession with fighting, bloodshed, ostentation and competition.'

91 Ville (1981), n. 145 on 425–6, suggests that 'gladiator' was added just as a term of infamy, that the word does not tie Commodus to the arena, that 'hook' relates to the charge of parricide, not to the gladiator reference. However, the *spoliarium* ties the insult to the arena. Moreover, Septimius Severus later remarked that among the senators who called Commodus a gladiator were men who fought as gladiators or bought some of Commodus' gladiatorial equipment: Dio 76(75).8.3.

92 Oliver and Palmer (1955), 324, note that, in light of the inscriptions they discuss, some historians feel that SHA *Comm.* 18–19 may contain genuine information from a documentary source (i.e. Marius Maximus). E.g. R. Syme, *Emperors and Biography* (Oxford: Oxford U., 1971) 117. B. Baldwin, 'Acclamations in the *Historia Augusta*', *Athenaeum* 69 (1981) 138–49 (reprinted in his *Studies on Late Roman and Byzantine History, Literature and Language* (Amsterdam: J. C. Gieben, 1984) 33–44), sees the passages as one of the biographer's 'more ambitious fake documents'. He notes that Dio places most of the acclamations as responses to the news of Commodus' burial but the SHA has most coming earlier, with fewer ones greeting the news of the burial. However, Baldwin, 141, does admit that Dio and the SHA agree on using epithets rather than the name of the emperor, and that 'Senatorial abuse of the late Commodus can be accepted as a fact.'

93 As noted above, dumping corpses into the river did not break the ancient taboo because the men were not buried or burned 'within the city'. There might be some need to appease the spirits of the Tiber (e.g. by elevation of victims, perhaps by the *cena libera*, to worthy sacrifices); but Roman religion was amenable to the state's wishes. As Bodel (1986), n. 110 on 102, observes, the sources of streams were sacred (cf. Tac. *Ann.* 14.22.6; Sen. *Ep.* 41.3), but the lower courses were less sacred and less regulated.

8

CHRISTIANS: PERSECUTIONS AND DISPOSAL

> For it seems to me God has made us apostles the last act in
> the show, like men condemned to death in the arena, a spec-
> tacle to the whole universe – to angels as well as men.
> (1 Corinthians 4.9, *Oxford Study Bible*)

At the village of St Ignace, Simcoe County, Ontario, Canada, in 1649 Jesuit Fathers Jean de Brébeuf and Jerome Lalement, missionaries to the Hurons, were captured and tortured to death by an Iroquois raiding party. First the Iroquois stripped both priests naked and bound each to a post. They tore out their fingernails, and beat them with sticks all over their bodies. Brébeuf inspired his fellow captives (Hurons) by saying that God was watching and would reward them with glory. In an unusual addition to the torments, a Huron rebel who had been baptized by Brébeuf but had now joined the Iroquois mocked and abused the priest by pouring a vessel of boiling water on his head three times, saying 'Go to Heaven, for thou art well baptized.' Brébeuf next had to bear a collar of red-hot hatchet heads bound together about his neck, a torment used on other prisoners. Then the Iroquois put a belt of bark, resin, and pitch on him and set fire to it. Brébeuf aston-ished the Iroquois by standing firm, apparently insensitive to the fire, preaching and trying to convert his tormentors, which enraged them so that they cut out his tongue and cut off his lips. Next they stripped flesh from his legs, thighs, and arms, and put it on to roast before him in order to eat it. They mocked him verbally, saying that he should be grateful to them for the glory that he would gain from God for their efforts. Brébeuf was then scalped alive, and as he was about to die one Iroquois cut out his heart, roasted it, and ate it. Other Iroquois drank of his blood saying that they wanted to acquire his bravery.[1] Filtered through a common cultural heritage, such accounts of the martyrdom of missionaries by 'savages' are strikingly reminiscent of descriptions of Amerindian ritual violence (see ch. 4 above), and many of the motifs are first found in Christian accounts of martyrdoms under Rome.

242

Persecutions: passions, procedures, spectacles, and disposal

Romans took spectacular executions for granted, but Christians immortalized the deaths and disposal of Christians in spectacles. Most history, indeed, is 'written by the victors', and when on top the Roman authors paid little attention to Christian suffering; but the Christians, when they triumphed, eagerly documented traditions about the heroism of saints and 'martyrs'. Rhetorical and fervent in their commonplaces and coloring, and heavily influenced by the ideologies of martyrdom and resurrection, Christian accounts (*acta* or *gesta* about interrogations and trials, *passiones* or *martyria* about last days and deaths) include both reliable contemporary records and later reconstructions with millennialist and apocalyptic tinges. Martyrology, hagiography, and historiography are intertwined, but Roman attitudes and rituals are revealed.[2]

We cannot know how many Christians died at Rome or beyond, and the intensity of persecutions varied with areas and leaders. The severest purges were in North Africa and the eastern Empire. Ironically, probably very few Christians died at Rome and fewer still in the Colosseum.[3] Contrary to popular opinion,[4] Christians probably did not outnumber pagan arena victims, but the persecutions produced famous examples of the death and disposal of *damnati* perceived as religious traitors and threats.[5] From sporadic and local incidents prior to the mid third century to systematic and general attacks, the persecutions adapted established procedures already used in executions and fatal charades.[6] However, concepts of resurrection, affected by the context of persecution, apparently influenced Romans to inflict especially harsh abuse on Christian corpses.

Tertullian (*Apol.* 37.1–2, 49.4) and others describe the violence against Christians as a combination of legal procedures and mob passions. Scholars have long debated which legal charges, if indeed there were specific charges, were brought against Christians. Early persecutions were possibly sanctioned only by the local power of a governor or the unlimited power of an emperor. Given the potential for abuse in the Roman legal system, a direct order or rescript on Christians before the third century seems unnecessary.[7] Existing laws and powers, notably those relevant to treason, would suffice. Rome, we must remember, did not know the modern separation of church and state. Pagan and Christian sources generally associate Christians with charges of both *sacrilegium* and *maiestas*,[8] and Tertullian (e.g. *Apol.* 35.6) tries to refute the common charge that Christians were disloyal because they did not pay homage to the emperor cult. Christian abstention (e.g. from the games, sacrifices, and the emperor cult) was seen as hostility to Rome, as religious treason threatening the *pax deorum*, and as insolence against the majesty and divinity of emperors. After Septimius Severus forbade conversion to Christianity in 202 (Euseb. *HE* 6.1.1; SHA *Sev.* 17.1) and the Edict of Caracalla of 212 spread citizenship and therefore the obligations of the imperial cult to all free males, Christians' exclusivist refusal to participate meant that treason and sacrilege overlapped in injurious, insulting defiance of the emperors, the gods, and the state. Christians were feared and vilified by the masses as public enemies and *noxii*: a Christian was 'a man guilty of every crime, the enemy of the gods, emperors, laws, morals, of all Nature together'.[9] Slanders applied to Christians (e.g. as the dregs of society, parricides, temple robbers, religious criminals, incestuous perverts) correspond to charges against arena *damnati*, and Christians were thought to deserve appropriately offensive punishments. They died in the arena, but not as gladiators; they were thrown to the beasts, but not as *bestiarii*. As cheap, non-bellicose *noxii*, they suffered the worst atrocities of *summa supplicia*. It was Christian sources and the ironies of the history of western civilization that turned Roman prosecutions for religious treason into Christian persecutions for faith.

Tacitus describes Nero's famous persecution of Christians as scapegoats to absolve himself of suspicions that he had ordered the great fire of 64 at Rome:

> Therefore, to scotch the rumor, Nero substituted as culprits, and punished with the utmost refinements of cruelty, a class of men, loathed for their vices, whom the crowd styled Christians. Christus, the founder of the name, had undergone the death penalty ... and the pernicious superstition was checked for a moment, only to break out once more, not merely in Judaea ... but in the capital itself ... First, then, the confessed members of the sect were arrested; next, on their disclosures, vast numbers were convicted, not so much on the count of arson as for hatred of the human race. And derision accompanied their end: they were covered with wild beasts' skins and torn to death by dogs; or they were fastened on crosses, and, when daylight failed were burned to serve as lamps by night. Nero had offered his Gardens for the spectacle (*spectaculo*), and gave an exhibition in his Circus, mixing with the crowd in the habit of a charioteer, or mounted on his car. Hence, in spite of a guilt which had earned the most exemplary punishment, there arose a sentiment of pity (*miseratio*), due to the impression that they were being sacrificed not for the welfare of the state but to the ferocity of a single man.[10]

Notorious for lavish shows, and overly sensitive to critical rumors, Nero was in a hurry, so the judicial system rounded up and convicted *damnati* to be punished as a spectacular entertainment. The 'immense multitude' (15.44.5, *multitudo ingens*) may be rhetorical,[11] and it was amassed only after a smaller and apparently insufficient number of self-acknowledged Christians were arrested (and undoubtedly tortured). Despite Tacitus' phrase (15.44.5, *novissima exempla*) and modern popular perception, the methods of execution (crucifixion, fire, beasts) were not invented by Nero specifically for Christians.[12] Trying to demonstrate order and control after disruption and disaster, Nero inflicted elaborate punishments on the Christians to heighten the torments and entertainment in order to make their guilt and his innocence more convincing. The 'fatal charades' of the early Empire had already developed a vast array of methods of torture, humiliation, and aggravated death. Later martyrology details hideous but not essentially new horrors.

Recording these events to excoriate Nero as a bad emperor, Tacitus agreed that the Christians were guilty and deserved ruthless punishment for their 'abominations' and their 'mischievous superstition'. Christians were thought to be guilty of 'hatred of mankind' (15.44.5, *odio humani generis*) in part because they shunned the sacrifices and spectacles – the very things Romans saw as essential for integration into society. After noting that the ever self-indulgent Nero made this his own and not the people's spectacle, by holding it in his own gardens, and that he made a spectacle of himself, by appearing inappropriately as a charioteer, Tacitus finally suggests that the victims were pitied because they suffered through Nero's brutality rather than in the national interest (15.44.5, 'non utilitate publica, sed in saevitiam unius').[13] When *damnati* were abused and humiliated in the people's arena, for their reassurance and amusement, the people were pleased. In the later persecutions, presented as 'for the public good', there was little compassion, except occasionally in the minds of martyrologists.

Nero's persecution was spontaneous, those killed were nameless and of uncertain number, and Tacitus mentions neither the idea of resurrection nor the ultimate disposal of the victims. We must turn to Christian sources to learn of the first known Christian to die in the Colosseum and of concern about disposal. Condemned to the beasts in 107 or 109, St Ignatius of Antioch wrote in one letter (noted above in ch. 6) of wanting to be eaten up by the beasts: 'Rather entice the wild beasts that they may become my tomb, and leave no trace of my body, that when I fall asleep I be not burdensome to any.' Another letter says that he longs for the beasts and that he will entice them to devour him – he will even force them if they are reluctant, as sometimes happens when they are afraid to touch victims. 'Let there come on me fire, and cross, and struggles with wild beasts, cutting, and tearing asunder, rackings of bones, mangling of limbs, crushing of my whole body, cruel tortures of the devil, may I but attain to Jesus Christ!' Ignatius expected complete somatic resurrection and (ideologically but not realistically) wished for complete destruction, perhaps so that his followers would not endanger themselves by trying to bury any remains.[14] Strictly speaking, Ignatius predates the phenomenon of martyrdom. As Bowersock has now clarified, martyrdom arose as something entirely new in the second century AD when the word-shift from the earlier meaning of 'witness' to 'dying for a cause' reflected 'a conceptual system of post-humous recognition and anticipated reward'. 'Martyrs' all refused to sacrifice when asked and persisted until death in their public confessions of their Christian faith.[15]

St Justin the Apologist and his companions, the first 'martyrs' to die at Rome, were tried around AD 165 and sentenced before the urban prefect (Q. Junius Rusticus) to be scourged and beheaded 'in accordance with the law' for refusing to sacrifice to the gods. Followers secretly took the bodies of Justin and his companions and buried them in a convenient place.[16] Apparently the bodies of Christians executed in normal fashion at the edge of town were not always simply handed over,[17] and the bodies of Christians killed in arenas often suffered additional abuse.

Rather than Rome, the lengthiest accounts and the greatest numbers of martyrdoms concern provincial cities.[18] Probably the earliest genuine Christian account of a martyrdom, the *Passion* of Polycarp at Smyrna (in or around AD 156), shows the spectacular treatment of martyrs.[19] According to Marcion, an eyewitness, several martyrdoms included scourging, fire, beasts, and other tortures (2). When a certain Germanicus refused to recant and even pulled a beast toward himself (3), the crowd demanded that Polycarp be arrested. Interrogated by the governor in the circus, Polycarp firmly refused to recant despite threats of fire and beasts. When he defiantly warned the governor that God would judge and punish him in the future, the crowd flew into a rage, chanting 'destroyer of our gods' and calling for lions (11–12).[20] The beast games had been officially closed, however, so Polycarp was to be burned alive. The crowd, with Jews taking a prominent role, gathered firewood, and Polycarp was bound to the pyre with his hands behind his back 'like a noble ram' selected for sacrifice. Miraculously, the fire did not kill him (15). 'Finally, when they realized that his body could not be destroyed by fire, the ruffians ordered one of the dagger-men (a *confector*) to go up and stab him with his weapon.'[21] As this was done a symbolic dove flew out of the body. Offended by Polycarp's achievement, the Evil One (17) 'proceeded to do his best to arrange that at least we should not get possession of his mortal remains, although members of us were anxious to do this and to claim our share in the hallowed relics'. After observing Christians about to draw the body from the fire, Jews, moved by Satan, wanted to appeal to the governor not to release the body 'in case they should forsake the Crucified and take to worshipping this fellow instead'. 'However, when the centurion saw that the Jews were spoiling for a quarrel, he had the body fetched out publicly, as is their usage, and burnt. So, after all, we did gather up his bones . . . and we laid them to rest in a spot suitable for the purpose' (18).[22] As well as the anti-Semitism apparent in this and other accounts, note here the Christians' anxiety about burial and relics, the concern of Jews and Romans about veneration of martyrs' remains, and the suggestion that, after *crematio*, Romans routinely burned such bodies in public.

Concerning Geta's birthday games at Carthage in AD 203, the *Passion of Perpetua and Felicitas* contains similar details.[23] Constant in their refusal to recant, Christian men and women refused to wear the robes of priests of Saturn or priestesses of Ceres (18.4, i.e. as roles in a fatal charade), one feature that has led scholars to see the events as human sacrifices to Saturn and Ceres as gods associated with the underworld and possible surrogates for Baal.[24] When Perpetua and Felicitas were exposed naked or in diaphanous robes, the crowd, perhaps touched by their ages and conditions (one was pregnant; one had recently delivered: 20.2), asked that they be clothed.[25] The victims did not try to defend themselves but rather cooperated by walking out and attracting beasts with signals. Perpetua even directed a young gladiator's trembling sword hand to her throat (21.8–10).[26] They were eager for the glory of martyrdom, preferring to die with their colleagues and not later with common criminals (15.2). When the martyrs warned the spectators and suggested that God would condemn the governor Hilarius as he had condemned them, the crowd (18.9) 'became enraged (*exasperatus*) and demanded that they be scourged before a line of gladiators'. When the martyrs rejoiced at this, the crowd remained angry, and it would later demand to witness the cutting of the martyrs' throats (21.7).[27] Thanks perhaps to the discretion of local magistrates or to dutiful followers the remains of these martyrs seem to have been buried.[28]

Such accounts reveal procedures of damnation, death, and disposal of Christians. Often punishment was demanded of prominent leaders rather than of all Christians. Sometimes in the arena itself, Christians were brought before a magistrate (a governor or the urban prefect at Rome) and told to recant. Those who refused were condemned to die.[29] The magistrates had some discretion about the type of execution, which took place immediately or after incarceration. The executioner (*carnifex*) took the victims to a place of execution, probably at the edge of town, or the victims went to the arena. In the arena various *summa supplicia* might be used after the victim was publicly denounced. Influenced by historical developments, the shift to systematic persecutions in the third century involved increased numbers, not greatly different methods of death and disposal.[30] Local circumstances and crowd passions were factors, especially when refusals to recant, public defiance, and Christian threats about the future enraged the spectators.[31] Miracles aside, death by fire or beasts did not involve total consumption. Victims often had to be finished off. Deaths might be confirmed by having the victims' throats cut by a *confector*, and a public display of the corpse seems to have been customary. How the bodies were disposed of, and whether they were permitted burial rites, seems to have been a matter of official discretion, of geography, or of the resourcefulness of followers, but corpses were not always simply turned over for proper burial.[32] Satan aside, concerns about Christian ideas of resurrection and the veneration of martyrs' relics apparently often led to a second complete burning of the body.[33] Only afterwards, probably at night and in secret, were followers able to gather minimal relics for burial.[34] Even then, burials might not remain secure. At times Christians were banned from cemeteries, and Tertullian records that their own cemeteries and their buried dead were attacked:

> How often do you wreak your fury on the Christians, in part obeying your own instincts, in part the laws? How often, too, without regard to you [magistrates], does the unfriendly mob on its own account assail us with stones and fire? Mad as Bacchanals, they spare not even the Christian dead; no! from the repose of the grave, from what I may call death's asylum, changed as the bodies may be, or mere fragments – they will have them out, rip and rend them.[35]

Since Christians were seen as enemies, their burial areas were not respected as holy ground,[36] but, as discussed below, abuse of Christian corpses and cemeteries was related to eschatological concerns.

Martyrs heroically endured horrible torments, but they probably provided more frustration than entertainment for spectators. In Christian eyes the volunteerism, even the enthusiasm, of martyrs for death 'sacralized' them as worthy of sacrifice and resurrection,[37] but in Roman eyes they were disturbing, threatening heretics. The martyrs' compliance in their own deaths and their defiance of authority infuriated spectators. After some initial novelty value, and even with costumes and spectacular forms of death, Christians provided a rather poor show. They were not skillful performers like gladiators, so they received no hope or privileges. Their use is best explained by Roman hatred or religious anxiety, as punitive executions or propitiatory sacrifices, not by their entertainment value.[38] A steady sequence of spectacles with Christians would soon become boring for most Romans. Christians 'would do' for an occasional novelty, or perhaps for human sacrifices in the provinces, but spectators at Rome would request the return of combative gladiators as soon as possible. Ironically, because the martyrs' conduct undermined the goals of the shows, and because too many 'voluntary' martyrs were coming forth, by roughly the 250s governors were trying to keep trials and executions unspectacular to avoid giving martyrs opportunities for prominent self-display. Governors went from theatricalizing or trivializing Christian deaths in charades to downplaying them as quiet decapitations outside the arena.[39]

Lyons and disposal by water

In one case Christians were apparently used because true gladiators or bellicose *damnati* were unavailable or too expensive. At Lyons in AD 177 Christians were supplied as a substitute resource for a show, they were abused to death, and their disposal suggests Roman concerns about Christian ideas of resurrection. Eusebius is the sole source for a supposed encyclical letter from Christian communities in Lyons and Vienne in Gaul to communities in Asia and Phrygia recounting this persecution.[40] This was a local incident involving mob fury and official acquiescence, but the abuse was carried out as a spectacle and the judicial and spontaneous actions were probably typical. Death and disposal here combined both instrumental and expressive violence, both pragmatism and emotionalism, both expiation and vengeance.

Eusebius says that the Christian victims (7) 'heroically endured all that the people en masse heaped on them: abuse, blows, dragging, despoiling, stoning, imprisonment, and all that an enraged mob is likely to inflict on their most hated enemies'. Victims were dragged into the forum and interrogated; those who confessed were imprisoned to await the governor (8). Christians were collected from the two communities when the prefect ordered a full-scale investigation (13). Coerced by soldiers, pagan servants of the Christians, fearing torture, falsely accused their masters of cannibal feasts and other atrocities (14). Then the people raged and gnashed their teeth at the Christians (15).[41] 'All the wrath of the mob' fell on the leaders, including the deacon Sanctus of Vienne. Christians under torture refused to blaspheme, arousing more anger in the governor and the torturers (16). Jailers tortured the Christians with the sort of indignities that they were 'accustomed to inflict on their prisoners' (27). An aged victim, Pothinus, defiant before the governor, was dragged and beaten, and bystanders attacked him with their hands and feet (29–31). At one point Eusebius says that most of the forty-eight victims in the persecution 'were strangled in prison' (27). Below (47) he notes that the emperor's order was that those who denied their faith were to be released, otherwise they were to be beheaded. He adds (47) that at the start of the festival the governor questioned the Christians again before the public tribunal; citizens he beheaded, and others he condemned to the beasts.[42]

Eusebius (37) says that a day of beast-fighting was specifically arranged for the Christians, but he initially mentions only four Christians (Maturus, Sanctus, Blandina, and Attalus) 'led into the amphitheater to be exposed to the beasts and to give a public spectacle of the pagans' inhumanity'. Preliminary torments followed (38): 'Once again they ran the gauntlet of whips (according to the local custom), the mauling of animals, and anything else that the mad mob from different places shouted for and demanded. And to crown all they were put in the iron seat, from which their roasted flesh filled the audience with its savour.' In the end (39) 'they were sacrificed after being made all day long a spectacle to the world to replace the varied entertainment of the gladiatorial combat'. 'Blandina was hung on a post and exposed as bait for the wild animals that were let loose on her.' None, however, would touch her (40).

Attalus was led around the arena with a sign declaring him a Christian; but when the governor found out he was a citizen, he was sent back to jail while the governor awaited a response to his inquiry to the emperor (43–4). The next day Alexander and Attalus, despite his citizenship, were brought to the arena (50–1): 'For to please the mob the governor was offering Attalus to the beasts a second time.'[13] Tortured on the brazen seat before being 'sacrificed', Attalus accused the crowd, rather than the Christians, of cannibalism (52).[44]

On the last day of the games Blandina and the boy Ponticus were brought back (53). When they refused to recant and condemned their persecutors, the crowd grew angry and showed no mercy. 'After the scourges, the animals, and the hot griddle, she was at last tossed into a net and exposed to a bull' (56). She was tossed to death, but the spectacle was not finished (57): 'But not even this was enough to satisfy their madness and their viciousness towards the Christians. For these wild and barbarous people once stirred up by the wild Beast were difficult to satisfy, and their wickedness found another special form in what they did to the bodies of the dead.' Death was not enough. Death was not the end of the spectacle.

Scholars have suggested a historical connection between the massacre at Lyons and the edict of AD 177 setting limits on the prices of gladiators and the expenses of shows. It is argued that, as a result of the decree, Christians were being substituted in the gladiatorial games for volunteers called *trinqui* used for ritual sacrifice at the annual festival of the Three Gauls. Oliver and Palmer support this interpretation from details in Eusebius' account: Christians were killed at a festival of the Three Gauls, like the *trinqui* of the inscriptions, with imperial permission (47); Christians were a substitute for gladiators (40, 53) just as the *trinqui* were in the inscriptions; and Christians were murdered like the *trinqui* in what passed for a sacrificial rite (40, 56).[45] They also suggest that the Christians fought with beasts (37) as *trinqui* perhaps did, but the the 'fighting' amounted simply to exposure. It is important to note, also, that the edict does not explicitly mention Christians.[46]

Whatever his personal reservations about gladiatorial shows, Marcus Aurelius was concerned about expenses and the frontier, and his action concerning Gaul was largely a matter of economics.[47] After the plague of AD 165–75 and in a time of economic stress, criminals, including Christians, were unpopular, cheap, and convenient, if rather uncombative, substitutes for *trinqui* (Ital. 58: <t>rin<quo>s; S 12) as arena victims. As *trinqui*, *damnati* were cheaper than even cheap gladiators: Ital. 56–8 shows that *damnati* were purchased by *lanistae* for six gold pieces and sold to priests for 2,000 HS (maximum). The cheapest gladiator went for 3,000 HS (maximum).[48] Without investing in training or maintaining them for long, the manager made a profit simply for delivery of capitally condemned criminals.[49] Any fighting of men or beasts by these victims was just to increase the show. Once the emperor opened the door, officials in Gaul took advantage of the edict.[50] Christians were being used coldly as an imperial resource, but local passions and the fear of resurrection took matters to extremes.

Eusebius' lurid description of the treatment of the Christian corpses at Lyons shows the spectators' emotional and religious intensity:

(59–60) At any rate, those that had been strangled in prison they threw to the dogs, watching sedulously both day and night lest we might bury any of the bodies. Then whatever was left of those who had been exposed to the beast or the fire, some charred and ripped apart as they were, with the heads off the rest and pieces of their bodies, all this they similarly left unburied and kept under guard of soldiers for days on end. Some men raged and ground their teeth at these bodies as though they were trying to take some further special revenge on them. Others laughed and mocked them, at the same time exalting their own idols, attributing their punishment to them . . .

(61) . . . but for our part there was great grief because . . . we could not bury the martyrs' bodies in the earth. For to this end neither was the night any help, nor did money persuade, nor did our supplications discomfort them. But they kept guard in every way as though they would derive great profit from depriving them of burial . . .

(62–3) And so the bodies of the martyrs, exposed in every possible way and left unburied for six days, were then burned and reduced to ashes by these vicious men and swept into the river Rhone which flows hard by, so that not a single relic of their bodies might be left on earth. And they did this as though they could overcome God and deprive the martyrs of their restoration, in order, as they themselves said, 'that they might have no hope in the resurrection in which they put their trust when they introduce this strange new cult among us and despise the torments, walking readily and joyfully to their death. Now let us see whether they will rise again, and whether their God can help them and rescue them from our hands.'[51]

Abused before and after death, the martyrs' bodies were exposed and guarded, thrown to dogs, and then burned, with the bones ground and the ashes dumped in the Rhone. The rhetorical nature of the text invites skepticism,[52] but the motifs of enraged, vengeful crowds, insult, abuse, exposure, denial, and ultimate disposal of remains by water are credible and characteristic. Burial was denied even though friends tried to get their bodies by night, money, or 'supplications'.[53] Whether Romans routinely denied burial to martyrs is uncertain, but early martyrologies indicate Christian fears of such insults.[54]

Recurring martyrological references, especially in Eusebius, indicate that provincial officials used water both as a form of execution (i.e. drowning)

251

and as a means of disposal, sometimes simultaneously. Perhaps because of the location of Caesarea by the sea, Eusebius' *Martyrs of Palestine* contains various examples.[55] Like his brother at Alexandria, Apphianus at Caesarea in 306 was tortured and then thrown, not yet dead, into the sea.[56] In 306, when Maximinus celebrated his birthday at Caesarea, the martyr Agapius, after having been exposed to a bear, was thrown the next day, still alive, into the sea with stones tied to his feet.[57] Eusebius' *Ecclesiastical History* provides further examples.[58] According to Eusebius, in 303 at Nicomedia some martyrs died by fire or the sword, but executioners bound some of the imperial servants, put them in small boats, and threw them into the sea. Ones already buried were dug up and also thrown into the sea, lest people worship them in their graves as gods.[59] Eusebius also says that bodies of Egyptian martyrs at Tyre, who were thrown to beasts and then killed by the sword, were not buried in the earth but were thrown into the sea.[60] Concern about Christian concepts of resurrection or martyr cults (see below) may have led Romans to compound abuses (e.g. beasts or fire, with water as the final act), but they were following traditional lines of punishment and disposal of perceived threats and religious contaminations.

The *Passion* of St Theodotus of Ancyra, which seems to be a reliable document (probably written soon after AD 360) concerning the persecution of Christians (probably Montanists) in Ancyra under Maximinus Daia in AD 311–13, contains several intriguing details. After collecting the remains of the martyr Valens, which had been thrown into the Halys River (10), Theodotus heard about seven Christian virgins who had refused to perform sacrifice. They were condemned and taken to a nearby lake, were weighted down with stones about their necks, and taken in a boat to a deep part of the lake and drowned (13–20). Soldiers were posted to guard the lake (17), but some left to attend a festival and others were driven away by a storm. Theodotus and another man took sickles to cut the ropes holding the stones, and, when the same storm exposed the bodies in the lake, they retrieved them and buried them. Subsequently the burials were discovered, and the bodies were exhumed and burnt (20).[61]

The disposal of martyrs by water at Rome itself is recalled in a painting by Ludovico Carracci, *St Sebastian Thrown into the Cloaca* (see jacket illustration), an exception to the usual scenes of St Sebastian in late medieval and Renaissance art as a young man pierced with arrows.[62] According to tradition, around AD 303–5 Sebastian was a tribune in the praetorians at Rome who declared his Christian faith. An attempt to kill him with numerous arrows failed. Left for dead, he was saved and nursed to health by Irene. He was recaptured or presented himself again to Diocletian, who ordered that he be beaten to death and his body dumped in a canal called the Euripus Agrippae. In order to provide the decent burial denied by the soldiers, Lucina, inspired by a vision, recovered his body from the drain (*cloaca*).[63] Alongside this drain, a church (San Bastianello) was later built in the twelfth century and dedicated to Sebastian, to be replaced by the present-day church of Sant'Andrea della Valle in the sixteenth century.[64]

Another late and suspect legend says that two brothers, Simplicius and Faustinus, refusing to sacrifice, were beheaded and thrown into the Tiber (another version says that they were drowned in the Tiber) in 303. The bodies were recovered by their sister Beatrice (Viatrix) and buried in the catacomb of Generosa on the road to Porto. Exposed in 304 as a Christian by a neighbor seeking her estate, Beatrice was strangled in prison and was buried with her brothers. Relics of all three were 'translated' by Pope Leo III in the seventh century to the church of Santa Bibiana and later to Santa Maria Maggiore.[65] The catacomb of Generosa was found in 1868 and yielded a fragmentary inscription: 'The martyrs Simplicius and Faustinus who suffered death in the Tiber River (*qui passi sunt in flumen* [*sic*] *Tibere*) and have been laid to rest in the cemetery of Generosa above Philippi'.[66] Although probably aprocryphal, such martyrological traditions recall a long familiarity with denial and disposal by water.

Relics and resurrection

Roman and early Christian attitudes and responses to death and burial must be understood against the history of Christian doctrines of resurrection. In her profound work, Bynum shows that early Christians' anxieties about proper (i.e. whole) burial were related to their belief in somatic resurrection. They feared that the treatment of the corpse might jeopardize or affect the state of the body when resurrected at the Last Judgement. Just as pagans imagined embodied souls in Hades, Christians feared that the resurrected body would bear the signs of abuse. There was an early and continuing assumption 'that formal and material continuity is necessary for the survival of body and that the survival of body is necessary for the survival of self'.[67]

St Paul used the metaphor of a seed to present the resurrected body as regrown whole from a seedling. There was continuity but also radical transformation: 'numerical identity through spatio-temporal continuity but not necessarily material continuity'.[68] In the continuing spiritualist–physicalist debate among early Christians, the end of the second century saw increased emphasis on bodily resurrection of the same flesh. The idea of organic regrowth from a seed was losing out to the idea of inorganic, mechanical reassemblage of pieces. Around AD 200 Tertullian wrote of the resurrection of the self in the physical and not merely the spiritual body. By a process of 'reassemblage' the pieces of the body were to recombine into the resurrected body as the embodied self – healed, purified, and whole.[69]

Fear of martyrdom, of agony, of decay, and of being eaten profoundly influenced Christian thinking. As Bynum explains, this concept of reassemblage of the original body relates to the context of persecutions and martyrdom. The resurrected body is that of the abused martyr, reassembled

253

whole – no matter what happened to it before, during, or after the martyr-dom.[70] Reassemblage thus allayed Christian fears of execution, abuse and denial of burial. It gave a guarantee of changelessness and peace. 'Resur-rection is victory over partition and putrefaction; it is both the anesthesia of glory and the reunion of particles of self. Resurrection guarantees not only the justice denied to the living; it guarantees the rest and reassemblage – the burial – denied to the dead.'[71]

Both Romans and Christians understood punishment and vengeance beyond death. The torments that Christian writers record or predict for their persecutors reflect traditional Roman patterns of abuse and damnation, but with their final scene being the fires of hell.[72] As Minucius Felix (*Oct.* 11.5, 34–5, Loeb) says, Christians 'promise themselves, as virtuous, a life of never-ending bliss after death; to all others, as evil-doers, everlasting punishment'. Denial of Christian burial surely lies behind remarks in Lactantius when he (incorrectly) says that Nero was denied burial, and when he (correctly) notes that Domitian suffered *damnatio memoriae* and that Decius was denied burial and stripped naked for the carrion animals.[73] Like Tertullian (*De spect.* 30) rejoicing in the spectacle to come of fire consuming persecutors in the apocalypse, Lactantius (*De mort. pers.* 50.7) rejoices in the poetic justice of abuse and denial coming to leaders who persecuted Christians: God justly punished the persecutors with 'the very things they had done to others'.

Condemning Christians for their monotheistic exclusiveness, their reli-gious treason, Romans were bewildered by their non-resistance and even enthusiasm for death. Christians felt that they were sacrificing themselves for God, but most Romans, in terms of their own culture, thought that they were excessive and suicidal. We have seen that Roman law allowed suicide in defense of acceptable principles, but spectators did not condone Christian suicide, which seemed to them to be without reason or accept-able principles.[74] In their eyes, these suicidal criminals deserved the same type of post-mortem damnation inflicted on those who committed suicide or suffered *summa supplicia*.

Christian anxieties about burial and bodily resurrection help explain refer-ences (especially early ones) to the retrieval, burial, or preservation of remains of martyrs. After around 200 Tertullian and others confidently claimed that whole resurrection was assured and that the fate of the corpse was irrelevant. For their part, Romans had always been concerned about honoring, appeasing, and keeping away the spirits of their own dead (e.g. via burial, rites, and offerings). Faced with Christian claims of somatic resurrection of the original bodies of martyrs, Romans reacted in a defensive and preven-tive manner. They went beyond execution to add further insult and abuse to Christian corpses, seeking to destroy and disperse the remains.[75] They attacked condemned Christians and even Christian cemeteries; their brutality was moved by rage and indignation but also by concerns about Christian resurrection. Roman abuses were both physically and spiritually apotropaic – they wanted to expel and keep away both the ghosts and the bodies of Christians. In both respects water presented a 'final solution'.

NOTES

1 These torments are attested in the *The Jesuit Relations* based on the information conveyed by Hurons, who escaped the Iroquois, to Christopher Regnaut, who brought the priests' remains back to the nearby Jesuit base at Fort Sainte Marie. Lalement suffered similar torments with Brébeuf and was killed the next day. *The Jesuit Relations*, vol. 34, *Lower Canada. Hurons: 1649*, ed. R. E. Thwaites (Cleveland: The Burrows Brothers, 1898) Doc. 69 by Christopher Regnaut, 25–37; E. J. Devine, *The Jesuit Martyrs of Canada*, 3rd ed. (Toronto: The Canadian Messenger, 1925) 46–52; Parkman (1867) 489–95. *The Jesuit Relations*, 33, adds a comment on Brébeuf's remains: 'The barbarians threw the remains of his body into the fire; but the fat which still remained on his body extinguished the fire, he was not consumed.'

2 Prudentius, a Christian poet of the late Empire, was eager to retell the agonies of early martyrs but admitted a paucity of records about them: *Perist.* 1.73. Surveys of the value and problems of using such texts as historical sources include: Musurillo (1972) xi–lvii; G. E. M. de Sainte-Croix, 'Aspects of the "Great" Persecution', *Harv. Theol. Rev.* 47 (1954) 75–113; T. D. Barnes, 'The Pre-Decian Acta Martyrum', *JTS* 19 (1968) 509–31; T. D. Barnes, *Constantine and Eusebius* (Cambridge, Mass.: Harvard U., 1981) esp. 148–63; Fox (1987) 434–41; and Bowersock (1995) 23–39. Most recently, Potter (1996), 144–7, notes that martyrology emerged around the same time as the development of Roman transcriptions of trials; even fictional narratives can be valuable when they give the appearance of transcription and reflect official procedures to suggest an air of authenticity.

3 Various martyrs are said to have been killed at Rome (e.g. Placidius, Telesphorus, Ptolemaeus, Justin, and others), and some martyrs are said to have died in the Colosseum (e.g. Ignatius, Eustace, Eleuterio), but no source reliably puts them there. See de Sainte-Croix (1954) 94–5, on the lack of contemporary written evidence for martyrdoms at Rome under the 'Great Persecution'; oral traditions circulated but were not put into writing until the late fifth or early sixth century. My discussion here is not comprehensive and it concentrates on the more reliable accounts up to Eusebius and Lactantius; selected incidents from persecutions are used to show procedures, attitudes, and methods of disposal. Valuable studies include: W. H. C. Frend, *Martyrdom and Persecution in the Early Church* (Oxford: Basil Blackwell, 1965); Fox (1987), esp. ch. 9, 'Persecution and Martyrdom', 418–92; H. Delehaye, *Les Origines du culte des martyrs* (Brussels: Bollandists, 1933); Peter Brown, *The Cult of the Saints: Its Rise and Function in Latin Christianity* (Chicago: U. Chicago, 1981); T. D. Barnes, 'Legislation against the Christians', *JRS* 58 (1968) 32–50; G. E. M. de Sainte-Croix, 'Why Were the Early Christians Persecuted?', *P&P* 26 (1963) 6–38. On Tertullian as a source for the arena, see Bomgardner (1989) 85–8. Recent works have noted theatrical and literary parallels to pagan performances in the way Christians viewed themselves as martyrs in the arena; see Bynum (1995) 44; Rouselle (1988) 107–31; Barton (1994); and Potter (1993).

4 L. Hertling and E. Kirschbaum, *The Roman Catacombs and their Martyrs*, rev. ed., trans. M. J. Costello (London: Darton, Longman and Todd, 1960) 82–3,

warn against believing fantastic numbers: 'There were certainly not tens of thousands, or hundreds of thousands of martyrs at Rome during the persecution of Diocletian since the Christian community at that time did not number a hundred thousand souls.' They suggest that executions of martyrs did not exceed, and were usually smaller than, groups of 40 or 50 in number. Fox (1987), 592, estimating that around 5 per cent of the population around 300 was Christian, feels, 315, that martyrdom was a rare occurrence. He, 434, notes that no governor in Africa is known to have executed Christians before 180, and he cites Origen's comment (*C. Cels.* 3.8) in the 240s that 'few' Christians had died for their faith. Following de Sainte-Croix (1954) 102, 104, Fox adds, 597, that the numbers who died in the 'Great Persecution' are uncertain, 'but the impact of a persecution was always greater than the numbers executed or sentenced to the mines'. Similarly, Rouselle (1988), 130–1, correctly notes that the numbers may not have been that large, but that the fear of persecution greatly influenced Christian ideas; see Bynum below.

5 Robinson (1995) 95–7, comparing the persecutions with pagan repression of cults such as the Bacchanalians and Druids, comments, 96–7, that 'the Romans treated the cults of Isis and Christ with equal indifference, and repressed them with equal brutality when it seemed expedient for public discipline'.

6 Bowersock (1995), 50, emphasizes that 'the martyrdom spectacles did not import something altogether new in the urban life of those spectacles in the amphitheater that were well established and much appreciated'. See below. MacMullen (1986a), n. 20 on 156, collects references showing analogies between pagan and Christian abuse, trial, and punishment. In Apuleius, *Met.* 10.10, when accused of homicide, the prisoner is racked, beaten, and burned; compare *Pass. S. Polycarpi* 2.4; Euseb. *HE* 3.32.6.

7 On the causes, motives, and legal basis, if any, for early persecutions, see Barnes (1968); Sainte-Croix (1963); O. F. Robinson, 'The Repression of Christians in the pre-Decian Period: A Legal Problem Still', *The Irish Jurist* 25–7 (1990–2) 269–92; Fox (1987) 422–8; Frend (1965) 165–8, 312–13. Robinson (1995), 80, 96–7, suggests that Christian groups could not be seen as legal associations (*collegia*) because they met more than once a month, but that Christianity was probably not an illegal religion until the edict of Decius in 250 or 251 demanded that all subjects sacrifice to the Roman gods.

8 Tert. *Apol.* 10.1: Christians would neither worship Roman gods nor sacrifice to emperors, so they were accused of 'sacrilege and treason together'; cf. 24.1, 28.2. At Smyrna (*Mart. Pionii* 15.2.1–2, 18.13–14) Christians were asked to offer sacrifice (and to eat of sacrificial meat) in the cult of Nemesis, associated with the emperor and with social order. Refusal was taken as both secular and sacral treason: see Hornum (1993) 130–1; Bowersock (1995) 29, 47, 53.

9 E.g. Tert. *Apol.* 2.16, Loeb; 7.1: 'the most criminal of men' (*sceleratissimi*); cf. 2.1: *nocentissimos*. Disasters were met with cries of 'Christians to the lions!': *Apol.* 40.1–2.

10 Tac. *Ann.* 15.44.3–8, Loeb. Suetonius, *Ner.* 16.2, Loeb, comments: 'Punishment was inflicted on the Christians, a class of men given to a new mischievous superstition (*superstitionis novae ac maleficae*).' Romans of the early Empire tended to see Christians as a variant sect of Judaism; see Robert L. Wilken, *The Christians as the Romans Saw Them* (New Haven: Yale U., 1984) 113–17, 184–5, 197–8. On a possible persecution of Christians, more probably of Jews, under Domitian, see Dio 67.14.1–2; cf. Fox (1987) 433. Of course, Rome had publicly abused Jews before the persecutions of Christians began. Philo, *In Flacc.* 85, says that in AD 39 in a morning 'spectacle' at a theater in Alexandria Jews were whipped, hung, turned on the wheel, tortured, and then led away through

the orchestra to execution; see Bowersock (1995) 48–9. Claudius had expelled Jews from Rome for causing disturbances at the instigation of 'Christus': Suet. *Claud*. 25.4. Wars in Palestine, as recounted by Josephus, had familiarized Romans with Jewish obstinacy; and, as noted in ch. 3 above, Titus sent Jewish captives to other provinces to be killed to celebrate his victory.

11 Cf. *ingens multitudo* in Tac. *Ann*. 14.8: a large number of people on seashore at Baiae congratulate Agrippina on surviving the collapse of her boat. Cf. *Ann*. 6.19.3: *immensa strages*: the immense mass killed by Tiberius, mentioned in ch. 7 above.

12 See n. 6 above. Crook (1984) 273: 'Now the summa supplicia were emphatically not an invention of the Principate, for all that they are associated primarily in everybody's mind with the Christian martyrdoms, including the first of them all.'

13 Like the 'fellowship' of men and beast attributed to spectators by Cicero in 55 BC (see ch. 1 above), any 'compassion' in AD 64 still saved no victims. On Nero's motives and legality, see Bauman (1996) 67, 86–7.

14 Ignatius *Ep. ad Rom*. 4.1–2, 5.2–3, trans. K. Lake, *Apostolic Fathers*, Loeb, 2:231–3. On destruction, see ch. 6 above; Bynum (1995) 27–8, and below.

15 Bowersock (1995) 5; 6: 'Ignatius betrays no knowledge of the language or concept of martyrdom.' Martyrdom's roots were in western Asia Minor rather than Greece (i.e. Socrates), Palestine (i.e. Maccabees), or Judaism; see Bowersock, 1–21. Bowersock, 41–58, explains the phenomenon in the context of Roman institutions (e.g. judicial procedures, spectacles) and the urban life (e.g. urban spaces and facilities, the imperial cult) of the Greco-Roman world. As he, 28, puts it: ' . . . Christianity owed its martyrs to the *mores* and structures of the Roman empire'.

16 *Act. SS. Justin et Sociorum* 6.2. See Musurillo (1972) text no. 4, pp. 52–3 of 42–62. Recension B.6 of the *Acts* says that after Justin and other martyrs were beheaded 'at the usual place' (Recension C.6, pp. 60–1, says 'the place of execution'), followers 'secretly took their bodies and buried them in a suitable place'. The Christians Ptolemaeus and Lucius had been condemned to death at Rome in the early 150s by the urban prefect (Q. Lollius Urbicus): Justin *Apol*. 2.2; but the fate of their bodies is unknown.

17 Frend (1965), 270–2, cites Ulpian, *Dig*. 48.24.1, saying that Christians would normally have the right to claim bodies, but see below on Christians' use of bribery and stealth to gather remains.

18 See n. 3 above. Bowersock (1995), 18–19, 41, points out that most early martyrdoms took place at important cities of the eastern Empire (e.g. Pergamum, Smyrna, Caesarea by the Sea, Carthage, Alexandria), an area especially fond of agonistic and amphitheatrical spectacles. As Fox (1987), 420, suggests, martyrdoms were 'exceptionally public events because Christians coincided with a particular phase in the history of public entertainment'. He also notes, 484–9, the significance of the urban locations of the governors' assize courts.

19 See Musurillo (1972), text no. 1, pp. 2–20. Bowersock (1995), 13, 17, identifies the *Passion* of Polycarp, probably written not long after the execution, as the earliest text with 'martyr' and 'martyrdom' (in the clear sense of 'death at the hands of hostile secular authority'), the 'first attested example of the word and act together'. On the authenticity of the account, and the date, see Barnes (1968) 510–14.

20 On crowds calling for the punishment of individuals by name, see Potter (1996) 153, 156–7, who, 157, stresses that the initiative at Smyrna came from the crowd: 'Polycarp was sacrificed on the altar of public opinion, against the inclination of leaders in local government and, it seems, that of the governor.'

21 On gladiators as executioners, see ch. 6 above, and below on Perpetua.

22 As became customary, Christians cared for Polycarp's remains and gathered at the grave (18.2–3) to celebrate the day of martyrdom as the *dies natalis* (the birthday into eternal life). On the Roman custom of celebrating the birthday of the departed at the grave, see Toynbee (1971) 63; Rush (1941) 72–90. Cf. Fox (1987) 446–9, 599–600, on the magical value of martyrs' bodies and relics as 'precious property'. As he says, 446, 'The race for skin and bones began early'; and, 448, 'Before long, church leaders were digging up corpses and breaking them into fragments.'

23 *Pass. Perp. et Fel.*, Musurillo (1972) text no. 8, pp. 107–31. Potter (1993), 57–8, sees this as a central hagiographic text and a model for other passions. L. Robert, 'Une vision de Perpétue martyre à Carthage en 203', *CR Acad. Inscr.* (1982) 228–76 (= *OMS* 5.791–839), compares the text to the testimony of art and inscriptions, and sees Perpetua's visions in her diary (e.g. God as an *agonothetes*, a fight with Satan as an Egyptian athlete) as a reflection of the procedures and terminology of athletic and amphitheatrical games at Carthage. On Perpetua and arena procedures, also see Bomgardner (1989) 88–91. With a detailed bibliography in n. 2 on 3, Shaw (1993) sees the diary as a rare survival of a piece of literature by a female. He discusses, 36–45, the redaction and editing of the account by male Christian writers influenced by the Church's gender concerns as a martyr cult to Perpetua and Felicitas developed at Carthage with annual celebrations and readings of the passion.

24 Wiedemann (1992), 87, compares Clement, *First Epistle* 6.2, with Christian women executed wearing costumes of Danaids and Dirce. Rouselle (1988), 112–21, compares this account to persistent traditions of child sacrifice in North Africa and notes sacrificial elements here: the request that the men wear robes of priests of Saturn and the women those of priestesses of Ceres, the cry by spectators that Saturus was 'well washed' by his own blood (see n. 8 in ch. 6 above), the eating of scraps of the victims' flesh by beasts, and the eating of the meat of arena beasts by spectators (see ch. 6 above). Rouselle suggests that the volition of the martyrs (accepting their punishment and agreeing to sacrifice themselves) is appropriate to sacrificial ritual, and that Tertullian's reference to the laughter at *meridiani* (*Apol.* 15.4) and his anticipation of Christian laughter at the persecution of foes in the Last Judgement (*De spec.* 30) are examples of ritual laughter appropriate to sacrifices. M. Leglay, *Saturne africaine: histoire* (Paris: É. de Boccard, 1966) 10, 236–7, 329–49, suggests that the execution of *noxii* in *munera* may have been used as a way to continue traditional human sacrifices to Baal and Tanit at Carthage. On Rome and human sacrifice, see ch. 1 above.

25 Like costuming them as pagan gods, stripping Christians added to their humiliation. Cf. 10.7: in a vision Perpetua sees herself stripped for a match with an Egyptian athlete. See Shaw (1993) 7–9, with parallels in n. 22 on 8, on the sexual dimensions of arena abuse (e.g. nudity, choice of bulls or cows) intended to dishonor females.

26 Bynum (1995), 45–6, explains the motif that martyrs do not feel pain: the glory of martyrdom was seen to act as an anesthesia that made the pain of the arena bearable.

27 Other demands by the crowd: 20.2–3, 20.7.

28 As Shaw (1993), 42 and nn. 87–9, explains, the bodies of Perpetua and Felicitas were said to have been buried at Carthage in the Basilica Maiorum north of the city: Victor Vitensis *Historia persecutionis Africanae provinciae* 1.3.9. Apparently but not conclusively, their tombs were discovered with conjoined sarcophagi and a memorial inscription: see Diehl, *ILCV* no. 2040 (= *CIL* 8.25038); cf. Musurillo (1972) n. 4 on 109. See R. P. Delattre, 'Sur l'inscription

des martyrs de Carthage, sainte Perpétue, sainte Félicité et leurs compagnons', *CR Acad. Inscr.* (1907) 193–5; cf. H. Leclercq, 'Carthage', Cabrol–Leclercq, *Dict. d'arch. chrétienne* 2 (1910) cols. 2233–52, on the excavations by Delattre. The identification of the church remains uncertain, the epigraphical evidence is late and heavily restored, and the cult of the saints led the early church to discoveries (often aided by visions) of previously forgotten or unknown relics, which were then identified and relocated.

29 On trials and interrogation procedures, see de Sainte-Croix (1963) 11–13; and Potter (1993) 64–5 and (1996) 147–55. Applying the sociology of spectacles, Potter (1993), 63–71, interprets the trials as contests in which martyrs defeated the state by refusing to sacrifice and paradoxically 'won' martyrdom. As Tertullian, *Scap.* 5, cited by Bowersock (1995) 20, said to a Roman governor, 'Your cruelty is our glory.'

30 Eusebius, *HE* 8.7–9, recounts a long list of horrible torments and executions of martyrs at Tyre and in the Thebais in the early years of the fourth century, including everything from beasts and crucifixion to the use of sharp potsherds to flinging naked women aloft by machines.

31 On the influence of the crowd, see Potter (1996) esp. 129, 152–3. MacMullen (1986a), n. 14 on 151, cites numerous examples of crowds calling for certain punishments of Christians.

32 E.g. at Caesarea in 310, when a household servant of the martyr Pamphilus asked to be able to bury the bodies of Pamphilus and his six companions, the governor Firmilianus confirmed that the youth was a Christian and put him to death: Euseb. *Mart. Pal.* 11.15–19. Maximus, the governor who tried St Tarachus, who died in the same persecution as Polycarp at Tarsus in 306, said that he would not destroy his body in such a way as to prevent a woman from giving his remains some rites (e.g. a winding sheet, ointment): *Act. SS. Tarachi, Probi et Andronici* 7, noted in Rush (1941) 123. Eusebius, *HE* 7.16.1, claims that Asturius, a senator, took away the body of martyred Saint Marinus on his own shoulders, prepared it in a splendid robe, and gave it a fitting burial.

33 Emerging from apocalyptic and teleological elements, the Christian notion of resurrection (discussed below) must have disturbed and baffled Romans. Min. Fel. *Oct.* 9.4, Loeb: 'To say that a malefactor put to death for his crimes, and the wood of the death-dealing cross, are objects of their [Christian] veneration is to assign fitting altars to abandoned wretches and the kind of worship they deserve.' Ibid., 11.2: Christians threaten the world with fire and destruction and 'say that they are born anew after death from the cinders and ashes'.

34 Frend (1965), 287–8, accepts as true various accounts of the destruction of bodies to counter notions of bodily resurrection. Concerning persecutions in Asia under Marcus Aurelius, Tatian, *Ad Gr.* 6.2, says that the flesh of Christians was consumed in various ways to dispel hopes of bodily resurrection, but Christians were assured of resurrection even if their bodies were torn by beasts or dispersed through rivers. Cf. August. *De civ. D.* 1.12, cf. 21–2, on the sack of Rome: God would raise up Christians even if unburied or eaten by beasts.

35 Tert. *Apol.* 37.2, Loeb; cf. Eusebius on Nicomedia below. Valerian's first edict in 257 ordered that Christian leaders sacrifice to the gods of the state or local communities would be forbidden to assemble or to enter their cemeteries: *Act. Proconsularia Cypriani* 1.7. See Frend (1965) 323–5, on Christian cemeteries near Carthage attacked by pagans (cf. Tert. *Scap.* 3.1). Hippolytus, *In Danielem* 4.51, claims that in the Severan persecution of 203 at Smyrna men were burned alive or thrown to the beasts, children were killed and left to be eaten by dogs, and 'cemeteries were robbed and destroyed, and the bones of the dead scattered'.

36 *Dig.* 47.12.4 (Paulus 27 ad ed.): 'sepulchra hostium religiosa nobis non sunt'; cited by Bodel (1986) n. 160 on 108.

37 Scornful reactions to Christian enthusiasm: M. Aurel. *Med.* 11.3; Epict. *Diss.* 4.7.6. Barton (1994), 56–7 and passim, stressing the importance of Christian volition, says that Christians adopted the *sacramentum* (e.g. Tert. *Ad Mart.* 3.1, *Scorp.* 4.5) and, in her terms, the 'sacralization' of the Roman soldier and gladiator, thus consecrating themselves and vindicating their honor in the manner of their deaths. Potter (1993), 56–63, explains that, inspired by Christ's model of suffering, sacred texts (e.g. the deaths of John, Peter, and Paul), and the hope of sitting in judgement over their persecutors, martyrs piously faced death without terror, thus foiling the intentions of producers of the shows.

38 Eusebius, *Mart. Pal.* 7.4, 8.2–3, cited by Millar (1992) 1995, reports that, of the Christians condemned in Palestine around AD 307 to fight as gladiators or to be sent to the beasts or mines, the ones condemned to be gladiators refused to be trained or even maintained by the imperial treasury.

39 Earlier, Trajan's policy had been to punish unrepentant Christians but not to seek them out: Plin. *Ep.* 10.96–7, noted by Tert. *Apol.* 2.6–9 and 5.7. From the late second century on, 'voluntary' martyrs challenged Rome and embarrassed the Church by seeking out ostentatious arena deaths. See de Sainte-Croix (1954) 101–4; and Fox (1987) 441–5, who, 425, 456–7, shows that Rome wanted religious conformity, lapsed Christians, and more worshippers of pagan gods – not martyrdoms. Potter (1993), 56–63, suggests that, in the context of third-century attacks on elite Church leaders, officials feared the social disruption of the imposition of slave penalties on non-lower-class individuals.

40 Euseb. *HE* 5.1.3–63, esp. 57–62; trans. Musurillo (1972) text no. 5, pp. 62–85. Cf. Frend (1965) 1–30; and Musurillo, xx and n. 13 on lxiv, on the account's authenticity.

41 Martyrologists suggest that the gnashing of teeth verged on cannibalism. Tannahill (1975), 9, 35, explains that cannibalism could be an act of hatred and ultimate vengeance, and that, similarly, in societies where cannibalism was forbidden, destruction of the body and denial of burial were acts of hatred and vengeance. Cf. the stoning of St Stephen (Acts 7.8–60) at Jerusalem after a defiant court appearance where members of the council 'ground their teeth with fury' at him (7.54). As Plass (1995), 144, says of rhetorical accounts of cannibalistic rage and orgiastic violence in Roman historiography, 'If the turn of phrase is rhetorical, there is no reason to dismiss the reality it dramatizes.' On charges of cannibalism, see ch. 6 above.

42 As Rouselle (1988), 117, explains, Roman citizens (with the exception of Attalus, discussed below) were killed outside the arena, free foreigners (non-citizens) were burned at the stake in the arena, and Blandina and some other slaves were exposed to beasts.

43 The crowd had demanded Attalus (5.1.43), and Potter (1996), 157–8, suggests that Attalus had an 'enemy in high places' at Lyons. He notes that only Christians associated with Attalus, and not the whole Christian community at Lyons, were punished; and he argues that the governor yielded to local hatred for Attalus and disobeyed the emperor's order that citizens be decapitated. P. Keresztes, 'The Massacre at Lyons in 177 A.D.', *Hist.* (1967) 75–86, sees the incident as an example of crowd pressures on a governor, one who violated the spirit and letter of Trajan's policy.

44 Cf. Prudent. *Perist.* 2.401–8, cited by Bowersock (1995) 60: Lawrence, roasted on a grill, joked to the prefect that his flesh was done: 'Eat it up and try whether it is better raw or roasted.' On charges of cannibalism, see ch. 6 above.

45 Oliver and Palmer (1955) 320–49; Piganiol (1923) 62–71, 'Les *Trinqui* gaulois,

gladiateurs consacrés' (a republication of his article in *Rev. Ét. Lat.* (1920) 283–90). Caesar, *B Gall.* 6.16.1, notes that Gauls felt that the sacrifice of criminals was especially welcome to their gods; on accounts of Gallic human sacrifice, see Rives (1995) n. 22 on 68.

46 Moreover, Barnes (1968), 518–19, points out that the Christians were executed by the governor alone, and priests of the imperial cult are not mentioned.

47 On the edict and on M. Aurelius and games, see ch. 3 above. Oliver and Palmer (1955) 325–6: 'In view of the barbarian invasions the loyalty of Gaul was critically necessary to him, and he doubtless never quite foresaw the excesses to which he was opening the way.'

48 Ital. 56–8, trans. Oliver and Palmer, 343: 'As for the Gallic provinces, (the same limits on prices for gladiators apply). But also for *trinqui*, who because of an ancient custom of sacred ritual [*veteri more et sacro ritu*] are eagerly awaited in the states of the most glorious Gallic provinces, let the *lanistae* not charge a higher price than 2,000 sesterces apiece, since their Majesties the Emperors have announced in their oration that the policy will be for a procurator of theirs to hand over to the *lanistae* at a price of not more than six pieces a man who has been condemned to death.' Ital. 57: *damnatum a<d> gladium*; S 11 *pro damnato ad gladium*.

49 Cf. Ital. 59–61: in some provinces *lanistae* were not used; priests took over gladiators bought and trained by previous priests, or free fighters who had bound themselves by contract. Such gladiators were not to be sold at higher than the rates set for *lanistae*. Clearly, if these gladiators were taken over or resold, they were not all or always killed. They were true gladiators and *auctorati*, distinct from the *trinqui* substitutes who were certain to be killed.

50 As Frend (1965), 5, says, 'The temptation of the priests of the Council of the Gauls to rid themselves of a largely alien and latently hostile group and at the same time to boost their own popularity and save their pockets may have proved too strong to resist'. Price limitations on the sale of victims delighted Gallic provincial priests, who (Ital. 16–18) no longer sought reprieve from their duty to put on shows.

51 Euseb. *HE* 5.1.57–63, trans. Musurillo (1972) text no. 5, pp. 80–3. Compare Eusebius' similar account, *Mart. Pal.* 9.8–11, of the treatment of three Christians executed at Caesarea in 309: the governor Firmilianus denied them burial and had the corpses exposed outside the city gate for several days to be abused by beasts, dogs, and birds; observers attended to make sure that the bodies were not stolen; animals ate of the flesh and scattered bones and remains about the area. Cf. *Mart. Pal.* 11.28: in 310 Firmilianus also ordered the bodies of Pamphilus and his companions exposed to beasts of prey, dogs, and birds for four days and nights, but, miraculously untouched, the corpses were later buried. Cf. Lactantius' account of disposal of remains after 'slow burning' in ch. 5 above, and see further below.

52 Musurillo (1972) xxi: 'The treatment of the Christian dead (1. 59–60) seems gratuitously cruel and may well have been invented'; cf. Frend (1965) 9: 'The condign punishment of the Christians was regarded as a necessary vindication of the gods and indeed a form of human sacrifice. There was a sense of triumph in the fact that the Christian god did not come to their aid.'

53 Christians apparently resorted to various means to get victims' bodies. Bribery: the companions of St Boniface, who was martyred at Tarsus in 306, were said to have paid a price for his body and then anointed it with unguents: *Act. S. Bonifatii Martyris* 15. Night: the body of St Cyprian, Bishop of Carthage, was removed by night and taken to burial: *Act. Proconsularia Cypriani* 5.6; Christians at Tarragona came at night with wine to the amphitheater to extinguish the

261

smouldering bodies of the martyrs Fructuosus and his deacons in 265: *Mart. Fructuosi* 6.1. (Christians preferred daytime burials, but during persecutions they buried corpses at night for safety; on the Roman customs of drenching ashes with wine and of daytime burial: Toynbee (1971) 46, 50.) Stealth: Christians secretly gathered and buried the remains of Sts Carpus, Papylus, and Agathonica at Pergamum: *Act. SS. Carpi, Papyli et Agathonicae* 46; at Lyons Christians stole the bodies of Sts Epipodius and Alexander and carried them secretly outside the city for burial: *Pass. SS. Epipodii et Alexandri* 12. On these examples, see Rush (1941) 122–3, 193–4, 205–6; with further bibliography cited by Bynum (1995) n. 115 on 49–50.

54 As well as references to Christian attention to remains, that Christians imputed motives of denial of burial (and resurrection) to Romans shows Christians' horror at corpse violation as a possible threat to literal resurrection. See Bynum (1995) 48–50 (and below); H. Leclercq, 'Martyr', Cabrol–Leclercq, *Dict. d'arch. chrétienne* 10 (1931) cols. 2425–40, esp. 2433 on disposal.

55 Leclercq, 'Martyr', col. 2429, sees drowning as an unusual capital punishment but cites a few cases. Also see examples from *Mart. Pal.* cited by Callu (1984) 333, and the excellent discussions in Barnes (1981) 152–8; and de Sainte-Croix (1954) 100–3.

56 *Mart. Pal.* 5.3, 4.13. Eusebius adds, 4.14–15, that miraculously the sea became disturbed and cast out the body at the gates of the city.

57 *Mart. Pal.* 6.7. Similarly, in 307 at Caesarea, Theodosia, a virgin from Tyre, was tortured and then condemned by the governor Urbanus to be thrown into the sea: 7.2. Eusebius also claims, 5.1, that a Christian at Tyre was shut up in an oxhide sack with a dog and a snake and thrown into the sea (i.e. like a parricide).

58 At Antioch, two virgins were executed by drowning; and, to prevent condemnation to a brothel, a mother and her two virgin daughters drowned themselves in a river: *HE* 8.12.4–5. Cf. *Mart. Pal.* 5.3 (in Alexandria a judge turned over modest women and even virgins to procurers); 8.5 (a woman provoked her execution to escape the threat of fornication); *Act. Agap. et al.* 5.8 (in AD 304 a prefect of Thessalonica ordered Irene exposed naked in a brothel, but supposedly no man would touch her).

59 *HE* 8.6.6–7. Of the same persecutions, Lactantius, *De mort. pers.* 15.3, speaks of martyrs cast into the water with millstones about their necks.

60 *HE* 8.7.6. Cf. 8.8.2, on martyrs in Egypt: some were given to the flames and others were engulfed in the sea. Cf. the *Martyrdom of Irenaeus, Bishop of Sirmium*; Musurillo (1972) text no. 23, pp. 299–301: in Pannonia in AD 304 the governor sentenced the bishop for disobedience to imperial commands (4.11); he was taken to a bridge over the Save River and beheaded, and his body was thrown into the river (5.6). Also, the *Martyrdom of Marian and James*; Musurillo (1972) text no. 14, pp. 209–11: sentenced by the prefect and awaiting the executioner in the prison, the martyrs were led out to a river valley near Cirta in Numidia for execution in AD 258 (11.10): 'Both forms of the sacrament would be present, since they would be baptized in their blood and washed in the stream.' Later (12.1–3) the text says that there were so many martyrs that the executioner had to get them to stand in rows for efficiency to save his arm and his sword: 'For if the executioner stood in one spot, there would accumulate an enormous pile of slaughtered bodies. Even the very river bed would have been choked if it were to be filled with this great heap of slaughter.' The sense is probably that the river would have been clogged if the mass of corpses were thrown in all at once, and hence they were killed and thrown in serially. Bowersock (1995), 32, comments: 'In the presence of the river the martyrdom could become literally, as it often was metaphorically, a second baptism.'

61 See S. Mitchell, 'The Life of St. Theodotus of Ancyra', *Anat. St.* 32 (1982) 93–113, esp. 94 and 102–7, with bibliography. Cf. *Pass. S. Quirini* 5, which says that Quirinus, Bishop of Sciscia, was thrown into the Save with a mill-stone about his neck. In the narrative Theodotus himself was arrested and executed at Ancyra, but a storm prevented the burning of his body; a priest from Malos provided wine, got the guards drunk, and took the body to Malos and buried it at a site which Theodotus had designated as a site for a martyrium (32–6). Mitchell locates both Malos and the site of the martyrium and defends the value of the text as a source, but cf. the reservations of Fox (1987) 599–600.

62 J. Paul Getty Mus., Malibu, inv. 71.PA.14, ca 1612. I thank Dr Mary Hart for directing me to this painting. Carracci chose to paint this rarely depicted episode because of the painting's intended (but never realized) location; see Andrea Emiliani, ed., *Ludovico Carracci*, essay and catalogue by Gail Feigenbaum (Fort Worth: Nuova Alfa Editoriale, Bologna, in association with Kimbell Art Museum, 1993) Cat. no. 70, pp. 152–4. Usual scene: e.g. Josse Lieferinxe, 'St. Sebastian Interceding for the Plague-Stricken', of 1497–9 (pierced with several arrows, Sebastian kneels before God above a plague scene); illustrated in Ariès (1982) between pp. 204 and 205. Cf. Lieferinxe's 'The Death of St. Sebastian', with a detail of soldiers throwing the saint into a round stone opening for a sewer (John G. Johnson Collection, Philadelphia); illustrated in Pearson (1973) 174. On depictions of Sebastian, see Louis Réau, *Iconographie de l'art chrétien* (Paris: Presses Universitaires de France, 1959) 3:1190–9, esp. 1198–9, with bibliography, on dumping the saint in a sewer or well.

63 For the *Pass. S. Seb.*, an inflated and unreliable fifth-century Greek martyrium, see Migne, *PG* 116:793–816. On the Euripus (or Euripus Thermarum Agrippae), which drained the Stagnum Agrippae in the Campus Martius and emptied into the Tiber, see Richardson (1992) 146–7. On the cult: B. Pesci, 'Il culto di san Sebastiano a Roma nell'antichità e nel medioevo', *Antonianum* 20 (1945) 177–220; F. L. Cross and E. A. Livingstone, eds, *Oxford Dictionary of the Christian Church*, 3rd ed. (Oxford: Oxford U., 1997) 1477; Everett Ferguson, ed., *Encyclopedia of Early Christianity* (New York: Garland Publishing, 1990) 837.

64 Under Constantine a basilica was built above the catacombs on the Appian Way and dedicated to the Apostles, but it later became known as the Basilica of San Sebastian, who was supposedly buried in the catacombs; Hibbert (1985) 69, n. 10 on 330.

65 On the relic cults and the shifting of bones from cemeteries to churches in Rome, Milan, and other church centers from the second half of the fourth century on, see Brown (1981); L. Cracco-Ruggini, 'Les Morts qui voyagent: Le Repatriement, l'exil, la glorification', 117–34, in Hinard (1995), esp. 125–34; and, in brief, Bynum (1995) 92–4, 104–8.

66 See Diehl, *ILCV*, no. 2000; Leclercq, 'Martyr', cols. 2498–9, fig. 7796; H. Leclercq, 'Tibre, Tigre', Cabrol–Leclercq, *Dict. d'arch. chrétienne* 15 (1949) col. 2300; A. Butler, *Butler's Lives of the Saints*, rev. ed., ed. H. J. Thurston and D. Attwater (Westminster, Md.: Christian Classics, 1981) 206; F. G. Holweck, *A Biographical Dictionary of the Saints* (Detroit: Gale Research Co., 1969, orig. 1924) 922. On medieval traditions in the *Gesta martyrum* that saints were thrown into the Tiber from a bridge near the Tiber Island, see Brucia (1990) 37, 129; and D'Onofrio (1980) 203.

67 Bynum (1995) 13. This section is heavily indebted to Bynum's convincing explication of the historical and intellectual developments. Also see Bernstein (1993) 172–7, 211, 328–9; John G. Gager, 'Body-Symbols and Social Reality: Resurrection, Incarnation, and Asceticism in Early Christianity', *Religion* 12 (1982) 345–63.

68 Bynum (1995) 7. Paul, I Cor. 15.20, 44, argued that resurrected Christians, reborn after the model of Jesus, are 'spiritual': they are immortal, but they are still bodies with sensations.

69 Tert. *De res.*; see Bynum (1995) 35–8, 41–3. For Tertullian we are all cadavers, whether eaten by beasts, birds, or fishes (*De res.* 8), and all corpses rot (*De anim.* 51–2). As Bynum explains, the resurrected body was victorious over death and decay, but Tertullian still condemned gladiatorial combat as an offense to the beauty of bodies created by God. Similarly, Bynum, 48, explains that Tertullian (*De anim.* 51–8) rejects the pagan idea that delay in burial hurts the soul or that those who die violently, prematurely, or without burial wander the earth as ghosts: all bodies are resurrected regardless of disposal or manner of death. Nevertheless, Christians felt that they should be buried like Christ and that they should treat corpses gently out of reverence for bodies as made in God's image and as the instrument of the soul: Min. Fel. *Oct.* 11.4, 34.10; Tert. *De cor. mil.* 11; see Nock (1932) 334–5; Rush (1941) 246–51. Christians maintained a fund of donations for burial of slaves and the poor (Tert. *Apol.* 39.6), and they were active in burying people, regardless of creed, even during plagues (Euseb. *HE* 7.22.9, 9.8.14).

70 See Bynum (1995) 43–51. As she, 43, says: 'The specific adjectives, analogies, and examples used in treatises on resurrection suggest that the palpable, vulnerable, corruptible body Christ redeems was quintessentially the mutilated cadaver of the martyr.' Also, 44: 'The paradox of change and continuity that characterizes theological and hagiographical descriptions of the risen body seems to originate in the facts of martyrdom.' Cf. Bernstein (1993), 111–15, who points out that Romans imagined post-mortem punishments in part from actual state punishments; see Lucr. 3.1014–19, on prison, the Rock, lashings, executioners, pitch, metal plates, and torches.

71 See Bynum (1995) 51–8, quote at 58. The debate on resurrection, change, and bodily integrity continued on through the third and fourth centuries with recurring spectacle images of torn and eaten flesh; see Bynum, 59–86.

72 In the Synoptic Gospels persecutors will be punished, body and soul, with damnation and fire, and part of their shame will be having their punishment visible to those whom they persecuted earlier. See Bernstein (1993) 228–47, esp. on Mark 9.43–48; Matt. 25.31–46; and Luke 16.19–31. Arena imagery recurs in Christian notions of hell's punishments and the Second Coming as a spectacle. Cf. Wiedemann (1992) 150: 'the mass execution of traitors, i.e. pagans, in a cosmic arena under the presidency of Christ. This was not a compassionate Christ, just as no compassion had been shown to those convicted of the crime of Christianity.'

73 Lactant. *De mort. pers.* 2.7 on Nero (cf. Suet. *Ner.* 50.4, 57.1), 3.3 on Domitian, 4.3 on Decius.

74 A governor of Asia in the late 180s, frustrated by the numbers and zeal of voluntary martyrs at his tribunal, said that if they were so eager to die they should leap off cliffs or use ropes to hang themselves – both means of suicide: Tert. *Scap.* 5. See Bowersock (1995) 59–74, on Christian self-sacrifice and Roman attitudes to suicide.

75 A final example, beyond our scope but not by much: Ammianus Marcellinus, 22.11.10, reports that in riots at Alexandria in AD 361 or 362 a mob killed George, an Arian bishop, and then took his corpse and others to the beach, burned them, and threw the ashes into the sea to prevent any collection and cult worship of remains. Cracco-Ruggini, op. cit., 125, cites the passage as representing 'la forme la plus radicale et irréversible d'"exil" du monde et de la mémoire des vivants'.

264

9

CONCLUSION: HUNTS AND HOMICIDES AS SPECTACLES OF DEATH

> Shame in death is the beginning of hell.
> (A. E. Bernstein, *The Formation of Hell* (1993) 167)

In the modern world the Holocaust, Vietnam, the former Yugoslavia, Rwanda, and more have made us reconfront human brutality. Examining our own violent nature drives us back further and deeper into our past, with a mandatory stop at Rome along the way. Rome makes us face our own violent legacy, our enduring predisposition to violence, and the banality of excessive violence in human history (and in the modern media).

Sadly, the contemplation of violence is essential to understanding human nature – what we have been and what we are, if not what we should become. Is violence dehumanizing or fundamentally human? Are civilization and violence antithetical, or does civilization depend on violence to control violence? Can the civilizing process succeed, or will man always know residual primitivism? Whatever its origin, for social order violence must be justified. Early man killed beasts to survive – to protect himself but mainly to eat; this killing became the sport of hunting and still retains its primitive justifications. The killing of men is justifiable for survival as well – to protect against foes and to punish criminals for prevention and revenge. To achieve its goals effectively in early societies, punishment had to be public, to be seen and sanctioned. The show had to go on. Public punishment of misbehavior regulated proper behavior by deterrence. It also reassured the community that it was protected and secure. As a violent, public, and imperial society, Rome took ritualized hunting and punishments to spectacular lengths. Even when men were tormented and killed for entertainment, the archaic justification persisted: 'that we may be safe'.

As ritualized versions of actions originally taken to ensure the survival and safety of the group, Roman blood sports legitimized, dramatically communicated, and reinforced the social and political order of the community. In the arena beasts were killed by men as if provisioning or protecting the clan or its field; men were killed by beasts as if being cast out defenseless into the wilds; and men killed other men, either in aggravated executions of doomed alien foes or domestic criminals, or in archaizing, staged duels by experts, who in the process might set a military example and achieve some redemption.

Arena disposal was a significant logistical matter and an even more significant symbolic problem. Rome's procedures concerning death and disposal of both men and beasts became ritualized over time as additional communicative functions were added; there was both continuity and change as the social order changed from an aristocratic republic to an autocratic empire. Power, protection, punishment, and patronage continued throughout. Whether we term the spectacles carnivals, ceremonies, festivals, hegemonic instruments of political control and diversion, or euergetism from Princeps to plebs, in special times and places the people of Rome had at least the illusion of sharing in the power, wealth, and privileges of Rome. Looking down from the stands felt better than looking up from the streets, and rites and punishment became entertainment and even sport. Moreover, an arena hierarchy emerged as some groups became structurally differentiated by having or lacking specialized skills, thereby meriting increased or decreased privileges. Conglomerate spectacles compounded performances formerly distinct by location and typology, and the scale and variety of the spectacles expanded over time and fluctuated with the fortunes of the empire.

In the arena humans killed humans, humans killed beasts, beasts killed humans, and beasts killed beasts. Concerning humans and animals killing animals, the Romans retained some symbolic links with the probable roots of the beast-fights as hunts. Traditional, natural hunts were transposed artificially and ritualized publicly in the arena. Domesticated animals were killed in blood sacrifices, but this was a step removed from hunts. In the arena the use of scenery and wild animals recalled original hunts, and, accordingly, at least some of the meat was consumed by the community. Beasts were killed to provision and protect the community; they were not gathered for punishment like criminals because they were not subject to human morals and laws.

The Roman mentality approached the supply, treatment, and disposal of both human and animal victims with its characteristic penchant for organization and efficiency. Both men and beasts were procured from near and far as the empire expanded. Seeking new sights Romans were presented with tigers and crocodiles, Nubians and Britons. Historically there was a development to increased centralization: friends, clients, and private entrepreneurs (e.g. hunters, *lanistae*) were increasingly replaced by official agents (e.g. governors, procurators) in the exploitation of imperial resources. Like the collection of beasts in great nets shown in mosaics of North Africa and Sicily, the legal system and the provincial administration gathered human fodder for the arena. The majority of the human and animal victims sent to Rome were not kept for very long – *vivaria* and prisons were just holding areas, and the state avoided the expense of maintenance by sending the victims to the arena with dispatch.[1] All victims in the arena, human and animal, were controlled by their handlers with whips and fire, and disobedience was not tolerated.

Permeating Roman society and its view of the human and animal worlds, inequality and hierarchy extended into the arena to death and even beyond. Animal as well as human victims were classified in various hierarchical categories according to talent, performance potential, and potential longevity. Romans might be impressed by creatures that faced death and died well (e.g. herbivores, Christians), but they more admired and associated themselves with predators and killers (e.g. lions, *bestiarii*). Exotic or skilled killers or performers (e.g. elite gladiators, tigers, elephants) might be spared or recaptured for later reuse if they showed virtue and lived up to their training. However, the vast majority of victims (i.e. docile beasts and generic *noxii*) were doomed to be slaughtered. Numbers of victims in both categories swelled as the taste for blood grew and crowds became jaded – or simply as the phenomenon became institutionalized and imperial resources became available. Under the Empire, the deaths of men or beasts or both, depending by then as much on availability as genre of spectacle, would do. As Seneca's spectators said: 'let not the arena be empty'. *Noxii* and beasts had no rights and no influential defenders. Aided by increased brutality and a discriminatory dual-penalty legal system that diminished even citizens' rights, increased numbers of condemned men, supplemented to some uncertain degree by Christians, were sent to Rome to die, or sold or killed by the state locally. Such analogies in the treatment of men and beasts, however, ended with death: dead beasts were a potential food source, but dead men were a potential source of pollution.

What do the facilities and procedures for death and disposal of human arena victims suggest about the many interpretations of the prominence of blood sports in Roman civilization? The treatment of the human body is fundamentally symbolic: whether respected or abused, what remains still represents what is gone or absent. Allowance, non-provision, and denial of burial were all expressions of the Romans' paradoxical attitudes to the games, and of their differential perceptions of their victims. The ritual of execution took on additional communicative functions and obligations – entertaining the people and demonstrating the power of imperial Rome. Rome wanted entertainment and inspiration from some victims, and reassurance and vengeance against others.

While upper-class writers wrote indignantly about injustices done to aristocrats and senatorials, little was written of the more numerous and facile injustices done to their social inferiors. Laws were made and enforced by the elite to insure the security of their families and property. In terms reminiscent of pagan senatorials writing of politicians, or of philosophers nobly invoking Republican principles when victimized by 'monstrous' despots, Christian writers heroized their peers and saints in arena martyrology as

virtuous men defiantly true to a new religion and victimized by a monstrous
state. Raised in a Roman world, however, Christian authors lacked sympathy
for pagan arena victims. As pagans, *noxii* were bound for hell – they were
not peers. Christians sought and even delighted in revenge against their
persecutors along remarkably Roman lines of vengeance and punishment,
and later Christian methods of punishing heretics owe much to Roman
legal precursors.

As in law, society, and burial at large, there was a hierarchy of status even
in the arena. Such hierarchies were socially embedded, but they could adapt
and reformulate over time, as in the elevation of gladiators above *noxii*. Status
affected removal and disposal, as in the hooking, dragging, and dumping
of despised *noxii* (and failed gladiators), and in the elevation and burial of
virtuous gladiators. Gladiators, in fact, once separated out from their original
status as mere *damnati*, were exceptional in their skills, their privileges (e.g.
costumes, weapons, freedoms), and their hopes for survival and burial.
Perhaps as in noble suicide, or probably because of their contribution to Rome
as specialized entertainers, they were allowed burial. Rather than being killed
at the funerals of noble Romans, as originally, these performers came to earn
their own obsequies. Obedient gladiators died nobly on the battlefield of the
arena, true to their word, like proper Roman soldiers of old, by the sword
after a good fight with their wounds in front, thus earning the soldier's right
of burial; but disobedient, threatening *noxii* were killed like captives and
criminals, earning neither rights nor rites.

More numerous than gladiators but less acknowledged by history, most
condemned victims sent to the arena were non-professionals, including criminals, slaves, and captives. Treated en masse as *noxii*, they faced the prospect
of not only certain and aggravated death, but perhaps also denial of proper
burial rites via dumping in pits, or denial of any burial at all via dumping
in the Tiber. Lowly victims usually had no property to be confiscated, so
Rome used their bodies. Without skill, training, or inclination, they put
on a poor show at best – as Seneca notes. They were killed in large numbers
to compensate for weak individual performances, and organizers of games
increasingly devised variations – such as naumachies and fatal charades –
to try to make things entertaining. As if Rome's wrath against *noxii* was
not sufficiently vented by their easy slaughter, ritualized violence went
beyond corporal to corpse abuse, beyond condemnation of their bodies to
damnation of their souls.

The fully developed phenomenon of the spectacles was multi-faceted and
remains subject to multiple interpretations. Pluralism must be acknowledged: elements of piety, performance, coercion, expiation, sport, and more
apply. However, as a conceptual framework making sense of disparate data
concerning human victims, the penal or punitive model works best.
Punishment and status differentiation were early and consistent themes, as
in the use of *damnatio* procedures, the social stigma and legislation against

elite participation, the gladiatorial oath's inclusion of acceptance of punishment, and views of the victims as worthless or worse. The reluctant gladiator of Ps. Quintilian (*Decl. Maj.* 9.6) says that people gathered for the 'spectacle of our punishment' (*ad spectaculum supplicii nostri*), and Martial's *On the Spectacles* applauds Titus' impressive transformation of fables into punishments. Even intellectuals, pagan and Christian, agreed that criminals had to be punished. As Hornum shows, the prevalence of the cult of Nemesis in relationship to spectacles had more to do with the theme of just punishment than capricious fortune. Whatever the origins of the blood sports, the victims were always seen as worthy of punishment.[2] Their presence in the arena, unless imperial abuse or obsession was involved, was taken as proof that their victimization was justified.

Except in the rare cases of bloodless dilettantes, participation in the arena itself was a punishment. Exceptional performers might redeem themselves to a degree, but they never entirely escaped the stigma of the arena. Penal spectacles, however, came to include punitive performance, for which some recognition of craft, sport, or entertainment value developed. Under the Republic convicted citizens appealed to the assembly; under the Empire spectacles became places of popular assembly and, with the decline of citizens' rights, the only reprieve from the masses went to elite gladiators via victory or release. Increasing brutality and the potential for abuse in legal history went hand in hand with increasingly violent spectacles.[3]

The ritual of punishment began as a response to insults, threats, and crises; it became institutionalized in spectacles in the Republic, but its original aim never disappeared, and it revived in future crises, especially the third century. The analogues among spectacles, traditional executions, proscriptions, reigns of terror, and Christian persecutions are striking and non-coincidental. Numerous incidents concerning both pagans and Christians show that *maiestas* and similar condemnations brought *summa supplicia* – not only death but corpse abuse and (often) denial of burial. *Maiestas* was not just political. It applied to traitors and conspirators, but also to personal insults (real or imagined) against individual emperors, or religious insults against the gods or the emperor cult. Rome disliked Christianity as both new and seditious in its exclusive monotheism. Offense was taken and then given in return. Punishment was seen as a justifiable use of violence entailing deep emotion. With the expansion of spectacles and possible shortages of potential victims, great numbers of persons were condemned to the arena for treason (and lesser crimes) by trial before a governor or urban prefect or by imperial whim. Punishment made some *damnati* useful, providing service in the arena, just as others provided labor in the mines. The enforcement of law and the production of spectacles were complementary and acted in complicity: the arena demonstrated the power of the legal system and the legal system supplied the needs of the arena. Given the banality of violence, things got worse before they got better.

CONCLUSION

Punitive spectacles combined cruelty and legal punishment with religious vengeance and purification. Rome's legal system damned victims to die in the arena, providing the raw material for violent entertainments; but after the killing, ritualized procedures were carried out, confirming the death, removing the bodies, and adding further damnation. Law took the criminal to the point of death, but thereafter punishment continued as vengeance. Corporal and spiritual torments added emotional involvement and catharsis. For the sake of expiation as well as entertainment, arenas became specialized spectator facilities, architecturally elaborate versions of the Forum and the Stairs of Mourning, facilitating the involvement of the people as witnesses, commentators, and judges.

As in other cases of ritualized killing, we must acknowledge the religious overtones of *munera* from early ties to funerals to later ties to the emperor cult. Concern about pollution was ubiquitous in antiquity, and execution rituals transcended secular homicide. In the XII Tables of early Rome criminals became *sacri* for Ceres, and at Puteoli in the first century BC logistical arrangements for removing bodies included religious rituals (e.g. caps and bells). Under the Empire bodies were 'claimed' in the arena by infernal powers, and Christian faith in resurrection was met with Roman ferocity in damnation. A moral and religious people, Romans were concerned about burial, afterlife, and ghosts. They needed to know that *damnati* were justly condemned and safely disposed of. In pagan antiquity a moral and religious community could – and in fact had to – hate, kill, and damn *noxii*. Public condemnation, repeated in the arena via announcements or placards, legitimized the denial of rights and rites to the victims, establishing an emotional distance and precluding empathy, and allowing non-burial and even denial of burial as exceptions to normal obligations. Like Greece, Rome did not have to fear divine displeasure (for breaking the divinely sanctioned law of burial) as long as the victims were properly condemned as traitors, temple robbers, parricides, and the like.

Blood sports were acceptable because institutionalized violence was essential to the formation and continuity of Roman culture. Neither the violence nor the institution was objectionable on the grounds of popular morality, religion, or tradition. Rome wanted vengeance and security, but it also had to be free of guilt and ghosts. Guilt (i.e. concerns about improprieties, blood guilt, haunting, and pollution) was allayed by the voluntary collusion of gladiators and by the formal condemnations of victims as *hostes* and *noxii*. Victims were killed symbolically by the emperor or *munerarius*, and there was communal involvement (in the crowd's witnessing, yelling about decisions, and reactions to deaths), but the victims were to be killed indirectly, at a social distance or in a disassociative way – by beasts, each other, or socially marginal gladiators.[4] Removal of *noxii* by hooks added further insult, but also avoided pollution (i.e. by touching the hostile corpse). At Rome condemned humans – pariahs and foes – were killed in public places

270

as a spectacle, the dead were displayed, and disposal probably followed traditional lines. Concerned about miasmatic pollution and the malevolent spirits, Rome wanted the corpses removed from the pure, sacred realm of the city. Rome wanted to cast the dead outside the community, and to keep them out – body and soul.[5]

For disposal of *noxii*, Roman pragmatism and rituals of punishment and purification point to use of the Tiber as economical, efficient, and psychologically reassuring. Disposal by water was not the only option, especially beyond Rome, but Rome was a river city in which spectacles of death were held 'downtown' close to the Tiber. Vengeance went beyond death to public exposure and more. Not burial but rather the height of insult, use of the Tiber meant non-provision and denial of burial for *noxii* since bodies were not likely to be recovered. Finally, Rome gained security from hostile spirits by the efficient and purgative use of the Tiber for disposal – it cleansed the city and completed the ritual of death, exorcism, and damnation. The offending bodies and their spirits were directed away by Dis and Mercury and the bodies were carried away by the purifying element of water. The lustral magic of the living water took away the pollution and brought purification against hostile spirits. Denial of burial extended punitive damnation beyond death, and disposal by water cleansed Rome of filth and ghosts.

NOTES

1   As Edmondson (1996), 82, says, 'Both groups [criminals and wild beasts] were seen as physical specimens of disorder, to be exhibited and marveled at by the Roman crowd before being put to death.'

2   Brown (1995), 384, comments: 'Even when a crowd was impressed by a fighter, it remembered that he was a being of the lower order, performing in a context signifying punishment. The arena symbolizes distance, killing, and control at least as much as it does acceptance, escaping death, and regaining social freedom.'

3   As Potter (1996), 152, writes: 'Penalties were horrific and painful ... Excruciating pain was the point of the exercise, for it was through its infliction that the crowd could feel that appropriate vengeance had been exacted on the condemned.'

4   Gunderson (1996), 134, explains that: 'Those dying on the sand have been exiled into the non-Roman space; their sufferings are those of the uncivilized world. In this sense, the *populus Romanus* is not even the agent of their destruction: beast, fellow criminals, or fellow gladiators are the overt agents, agents of that other world and not the Roman state.'

5   Rituals of abuse and denial are best understood in terms of the performers (and witnesses) rather than the sufferers. The issue is not the effect on the victims as much as the psychological functions for the victimizers: they believed that victims could suffer beyond death and that water and distance offered purification and security. Beyond legal punishment and deterrence, such rituals offered emotional vengeance and reassurance.

REFERENCES

Anderson, J. K. (1985) *Hunting in the Ancient World*, Berkeley: University of California Press.

Ariès, P. (1974) *Western Attitudes Toward Death*, trans. P. M. Ranum, Baltimore: Johns Hopkins University Press.

—— (1982) *The Hour of Our Death*, trans. H. Weaver, New York: Vintage Books (original French ed., Paris: Éditions du Seuil, 1977).

Aubert, J.-J. (1994) *Business Managers in Ancient Rome: A Social and Economic Study of Institutores, 200 B.C.–A.D. 250*, Leiden: Brill.

Auguet, R. (1972) *Cruelty and Civilization: The Roman Games* (Engl. trans., London: George Allen and Unwin; original French ed., Paris: Flammarion, 1970; reprint ed., London: Routledge, 1994).

Aurigemma, S. (1926) *I mosaici di Zliten*, Africa italiana II, Collezione de monografie a cura del ministero delle colonie, Rome: Società editrice d'arte illustrata.

Aymard, J. (1951) *Essai sur les chasses romaines des origines à la fin du siècle des Antonins (Cynegetica)*, Bibliothèque des Écoles françaises d'Athènes et de Rome, fascicule 171, Paris: E. de Boccard.

Balsdon, J. P. V. D. (1969) *Life and Leisure in Ancient Rome*, London: Bodley Head.

—— (1979) *Romans and Aliens*, Chapel Hill: University of North Carolina Press.

Baltrusch, E. (1988) 'Die Verstaatlichung der Gladiatorenspiele', *Hermes* 116: 324–37.

Barber, P. (1988) *Vampires, Burial, and Death: Folklore and Reality*, New Haven: Yale University Press.

Barnes, T. D. (1968) 'The Pre-Decian Acta Martyrum', *Journal of Theological Studies* 19: 509–31.

—— (1981) *Constantine and Eusebius*, Cambridge, Mass.: Harvard University Press.

Barton, C. A. (1989) 'The Scandal of the Arena', *Representations* 27: 1–36.

—— (1993) *The Sorrows of the Ancient Romans: The Gladiator and the Monster*, Princeton: Princeton University Press.

—— (1994) 'Savage Miracles: Redemption of Lost Honor in Roman Society and the Sacrament of the Gladiator and the Martyr', *Representations* 45: 41–71.

Bartsch, S. (1994) *Actors in the Audience: Theatricality and Doublespeak from Nero to Hadrian*, Cambridge, Mass.: Harvard University Press.

Bataille, G. (1988) *The Accursed Share: An Essay in General Economy*, Vol. 1, *Consumption*, trans. R. Hurley, New York: Zone Books.

Bauman, R. A. (1967) *The Crimen Maiestatis in the Roman Republic and Augustan Principate*, Johannesburg: Witwatersrand University Press.

—— (1974) *Impietas in Principem: A Study of Treason against the Roman Emperor with Special Reference to the First Century AD*, Munich: Beck.

—— (1996) *Crime and Punishment in Ancient Rome*, London: Routledge.

Berger, A. (1953) *Encyclopedic Dictionary of Roman Law*, Transactions of the American Philosophical Society, 3.2, Philadelphia: American Philosophical Society.

Bernstein, A. E. (1993) *The Formation of Hell: Death and Retribution in the Ancient and Early Christian Worlds*, Ithaca: Cornell University Press.

Bertrandy, F. (1987) 'Remarques sur le commerce des bêtes sauvages entre l'Afrique du Nord et l'Italie (IIe siècle avant J.-C.–IVe siècle après J.-C.)', *Mélanges d'Archéologie et d'Histoire de l'École Française de Rome* 99: 211–41.

Bodel, J. (1986) 'Graveyards and Groves: A Study of the Lex Lucerina', *American Journal of Ancient History* 11: 1–133 (appeared 1994).

Bomgardner, D. L. (1989) 'The Carthage Amphitheater: A Reappraisal', *American Journal of Archaeology* 93: 85–103.

Bonfante, L. (ed.) (1986) *Etruscan Life and Afterlife*, Detroit: Wayne State University Press.

Boone, E. (ed.) (1984) *Ritual Sacrifice in Mesoamerica*, Washington, D.C.: Dumbarton Oaks University Press.

Bowersock, G. W. (1995) *Martyrdom and Rome*, Cambridge: Cambridge University Press.

Bradley, K. R. (1981) 'The Significance of the *Spectacula* in Suetonius' *Caesares*', *Rivista storica dell'Antichità* 11: 129–37.

Briquel, D. (1984) 'Formes de mise à mort dans la Rome primitive: Quelques remarques', 225–40, in *Châtiment* (see L'École française de Rome below).

Broughton, T. R. S. (1951–2) *The Magistrates of the Roman Republic*, 3 vols., New York: American Philological Association, repr. ed. Atlanta: Scholars Press, 1986.

Brown, P. R. L. (1981) *The Cult of the Saints: Its Rise and Function in Latin Christianity*, Chicago: University of Chicago.

Brown, S. (1992) 'Death as Decoration: Scenes from the Arena on Roman Domestic Mosaics', 180–211, in A. Richlin (ed.) *Pornography and Representation in Greece and Rome*, Oxford: Oxford University Press.

—— (1995) 'Explaining the Arena: Did the Romans "Need" Gladiators?', *Journal of Roman Archaeology* 8: 376–84.

Brucia, M. A. (1990) 'The Tiber Island in Ancient and Medieval Rome', unpublished Ph.D. diss., Fordham University.

Burkert, W. (1983) *Homo Necans*, trans. P. Bing, Berkeley: University of California Press.

Bynum, C. W. (1995) *The Resurrection of the Body in Western Christianity, 200–1336*, New York: Columbia University Press.

Callu, J.-P. (1984) 'Le Jardin des supplices au Bas-Empire', 313–59, in *Châtiment* (see L'École française de Rome below).

Cantarella, E. (1991) *I supplizi capitali in Grecia e a Roma*, Milan: Rizzoli.

Carcopino, J. (1975) *Daily Life in Ancient Rome*, ed. H. T. Rowell, trans. E. O. Lorimer, Harmondsworth: Penguin (original 1941).

Cartmill, M. (1993) *A View to a Kill in the Morning: Hunting and Nature through History*, Cambridge, Mass.: Harvard University Press.

Cavallaro, M. A. (1984) *Spese e spettacoli: Aspetti economici-strutturali degli spettacoli nella Roma giulio-claudia*, Antiquitas 34, Bonn: Habelt.

Clavel-Lévêque, M. (1984a) *L'Empire en jeux: Espace symbolique et pratique sociale dans le monde romain*, Paris: Éditions du CNRS.

—— (1984b) 'Rituels de mort et consommation de gladiateurs: Images de domination et pratiques imperialistes de reproduction', 189–208, in Hélène Walter (ed.) *Hommages à Lucien Lerat*, Annales littéraires de l'Université de Besançon, 29, Paris: Les Belles Lettres.

—— (1986) 'L'Espace des jeux dans le monde romain: Hégémonie, symbolique et pratique sociale', *Aufstieg und Niedergang der römischen Welt* 2.16.3: 2406–563, Berlin: De Gruyter.

Clendinnen, I. (1991) *Aztecs: An Interpretation*, Cambridge: Cambridge University Press.

Cloud, J. D. (1971) 'Parricidium, from the Lex Numiae to the Lex Pompeia de

LIST OF REFERENCES

Parricidiis', *Zeitschrift der Savigny-Stiftung für Rechtsgeschichte, romanistische Abteilung* 88: 1–66.

Coleman, K. M. (1990) 'Fatal Charades: Roman Executions Staged as Mythological Enactments', *Journal of Roman Studies* 80: 44–73.

—— (1993) 'Launching into History: Aquatic Displays in the Early Empire', *Journal of Roman Studies* 83: 48–74.

—— (1996) 'Ptolemy Philadelphus and the Roman Amphitheater', 49–68, in W. J. Slater (ed.) *Roman Theater and Society*, E. Togo Salmon Papers I, Ann Arbor: University of Michigan Press.

Colini, A.-M. and Cozza, L. (1962) *Ludus Magnus*, Rome: Monte dei Paschi di Siena.

Corbier, M. (1989) 'The Ambiguous Status of Meat in Ancient Rome', *Food and Foodways* 3: 223–64.

Crook, J. (1984) *Law and Life of Rome*, Ithaca: Cornell University Press (orig. 1967).

Cumont, F. (1922) *After Life in Roman Paganism*, New Haven: Yale University Press (repr. ed. New York: Dover, 1959).

—— (1949) *Lux Perpetua*, Paris: Geunther.

David, J.-M. (1984) 'Du Comitium à la Roche Tarpéienne: Sur certains rituels d'exécution capitale sous la République, les règnes d'Auguste et de Tibère', 131–76, in *Châtiment* (see L'École française de Rome below).

Davies, N. (1981) *Human Sacrifice in History and Today*, New York: William Morrow.

—— (1984) 'Human Sacrifice in the Old World and the New: Some Similarities and Differences', 211–16, in E. Boone (ed.) *Ritual Sacrifice in Mesoamerica*, Washington, D.C.: Dumbarton Oaks University Press.

Decker, W. (1992) *Sports and Games of Ancient Egypt*, trans. A. Guttmann, New Haven: Yale University Press (original 1987).

Dill, S. (1956) *Roman Society from Nero to Marcus Aurelius*, New York: Meridian (original 1904).

Domergue, C., Landes, C. and Pailler, J.-M. (eds.) (1990) *Spectacula -I: Gladiateurs et amphithéatres: Actes du colloque tenu à Toulouse et à Lattes les 26, 27, 28 et 29 mai 1987*, Lattes: Éditions Imago, Musée archéologique Henri Prades.

Dunbabin, K. M. D. (1978) *The Mosaics of Roman North Africa*, Oxford: Clarendon Press.

Dupont. F. (1985) *L'Acteur-roi, ou, Le Théâtre dans la Rome antique*, Paris: Les Belles Lettres.

—— (1989) *Daily Life in Ancient Rome*, trans. C. Woodall, Oxford: Basil Blackwell.

Eckstein, A. M. (1982) 'Human Sacrifice and the Fear of Military Disaster in Republican Rome', *American Journal of Ancient History* 7: 69–95.

L'École française de Rome (1984) *Du châtiment dans la cité: Supplices corporels et peine de mort dans le monde antique*, Table ronde organisée par l'École française de Rome avec le concours du Centre national de la recherche scientifique (Rome, 9–11 novembre 1982), Collection de l'École française de Rome 79, Paris: Palais Farnèse.

Edmondson, J. C. (1996) 'Dynamic Arenas: Gladiatorial Presentations in the City of Rome and the Construction of Roman Society during the Early Empire', 69–112, in W. J. Slater (ed.) *Roman Theatre and Society*, E. Togo Salmon Papers I, Ann Arbor: University of Michigan Press.

Edwards, C. (1993) *The Politics of Immorality in Ancient Rome*, Cambridge: Cambridge University Press.

Farb, P. and Armelagos, G. (1980) *Consuming Passions: The Anthropology of Eating*, Boston: Houghton Mifflin.

Farron, S. (1985) 'Aeneas' Human Sacrifice', *A. Class.* 28: 21–33.

Finley, M. I. (1973) *The Ancient Economy*, Berkeley: University of California Press.

—— (1985) *Ancient History, Evidence and Models*, New York: Viking.

Flower, B. and Rosenbaum, E. (1958) *The Roman Cookery Book: A Critical Translation of the Art of Cooking by Apicius*, London: Harrap.

Foucault, M. (1977) *Discipline and Punish: The Birth of the Prison*, trans. A. Sheridan, New York: Pantheon.

Fox, R. L. (1987) *Pagans and Christians*, New York: Knopf.

Frasca, R. I. (1980) *Ludi nell'antica Roma*, Bologna: Pàtron Editore.

Fraschetti, A. (1984) 'La sepoltura delle Vestali e la Città', 97–129, in *Châtiment* (see L'École française de Rome above).

Frazer, J. G. (1957) *The Golden Bough: A Study in Magic and Religion*, abridged ed., London: Macmillan (original 1922).

Frend, W. H. C. (1965) *Martyrdom and Persecution in the Early Church*, Oxford: Basil Blackwell.

Friedländer, L. (1965) *Roman Life and Manners Under the Early Empire*, trans. J. H. Freese and L. A. Magnus, 4 vols., New York: Barnes and Noble, of *Sittengeschichte Roms*, 7th ed., ed. G. Wissowa, Leipzig (1921–2).

Gager, J. G. (1992) *Curse Tablets and Binding Spells from the Ancient World*, Oxford: Oxford University Press.

Gardner, J. F. and Wiedemann, T. (1991) *The Roman Household: A Sourcebook*, London: Routledge.

Garland, R. (1985) *The Greek Way of Death*, Ithaca: Cornell University Press.

Garnsey, P. (1968) 'Why Penalties Became Harsher: The Roman Case, Late Republic to Fourth-Century Empire', *Natural Law Forum* 13: 141–62.

—— (1970) *Social Status and Legal Privilege in the Roman Empire*, Oxford: Clarendon Press.

—— (1988) *Famine and Food Supply in the Greco-Roman World*, Cambridge: Cambridge University Press.

Geertz, C. (1974) 'Deep Play: Notes on the Balinese Cockfight', 1–37, in C. Geertz, ed., *Myth, Symbol, and Culture*, New York: Norton, copyright 1971 (= *Daedalus* 101.1 (1972) 1–37), repr. in P. Rabinow and W. Sullivan, ed., *Interpretive Sociology: A Second Look*, 195–240, Berkeley: University of California Press, 1987.

van Gennep, A. (1960) *The Rites of Passage*, trans. M. Vizedom and G. Caffee, Chicago: University of Chicago Press.

Girard, R. (1977) *Violence and the Sacred*, trans. P. Gregory, Baltimore: Johns Hopkins University Press, paperback (original 1972).

Gnoli, G. and Vernant, J.-P. (eds.) (1982) *La Mort, les morts, dans les sociétés anciennes*, Cambridge: Cambridge University Press.

Golvin, J.-C. (1988) *L'Amphithéâtre romain: Essai sur la théorisation de sa forme et de ses fonctions*, préf. Robert Etienne, 2 vols., Publications du Centre Pierre Paris 18, Paris: De Boccard.

Golvin, J.-C. and Landes, C. (1990) *Amphithéâtres et gladiateurs*, Paris: Éditions du CNRS.

Gowers, E. (1993) *The Loaded Table: Representations of Food in Roman Literature*, Oxford: Clarendon Press.

—— (1995) 'The Anatomy of Rome from Capitol to Cloaca', *Journal of Roman Studies* 85: 23–32.

Grant, M. (1967) *Gladiators*, London: George Weidenfeld & Nicolson (reprint, New York: Barnes and Noble, 1995).

Green, P. (1988) *Classical Bearings*, London: Thames and Hudson.

Gregori, G. L. (1989) *Epigrafia anfiteatrale dell'Occidente Romano II: Regiones Italiae VI–XI*, 'Vetera' 4, Rome: Edizioni Quasar.

Griffin, J. (1980) *Homer on Life and Death*, Oxford: Clarendon Press.

Grisé, Y. (1982) *Le Suicide dans la Rome antique*, Paris: Les Belles Lettres.

Grodzynski, D. (1984) 'Tortures mortelles et catégories sociales: Les *Summa Supplicia* dans le droit romain au IIIe et au IVe siècles', 361–403, in *Châtiment* (see L'École française de Rome above).

Gruen, E. S. (1968) *Roman Politics and the Criminal Courts, 149–78 BC*, Cambridge, Mass.: Harvard University Press.

Gunderson, E. (1996) 'The Ideology of the Arena', *Classical Antiquity* 15: 113–51.

Guttmann, A. (1986) *Sports Spectators*, New York: Columbia University Press.

Hammerton-Kelly, R. G. (ed.) (1987) *Violent Origins: Walter Burkert, René Girard, and Jonathan Z. Smith on Ritual Killing and Cultural Formation*, Stanford: Stanford University Press.

Harmon, D. P. (1978) 'The Public Festivals of Rome', *Aufstieg und Niedergang der römischen Welt*, Berlin: De Gruyter 2.16.2: 1440–68.

Harris, M. (1978) *Cannibals and Kings: The Origins of Culture*, New York: Random House.

—— (1984) *Cows, Pigs, Wars. and Witches: The Riddle of Culture*, New York: Vintage Books.

Harris, W. V. (1979) *War and Imperialism in Republican Rome 327–30 B.C.*, Oxford: Clarendon Press.

Häuber, R. C. (1990) 'Zur Topographie der Horti Maecenatis und der Horti Lamiani auf dem Esquilin in Rom', *Kölner Jahrbuch für Vor- und Frühgeschichte* 23: 11–107.

Heaton, J. W. (1939) *Mob Violence in the Late Roman Republic 133–49 B.C.*, Urbana: University of Illinois Press.

Hemingway, E. (1960) *Death in the Afternoon*, New York: Scribners (original 1932).

Hengel, M. (1978) *Crucifixion in the Ancient World and the Folly of the Message of the Cross*, Philadelphia: Fortress Press.

Hertling, L. and Kirschbaum, E. (1960) *The Roman Catacombs and their Martyrs*, rev. ed., trans. M. J. Costello, London: Darton, Longman and Todd.

von Hesberg, H. and Zanker, P. (eds.) (1987) *Römische Gräberstraßen*, Bayerische Akademie der Wissenschaften, Philosophisch-Historische Klasse, Neue Folge 96, Munich: Bayerische Akademie der Wissenschaften.

Hibbert, C. (1985) *Rome: The Biography of a City*, Harmondsworth, Penguin.

Hinard, F. (1984) 'La Male Mort: Exécutions et statut du corps au moment de la première proscription', 295–311, in *Châtiment* (see L'École française de Rome above).

—— (1985) *Les Proscriptions de la Rome républicaine*, Collection de l'École française de Rome 83, Rome: École française de Rome.

—— (ed.) (1987a) *La Mort. les morts, et l'au-delà dans le monde romain*, Caen: Centre de Publications de l'Université de Caen.

—— (1987b) 'Spectacle des exécutions et espace urbain', 111–25 in *L'Urbs: Espace urbain et histoire (Ier siècle av. J.-C.–IIIe siècle ap. J.-C.)*, Actes du colloque international organisé par le Centre national de la recherche scientifique et l'École française de Rome (Rome, 8–12 Mai 1985), Collection de l'École française de Rome 98. Rome: Palais Farnèse.

—— (ed.) (1995) *La Mort au quotidien dans le monde romain*, Paris: De Boccard.

Holland, L. A. (1961) *Janus and the Bridge*, Papers and Monographs of the American Academy in Rome, vol. 21, Rome: American Academy in Rome.

Hönle, A. and Henze, A. (1981) *Römische Amphitheater und Stadien: Gladiatorenkämpfe und Circusspiele*, Zurich: Atlantis.

Hopkins, K. (1983) *Death and Renewal*, Sociological Studies in Roman History Vol. 2, Cambridge: Cambridge University Press.

—— (1987) 'Graveyards for Historians', 113–26 in F. Hinard (ed.) *La Mort, les morts, et l'au-delà dans le monde romain*, Caen: Centre de Publication de l'Université de Caen.

Hornum, M. B. (1993) *Nemesis. the Roman State, and the Games*, Leiden: Brill.

276

Hughes, D. D. (1991) *Human Sacrifice in Ancient Greece*, London: Routledge.

Hughes, J. D. (1994) *Pan's Travail: Environmental Problems of the Ancient Greeks and Romans*, Baltimore: Johns Hopkins University Press.

Humphrey, J. H. (1986) *Roman Circuses: Arenas for Chariot Racing*, Berkeley: University of California Press.

Humphreys, S. C. and King, H. (eds) (1981) *Mortality and Immortality: The Anthropology and Archaeology of Death*, London: Academic Press.

Hyland, A. (1990) *Equus: The Horse in the Roman World*, New Haven: Yale University Press.

Jennison, G. (1937) *Animals for Show and Pleasure in Ancient Rome*, Publications of the University of Manchester CCLVII, Manchester: Manchester University Press.

Johnson, A. C., Coleman-Norton, P. R., and Bourne, F. C. (1961) *Ancient Roman Statutes: A Translation with Introduction, Commentary, Glossary, and Index*, Austin: University of Texas Press.

Jones, C. P. (1987) '*Stigma*: Tatooing and Branding in Graeco-Roman Antiquity', *Journal of Roman Studies* 77: 139–55.

—— (1991) 'Dinner Theater', 185–99, in William J. Slater (ed.) *Dining in a Classical Context*, Ann Arbor: University of Michigan Press.

Kunkel, W. (1966) *An Introduction to Roman Legal and Constitutional History*, trans. J. M. Kelly, Oxford: Clarendon Press.

Lactantius (1984) *De Mortibus Persecutorum*, ed. and trans. J. L. Creed, Oxford Early Christian Texts, Oxford: Clarendon Press.

Lafaye, G. (1896) 'Gladiator', in C. Daremberg, E. Saglio, and M. Pottier (eds.) *Dictionnaire des antiquités grecques et romaines d'après les textes et les monuments*, Paris: Hachette, 1877–1919, 2:1563–99.

—— (1914) 'Venatio', in C. Daremberg, E. Saglio, and M. Pottier (eds.) *Dictionnaire des antiquités grecques et romaines d'après les textes et les monuments*, Paris: Hachette, 1877–1919, 5:680–709.

Lanciani, R. (1888) *Ancient Rome in the Light of Recent Discoveries*, London: Macmillan.

—— (1897) *The Ruins and Excavations of Ancient Rome*, Boston: Houghton Mifflin, repr. New York: Bell, 1979.

Lattimore, R. (1942) *Themes in Greek and Latin Epitaphs*, Urbana: University of Illinois.

Le Gall, J. (1939) 'Notes sur les prisons de Rome à l'époque républicaine', *Mélanges d'Archéologie et d'Histoire de l'École Française de Rome* 56: 2–22.

—— (1952) *Le Tibre, fleuve de Rome dans l'antiquité*, Paris: Presses Universitaires de France.

—— (1953) *Recherches sur le culte du Tibre*, Paris: Presses Universitaires de France.

—— (1980–1) 'La Sépulture des pauvres à Rome', *Bulletin de la Société Nationale des Antiquaires de France* (1980–1): 148–63.

Leon, H. J. (1939) 'Morituri te salutamus', *Transactions of the American Philological Association* 70: 46–50.

Levick, B. (1976) *Tiberius the Politician*, London: Thames and Hudson (repr. London: Croom Helm, 1986).

—— (1983) 'The *Senatus Consultum* from Larinum', *Journal of Roman Studies* 73: 97–115.

—— (1990) *Claudius*, New Haven: Yale University Press.

Lincoln, B. (1985) 'Of Meat and Society, Sacrifice and Creation, Butchers and Philosophy', *L'Uomo* 9: 9–29.

—— (1986) *Myth, Cosmos and Society: Indo-European Themes of Creation and Destruction*, Cambridge, Mass.: Harvard University Press.

Lintott, A. W. (1968) *Violence in Republican Rome*, Oxford: Clarendon Press.

Luck, G. (1985) *Arcana Mundi: Magic and the Occult in the Greek and Roman Worlds*, Baltimore: Johns Hopkins University Press.

McGowan, A. (1994) 'Eating People: Accusations of Cannibalism Against Christians in the Second Century', *Journal of Early Christian Studies* 2: 413–42.

MacMullen, R. (1966) *Enemies of the Roman Order: Treason, Unrest and Alienation in the Empire*, Cambridge, Mass.: Harvard University Press.

—— (1986a) 'Judicial Savagery in the Roman Empire', *Chiron* 16: 147–66.

—— (1986b) 'What Difference did Christianity Make?', *Historia* 35: 322–43.

Magdelain A. (1984) '*Paricidas*', 549–71, in *Châtiment* (see L'École française de Rome above).

Mau, A. (1899) *Pompeii: Its Life and Art*, London: Macmillan.

Metcalf, P. and Huntington, R. (1991) *Celebrations of Death: The Anthropology of Mortuary Ritual*, 2nd ed., Cambridge: Cambridge University Press.

Millar, F. (1984) 'Condemnation to Hard Labour in the Roman Empire, from the Julio-Claudians to Constantine', *Papers of the British School at Rome* 52: 125–47.

—— (1992) *The Emperor in the Roman World*, Ithaca: Cornell University Press (original 1977).

Mitchell, T. (1991) *Blood Sport: A Social History of Spanish Bullfighting*, Philadelphia: University of Pennsylvania Press.

Mommsen, T. (1899) *Römisches Strafrecht*, Leipzig: Dunker und Humblot, repr. Darmstadt: Wissenschaftliche Buchgesellschaft, 1961.

Morris, I. (1992) *Death-Ritual and Social Structure in Classical Antiquity*, Cambridge: Cambridge University Press.

Mustakallio, K. (1994) *Death and Disgrace: Capital Penalties with Post Mortem Sanctions in Early Roman Historiography*, Annales Academiae Scientiarum Fennicae Dissertationes Humanarum Litterarum 72, Helsinki: Suomalainen Tiedeakatemia.

Musurillo, H. A. (1972) *The Acts of the Christian Martyrs*, Oxford: Clarendon Press.

Nagy, B. (1985) 'The Argei Puzzle', *American Journal of Ancient History* 10.1: 1–27 (appeared 1992).

Nash, E. (1961–2) *Pictorial Dictionary of Ancient Rome*, 2 vols., New York: Praeger.

Newbold, R. F. (1975) 'Cassius Dio and the Games', *L'Antiquité Classique* 44: 589–604.

Nippel, W. (1995) *Public Order in Ancient Rome*, Cambridge: Cambridge University Press.

Nock, A. D. (1932) 'Cremation and Burial in the Roman Empire', *Harvard Theological Review* 25: 321–59.

Oakley, S. P. (1985) 'Single Combat in the Roman Republic', *Classical Quarterly* 35: 392–410.

Oldfather, W. A. (1908) 'Livy i, 26 and the *Supplicium de More Maiorum*', *Transactions of the American Philological Association* 39: 49–72.

Oliver, J. H. and Palmer, R. E. A. (1955) 'Minutes of an Act of the Roman Senate', *Hesperia* 24: 320–49.

D'Onofrio, C. (1980) *Il Tevere*, Rome: Romana Società Editrice.

Parker, R. (1983) *Miasma: Pollution and Purification in Early Greek Religion*, Oxford: Clarendon Press.

Parkin, T. G. (1992) *Demography and Roman Society*, Baltimore: Johns Hopkins University Press.

Parkman, F. (1867) *The Jesuits in North America*, Boston: Little, Brown, 1963, repr. of 1867 original.

Pearson, J. (1973) *Arena: The Story of the Colosseum*, New York: McGraw-Hill.

Peters, E. (1985) *Torture*, New York: Basil Blackwell.

Piganiol, A. (1923) *Recherches sur les jeux romains*, Publications de la Faculté des lettres de l'Université de Strasbourg, Fasc. 13, Strasburg: Librairie Istra.

Plass, P. (1995) *The Game of Death in Ancient Rome: Arena Sport and Political Suicide*, Madison: University of Wisconsin Press.

Platner, S. B. and Ashby, T. (1929) *A Topographical Dictionary of Ancient Rome*, London: Oxford University Press.

Potter, D. (1993) 'Martyrdom and Spectacle', 53–88, in R. Scodel (ed.) *Theater and Society in the Classical World*, Ann Arbor: University of Michigan Press.

—— (1996) 'Performance, Power, and Justice in the High Empire', 129–160, in W. J. Slater (ed.) *Roman Theater and Society*, E. Togo Salmon Papers I, Ann Arbor: University of Michigan Press.

Price, S. (1984) *Rituals and Power: The Roman Imperial Cult in Asia Minor*, Cambridge: Cambridge University Press.

Purcell, N. (1987) 'Tomb and Suburb', 25–41, in H. von Hesberg and P. Zanker (eds.) *Römische Gräberstraßen*, Bayerische Akademie der Wissenschaften, Philosophisch-Historische Klasse, Neue Folge 96, Munich: Bayerische Akademie der Wissenschaften.

Quennell, P. (1971) *The Colosseum*, New York: Newsweek.

Radin, M. (1920) 'The Lex Pompeia and the Poena Cullei', *Journal of Roman Studies* 10: 119–30.

Reggiani, A. M. (ed.) (1988) *Anfiteatro Flavio: immagine, testimonianze, spettacoli*, Rome: Edizioni Quasar.

Reid, J. S. (1912) 'Human Sacrifices at Rome and Other Notes on Roman Religion', *Journal of Roman Studies* 2: 34–45.

Richardson, L., Jr (1988) *Pompeii: An Architectural History*, Baltimore: Johns Hopkins University Press.

—— (1992) *A New Topographical Dictionary of Ancient Rome*, Baltimore: Johns Hopkins University Press.

Rives, J. (1995) 'Human Sacrifice among Pagans and Christians', *Journal of Roman Studies* 85: 65–85.

Robert, L. (1940) *Les Gladiateurs dans l'Orient grec*, Bibliothèque de l'École des hautes études, fasc. 278, Paris: Librairie ancienne Honoré Champion (reimpression with additions: Amsterdam: Hakkert, 1971).

—— (1968) 'Enterrements et épitaphs', *L'Antiquité Classique* 37: 406–48.

—— (1982) 'Une vision de Perpétue martyre à Carthage en 203', *Comptes Rendus de l'Académie des Inscriptions et Belle-Lettres*, 228–76 (= *OMS* 5, 791–839).

Robinson, O. F. (1975) 'The Roman Law on Burials and Burial Grounds', *The Irish Jurist* 10: 175–86.

—— (1995) *The Criminal Law of Ancient Rome*, Baltimore: Johns Hopkins University Press.

Rohde, Erwin (1925) *Psyche*, 5th ed., trans. W. B. Hillis, London.

Roueché, C. (1992) *Performers and Partisans at Aphrodisias in the Roman and Late Roman Periods*, London: Society for the Promotion of Roman Studies.

Rouselle, A. (1988) *Porneia: On Desire and the Body in Antiquity*, trans. F. Pheasant, Oxford: Basil Blackwell.

Rush, A. C. (1941) *Death and Burial in Christian Antiquity*, Washington, D.C.: Catholic University of America Press.

Sabbatini-Tumolesi, P. (1980) *Gladiatorum paria: Annunci di spettacoli gladiatorii a Pompeii*, 'Vetera' 2, Rome: Edizioni Quasar.

—— (1988–) *Epigrafia anfiteatrale dell'Occidente Romano, I: Roma*, 3 vols to date, Rome: Edizioni Quasar.

Le Sacrifice dans l'antiquité (1981) Entretiens Hardt sur l'Antiquité Classique 27, Geneva: Fondation Hardt.

de Sainte-Croix, G. E. M. (1954) 'Aspects of the "Great' Persecution" ', *Harvard Theological Review* 47: 75–113.

—— (1963) 'Why Were the Early Christians Persecuted?', *Past and Present* 26: 6–38.

Saylor, C. (1987) 'Funeral Games: The Significance of Games in the *Cena Trimalchionis*', *Latomus* 46: 593–602.

Schele, L. and Friedel, D. (1990) *A Forest of Kings: The Untold Story of the Ancient Maya*, New York: William Morrow.

Schele, L. and Miller, M. E. (1986) *The Blood of Kings: Dynasty and Ritual in Maya Art*, New York: George Braziller and the Kimbell Art Museum.

Schneider, K. (1918) 'Gladiatores', in A. Pauly and G. Wissowa (eds.), *Realencyclopädie der classischen Altertumswissenschaft* (Stuttgart: J. B. Metzler), Suppl. 3: 768–84.

Scobie, A. (1986) 'Slums, Sanitation and Mortality in the Roman World', *Klio* 68: 399–433.

—— (1988) 'Spectator Security and Comfort at Gladiatorial Games', *Nikephoros* 1: 191–243.

Scullard, H. H. (1981) *Festivals and Ceremonies of the Roman Republic*, Ithaca: Cornell University Press.

Segal, C. (1971) *The Theme of the Mutilation of the Corpse in the Iliad*, Mnemosyne Supplement 17, Leiden: Brill.

Shaw, B. D. (1993) 'The Passion of Perpetua', *Past and Present* 139: 3–45.

Shelton, J.-A. (1988) *As the Romans Did: A Sourcebook in Roman Social History*, Oxford: Oxford University Press.

Slater, W. J. (ed.) (1996) *Roman Theater and Society*, E. Togo Salmon Papers I, Ann Arbor: University of Michigan Press.

Stambaugh, J. E. (1988) *The Ancient Roman City*, Baltimore: Johns Hopkins University Press.

Tannahill, R. (1975) *Flesh and Blood: A History of the Cannibal Complex*, New York: Dorset Press.

Thomas, Y. (1984) '*Vitae necisque potestas*: Le Père, la cité, la mort', 499–548, in *Châtiment* (see L'École française de Rome above).

Thome, G. (1992) 'Crime and Punishment, Guilt and Expiation: Roman Thought and Vocabulary', *Acta Classica* 35: 73–98.

Thuillier, J.-P. (1985) *Les Jeux athlétiques dans la civilisation étrusque*, Rome: Palais Farnèse.

Toynbee, J. M. C. (1971) *Death and Burial in the Roman World*, Ithaca: Cornell University Press.

—— (1973) *Animals in Roman Life and Art*, Ithaca: Cornell University Press.

Treggiari, S. (1969) *Roman Freedmen during the Late Republic*, Oxford: Clarendon Press.

Tzaferis, V. (1985) 'Crucifixion – The Archaeological Evidence', *Biblical Archaeology Review* 11.1: 44–53.

Van Hooff, A. J. L. (1990) *From Autothanasia to Suicide: Self-Killing in Classical Antiquity*, London: Routledge.

Versnel, H. (1970) *Triumphus: An Inquiry into the Origin, Development and Meaning of the Roman Triumph*, Leiden: Brill.

—— (1981) 'Self-Sacrifice, Compensation, and the Anonymous Gods', 135–85, in *Le Sacrifice dans l'antiquité*, Entretiens Hardt sur l'Antiquité Classique 27, Geneva: Fondation Hardt.

—— (1994) *Inconsistencies in Greek and Roman Religion*, vol. 2, *Transition and Reversal in Myth and Ritual*, 2nd ed., Leiden: Brill.

Veyne, P. (1990) *Bread and Circuses: Historical Sociology and Political Pluralism*, abridged with an Introduction by O. Murray, trans. B. Pearce, London: Allen Lane, Penguin (*Le Pain et le cirque: Sociologie historique d'un pluralisme politique*, Paris: Éditions du Seuil, 1976).

Ville, G. (1960) 'Les Jeux de gladiateurs dans l'empire chrétien', *Mélanges d'Archéologie et d'Histoire de l'École Française de Rome* 72: 273–335.

—— (1981) *La Gladiature en Occident des origines à la morte de Domitien*, ed. P. Veyne, Bibliothèque des écoles françaises d'Athènes et de Rome, no. 245, Rome: Palais Farnèse.

Vismara, C. (1987) 'Sangue et arena: Iconografie di supplizi in margine a: *Du châtiment dans la cité*', *Dialoghi di Archaeologica* 5.2: 135–55.

—— (1990) *Il supplizio come spettacolo*, Vita e costumi dei Romani antichi II, Rome: Edizioni Quasar.

de Visscher, F. (1963) *Le Droit des tombeaux romains*, Milan: Guiffrè Editore.

Voisin, J.-L. (1979) 'Pendus, crucifiés, *oscilla* dans la Rome païenne', *Latomus* 38: 422–50.

—— (1984) 'Les Romains, chasseurs de têtes', 241–93, in *Châtiment* (see L'École française de Rome above).

—— (1987) 'Apicata, Antinous et quelques autres', *Mélanges d'Archéologie et d'Histoire de l'École Française de Rome* 99.1: 257–80.

Watson, A. (1987) *Roman Slave Law*, Baltimore: Johns Hopkins University Press.

Welch, K. (1991) 'Roman Amphitheatres Revived', *Journal of Roman Archaeology* 4: 272–81.

—— (1994) 'The Roman Arena in Late-Republican Italy: A New Interpretation', *Journal of Roman Archaeology* 7: 59–80.

Wiedemann, T. (1981) *Greek and Roman Slavery*, Baltimore: Johns Hopkins University Press.

—— (1989) *Adults and Children in the Roman Empire*, London: Routledge.

—— (1992) *Emperors and Gladiators*, London: Routledge.

Wistrand, M. (1990) 'Violence and Entertainment in Seneca the Younger', *Eranos* 88: 31–46.

—— (1992) *Entertainment and Violence in Ancient Rome: The Attitudes of Roman Writers of the First Century A.D.*, Göteborg, Sweden: Acta Universitatis Gothoburgensis.

Yavetz, Z. (1958) 'The Living Conditions of the Urban Poor in Republican Rome', *Latomus* 17: 500–17.

—— (1988) *Plebs et Princeps*, reprint with a new Preface, New Brunswick N.J.: Transaction Books (London: Oxford University Press, 1969).

Zanker, P. (1988) *The Power of Images in the Age of Augustus*, trans. A. Shapiro, Ann Arbor: University of Michigan Press.

INDEX

Note: this selective index concentrates on topics, terms and names in the text. Citations of pages are understood to include the notes associated with those pages.

devotio 45–6, 81, 87
Dio (Cassius) 14, 77, 94, 159, 186, 219, 221, 225–7
Diocletian 252
disposal of the dead: as a problem 11–14, 17, 19, 76, 79, 159–60, 162, 187, 213, 266; options 13, 159–71; *see also* burial; consumption; Esquiline; Tiber River etc.
dogs *see* carrion animals
Domitian 90, 98, 191, 226, 254
dumping of corpses and garbage 163–4, 168, 193; *see also* Esquiline
Dupont, F. 11

eating *see* consumption
Eckstein, A. 38
Edmondson, J. 89
effigies 37, 131, 216
Egypt 130
Elias and Dunning *see* civilizing process
Elagabalus 192, 223
elephants 4, 42, 46, 49, 78, 187, 193, 267
emperor cult 52, 77, 84, 100, 243–4, 270
emperors *see* by name
Ephesus 169
epitaphs 160–1; *see also* burial; gladiators, burial
Esquiline 19, 99, 163–8, 187
Etruscans 37–8, 41, 44–5, 188
Euripides 135
Euripus Agrippae 252
Eusebius 14, 185–6, 249–52
evidence 14, 49, 79, 89, 92, 155–7, 185, 267–8; *see also* authors by name; mosaics; martyrology
executioner (*carnifex, confector*) 246–7
executions: 40–1, 46, 49, 79, 95, 102, 133–4, 156, 164–5, 219, 246, 265, 267; shift to arena 49, 82, 100, 102, 157, 168, 213; *see also* crucifixion; fatal charades; fire; Forum; *poena cullei; summa supplicia*
exposure: of corpses *see* Christians; Forum; Stairs of Mourning; of infants 168

facilities for spectacles *see* Forum; amphitheater etc.

fatal charades (theatricalized executions) 9, 54–5, 170, 243, 245, 247, 268
festivals (*feriae*) 35–6, 41, 77; *see also* by type (e.g. *ludi*) and name
Finley, M. 7
fire 53, 168–71, 222; *see also* cremation
fish 42–3, 190
Floralia 43
Florus 49, 82
food 190–5, 221; *see also* consumption; largesse; meat
Forum 37, 41–3, 46, 49–50, 132, 168, 185, 187, 214, 217–20, 270; Forum Boarium 38, 46
Foucault, M. 9, 133–4
Fulvius 220
Fucine Lake 94
funerals *see* burial

Gager, J. *see* curses
Galen 193
Galerius 185
garum 190
Gaul 94, 249–50; *see also* Lyons; *trinqui*
Gérôme, J. 3, 156
Geta 247
Geertz, C. 133, 190
Gibbon, E. 3
gladiators: 55, 79–91, 94; ambivalent attitudes to and status of 3–4, 9–10, 47–8, 80–5, 89–90, 161–2; burial and epitaphs 19, 89, 160–2, 268–9; definition 78–9, 157, 160, 227; female 89; military virtues of 49–50, 80–1, 83, 85, 101, 268; oath (*sacramentum*) 79, 87, 162, 269; origins *see munera*; prices, sale, contracts 84, 86, 94–5, 160, 250; privileges, professionalism 83–4, 89, 91, 160–2, 268 ; survival (odds, retirement) 79, 85–6, 89, 162, 267–8; volunteers 17, 79, 81, 87, 89, 161–2; *see also auctoratus; missio; munera* etc.
gods: Baal 247; Ceres 41–3, 45, 247, 270; Diana 189; Dis Pater 157, 271; Minerva 52; Mother Earth 222; Saturn 37, 40, 247; Venus 167; *see also* Charun; Hercules; Nemesis etc.

Made in the USA
Las Vegas, NV
10 February 2021